# SOCIOLOGICAL THEORY

# SOCIOLOGICAL THEORY

## Explanation, Paradigm, and Ideology

**William D. Perdue**
Eastern Washington University

Mayfield Publishing Company
Palo Alto, California

11-8-94

Library of Congress Catalog Card Number: 86-061124
International Standard Book Number: 0-87484-693-5

Manufactured in the United States of America
10 9 8 7 6 5 4 3 2

Mayfield Publishing Company
285 Hamilton Avenue
Palo Alto, California 94301


*Sponsoring editor:* Franklin C. Graham
*Manuscript editor:* Marie Enders
*Managing editor:* Pat Herbst
*Art director:* Cynthia Bassett
*Designer (interior and cover):* Adriane Bosworth
*Production manager:* Cathy Willkie
*Compositor:* G & S Typesetters, Inc.
*Printer and binder:* Malloy Lithographing, Inc.

To Diane, and My Three Sons of Promise

# ∎ Contents

UNIT TWO
# A Call to Order

*UNIT FOUR*
# Conflict and Change

# ■ Preface

Theoretical sociology emerges from the dynamic interplay of ideas and events in history, mediated through the biographies of men and women of imagination. What we recognize as social thought, however, is not merely the work of seminal thinkers; it is drawn instead from the ways, movements, and organizations of people seeking to resolve the societal puzzles of production and commerce, rules and power, stability and change. Althusser described this relationship well when he wrote of Marx, "He has given back to the workers' movement in a theoretical form what he took from it in a political and ideological form." Hence, even the master is more medium than creator.

This book is intended to be more than a survey of social thought. It is also presented as an analytic framework to help its users to think sociologically. Toward that end, I present my own conception of the paradigmatic traditions that together comprise the craft of sociology. My hope is to encourage readers to compare and contrast the three major paradigms (order, pluralist, and conflict) that mark our discipline. Each of these paradigms is based on distinctive and interrelated assumptions about human nature and the nature of society and theoretical human science.

To help with the somewhat dialectical process of comparing these paradigms, I have developed an organizational format informed by the spirit of the critique and perhaps best exemplified in the work of the Frankfurt School. But other modern classics are also basic to this attempt to fashion some logical unity: *The Structure of Scientific Revolutions* by the philosopher of science Thomas Kuhn, *Ideology and Utopia* by Karl Mannheim, and *Class and Class Conflict in Industrial Society* by Ralf Dahrendorf.

The organization of the text thus reflects Kuhn's argument that science is neither uniform nor unified but has been shaped by competing paradigms that yield "incommensurable ways of seeing the world and practicing science in it."

This is to say that schools of thought do not necessarily share a common standard or measure for constructing theory, devising research methods, and drawing conclusions.

I draw from Mannheim to establish correlations between social structures and modes of knowledge, between the events and ideas of history and the biographies of those who conceive our images, our precepts, and our visions. From Dahrendorf's models of society, I take a distinctively sociological focus, for the "incommensurable ways of seeing" among sociologists can often be traced to different assumptions about the role of consensus and power in making society possible. But where Dahrendorf (by my definition a pluralist) sees only two models of society, I argue the existence of three.

Thus, some theorists hold an image of social *order* founded in commonly shared values. Others see society as a form of antagonistic equilibrium where a *plurality* of shifting and competing economic, political, and social groups struggle for dominance in a context of countervailing power. And still others assume a class-based *conflict* with a self-replicating ruling class that employs state and ideological coercion to bind together a society "where the center does not hold."

There are already numerous definitions of "paradigm" and "model" among sociologists. In my view, however, "paradigm" as used by Kuhn centers on the dominant assumptions within "communities of scientists" about the nature of their field. Dahrendorf's "models" speak specifically to the nature of society. In sociology, these concerns are quite clearly intertwined. But because the focus here is not just on assumptions about society, I have borrowed Kuhn's broader conception of "paradigm" and fitted it for the analysis of sociological theory.

The text is divided into four units. Unit One, "Human Nature, Society, and Sociology," foreshadows the balance of the work. Units Two, Three, and Four review the order, pluralist, and conflict theories of society, respectively. Each unit opens with a chapter that presents the more or less common assumptions about human nature, society, and sociology that constitute the paradigm at hand. Subsequent chapter titles reflect the distinctive societal issues addressed by the theorists discussed within. The theoretical exemplars for each paradigmatic tradition are featured, of course: The preeminent orderist is Durkheim; the pluralist, Weber; and the conflict thinker, Marx.

Where appropriate, the subsections in each chapter take us first through a discussion of *history and biography,* to provide a context for the particular system of thought under consideration. Next, the *assumptions* for each system are analyzed to demonstrate why it "fits" a certain paradigm. Each analysis is followed by an explication of the *theoretical content* or formal body of the system. And, finally, we find a *critique* that includes an ideological analysis of each theory.

My hope is that readers of this book will come to appreciate the importance to sociology of widely different bodies of thought. In the process, they may experience an internal sociological passage. I believe that the dialectic in the social world is reproduced whenever we engage in thinking sociologically. First, we are struck by the thematic order that binds seemingly distinctive theories into discernible paradigms. Next, as we seek to understand how those of each tradition interpret the social reality, we take the role of the other and see society undergo a metamorphosis. And, finally, as we compare theories within paradigms and contrast each paradigm with its alternatives, we develop a sense of how "truth" comes into being: It is routinely extracted from the clash of contradictory conceptions of social life, and, thus, it appears not as pure, hard, and absolute, but as emerging, dynamic, and exciting.

# ■ Acknowledgments

Just as theoretical systems have many makers, this work has many authors. These are real people, and their lives are rooted in the specific conditions and social categories of history. These people include my working-class father for whom death came at an early age, my Native American mother who struggled to raise two sons alone, and my wife Diane whose intelligence and compassion have left indelible marks. They include students in every class who know that asking the right questions is more important than repeating the right answers. They include the people in international movements for peace and justice. And they include my colleagues in the total community of sociology who struggle to keep the human sciences alive in an era of privatism.

Bruce Throckmorton and Bill Hoekendorf have supported this work by defending the integrity of Letters and Sciences. Pat Herbst pushed this project through production, on time and on track. Don Palm was a source of patient insight. Elaine Wang solved various production problems. Marie Enders was an exceptional copyeditor, and Bette Tingley offered typing skills, dependability, and heart.

I appreciated the often salient comments of the reviewers: Carol Andreas, University of Oregon; Douglas Gwynn, University of California at Davis; Russell W. Hansen, Central Washington University; Barbara A. Owen, University of California at Santa Cruz; Geoffrey A. Tootell, San Jose State University; John Williamson, Boston College; Stan L. Albrecht, Brigham Young University; Satoshi Ito, College of William and Mary; Scott G. McNall, University of Kansas; and Hugh Barlow, Southern Illinois University at Edwardsville.

I am especially grateful to Carol Andreas who provided a rigorous critique fashioned after studies of women's movements of the Third World; to Doug Gwynn for his understanding of paradigms and development; to Barbara Owen for her lucid grasp of interactionism; and to Russ Hansen for the sweep of his sociology.

I owe a special debt to Jeffers Chertok for his classicism and eloquence; to Bilal Hashmi for a prescience born of intelligence, sociology, and neo-colonialism; and to Themba Sono, for inspiration forged in resistance to all forms of apartheid.

And, finally, I wish to acknowledge my editor, Frank Graham: humanist, intellectual, and brave.

William D. Perdue

# SOCIOLOGICAL
# THEORY

# Human Nature, Society, and Sociology

# CHAPTER 1

# ■ The Vision

*But if the division of labor produces solidarity, it is not only because it makes each individual an* exchangist *as the economists say; it is because it creates among men an entire system of rights and duties which link them together in a durable way. Just as social similitudes give rise to a law and a morality which protect them, so the division of labor gives rise to rules.* (Émile Durkheim in *The Division of Labor in Society*)

*. . . there may exist at the same time different interpretations of the meaning of the [social] order. In such cases, for sociological purposes, each can be said to be valid insofar as it actually determines the course of action. The fact that, in the same social group, a plurality of contradictory systems of order may all be recognized as valid, is not a source of difficulty for the sociological approach. . . . The same individual [may] orient his action to contradictory systems of order.* (Max Weber in *Economy and Society*)

*The history of all hitherto existing society is the history of class struggles. Freeman and slave, patrician and plebeian, lord and serf, guild-master and journeyman, in a word, oppressor and oppressed, stood in constant opposition to one another, carried on an uninterrupted, now hidden, now open fight, a fight that each time ended either in a revolutionary reconstitution of society at large or in the common ruin of the contending parties.* (Karl Marx and Friedrich Engels in *The Communist Manifesto*)

Society is the ultimate paradox. Its nature is that of a three-dimensional contradiction evident in the classic statements above. In the Durkheimian view, society emerges from a division of labor as a system of continuity, consensus, and equilibrium. It has a history, seems to represent what "we the people" want, and offers the security of an integrated social existence. Its rules carry both the force of tradition and the stamp of group approval. Yet, if we look through the Weberian prism, all is not *order*. Instead, society now appears as more heterogeneous. Its structure reveals great diversity, including striking differences in language, custom, and status. No longer does it have the appearance of a system imposed from the outside. Rather, that which we term society seems created and recreated, produced and reproduced through the mindful interaction of its members. It represents in large measure a quest for the "meaning of social order."

If we look still a third time, we may decide that there is more to society than this *pluralist* and dynamic nature. From the Marxian vantage point, there is indeed variety in the human condition, but such variety now goes beyond differences in culture or status. Instead, that which is called society is a place for contention and strife. Such *conflict* is not a simple product of Weber's *shifting* and "contradictory systems of order." Instead, this third vision of social life directs our attention to the use of power and coercion by ruling forces. Now we see *durable* forms of class inequality, irreconcilable differences between those who have great wealth and those who do not, and open or dormant clashes between the holders of state power and the masses they rule. Such a view necessarily attaches great importance to the subject of social change.

It thus appears that society is at once homogeneous and heterogeneous, both a product and a process, with its members simultaneously united by core values and divided by dissent. It is both imposed from without and developed from within. And it is certainly true that society forms an arena in which fraud, coercion, and exploitation mark a struggle for existence. Given such contradictory visions, we should not be surprised to find an inherent tension in the discipline of sociology.

Those theorists seeking to explain society as a whole have not developed a comprehensive system of thought that provides equal emphasis to all sides. Each routinely (if not always consciously) adopts implicit assumptions that portray the nature of society as *predominantly* one of order or pluralism or conflict. The reasons for this are both logical and ideological. For example, if society is assumed to be an integrated system founded on widespread consensus, a sociologist might logically explore how each part of society contributes to the whole. Furthermore, given such order, major change should not be expected to occur. In fact, serious social change should logically appear as a threat to the natural equilibrium of social life. It should also be apparent that social thought which focuses on the issues of integration, stability, and consensus has conservative ideological implications.

Other theorists attempt to explain society in more intimate terms, centering on the actions and interactions of individuals. These sociologists assume a form of antagonistic cooperation among groups with different interests. Pluralist sociology stresses the processes through which institutions, norms, and self-image are constructed. This focus is obviously at variance with the vision of an externally imposed social system with a life of its own. And of course, the portrait of a self-conscious social actor shaping his or her fate in an open and diverse world is a hallmark of liberal ideology.

If the nature of society is expressed in conflict imagery, the sociologist might logically explain the ways in which dominant groups rule. Such a focus might include an analysis of state power, the concentration of wealth, or patterns of domination among world systems. This form of social thought is often implicitly critical of the existing order and is favorably disposed toward institutional (especially economic and political) change. On the ideological side, conflict sociology has more radical implications for the old societal or global order.

There are other reasons why one vision of a society prevails over others for a particular sociologist or a particular body of social thought. One such reason is that order, pluralist, or conflict issues may seem to best fit the conditions of a specific society during a specific period of history. Hence, the events and ideas that dominate a historical era find their way into social thought. However, in so doing, they must pass through a human mind that defines and explains, a mind at least somewhat influenced by biographical conditions.

It was Karl Marx who argued that "being determines consciousness"; that one's total social position would strongly shape the processes of awareness and what one conceived of as "truth." Thus, how sociologists view the world will be influenced variously by such things as academic training, class origins, sex, and race. We will rejoin such issues later when we examine the sociology of knowledge.

# ■ Assumptions and Paradigms: The Sociological Prism

The term *assumption* denotes a preconception or "given." In common parlance, it refers to something that is taken for granted. In this sense, the term acquires meaning when it is associated with some specific reference point. For example, in the preceding discussion we referred to "assumptions about society." These are (often) unstated suppositions about the natural state of this important form of social organization. Stated a different way, an assumption is also an implied answer to a question. Order sociologists answer the question "what makes a society possible" in part with the supposition "a consensus of its members."

Assumptions in sociology are not limited to preconceptions about society. Also crucial to the development of social thought are the suppositions that "answer" questions about human nature, as well as those of sociology and its theories. Underlying some social thought is the assumption that human nature is competitive, private, and self-absorbed. Other assumptions are more benign, stressing the cooperative nature of social being. As to questions concerning the essence of the discipline, some sociologists imagine a quest for laws (as with physics, chemistry, and other "true" sciences). Others see sociology more as a soft and descriptive discipline, and still others look to history for truth. As we shall see, these by no means exhaust the possibilities, but they are examples of the different assumptions that underlie sociological inquiry.

Sociological assumptions are not confined to human nature, the nature of society, and the essence of science. However, these are certainly important to an understanding of where sociologists are coming from. Also fascinating is the fact that assumptions can be systematized into larger structures of thought. This means that a certain preconception about what makes a society possible can be shown to cohere with specific suppositions about human nature, as well as science. We shall refer to such interrelated sets of assumptions as sociological *paradigms*.

In *The Structure of Scientific Revolutions* (1970), a work on the history of natural science, Thomas S. Kuhn sought to explain the advance of scientific thought. In so doing he rejected the prevailing view that science emerges painstakingly in a cumulative and developmental fashion. Instead, Kuhn observed a "revolutionary" process. This was founded not so much in momentous breakthroughs and great minds but in the often social and political conditions that either liberate or restrain new ideas. Kuhn argued that unraveling the conditions of such revolutions signified a new role for the historians of science.

> Rather than seeking the permanent contributions of an older science to our present vantage, they attempt to display the historical integrity of that science in its own time. They ask, for example, not about the relation of Galileo's views to those of modern science, but rather about the relationship between his views and those of his group, i.e., his teachers, contemporaries, and immediate successors in the sciences. Furthermore, they insist upon studying the opinions of that group and other similar ones from the viewpoint . . . that gives those opinions the *maximum internal coherence and the closest fit to nature*. (Kuhn, 1970: 3; italics added)

Now consider for a moment the phrase "maximum internal coherence and the closest fit to nature." By this Kuhn meant that groups or communities of scientists hold a well-integrated body of beliefs or opinions. They have to do with such questions as the nature of the universe, how the entities that are thought to comprise the universe interact, how the universe can best be perceived by the senses, what techniques or methods can be employed in the search for solutions. Many of these opinions, Kuhn argued, are somewhat arbitrary. But they are often embedded in the training that educational institutions offer professional scientists. Such opinions are also upheld by a strongly developed consensus among those with similar experiences. When other arbitrary elements such as personal and historical accident are thrown in, science emerges as a distinctively human enterprise, not a fail-safe method (Kuhn, 1970: 4–8).

Put simply, throughout history scientific schools have developed vastly different *assumptions* about both the nature of the physical universe and the nature of science. As a type of social organization, *scientific communities* have developed conceptions of scholarly life binding on their members. Kuhn argued that communities of various scope exist. All natural scientists might represent one grouping, but various specialties represent others. Each community shares similar goals, employs acceptable techniques, and trains those who would enter the fold. In the modern era, each community backs up this gatekeeping power by developing its own specialized journals and other publishing resources that can be expected to print the right stuff, that is, *real* science. Networks and contacts are developed and a status hierarchy is often present.

Kuhn used the term *paradigm* rather loosely. However, a central meaning was that scientific communities develop strongly held preconceptions about models of the universe, as well as "correct" methods for uncovering truth. The pragmatic significance of this is self-evident. Schools holding competing paradigms can be expected to quarrel among themselves. Perhaps more importantly, a scientific argument or finding that falls outside the dominant paradigms may be expected to face tough going, unless or until the new view acquires converts among those regarded as legitimate scientists.

Kuhn (1970: 115–117) employed a simple example from astronomy to show how a dominant paradigm served to influence the development of this field. The planet Uranus was "discovered" by Sir William Herschel in 1781. However, the same body had been observed on at least 17 other occasions beginning in 1690. Despite the fact that its motion meant that it could not be a star, it was so defined for almost a century. Why? Even though earlier astronomers possessed the technology (telescopes) necessary to chart the motion, a new planet simply *did not fit* into the well-entrenched model of the heavens. Even Herschel first defined the planet as a comet. Another astronomer by the name of Lexell correctly noted that the motion did not fit that of a comet and that the only remaining explanation for the orbit was planetary.

The power of paradigms can also be demonstrated in the "unnatural" science of sociology. Today, it is commonplace to find the work of C. Wright Mills (see Chapter 16) dutifully noted in a wide range of sociology textbooks and widely cited in sociological research. Many introductory works include a passage from his "sociological imagination" to press upon students the importance of connecting history and biography and understanding that public issues (such as unemployment) are frequently wrongly interpreted as private troubles (i.e., the jobless merely lack ambition or the right training).

Yet during the 1950s, when Mills's work on *The Power Elite* and *White Collar* was new, it was severely criticized in the sociology community. His portrayal of the dominance of the United States by a small, often interlocking and self-replenishing ruling elite was radically at variance with consensual and pluralist models of society. His corresponding description of the empty lives of a new working class offered yet another critique. Moreover, taken together, his works presented a dilemma to the most cherished beliefs of a self-proclaimed democracy. Perhaps it required the events of the 1960s and early 1970s, as well as the emergence of a new generation of sociologists, before the thought of Mills could be "rehabilitated" (at least in the minds of some).

We should not conclude that sociologists simply believe what they want to believe. However, it is crucial to remember that social thought does not emerge full-blown and pure. It makes its way, instead, through a tortuous maze. It competes, not always successfully, with the power of ideology, the constraints of tradition, and the norms of truth makers. Knowledge, including that developed by human science, is refined in an all-too-human crucible. Our best hope to understand sociological conceptions of society is to understand that crucible.

It should be evident by now that we share Kuhn's convictions concerning the power of paradigms. In the human science of sociology there also exists a *pretheoretical* base including but not restricted to a model of society. In other words, "communities" of sociologists are also united by their distinctive paradigms. Paradigms consist of assumptions that together constitute a "maximally coherent" view—of the social world, of its inhabitants (including sociologists), and of the practice of human science. Ironically, these assumptions are typically unstated, and routinely unexplored, even by those who hold them. Be that as it may, paradigms specify the issues and questions that lead to formal sociological explanations.

For example, two American sociologists, Kingsley Davis and Wilbert Moore (1945), developed a "functional theory of stratification." Their essential position was that a social hierarchy is necessary to the maintenance of society and, further, that those with greater status and rewards are there because they are doing the most important work. Thus, stratification systems exist because they ensure that the most qualified people fill the most important positions. Now this argument appears logical (especially to those who are well positioned in the hierarchy). However, if we probe a bit we may discover an underlying assumption. Davis and Moore *began* with the given that the natural state of society is one of *integration*. And within an integrated order, enduring social patterns are assumed to contribute to the maintenance of the whole. Hence, Davis and Moore were asking the question: "How does stratification contribute to the integration of society?"

Such a view of stratification systems is not uniformly shared by sociologists working in this area. In the influential nineteenth-century work *Das Kapital,* or *Capital* (1967, originally published 1867–1895), Karl Marx observed that economic and political hierarchies are not very functional for those on the bottom. History appeared to him as a struggle of classes, as an ongoing clash between the haves and have-nots. In his work on the capitalist system, Marx explained stratification as a class system founded in structural inequality. Classes emerge not from some universal societal requirement or merited reward but from the relationships of people to the means of production. Those who own and control the land, factory systems, and natural resources also own the jobs, while workers are left to sell their labor. The Marxist interrogative was: "How does the class hierarchy contribute to the coercive nature of capitalist society?"

# ■ A Note on the Sociology of Knowledge

To this point we have addressed in general the meaning of paradigms. As we move in the next chapter to identify specific sociological paradigms, we will have at hand a means of comparing and contrasting different systems of social thought. However, the assumptions that comprise sociological paradigms, as well as particular bodies of social thought loosely termed *theory,* do not exist in a vacuum. A richer appreciation of both the enduring ideas of sociology and their underlying assumptions can be had through an approach known as the sociology of knowledge. Here it is imperative to understand something of the historical conditions that have shaped both "truth" and "truth maker."

One important figure in the development of the sociology of knowledge was Karl Mannheim. From his vantage point, there is more to knowledge than its inherent character (that is, chemistry knowledge differs from philosophy and so forth). There is also more to knowledge than the specific method by which it is constructed (such as intuition, revelation, logic, systematic observation, and so forth). At quite another level, knowledge is a social product. This means we lay aside for a moment the general criteria by which we decide that certain ideas are correct or at least important. Rather, we view those ideas as reflections, as revealing something about the age in which they arose or in which they were dominant. Mannheim's treatment of this problem of *relationism* is vital, and to explain it he resorted to a metaphor, that of the constellation.

> The term "constellation" comes from astrology; it refers to the position and mutual relationship of the stars at the hour of . . . birth. One investigates these relationships in the belief that the fate of the new-born child is determined by this "constellation." In a wider sense, the term "constellation" may designate the specific combination of certain factors at a given moment. . . . [Thus] the simultaneous presence of various factors is responsible for the shape assumed by that one factor in which we are interested. (1971: 59)

Throughout this book, the "one factor in which we are interested" will be specific systems of social thought (loosely termed theory), including their underlying paradigm. However, it is not enough merely to review the content of theory or the implicit assumptions that shape it. Also of interest are *contextual questions* of a sociology of knowledge. For example, what were other social thinkers and intellectuals thinking during the time that specific bodies of theory emerged? What specific events marked the historical era during which the theorist worked? What were the social relationships during a particular era? More specifically, what discernible groups held political power, economic control, and status based on honor? What movements appeared to challenge the legitimacy of the status quo? And where were the thinkers in question positioned in this milieu? Such issues will not be mechanically raised for every figure who follows, but where appropriate, the joining of history and biography will provide a matrix for specific systems of thought.

All such questions enrich our understanding—of the coming of some ideas and the passing of others, of the embracing of one vision and the scorning of alternatives, of golden and dark ages, of renaissance and technocracy. Knowledge, including that of theoretical sociology, obeys no inherent law of development. Whether it flourishes or stagnates and whatever the purposes to which it is put are questions of history. This knowledge, like all other, is context bound.

# ■ *Bibliography*

Davis, Kingsley, and Wilbert E. Moore
1945                    "Some Principles of Stratification." *American Sociological Review* 10:242–249.

Durkheim, Émile
(1893) 1960             *The Division of Labor in Society.* Translated by George Simpson. New York: Macmillan.

Kuhn, Thomas S.
1970                    *The Structure of Scientific Revolutions.* Chicago: Chicago University Press.

Mannheim, Karl
1936                    *Ideology and Utopia.* New York: Harcourt, Brace & World.
1971                    "The Problem of a Sociology of Knowledge." In Kurt H. Wolff (Ed.), *From Karl Mannheim.* New York: Oxford University Press.

Marx, Karl
(1867–1895) 1967     *Capital: A Critique of Political Economy.* 3 vols. New York: International Publishers.

Marx, Karl, and Friedrich Engels
(1848) 1971            *The Communist Manifesto.* New York: International Publishers.

Weber, Max
(1922) 1968            *Economy and Society: An Outline of Interpretive Sociology.* 4th ed. 3 vols. Edited by Guenther Roth and Claus Wittach and translated by E. Fischoft et al. Totowa, N.J.: The Bedminster Press.

# CHAPTER 2

# ■ A Puzzle-solving System

With some appreciation of the general nature and importance of paradigms in hand, our next task is to elaborate them as they exist in sociology. Consistent with our earlier description, these paradigms shall be termed *order, pluralist,* and *conflict* because of the distinctive imagery each employs in its contrasting vision of society. However, these models also address assumptions on the nature of human being and the nature of sociology and its theories. Although we shall preview these now, each paradigm is the subject of an introductory chapter to each of the three units that follow.

## ■ Images of Society

Our treatment of the contrasting images of society is a bit more formal here, but it follows closely our previous description of the *paradox* of society. To review, one of these visions addresses the conditions for societal harmony and equilibrium. Sociologists who hold order assumptions presuppose that society is a persistent and stable entity or system enduring over time. This social system is composed of interrelated elements, each of which functions to maintain the whole. Finally, this orderly system with its interdependent institutions, customs, and groups is based on consensus. That is, the members of a society are assumed to be in essential agreement on the values that support the social order.

A quite different image of society is held by a second community of sociologists. Pluralists argue that the members of a society do not share a single world of meaning. Rather, in a heterogeneous, segmented social reality, one finds many cultures and interests. People may also strongly differ in terms of social heritage and life-style. Not all groups have the same influence or power, but many are organized so they can veto their rivals before they establish an enduring form of tyranny. Religious affiliation or dogma, political party, and bureaucratic regulation all represent *multiple social realities* (see Chapter 13, especially the work of Alfred Schutz). Finally, despite such distinctive worlds, most members may be assumed to share the truly important meanings that unite the society.

Taken together, the above are descriptions of the *pluralist model* of society. This model is distinctive in its portrayal of *antagonistic cooperation* on the part of the constituent interest groups and various cultures of society. Pluralists recognize differentials in social power. However, they stop short of embracing conflict imagery, as we shall see.

For example, the pluralist model stresses the heterogeneity of society and attaches positive value to the liberal ideal of diversity, especially at the cultural level. Pluralists tend to be critical of such things as cultural domination (as with the entrenchment of WASP customs), the problems of modernity (as with bureaucratization, urbanization, and the abuse of technology), and interest groups (which seek to influence politics and the law). Ideologically, they are often sympathetic to powerless groups and the social movements such groups form to obtain social justice. However, because many of these concerns have something to do with social conflict, one might be forgiven for confusing pluralist and conflict sociology. How do we avoid such an error?

Clear distinctions between pluralist and conflict sociology follow when we remember that the latter view of society implies the need for serious institutional change. Pluralist sympathy toward the plight of the underdog does not go that far. Conflict sociology holds that master institutions (especially the political and economic) are organized inherently to serve the interests of the higher circles. Hence the *existing order is the problem*. Pluralist sociology believes that the system can be redeemed, that its benefits can be extended to traditionally powerless groups who can then negotiate a better deal for themselves.

For example, John Stuart Mill's *The Subjection of Women* (1929) is a classic argument founded in pluralist assumptions on the nature of society. Here he argued that men held despotic power over women in the home as well as in the larger institutional order. His solution was to call for a redefinition of marriage as a *business partnership, with equality for women to be ensured lawfully.* In other words, women should have the same rights and opportunities men enjoy in the existing system. First of all, they should be equal partners in the family. Further, they should be able to negotiate freely their position in the social order. In sum, Mill advocated extending the rights of Rousseau's social contract (see Chapter 9) to women.

On the conflict side, Friedrich Engels during the same century wrote *On the Origin of the Family, Private Property and the State* (1972). Although he also called for an end to the legal tyranny under which women suffered, his view of the issue was somewhat broader. Engels argued that social relations within the family reflected the specific conditions of the capitalist mode of production.

For Engels, women in the home became the *proletariat* while men were the *bourgeoisie*. Among the propertied classes of the time, women did not work outside the privatized family and were totally dependent on their husbands. Among the working classes, both men and women were cruelly exploited by a factory system in private hands. Thus, in capitalist society unequal social relationships emerged as a logical consequence of the class system. Simply put, this meant that people were engaged in a competitive struggle for existence, accepted the class hierarchy as natural, and in the process viewed and treated one another as objects. Given this reality, equality under the law (and other political rights of the social contract) would not be enough to emancipate women specifically or the proletariat generally. Only when both sexes worked on equal footing in socially owned industry would one essential precondition of women's liberation be met.

# ▪ Images of Human Nature

So, the first "paradigmatic component" refers to those assumptions about society that inform the makers of social thought. If you recall our earlier comments, a second kind of supposition centers on images of human nature. By this we mean that a conception of the *essential character* of people can be gleaned from sociology. Human nature is another abstraction from reality. It refers to those qualities that would be left if all external influences were stripped away. In sociology, and elsewhere, such assumptions center on such issues as determinism and voluntarism, self-interest and social being, reason and emotion, hedonism and humanism.

The issue of determinism and voluntarism has been historically central in sociology. This issue refers to the explanation of phenomena in terms of antecedent causes. When phenomena include such things as social behavior, the issue of human freedom is joined. Put simply, the question is the extent to which our choices are self-produced. The issue of self-interest and social being focuses on whether human beings are basically private, contentious, and selfish or whether they are prone toward cooperative social relations with others. If the former is assumed, then powerful and enduring social institutions are necessary to maintain order. If the latter is assumed, institutions should be egalitarian tools and open to change.

A third concern contrasts a rational conception of the thinking creature, weighing options and projecting the course of future events, with a being whose passion may both enrich life and blind judgment. And finally, comes the portrait of the hedonistic being who is assumed to respond to pleasure and pain. This may be contrasted with a humanist vision, wherein decisions and behavior are based on broader intellectual criteria that often result in greater personal pain or reduced pleasure.

In the chapters that follow, we will raise these and other issues of human nature. For example, we will discover that the sociology of Émile Durkheim (1858–1917) bore the imprint of the intellectual undercurrents of his day. British in origin, a certain conception of rule by self-interest had survived since the classical works of Thomas Hobbes (Horton, 1964). In *The Leviathan,* Hobbes argued that the modern state is a contractual response to the unbridled passions that together constitute human being. Left uncontrolled, this natural pursuit of selfish ends will destroy society.

For his part, Durkheim also viewed a strong normative system as crucial to social order. Otherwise, human beings would revert to something resembling the Hobbesian state of nature: "solitary, poor, nasty, brutish and short." Durkheim expressed his views in his conception of *anomie* (1951, originally published 1897). This term, literally translated as "normlessness," refers to the breaking down of traditional rules in the wake of too rapid social change. Given his image of human nature, this could only result in the unleasing of unrealistic and antisocial wants.

Turning next to a representative of the pluralist position, we find a contrasting image of human nature. In some important ways a caretaker of the Enlightenment tradition, Max Weber (1864–1920) was committed to the role of reason and freedom in human affairs. Such ideas were expressed sociologically in his argument that human conduct is rooted in ongoing interpretation by social actors who give meaning to their world (1957: 88, originally published 1922). Not only is the species capable of self-reflection, but its members consider, define, and orient themselves to their historical era. Such interpretations become the basis for subsequent behavior. For example, early Protestants, who believed that hard work and material success were favored by God, were thought by Weber to have strongly advanced the institutions of modern capitalism.

However, for Max Weber, a disturbing trend within the Western world threatened to degrade the heritage of the Enlightenment on which it was founded (see Chapter 10). In his sociology, the human propensity for rational action faced an intricate puzzle: that of managing an increasingly complex industrial world. The solution was to create the "iron cage" of the bureaucracy with its standardized operating procedures, its division of labor, and its routine. And as it expanded, this structure threatened to imprison its makers and threaten human freedom. Weber retained his *voluntaristic* conception, never truly ascribing deterministic power to the bureaucracy or any other aspect of an objective social world. However, contrary to the optimism of later pluralists working in the United States, Weber grew ever darker in his outlook.

A final contrasting example of human nature comes from the writings of Karl Marx (1819–1883). Marx joined a devastating critique of societal inequality with a utopian conception of human nature. Now, as with pluralist imagery, the conflict vision emphasizes rationalism. However, there is more. Pluralist sociologists, just like their Enlightenment predecessors, wrap their conception of freedom in the shroud of *individualism*. Conflict thinkers in general, and Marx in particular, conceive of human freedom in *collective* terms. It is perhaps in Marx's work on alienation that we can find the clearest evidence of this distinction.

In 1844 Marx described alienation as a multifaceted emptiness for the worker who toils under the conditions of industrial capitalism. Under the economic, political, and social conditions of this system, both the product of the worker's labor and the process of work itself come to confront the person as an alien force. As workers are exploited for profit, they become objects in a system of production owned and controlled by others. With workers pitted against one another, and hostage to arrangements that threaten lives and livelihood, their cooperative nature can only be subjugated to a struggle for existence.

For Marx, human freedom presupposes cooperative interaction with others. Freedom can thus flourish only under the specific societal conditions that nurture this uniquely social being. When the producer is subservient to the product, when the worker invests time in a mindless process, when all are expendable in the face of market needs, then freedom gives way to alienation. (There is much more to alienation, as we shall see in Chapter 15.)

# ■ Images of Sociology and Sociological Theory

We have established that there are differences among sociological paradigms on the assumed nature of human being and society. Consequently, we should not be surprised to find corresponding differences on the assumed nature of the discipline itself. More specifically, we will find that there are at least three contrasting visions of sociological theory. Put simply, suppose we ask for an in-depth response to the question "What is the nature of sociology and sociological theory?" In the various systems of social thought that we explore in later chapters, we shall discover strongly different answers to that question. Stated in the terms of Thomas Kuhn, different "communities" of sociologists have emerged, each with varying positions on what "real" sociology is all about. One of these argues a formal or natural conception of science, and as we briefly outline this argument, we will see that it fits the order paradigm.

One influential book on theory construction was written by Hans Zetterberg (1966). In it he argued that real sociology ought to conform to the precise logic and methods of natural science. Basic to Zetterberg's position is an imagined sense of regularity, recurrence, and predictability in society waiting to be discovered. Put succinctly, as with the physical world, there is order in the social universe. Such an order consists of the more or less enduring relationships between and among the variables of social life. A *variable* in turn refers to some aspect of social life that varies quantitatively and can be measured. For example, perhaps there is a relationship between income and political views. One might reason, perhaps as a part of a larger theory of stratification, that high-income groups will be more conservative in their outlook than low-income groups. Research could then be undertaken to test this relationship.

What, then, is the nature of sociological theory? For Zetterberg, in order to be truly scientific, theory should assume the nature of a *formal explanatory system that conforms to certain logical rules.* More precisely, theory should be axiomatic and deductive in form. This means that (1) general propositions should assume the nature of an axiom or self-evident truth, and (2) from such general propositions, more specific statements of relationships should be derived. The nature of Zetterberg's formal explanatory system becomes clear when it is imposed on some of Émile Durkheim's theoretical work. (See box.)

Now if this leaves you with the logical impression that sociological theories of order are routinely packaged in Zetterberg's axiomatic-deductive form,

---

Hans L. Zetterberg
**On Axiomatic Theories:
An Illustration**

---

I. The greater the division of labor, the greater the solidarity.

II. The greater the solidarity, the greater the consensus.

III. The greater the number of associates per member, the greater the division of labor.

IV. The greater the solidarity, the smaller the number of rejections of deviants.

These four Durkheimian propositions can be used to derive other relationships, which thus become theorems.

I and II render: The greater the division of labor, the greater the consensus.

I and III render: The greater the solidarity, the greater the number of associates per member.

II and IV render: The greater the consensus, the smaller the number of rejections of deviants.

I and IV render: The greater the division of labor, the smaller the number of rejections of deviants.

Source: H. L. Zetterberg, *On Theory and Verification in Sociology* (Totowa, N.J.: The Bedminster Press, 1966), pp. 159–161.

you are in error. What is important is his focus on objective and elemental social variables and their supposedly orderly relationships. As we shall see, various theories of society share this vision of a patterned interdependence among the elements of a social system. Many also stress that the discovery of such order will make *prediction* possible.

As you might expect, that which we term the pluralist paradigm also advances distinctive assumptions on the nature of sociological theory. However, before we preview that imagery, a note of explanation is in order. One of the important divisions within the various pluralist theories centers on the use of *history*. For Max Weber and other sociologists wed to the tradition of German idealism (see Chapter 10), social theory is to recognize not only the subjective aspects of human experience but the historical context within which they occur. For example, in *The Protestant Ethic and the Spirit of Capitalism* (1958, originally published 1904–1905), Weber sought to "get inside" the social world of early Protestant believers. From this imagined vantage point, he argued (as you may recall) that religiously dominant ideals (such as the moral imperatives of hard work, material success, and asceticism) would motivate the faithful to create the conditions for the emergence of modern capitalism.

In the United States, this emphasis on the world of ideas was reduced to a more *social-psychological* level. Among others, symbolic interactionists at the University of Chicago often ignored the broader ground of history. Instead, they focused on the reciprocal exchanges of human behavior, especially the use of language in making sense of social action. One such interactionist was Herbert Blumer (1969). While his assumptions leave little room for history, his argument on "sensitizing concepts" appeals to Weberian and Chicagoan alike.

Taking one cue from Max Weber, Blumer argued that the subject matter of sociology is quite different from that of the physical world. (Physicists, for example, do not have to concern themselves with the subjective world of particles.) It therefore follows that qualitatively different realities require distinctive explanatory systems. Remember too that the pluralist paradigm features a somewhat *voluntaristic* conception of human nature. Hence, pluralist assumptions about the nature of theory must be consistent with this portrayal.

From the pluralist vantage point, sociology is distinctive by virtue of its human focus, a focus that includes primary roles for interpretation and choice on the part of a social actor. (In threading all of this together, remember that the actor is actively engaged in the construction and reconstruction of the social environment.) This emphasis on process defies the limitations of fixed and orderly relationships between rigidly defined variables. Nor is it amenable to a quest for lawful properties expressed in a neat explanatory system.

The concepts of pluralist theory are not to be imposed in a mechanical fashion upon an objectively based social order simply because that order is assumed to be constantly evolving. Instead, as Blumer argues, the central ideas of theory must enable sociologists to understand salient aspects of creative and changing social acts. Hence, while some modern order theorists insist on *operational definitions* for central concepts, Blumer holds that concepts are more

---

Herbert Blumer
**On Sensitizing Concepts**

A sensitizing concept . . . gives the user a general sense of reference and guidance in approaching empirical instances. Whereas definitive concepts provide prescriptions of what to see, sensitizing concepts merely suggest directions along which to look. The hundreds of our concepts— like culture, institutions, social structure, mores, and personality—are not definitive concepts but are sensitizing in nature. They lack precise reference and have no benchmarks which allow a clean-cut identification of a specific instance and its content. Instead, they rest on a general sense of what is relevant.

Source: Herbert Blumer, *Symbolic Interactionism: Perspective and Method* (Englewood Cliffs, N.J.: Prentice-Hall, 1969), p. 148.

---

*sensitizing* than definitive. The operational definition is measurement bound (for example, intelligence may be defined as what intelligence tests measure). The sensitizing concept has no precise empirical reference but directs inquiry along qualitative lines. (See box.)

A final set of assumptions provides yet a third general answer to the question "What is the nature of sociology and sociological theory?" At a superficial level, there is similarity between this vision and that of the pluralists. For example, Mills called for the development of a "sociological imagination" that "enables its possessor to understand the larger historical scene in terms of its meaning for the inner life and the external career of a variety of individuals" (1959: 5). However, it quickly becomes clear that Mills sought to understand private lives in a manner quite removed from the subjective vantage point of the social actor.

For Mills, the task of understanding society commands a broader view, sufficient to grasp the intricacies of historical events and ideas. He argued that the biographies of individuals are shaped by something more than meaningful interaction. Put succinctly, private lives are not that at all. Each person shares his or her circumstances with broad social categories (such as societies, classes, races, and the sexes). Therefore, to understand sociologically is to transcend the puzzles of character rooted in "immediate relations with others." Such privatized conceptions of "what's wrong" leave us unable to grasp "structural issues." This is evident in the following example from Mills.

> Consider war. The personal problem of war, when it occurs, may be how to survive it or how to die in it with honor; how to make money out of it; how to

climb into the higher safety of the military apparatus; or how to contribute to the war's termination. . . . But the structural issues of war have to do with its causes; with what types . . . it throws up into command; with its effects upon economic and political, family and religious institutions, with the unorganized irresponsibility of a world of nation-states. (1959: 8–9)

It should be apparent that sociology and its theories emerge for Mills from the practice of one's craft, which when mastered raises systematic criticism to the highest level. It is a means of analyzing and explaining the institutions and institutional power. It is a device for joining history and biography, and for grasping the often opposing forces of change. Conflict theories of society seek neither lawful regularities among elemental variables nor careful elaboration of ever-emerging social acts. Rather, they are distinctive by their assumptions that no element of social life can be understood in isolation and that no single event or idea can be comprehended as a disembodied entity. Instead, each must be set within history as a whole and related to an institutional structure with global implications. (See box.)

*If we synthesize our thought to this point, we can argue that each of our three sociological paradigms consists of assumptions yielding contrasting images on the nature of (1) human being, (2) society, and (3) sociology and its theories. Therefore, what we term the order paradigm refers to more than an integrative model of society. It also represents a unique way of conceptualizing human nature (often in privatized terms) and theory (as a logical system which constructs empirical relationships). The pluralist paradigm portrays society as heterogeneous; sufficiently elastic to contain a struggle born*

---

C. Wright Mills
### On Intellectual Craftsmanship

Do not study merely one small milieu after another; study the social structures in which milieux are organized. (224)

Try to understand men and women as historical and social actors, and the ways in which the variety of men and women are intricately selected and intricately formed by the variety of human societies. (225)

Do not allow public issues as they are officially formulated, or troubles as they are privately felt, to determine the problems that you take up for study. . . . Know that many personal troubles cannot be solved merely as troubles, but must be understood in terms of public issues—and in terms of the problems of history-making. (226)

Source: C. Wright Mills, *The Sociological Imagination* (New York: Oxford University Press, 1959).

*of different interests among groups who share distinctive worlds of meaning. Corre-
spondingly, it is human nature to make sense of social acts, and in the process to construct
a social reality. Here, theory is viewed as more a gyroscope than a system of explanation. And finally, the conflict paradigm joins assumptions about the social nature of
human being and the repressive nature of society with a critical/structural approach to
theory.*

# ■ Thinking Theoretically: A Cautionary Note

Given our argument to this point, how would you answer the question
"What is sociological theory?" By now you should be able to respond with a
sophisticated answer that begins, "That depends on our assumptions." You can
then proceed by developing three contrasting positions, one for each of our
sociological paradigms: order, pluralist, and conflict. Likewise with the question "What is good theory?" The criteria for evaluating a theory are also
paradigm-based as we shall see in later chapters. For example, an order sociologist might say that a good theory is one whose hypotheses resist falsification. A pluralist might cite the richness and analytic worth of its "ideal types,"
and a conflict sociologist would be prone to consider historical specificity and
the value of oppositional thinking in transcending the "illusions of the day."
Having said this, however, you might include in your argument some of the
following thoughts.

First of all, theory is not a synonym for guesswork, speculation, or opinion. Often when people are asked what theory means, they contrast theory and
*fact*. Implicitly this response assumes that the latter is true and the former mere
conjecture. Please remember that facts are meaningless unless they are interpreted, and theory represents a conceptual system for interpretation.

Also, sociological theories differ in terms of their level of abstraction.
Macrotheory focuses on such things as society as a grand system, or political
economy (as with the role of the state in capitalist society), or even a conception of world systems that transcend nation-states. Its concerns are typically
institutional and/or cultural. Microtheory is ordinarily concerned with lesser
units, centering on such issues as interaction or more narrowly drawn relationships among variables.

It follows that macrotheory tends to explain society from the outside in,
from higher levels of abstraction to lower ones. Microtheory reverses this
order, arguing that society is built from the inside out. For example, some sociological theory is centered in a discussion of the social world of everyday life.
Other sociological theory holds that sociology is a corollary of psychology,
that society and its institutions are ultimately rooted in the reinforcement of
behavior.

As we shall discover, theories based on conflict assumptions are macro-sociological. On the other hand, pluralist theories tend toward the micro level (as we have seen, some are social-psychological while others place the actor's interpretations in a broader historical/comparative context). Interestingly enough, order theory is not confined to one or the other level of abstraction. Some such systems of thought find integration and stability to be properties of the social system as a whole. Others seek to discover order in the learning of social behavior or the relationships of specifically defined group variables.

Generally stated, sociological theory (whatever the underlying paradigm) is an attempt to *explain* a distinctively social (as opposed to a physical or metaphysical) reality. Stated more formally, sociological theory is a set of conceptions or propositions relating to the nature, action, cause, or origin of societal structure and processes. Ideally, each explanatory conceptual system is a rigorous, internally consistent set of arguments that answers the question "Why?" Theoretical concepts should be refined, logically arranged, and stated in clear language. They should be powerful enough to generate serious thought and research.

In reality, not all the theory we examine will measure up. Sometimes the key ideas remain fuzzy. On other occasions, the interpretations of theory by different sociologists clash (your author's included). Some theory appears more an ideological brief than explanation, though all systems of thought have political implications. But through it all, the ideas we explore in the pages to come have endured, making their mark on the discipline and those who would master it.

This does not mean that we will examine only the most intellectually sophisticated thought. That is because some sociological theory is important primarily because of what it reveals about the development of knowledge and its relationship to history. For example, a strong case could be made to disregard the somewhat feeble work of William Graham Sumner on "social Darwinism." But to do so would eliminate from this book one of the recurring issues of this century, and with it the debate that has resurfaced with a vengeance in our time.

# ■ Synthesis: A Puzzle-solving System

A few summary remarks are in order before we conclude this orientation to the work to come. Sociological theories with their underlying paradigms should not be *reified*. Neither they nor the phenomena they examine represent concrete, material objects. The theoretical systems that await constitute neither a blueprint depicting the structure of a society nor a looking glass through which we peer at the processes of emergence and change. Instead, each is a sextant by which we steer through one strait and then another of the sociological passage.

As we approach the understanding of society, we can take stock of the rich and varied history of social thought. We can come to know that society consists of men and woman forming groups, making rules, and becoming human. However, there is more to this puzzle than associates, friends, communities, nations, and even global systems. When people unite, merge, or commune together, and when they become part of a wider interdependent whole, they are shaped by the legacy of past generations, the power of present forces, and the anticipation of things yet to come. We live out our biography not in the shelter of some altogether private existence but rather in the company of players on the stage of history. What has happened and continues to happen in the life of a people comes to bear on the life of a person.

Some would argue that sociology need not be historical. But it is certain that we must have more than a disembodied understanding of ideas. This necessitates at least a glimpse into the age of their origin. History records human attempts to resolve the questions of power and influence, to make and distribute wealth, to transmit knowledge and the mysteries of dieties, along with the regulation of the societal responsibilities of kin. What have been preserved as state, economy, education, religion, and family represent more than attitudes and behaviors. Rather these social institutions are formed and reformed, taking on the imprint of the varying events, ideas, and customs of changing historical periods. Such patterns by their nature favor the past but succumb daily to the forces of change. And those sociologists now recognized as theorists of society have not somehow been cosmic observers of such forces, traveling a course outside the social history of their age. They wrote then as now from inside their milieu.

Keep foremost in mind the value of history and our brief in Chapter 1 on behalf of the sociology of knowledge. Consider society as a puzzle to be unraveled. Finally, understand paradigm and theory as a puzzle-solving system. And whether you are moved by the mysteries of equilibrium and order, of the self and reciprocity, of inequality and change or by any of the myriad of societal issues, you will find that each intricate riddle commands the attention of a number of masters. Such issues hold fascination not for the sociologist alone but for all who have pondered the intricacies, the labyrinth, the paradox of collective life.

# ■ *Bibliography*

Blumer, Herbert
1969                    *Symbolic Interactionism: Perspective and Method.* Englewood
                       Cliffs, N.J.: Prentice-Hall.

Durkheim, Émile
(1897) 1951            *Suicide: A Study in Sociology.* Glencoe, Ill.: The Free Press.

Engels, Friedrich
1972                    *On the Origin of the Family, Private Property and the State.*
                       New York: Pathfinder Press.

Horton, John
1964                    "The Dehumanization of Anomie and Alienation: Prob-
                       lems in the Ideology of Sociology." *British Journal of
                       Sociology* 15:283–300.

Marx, Karl
(1844) 1961            *Economic and Philosophic Manuscripts of 1844.* Moscow:
                       Foreign Languages Publishing House.

Mill, John S.
1929                    *The Subjection of Women.* New York: E. P. Dutton.

Mills, C. Wright
1959                    *The Sociological Imagination.* New York: Oxford Univer-
                       sity Press.

Weber, Max
(1904–1905) 1958       *The Protestant Ethic and the Spirit of Capitalism.* New York:
                       Charles Scribner's Sons.
(1922) 1957            *The Theory of Social and Economic Organization.* Translated
                       and edited by A. M. Henderson and Talcott Parsons.
                       Glencoe, Ill.: The Free Press.

Zetterberg, Hans L.
1966                    *On Theory and Verification in Sociology.* Totowa, N.J.: The
                       Bedminster Press.

# A Call to Order

# CHAPTER *3*

# ■ The Order Paradigm

Two premises guide the development of this and later chapters of this book. The first is that every sociologist writing about theoretical issues is not necessarily "doing" theory. Many of the masters are often remembered more for developing their assumptions about the nature of human being, or society, or sociological explanation than for the content of their theory.

Another way of saying this is that theoreticians have contributed as much or more to the paradigms of sociology as to theory proper. Of course the assumptions of a paradigm are certainly related to the propositions of a theory. Both are elements of a logical system of thought. Thus, when you read the chapters on equilibrium and prediction, the connection between those issues and the content of this chapter should be clear. Still, it is useful to separate out what one says or implies about the essence of sociology—or how theory is connected to research, or how theory should be constructed—from what a theory actually proposes about society's puzzles.

As we shall see, when Comte identified three states of intellectual development, he was not raising a theoretical proposition to be verified. He was instead arguing that a particular way of thinking (looking for certainty in relationships) could be applied successfully to society. Likewise, when Hobbes (a social philosopher, not formally a sociologist) imagined the natural state of the human species to be contentious, he was not setting forth an argument that could be confirmed by the evidence. The same is true for the philosopher Rousseau's image of the "free" person in a state of nature. In reality, it is difficult if not impossible to find one who lives somehow independent of social order. Thus one cannot verify the essential nature of the species apart from social forces. However, such pure assumptions offer contrasting views of what *at the core* people really are. And these assumptions, as we shall soon understand, lead to different conceptions of what a society must be and how it can be explained.

A second premise has to do with the scope of our understanding. All theory develops a logically interrelated set of concepts, showing the relationships between ideas. Such relationships, taken as a whole, constitute an explanatory system. Good theory gives meaning to the facts of social life and guides, formally or informally, the research process. However, the theories we shall examine in this and later units are distinctive. Each centers on the explanation of *societal* puzzles rather than narrower issues.

The theories presented in this unit will seek to answer broad and sweeping questions of order in social life: What makes society possible? How do often divergent groups of people ever manage to live together? Why and how do they form institutions? What are the social origins of norms, rules, and standards? And perhaps above all, What *purposes* are served by this complex and cohesive array of customs, organizations, and patterns?

Major theoretical efforts at a societal level have influenced the development of explanatory systems that are more narrowly drawn. For example, functionalist theories of society (based on the order paradigm) have influenced the construction of various functionalist theories of crime, deviance, and stratification among others. While we may use these specialized theories as examples from time to time, the major emphasis in this book will be on the "larger order."

To understand the relationship between paradigm and theory, we shall turn in sequence to the major elements that constitute a paradigm. These are again *images,* first of human nature, then of society, and finally of sociological thought. In the pages that follow, we will discover that paradigmatic assumptions are frequently rooted in systems of thought that predate Auguste Comte's "founding" of sociology. However, there will be no attempt to offer a comprehensive review of such presociological work. Our purpose will be served through the selection of *exemplars.* These are various thinkers whose arguments clearly develop the imagery that prevails in the paradigm in question.

One of the contributions made to sociology by Max Weber (Chapter 10) is an analytic conception known as the *ideal type.* This device calls for the reduction of a category of related cases to a "typical description." The result is a representation of the most essential properties of a social phenomenon. For example, Weber described the bureaucracy as an iron cage while noting its rational procedures, impersonalization, and formal organization. Of course not every specific bureaucracy conforms to the type in identical fashion.

A strong case can be made that the imagery of human nature set forth by Thomas Hobbes is an ideal type. As such, Hobbes's assumptions represent a somewhat exaggerated yet analytically useful picture of people in a "state of nature." Now, the utilization of Hobbes as an exemplar and his image of human nature as an ideal type does not mean that order theorists in sociology have avidly studied this early thinker. Nor does it mean that each assumes the image in some exact manner. Hobbes's ideal type is simply typical in some essential respects of the image of human nature in order sociology.

# ■ The Hobbesian Conception of Human Nature

Thomas Hobbes (1588–1679) was a British political philosopher who contributed to a mechanistic view of the universe and advanced mathematical reasoning as the primary basis for philosophical thought. Born the son of a clergyman, Hobbes attended Oxford and became tutor to Lord Hardwick, later Earl of Devonshire. At this time, intellectuals who were not people of property were supported by means of a system of patronage. Hobbes was materially sustained throughout his life by Lord Hardwick and his family (the Cavendishes).

The first work of Thomas Hobbes was not in political philosophy but rather a translation of *History* by Thucydides. This effort offers substantial insight to those seeking to understand Hobbes. Thucydides presented an analysis of the dissipating consequences of political strife. It was viewed favorably by Hobbes as a clear example of the practical applications of history. History is not a tale of events, personalities, and ideas. It is rather to be viewed pragmatically: as political instruction for the aristocracy. For Hobbes, the class that governs can hope to learn sound judgment through understanding the past (Aubrey, 1957: 147–159, originally published 1669–1690).

Hobbes's seventeenth-century world was one of growing mercantilism. In a general sense, the commercial interests of the time necessitated the protection of state power, the development of transportation, and the rise of finance. However, more specific events contributed to his turn to political philosophy from history. In March 1625, some four years before the publication of Hobbes's translation of Thucydides, Charles I became king of England. His ascension to the throne marked the beginning of a divisive constitutional struggle between parliament and the crown. No greater example of injudicious rule could be found. Charles had the rather unpleasant habits of religious zeal (marked by state persecution of Roman Catholics), a staunch belief in the divine right of kings, isolation from others, and a remarkable propensity to negotiate with and then betray all sides. He was executed by Cromwell and his parliamentarians in 1649. Two years after the death of Charles I, Thomas Hobbes's classic, *The Leviathan,* was published.

In addition to the events of his period, the prevailing ideas about philosophy had an impact on Hobbes. *The Leviathan* (1909, originally published 1651) was written under the influence of the emerging science of the times. Thus to understand this work is to first comprehend the Hobbesian view that philosophy has three distinctive divisions. One centers on general questions of existence, another centers on the human being as a distinctive natural entity, and the third addresses the commonwealth. The last of these is human-made, called into existence by reason. Hobbes believed that the state and society can be studied and statecraft can be practiced in a scientific fashion.

For Hobbes, science has an impact on philosophy by means of its conception of cause and effect. Yet it was too early for him to be referring to formal verification through experiment. The identification of cause and effect was to be made through impeccable reasoning, supported by ordinary experience. Ironically, Hobbes had greater faith in the science of politics than in the science of the natural world. Whereas the latter reveals only probable cause, "civil philosophy is demonstrable because *we* make the commonwealth" (1966: 184, originally published 1656). Hobbes believed a science of politics is not only conceivable but was at hand in his works. All that is necessary are general propositions from which one can deduce the more specific principles by which society can exist in harmony.

The point of departure for Hobbesian political philosophy is a conception of human nature. He argued that the person in essence is an assortment of wants, desires, and passions that place self-interest above all other considerations. Morality is in danger of becoming simply a matter of convenience redefined to fit individual aspirations: That which is desirable becomes good while that which represents anxiety or frustration becomes evil. Left unchecked, such impulses can only lead to personal destruction. It follows that some compromise is in order to ensure self-preservation.

The Hobbesian compromise was to come in the form of a covenant. It was not born of innate social impulses or even a natural desire for order over anarchy. Anarchy as a lawless state of nature would mean that the only legitimate authority would come from the power of some individuals to ruthlessly subjugate others. Or as Hobbes pointed out, the weakest person is perfectly able to kill the strongest. Now this philosopher was not concerned with the historical fact of such a state in which the unchained beast preys on fellow creatures. He *imagined* such a condition as the only alternative to the commonwealth. Contrary to the critical view of state power espoused centuries later by sociologists of the conflict community, Hobbes viewed political coercion as the sole alternative to the worst imaginable jungle:

> In such condition, there is no place for industry; because the fruit thereof is uncertain: and consequently no culture of the earth; no navigation, nor use of the commodities that may be imported by sea; no commodious building; no instruments of moving and removing, such things as require much force; no knowledge of the face of the earth; no account of time; no arts; no letters; no society; and which is worst of all, continual fear, and danger of violent death; and the life of man, solitary, poor, nasty, brutish and short. (Hobbes in Sennett, 1977: 247)

Now it may be clear that Hobbes was not exactly the most optimistic of men. However, against the spectre of this grim supposition, Hobbes raised the one redemptive faculty of human nature: *reason*. It is simply unreasonable that a thinking being who can form judgments and draw conclusions would choose chaos and death. Thus the lawless liberty of the state of nature would be abandoned and freedom would be defined in a distributive sense of justice. That is to say, the exercise of one person's liberty should not infringe on that of another.

By what means then should this great compromise wrought by the reasonable constraint of self-interest come to pass? The seeking of peace (and subsequently survival, art, commerce, trade, and other social imperatives) is conditional on the establishment of a covenant between the part (the members) and the whole (the society). And yet this contract is far more than a simple agreement by all to beat their swords into ploughshares. Ultimately reason will prove subordinate to passion unless formally institutionalized. Therefore appealing to one's best interests is not enough. The interests of the whole nation can be ensured only through the willful surrender of "natural" liberty to the power of the *sovereign*.

*Leviathan* refers to a huge and awesome aquatic animal, perhaps a whale or reptile, described in the book of Job in the Old Testament. Used as a metaphor for the state, the imagery is one of magnitude, force, and power. However, the political sovereign or the governing classes, which have at their disposition the majesty of law, the strength of arms, and the other instruments of coercion, do not rule by caprice. For Hobbes, their decisions, including the infliction of punishment, bear the legitimacy of consent on the part of the many. The union of private interests with the public good is sealed by bargains struck between subjects and the crown, citizens and lawmakers, serfs and lords. Once these powers necessary to maintain order have been transferred by compacts, they take precedence over private rights. It matters not what the form of government may be; Hobbes argued that its necessary powers are absolute and grounded in the strength of the sword.

Necessary powers include any and all force and influence required to maintain peace and order. Hobbes was not swayed by the argument that government characterized by one-way communication is tyranny. Sovereign rule is authorized by the members of the commonwealth. In concrete terms it means the absence of legal restraint, the will to make law, the authority to decide on war and peace, and the power to determine the conditions of property ownership. The sovereign of course will not exercise such entitlements unjustly but in accordance with the aforementioned logical derivation of political norms.

In the face of such power, subjects retain the right of self-preservation, ironically even to the point of refusing to serve in war. There is also no obligation to obey a command not in the legitimate interest of maintaining social harmony. According to Hobbes, sovereign rule means the exercise of duty and justice toward the subject population. Failure in such respects will be followed by a breakdown of order and the possibility of rebellion.

It has been Thomas Hobbes's assumptions about a contentious human nature and the solution of the commonwealth that have intrigued us to this point. Yet one final observation remains to be made. His was a particularly influential form of seventeenth-century rationalism. The commonwealth was not born of the power of God or passion but of the ability to reason. Hobbes believed that science along with its mathematical and philosophical logic would bring to pass a society of reason (peace and harmony). As we shall see toward the end of this chapter, in the nineteenth century this conception of human-made order was resurrected and refined in the form of "positivistic sociology." It was then that a scientific approach to the problem of society came to have a clear impact on the nature of sociological thought.

# ■ Plato's Republic: A Society of Order

It should be clear that Hobbes's political philosophy presents us with more than an image of human nature. Hobbes also portrays his conception of the nature of scientific thought. In another vein, it requires little effort to see that "the commonwealth" qualifies as a representative answer to the question "What is the essence of society?" However, another philosopher has offered a fascinating image of this largest form of social organization. In keeping with the earlier discussion, we will briefly examine Plato's *Republic* as an ideal type. We believe that this classical vision of society contains certain essential features that are often reflected in later sociological theories of the order tradition.

Perhaps no other singular philosophy has had so great an impact on the course of Western social thought as that of Plato (427 B.C.–347 B.C.). Born into Athenian nobility, Plato might well be considered the actual founder of sociology. However, the segmented division of thought that we refer to as specialized knowledge did not even exist in his lifetime. While his views have been criticized as authoritarian and collectivist, they are clearly reflected in what we shall later term functionalist theories of society.

Unlike Hobbes, who was dependent on the support of a family of the British elite, Plato's father was a descendant of the king of Athens. Thus personal wealth sustained Plato's more scholarly pursuits. However, his family also viewed political involvement as a special obligation of the nobility. Thus realpolitik was to shape Plato's philosophical system.

Plato, like Hobbes long after, lived a life marked by the turbulence of history. From 431 B.C. through 404 B.C., the Peloponnesian War set two rival empires in a fierce struggle for dominance. Sparta with its militarism faced Athens in a conflict to control the Greek world. When Sparta occupied Athens (404 B.C.), a group of leading citizens of the city were appointed to administer its affairs. Known as the Thirty Tyrants, they served as political surrogates for the Spartans and under their protection initiated a short-lived reign of terror. Ironically, two of the "dirty thirty" were Plato's uncles. In a period of less than a year, large numbers of Athenians were put to death. However, the resistance continued and the puppet government was unable to maintain order. Sparta, under King Lysistratus, withdrew its protection, and those tyrants who remained were defeated. Plato's uncles had already lost their lives in battle.

Faced with explaining and purging the forces who had supported the Spartans, the resurgent Athenians identified a scapegoat. Certain of the Thirty

Tyrants, including Plato's uncles, had been instructed by Socrates. This philosopher, whose students also included Plato, was accused of corrupting the youth of the city. Such was perhaps predictable given the stance of critical skepticism so essential to his method of logically founded questioning. At any rate, Socrates chose the hemlock rather than renounce the right of unfettered thought and speech (Bluck, 1951).

It appears impossible to separate Plato's thought from the storm of warfare, his own class position, and the death of Socrates. Convinced by his teacher that truth and goodness can be discerned and that virtue is dependent on knowledge, Plato sought to develop a theory of society. In the model human community, the spectacle of political degeneration that marked the first quarter century of his life would disappear. As we shall see, the alternative vision of society advanced by Plato was based on what appeared to him to be inescapable reason. However, the nature of Plato's society leads to a point of criticism. In some important ways, the *Republic* is founded on the premise of social inequality. If such is a condition of injustice, then it follows that for this philosopher justice is incidental to order.

Plato's early works were devoted to a revelation of the character of Socrates by means of a series of famous dialogues. Ironically, the latter's conception of perfectible human nature and democratic social order were abandoned by Plato in *The Republic* (1974, written approximately 377 B.C.). In his view the mob, in the guise of democracy, had sent Socrates to his death. The ideal society would not repeat the mistake of a false equality. Later, in *The Laws* (1926: #609, written approximately 360 B.C.), he was to write that "the wise shall lead and rule and the ignorant shall follow."

Above all, Plato's image envisioned an ideal society headed by ideal leaders. His was a state in which the philosophers resided not as inhabitants of misunderstood and scorned ivory towers but as holders of political power. His interests went beyond Socratic dialogue or understanding the social and physical worlds. For Plato the love of wisdom was meaningless without institutionalized influence. His proposal was that philosophers should do more than comprehend the world. Their purpose was to rule it. Until that day, the savagery of unrestrained individualism would constantly threaten the fabric of human societies.

Plato developed in detail a *theory* of society, but his republic was founded on two major assumptions. These conceptions of social order were for Plato so reasonable, so compelling, so verifiable through common experience that no intelligent being would question them. While we shall show how they came to be interwoven in his formal theory, it is these givens that came to underlie sociological theories of order yet to be written.

The first assumption for Plato can be expressed in a metaphor, that of *organicism*. By this we mean that he viewed society as a necessary and complex interrelationship of elements similar in nature to living things. Given the ideas of his age, it is not surprising that Plato sought to unify the concepts of the soul and the body, the individual and the community, the mind and the political order. He argued that the source of energy, motion, and direction for the body is the soul, the virtues of which are wisdom, justice, courage, and harmony. Further, he argued that while the person is part of the community, the interests of the whole take precedence over the needs of the individual. Finally, in Plato's scheme of unification, the *Republic* as an organism represented the political supremacy of the mind. Thus individual ethics were not to be separated from societal politics. Unity, truth, beauty, and goodness were both a universal and moral system for the individual and the value basis for social order.

While Plato's body had various members, they were not all created equal. A second assumption that came to play a prominent role in Plato's formal theory of society was that of the inherent and fundamental differences in the abilities of human beings. Upon this premise he constructed a hierarchical division of labor, a social system that reflected a natural order of dominance.

Plato's *Republic* represented an ideal society in which the virtues of the soul were institutionalized in a system of stratification. Such a natural division was viewed as necessary to the maintenance of the social body. At the upper stratum were the *guardians* whose function it was to acquire, preserve, and transmit knowledge. Concretely, they could be seen as teachers and philosophers. Indeed, Plato envisioned an order in which the kings would be philosophers and the philosophers would be kings. As rulers, they would have the best of higher education. In the republic, wisdom was to be the highest virtue.

Below the guardians was a class committed to political service including the military role. Termed the *auxiliaries,* they were to be committed to courageous actions in the face of all obstacles. On the lower tier were to be found the *artisans*. As workers, these members were to produce the material basis for the sustenance of the community.

While Plato did not embrace the Hobbesian conception of the upright beast, he had grave misgivings about the natural abilities of the masses of human beings. Thus, as we shall see, reason was thought to be in short supply and concentrated in the hands of the few. However, in *The Republic* Plato envisioned an early day meritocracy. That is to say, one could not identify the best and the brightest at birth. Rather, it was necessary to provide the opportunity for the cream to rise to the top. This could be done by providing universal access to education and political office, affirming the rights of women as citizens, eliminating the extremes of great wealth and vast poverty, and requiring the guardians to hold property, spouses, and children in common. Plato was probably one of the earliest thinkers to advocate equal opportunity in lieu of equality.

Now a society organized along these lines would, for Plato, exist in harmony. It would be the duty of each stratum to exercise the appropriate role. In so doing, the social welfare would be upheld. Through unity the divisiveness of factions could be avoided. In his later work *The Laws,* Plato wrote that "You are created for the sake of the whole, and not the whole for the sake of you" (1926: #903c). It is critical to note that Plato was not defending the rights of the *many* or the rights of the *individual*. To the contrary, the welfare of the social order as an entity, that is to say, the whole body, transcends the rights or interests of the people within that order.

In *The Republic* Plato made clear that the lower levels were unable to rule. Further, should the kings or rulers govern without intellectual purpose they could no longer be philosophers. With the decline of the guardians, rule would be passed to the parasites who would be unable to use it wisely and justly. It should be apparent by now that Plato was not a proponent of the democratic theory of political organization.

It might be argued that Plato's vision was more reactionary than progressive. He possessed a rather romanticized vision of the past glory of the Greek city-states with their tradition of hereditary governance, in which the rulers were supported by advisers and officials as well as the wisest and most courageous soldiers and loyal workers. For Plato, such an early vision of Camelot degenerated first to aristocracy (rule by nobility), then to democracy (mob rule), and finally to tyranny. The republic, it appears, represented a resurrection, a refined version of a lost ideal (Strauss, 1975).

Plato's society, then, is a solution to the decline and fall of a sensible social hierarchy; a reasonable order based on merited division of labor. In restoring a perfected past it would be crucial for future rulers (ideally, philosopher-kings) to avoid the pitfalls that had ushered in an era of chaos. Plato was convinced that the winds of change are ordinarily destructive. Whether change is embodied in false conceptions of democracy, population growth and concentration, or the conflict of cultures, the result is an untenable social disorganization. But among all the forces of instability, one is supreme: the degeneration of a ruling class. Thus in essence, *The Republic* is a clarion call to identify, unify, and educate the guardians and to hold tight to the ballast of tradition.

# ■ The Order Conception of Human Science

With some understanding of the order conception of society in hand, let us turn to the final paradigmatic element. Throughout sociology's brief history, its makers have entertained and contested contrasting images of theoretical science. Taken together these are the answer to the question What is the ultimate nature of sociological explanation? As we shall see, two distinctive yet related sets of assumptions constitute the order imagery.

The assumptions of the order paradigm are reflected in two major theoretical traditions in sociology. These are by convention termed functionalism and positivism. We are not primarily interested here in the content of such theoretical systems. An examination of how each approaches the central puzzles of society and the specific explanations they offer will be left for later. At this point we want to examine the vision of human science constructed by the exemplars we have chosen. Thus we are interested in the *approach* to theory rather than the theories per se.

One useful way to understand the differences in theories can be derived from earlier discussions of the major puzzles addressed by theory. The puzzles we focus on in this book are societal in scope. Thus even the microsociologists examined herein will be attempting to account for the larger patterns in human existence. However, let us change just a bit of the conception of a puzzle. Perhaps we can focus on a particular unit in society to see how those in the order tradition solve the inherent puzzle that the existence of that unit represents. Later we can use the same unit to see how it might be analyzed from the pluralist and conflict perspectives. The question before us, then, is how shall the sociologists of the order community address the puzzle of the *family?*

# ■ Positivism

Recall for a moment the brief introduction to images of sociology in Chapter 2. There we found that some sociologists believe social relationships to have *lawful* properties. In other words, social life is thought to reflect the supposed predictability and order of the natural universe. Thus, the discipline is conceived as "natural science sociology." How does this image of human science affect the study of the most intimate of social relationships? The following quotation addresses one aspect of family life, that is, the role of women:

> Biological analysis presents the female sex, in the human species especially, as constitutionally in a state of perpetual infancy, in comparison with the other; and therefore more remote, in all important respects, from the ideal type of the race. Sociology will prove that the equality of the sexes, of which so much is said, is incompatible with all social existence, by showing that each sex has special and permanent functions which it must fulfill in this natural economy of the human family. (Comte, 1896: 284, originally published 1853)

Auguste Comte, the "father of sociology," attempted to find the basis for the social subjugation of women in the natural order of biology. (We shall postpone an account of his life until later, when we review his theoretical position.) In his three-volume work, *The Positive Philosophy of Auguste Comte* (1896, first published 1853), he argued that the subordination of women in the home is a natural extension of the intrinsic traits of the sexes. That is, women are "unfit . . . for the . . . intensity of mental labour" (285). According to Comte, male dominance is to be found under any and all cultural and social conditions and is hence tantamount to an expression of social law.

This description of the family position of women was presented in the context of the Western European society of the mid-nineteenth century. While a number of influential women and men were arguing for the equality of the sexes, Comte's reaction was typical for his time. His error was to attempt to elevate a common social condition (the subjugation of women) to the status of unvarying uniformity. Comte's conception of the social relationship conformed with the meaning of law in mathematics, that is, *a general principle to which all applicable cases must conform.* By the same logic, others have argued the natural inferiority or superiority of races, classes, nations, and civilizations. The tendency to define what *is* as what *must be* is ideology, not science.

You should not draw the conclusion that Comte's views on women and his eagerness to find lawful social arrangements were typical of those working in the natural science tradition. John Stuart Mill, another nineteenth-century philosopher (not sociologist), was both an important contributor to the tools of the research process associated with this type of sociology and an ardent champion of women's equality. However, Comte's work represented an early attempt to impart the rigor and precision of science to the study of the social universe. It remained for others to advance that dream.

Comte first used the term *sociology* in print in 1838. While there were many before him (including Hobbes) who thought that science should be used to make a society of reason, Comte argued for an independent discipline that would approach society in a manner analogous to the astronomer studying the stars or the chemist analyzing compounds.

In his efforts to envision this new way, Comte developed a historical account of the development of knowledge. All thought, he argued, passes through three stages: theological, metaphysical, and positivistic. The first stage refers to the human propensity for supernatural explanations. The second seems to mean an abstract and speculative philosophy. The positive stage was for Comte the coming of science. Under it, all phenomena including the social are viewed as governed by natural laws. The discovery of lawful relationships between events can be made through scientific observation and experimental research.

What specifically is positivism? We will attempt only a brief overview of the more essential properties of this tradition here. While there is always a danger of oversimplification, we can make an important beginning by focusing on the meaning of the word *positive*. Certain synonyms then come to mind such as *specific, certain, precise,* and *beyond doubt.* That these words represent the *imagery* of what, for most people, is meant by *science* is not accidental. Positivism lays claim as the *philosophy* of science.

The word *philosophy* is from the Greek *philos* for "loving" and *sophos* for "wise." Generally it refers to a study of the principles governing thought and conduct. As a philosophy of science, positivism represents a way of guiding (1) the development of logically connected ideas (theory) and (2) the design of research (ways of looking for evidence to test those ideas). While positivism is largely preeminent in the natural sciences (for example, physics and chemistry), the attempt to apply it to the social universe has been criticized in many quarters. However, the development of research tools common to much sociological inquiry has strongly benefited from this legacy.

Positivism in sociology, then, refers to an approach to the field modeled upon the natural sciences. Other positivistic philosophers, unlike Comte, have rarely been concerned with sociology. They are primarily interested in the more general knowledge that represents their field. Likewise, only a minority of sociologists consider themselves positivists, though many are more indebted to this tradition than they may realize.

If positivism reflects a commitment to certainty, how is this objective to be realized? First of all, this approach in sociology focuses on the world of disciplined and tested experience and observation. This emphasis on what can be seen or shown means that a *subjective world of meaning is defined as outside the proper domain of science.* Thus, the very concerns that are fundamental to the pluralist paradigm quickly take their leave.

For those influenced by this theoretical legacy in sociology, science begins with clearly stated propositions. For example, if one suspects a relationship between two variables, say, income and education, the nature of that relationship must be stated in specific fashion so that it may be tested in the real world of observable experience. If one states that those who have more education will have more money, then both education and having money must be defined so that the proposition may be verified.

Although this appears simple, certain questions do appear. What is meant by education? Is it formal years of schooling? The completion of certain degrees? The awarding of diplomas? What then of those societies in which education is not conducted in a formal school system? Further, it may become obvious that money may come from several sources. It may be earned through labor, acquired through investments (in societies where the economy is in private hands), or inherited. Thus the *clarity* of the relationship is improved when we specify something like the following: In Western industrialized societies, those completing more years of formal education will receive more income in the form of wages and/or salary from their jobs. Statistical data on income and education can then be assembled and analyzed to test this hypothesis.

As this procedure demonstrates, positivism is about breaking down the complexities of ideas into their logical elements. When modern positivism is applied to society and other social relationships, it means that the ultimate nature of science is to find orderly patterns of variables. In his presidential address to the members of the American Sociological Association, Hubert Blalock stated:

> Reality is sufficiently complex that we will need theories that contain upwards of fifty variables if we wish to disentangle the effects of numerous exogenous and endogenous variables on the diversity of dependent variables that interest us. (1979: 881)

In other words, the search for true "causes" and reliable predictions necessitates the systematic elimination of extraneous factors that do not contribute to theoretical explanation.

For the positivists, the underlying image of society is one of a vast compound of interdependent variables that can be identified and measured, isolated and combined. It is not surprising that positivistic sociology has been called into question by critics who argue that when the richness and complexity of social life are fragmented into simple testable versions of the relationships among variables, something is lost in translation.

# ■ Functionalism

A second tradition in sociology can also be said to exemplify order assumptions about the nature of theoretical science. As the subsequent analysis unfolds, we should be sensitive to the distinctive way in which the arguments about the family are constructed. Positivists old and new look for order in the lawful arrangement of variables into patterns. For these sociologists, theoretical explanation ultimately makes possible prediction and control. Functionalists are also concerned with orderly relationships. However, the theoretical task is different. At a typically macrosociological level, functionalists demonstrate that practices, customs, and existing arrangements fit into the total structure of society. This constant quest to find the larger system or body that makes sense of a social fact demonstrates another image of science for the order paradigm.

Let us return to our examination of the family, with yet another description of the place of women.

> As we advance to modern times, we see marriage developing. The circle of ties which it creates extends further and further; the obligations that it sanctions multiply. The conditions under which it can be contracted, those under which it can be dissolved are limited. . . .
>
> Sexual (sex-role) labor is more and more divided. . . . Long ago, woman retired from warfare and public affairs, and consecrated her entire life to her family. Since then, her role has become even more specialized. Today, among cultivated people, the woman leads a completely different existence from that of man. One might say that the two great functions of the psychic life are thus dissociated, that one of the sexes takes care of the affective (emotional) functions and the other of intellectual functions. (Durkheim, 1933: 59–60, originally published 1893)

At first glance, this description of marriage, family, and "woman's place" appears very similar to the position of Auguste Comte. Yet if we examine Émile Durkheim's words (written in 1893) carefully, we find a fundamental difference. Stated simply, the place of women in marriage and the family is not necessarily due to the inborn traits or biological predisposition of women as Comte argued. For Durkheim (1858–1917), woman's place was *functional*, that is, a *necessary* part of the more complex division of labor which tended to emerge with the modernization of society. That women provided the emotional labor and men the intellectual only made "sense." To be clear, the division of labor in the family simply reflected the increasing role specialization that was developing in the broader society.

The same could be said for marriage. At one time, Durkheim argued, the marriage relationship was somewhat loose or nonexistent because there was no clear division of tasks and functions between the sexes. Women were more independent, participating broadly in economic life, government, and occasionally warfare (Durkheim, 1933: 56–58). As societies grew more heterogeneous, its tasks became more diversified, which in turn demanded specialization of its members. Such a state invariably produced a greater *dependence* of each member on the society or each partner in a marriage on the other. Thus, binding laws and obligations were then necessary to preserve the marriage unit and the delicate division of labor that it represented.

Of course to Durkheim (and to many people today) it appeared altogether "logical" that women would offer emotional support while men took care of intellectual business. Likewise, one might argue that women were and are functional when they are the primary suppliers of nurture and affection and confine their role to the home. The question to be explored, however, is—functional for whom? That men and women could be *socially* defined so that their humanity, wholeness, and potential might be seriously jeopardized appears to have escaped Durkheim's argument. Moreover, most contemporary anthropologists would take serious issue with Durkheim's position that family and kinship obligations were less complex in tribal societies than in later industrialized ones. Finally, despite the growth of specialization in the division of labor in Western societies, the marriage relationship does not show the increasing solidarity that Durkheim's logic predicted.

*But again, the critique of a particular functionalist position on the family or of this tradition in general should not obscure the point. For Durkheim, the marriage state and the institution of the family reflected the nature of society, not the consequences of biology.* However, this early sociologist did turn to biology for an analogy, that of the *organism*. This metaphor, you will recall, is also appropriate to describe Plato's conception of society.

To Durkheim and other early functionalists, society in its complexity appeared somewhat like a living thing. Just as every part of an organism contributes to the well-being of the biological whole, early functionalists thought that the patterns, rituals, and role divisions in a society are also necessary to the integration or well-being of the social whole. This particular description was to be replaced later by a mechanical metaphor, that of a *system* (Parsons, 1937). Whether organism or system, society was viewed in the sense of an essentially self-correcting equilibrium. Those operating in the functionalist/systems tradition have shown an abiding interest in relating whatever the element under scrutiny to other elements or to some aspect of the entire social order.

You may have concluded by now that the primary concern of functionalism is *order,* that is, with how a society fits together. Indeed, the readily identifiable questions that guide theory construction in this tradition center on such things as consensus (agreement), continuity, and effective socialization. For functionalists, things are the way they are because most people agree that existing patterns are the best. In turn, the emphasis is on understanding the *necessary* part each custom, pattern, or ritual plays in the continuation of the present order. Given this state of equilibrium based on consensus, any fundamental dissenting behavior is interpreted in terms of an inappropriately socialized minority who have not learned the rules (Chambliss, 1973).

The critics of functionalism have pointed to the *conservative* nature of this tradition. It must be admitted that if every part is related to and works to support other parts, then the organism or system should experience neither conflict nor change. Further, if these patterns exist because of consensus, and if each is truly necessary to the whole, it follows that intervening to change an element is a threat to the whole. Change may therefore be defined in terms of deviance or disorganization.

It appears that a major fault of the functionalist approach has been the tendency of adherents to find some sort of necessity in whatever exists. We might recall that Durkheim saw the clear distinctions in sex roles as necessary given the more specialized division of labor in industrial society. Yet a willingness to explore the often latent or unintended consequences of social patterns need not simply be a matter of legitimating the status quo.

For example, the ideology of racial inferiority was quite "functional" in the period of Western colonialism. This is to say that racism played a role in maintaining or at least legitimating the expansion of European empires (Van den Berghe, 1967). Such an observation, however, need not provide hidden ideological sanction to either colonialism or racism. It simply suggests that the latter may have been a historical function of the former. Unfortunately, functionalism as an explanatory system in sociology goes beyond this point.

Perhaps a distinction can be made that will enhance our understanding. As a form of *analysis,* a functionalist approach represents both science and logic as a means of identifying connections, associations, and relationships that might otherwise be overlooked. However, when functionalism is presented as theoretical *explanation* (as with Durkheim and his heirs), a troublesome shift occurs. Now, a pattern is thought to prevail because it is necessary to the whole, reflects underlying social needs, and is founded on a consensus of society's members. Figure 3.1 may be useful in separating out functionalist explanation (theory) and its criticisms from the functionalist analysis that in some form is common to all science.

As with Comte, we shall delay a discussion of the historical context in which Durkheim's life was formed. To this point we should understand enough about Durkheim's functionalism to know that he viewed human science in a distinctive fashion. It is the responsibility of the sociologist to explain the natural order of things, to reveal how seemingly independent and random events and customs are part of a larger pattern. To Durkheim, the major problem faced by the human community is a threat to its solidarity. Individualism and change are evils twinborn.

Durkheim's assumptions about the nature of human science logically flow from his conceptions about the social milieu. At base, he assumed that society

---

**Figure 3.1**   Distinguishing Functional
Analysis from Functional Explanation

While functional analysis means simply searching for relationships, functional explanation frequently leaves the impression that whatever exists must be there for some
socially beneficial purpose. However, the major problem for functionalist explanation
is social change. If the existing order is based on consensus and forms an interdependent system, social change can only be seen as threatening.

| FUNCTIONAL ANALYSIS | FUNCTIONAL EXPLANATION |
|---|---|
| 1. Is common to science. | 1. Is specific to functionalism. |
| 2. Searches for connections between or among events, conditions, ideas. | 2. Tends to transform connections into causes. |
| 3. Makes no assumption that the existence of a social practice is proof of its necessity. | 3. Assumes whatever exists plays a necessary role in the larger social order. |
| 4. May ask *for whom or what* something is functional. | 4. Assumes whatever exists is based on *consensus* among the members of a society. |
| 5. Does not preclude social change. | 5. Views social change as a threat to societal cohesion. |

---

and its norms reflect the needs of its members. Further, society is a consequence of consensus. Once established, its institutions and normative system
acquire a being of their own. For Durkheim, as for Plato, the interests of the
whole body transcend those of individual members.

Although society, its institutions, and norms flow from a consensus of
the people, social phenomena represent more than a blending of individual
minds. By this Durkheim meant that these and other social phenomena constitute a reality *sui generis*. That is, social reality represents a class alone, a special
state of its own kind. This distinctive and unique existence has both empirical
and subjective properties.

Durkheim's *The Rules of the Sociological Method* (1958, originally published 1895) did far more than Comte's polemic to bring about a truly distinctive human science. Durkheim argued that on the one hand, the social milieu
can be studied by means of observation, experience, and experiment. On the
other, this unique reality can be bridged from the vantage point of its members. To Durkheim, the social world contains its own truths, its own actual
forces. These *social facts* are as real as the phenomena studied by the natural
scientist though the social milieu is clearly independent of the physical environment. This independent social world demonstrates its reality to its members on an ongoing basis. Social facts not only appear as something real out
there (exteriority); they also serve to control the behaviors of people in society

(constraint). For example, social facts such as values and norms can be experienced and observed in socialization practices. They also serve to ensure societal cohesion by controlling unrestrained self-interest.

Durkheim cautioned against trying to explain this unique reality by means of psychological concepts. Any attempt to account for society and other social phenomena in terms of the wishes, instincts, or minds of individuals represents a form of psychological reductionism. Society is simply not analogous to the human psyche. Thus a new science was required to address social relationships. The theoretical conceptualizations of that science would for Durkheim identify, explain, and clarify the following:

1. A society assumed to be organic, collective, and cohesive

2. The regularities, continuity, and interdependence of social life

3. How each part of the whole represents underlying social needs

4. The problem of order at a macrosociological level

5. Threats to harmony—specifically, deviance and revolutionary change

6. An evolutionary conception of social change

# ■ Assumptions of the Order Paradigm

Putting Comte and Durkheim aside and summarizing what has been presented to this point, we can set forth the major assumptions of the order paradigm. As a composite this model portrays a striking and unique image of human nature, the nature of society, and the nature of human science.

*Human Nature*

1. Human nature is more private than public, individualistic than social, competitive than cooperative. Left unchecked, the force of self-interest may reduce a community of people to a mob of strangers.

2. The order conception of human nature is one of the power of reason. While subject to the dangers of unbridled passion or undisciplined wants, the species is capable of establishing those controls necessary to ensure survival. The principle of existence is embodied in a rationalism by which people surrender to social authority those reasonable powers essential to societal cohesion.

3. Personal inequalities are a part of the natural order. That is, there are fundamental and innate differences in talent, potential, and ultimate social worth.

*The Nature of Society*

1. Given the natural human disposition toward disorder, survival can be ensured only through the coming of powerful and integrated social institutions. Such institutions must be preserved because anarchy is tantamount to the mutual destruction of society and the individual.

2. Given the natural conditions of personal inequality, the good society will divide its tasks so as to reflect these innate differences (Durkheim, 1933: 28; Plato, 1974).

3. The nature of society is that of interdependent institutions and a supportive normative system that constrains private behavior. Remember that Plato, Durkheim, and others conceived society in *organismic* terms, while Talcott Parsons (see Chapter 7) employed the mechanical metaphor of a *system*. The natural state of society is therefore one of equilibrium, with each part or element contributing to the maintenance of the whole.

4. Institutions and norms exist in any given society because of a consensus on the part of members of that society.

5. Given a consensually validated social order, all members of a society should be expected to conform. Thus legitimacy logically follows the assumption of consensus.

6. Given the legitimacy of the existing order and the naturally adaptive properties of the social system, social change assumes a primarily evolutionary nature.

7. Forced social change represents a clear and present danger to the cohesiveness of society and the solidarity of its members.

*The Nature of Science*

1. As there is systematic order in the natural universe, so there is system and order in the social universe. Social relationships reflect unique properties that can be discovered through the methods of science.

2. A positive science of society commands a search for certainty in relationships. Sociology shares with the natural sciences a quest for laws that yield prediction and control.

3. A science of society is empirical. Sensory-based knowledge and rigorous observation replace detached rationalism with its emphasis on pure reason.

4. Social facts have quantitative properties. Such may be measured and assigned numerical value. Quantitative change in one or more social facts (now variables) may be directly or indirectly connected to change in others. Thus lawful relationships may assume mathematical form.

5. The social milieu is distinctive and independent of the physical environment. However, a science of society need not be unique. The phe-

**Figure 3.2** The Order Paradigm

| PARADIGMATIC ELEMENTS | ASSUMPTIONS | IDEAL TYPES |
| --- | --- | --- |
| Image of human nature | Reason, self-interest, personal inequality | Hobbes's state of nature |
| Image of society | Cohesion, integration, consensus, self-correcting, social inequality | Plato's republic |
| Image of science | Systematic, positive, empirical, quantitative, predictive | Comte's positivism Durkheim's functionalism |

nomena under examination may vary, but the nature of science does not. Chemists may study compounds, physicists thermodynamics, and sociologists society. Science does not alter its nature or methods simply because of a difference in the subject matter.

6. Theoretical relationships should be stated in clear language with all terms clearly defined. Modern positivists call for *operational definitions* that allow key concepts to be measured and uniformly understood by those testing theoretical propositions through research. To illustrate, if in a theory on human learning intelligence is a key concept, then the operational definition of intelligence might be: what *intelligence tests* measure.

The paradigmatic elements, assumptions, and ideal types that together comprise the order paradigm are outlined in schematic form in Figure 3.2. The task before us is to comprehend the linkages between such imagery and the content of the theoretical systems that follow.

# ■ *Bibliography*

Aubrey, John
(1669–1690) 1957  *Brief Lives*. Ann Arbor: University of Michigan Press.

Blalock, H. M.
1979                "The Presidential Address: Measurement and Conceptualization Problems: The Major Obstacle to Integrating Theory and Research." *American Sociological Review* 44:881–894.

Bluck, Richard S. H.
1951            *Plato's Life and Thought.* Boston: Beacon Press.

Chambliss, William
1973            *Sociological Readings in the Conflict Perspective.* Reading,
               Mass.: Addison-Wesley.

Comte, Auguste
(1853) 1896     *The Positive Philosophy of Auguste Comte.* Freely translated
               and condensed by Harriet Martineau. 3 vols. London:
               George Bell and Sons (Ann Arbor, Mich.: University Mi-
               crofilms, 1971).

Durkheim, Émile
(1893) 1933     *The Division of Labor in Society.* Translated by George
               Simpson. New York: Macmillan.
(1895) 1958     *The Rules of the Sociological Method.* Edited by George
               E. G. Catlin. Glencoe, Ill.: The Free Press.

Hobbes, Thomas
(1629) 1975     *Thucydides.* Edited by Richard Schlatter. New Brunswick,
               N.J.: Rutgers University Press.
(1651a) 1909    *The Leviathan.* Oxford, England: The Calendar Press.
(1651b) 1977    "Leviathan." In Richard Sennett (Ed.), *The Psychology of
               Society,* pp. 242–247. New York: Random House.
(1656) 1966     *The English Works of Thomas Hobbes of Malmesbury.* Edited
               by Sir William Molesworth. Aalen, Germany: Scientia.

Merton, Robert
(1949) 1968     *Social Theory and Social Structure.* New York: The Free
               Press.

Parsons, Talcott
1937            *The Structure of Social Action.* Glencoe, Ill.: The Free
               Press.

Plato
(c. 377 B.C.) 1974  *The Republic.* Translated by G. M. A. Grube. Indianapolis:
               Hackett Publishing Company.
(c. 360 B.C.) 1926  *The Laws.* The Loeb Classical Library, vols. 9, 10. New
               York: G. P. Putnam's Sons.

Strauss, Leo
1975            *The Argument and the Action of Plato's Laws.* Chicago: Uni-
               versity of Chicago Press.

Van den Berghe, Pierre
1967            *Race and Racism: A Comparative Perspective.* New York:
               The Free Press.

# CHAPTER 4

# ■ Organicism

With an understanding of the paradigm to guide us, we now turn to a particular set of order theories. At the outset, please remember that there is no line of demarcation between paradigm and theory. However, the broad sweep of the former with its imagery and assumptions can be distinguished from the more conceptually precise and focused nature of the latter. At base, a paradigm identifies what is common in some essential respects to the various theories it envelops. The particular puzzle at issue in this chapter is societal evolution. However, there are a number of ways of conceiving this problem of order. For Auguste Comte, Herbert Spencer, and William Graham Sumner, society is akin to a special *organism* obeying its own laws of "progress." These three men are further joined by common adherence to a Platonic theme: The natural order of all societies is one of *hierarchy*.

# ■ Auguste Comte (1798–1857): On Positive Philosophy

Auguste Comte, the founder of "positive philosophy" who gave sociology its name, was born in 1798 in Montpellier, France. His father was a lower level government functionary, and his family was both Roman Catholic and strongly supportive of the monarchy. Early in his adolescence, Comte broke with both the faith and his family's traditional allegiance to royalist politics. However, as with other notable French intellectuals (including Saint-Simon and Durkheim), Comte was to issue a *call to order* in society and in the new discipline he sought to establish. And, as we shall see, his "positive sociology" replaced (theoretically) the old royalty with a new elite.

In 1814 the precocious Comte was admitted to the École Polytechnique, a center of scientific education that was renowned in France. Even at the tender age of 16, his religious and political beliefs had already estranged him from his family. Although the formal curriculum at the École Polytechnique was technical, many of its students (including Comte) and some professors developed an intellectual and political opposition to both the Napoleonic empire and the kings of the Bourbon ruling family. (It is interesting to note that the entire student body was expelled for radicalism in 1816. The incident was sparked not by revolutionary fervor per se but by a protest against the traditionally rigid forms of examination) (Ferré, 1970: vii–xii).

## History and Biography

The events and ideas that were to so heavily influence Comte and other early European sociologists do not simply coincide with their life spans. Instead, it proved to be the political, class, and nationalistic movements of the previous century that marked the decline of the aristocracy, the expansion and contraction of empires, the rise of commercial and industrial nouveaux riches, and the emergence of a well-defined working class. Such forces were undergirded by the strong philosophical current known as the Enlightenment. The changes these movements produced were not to be confined. They swept onward into the next century eliciting revolution and reaction, war and peace, dogma and knowledge. However, the specific conditions in Europe were to leave a special mark on subsequent theories of order. It is for this reason that we will examine the history of this era in this chapter and others to come.[1]

In eighteenth-century England, the monarchy was already coming to be constrained by the rising commercial elite, who demanded free entry into a competitive marketplace. However, under Louis XV (1715–1774), France had surrendered most of its colonial empire in wars with the British. In the process, it lost much of its potential for economic expansion. The church and nobility held most of the land, and French investors were forced to seek a return on their profits by lending money to the crown. Louis expanded the royal debt making interest payments by borrowing.

In this context of bankruptcy, Louis XVI ascended the throne in 1774. The fiscal crisis he inherited from his father had alienated the merchants, leaving the Bourbon royalty aligned only with the nobility. Many of the aristocrats were holders of little more than titles, while those who had wealth were frequently land rich and cash poor. In the turbulance of the era, the center of economic power was rapidly passing to the disenchanted bourgeoisie.

The decaying institutions of the old order came to be symbolized in the

---

[1] The following sources are useful in understanding the historical period in question: Goodwin, 1966; Lefebre, 1962–1964; and Price, 1972.

person of Louis and his queen, Marie Antoinette. The mindless extravagance of the court and its mistress became the cause célèbre of a growing revolutionary movement. In the summer of 1789, a segment of the Parisian population stormed the Bastille, provoking a mass emigration by French nobility. In the rural areas, the revolution took the form of peasant uprisings known as the *great fear.* These forces led to the founding of the First Republic (1792). Louis XVI and Marie Antoinette kept a rendezvous with Mademoiselle Guillotine, and in the spring of 1793 the Jacobins, so-called because they met secretly in a Jacobin monastery in Paris, took the power of the state. Believers in a "rational society" in which position would be determined by merit, they were led by the infamous Robespierre.

The last decade of the eighteenth century saw the unleashing of the Jacobin Reign of Terror, the ascension of Napoleon Bonaparte as first consul of the First Republic, and the birth of Auguste Comte. Although Comte was quite literally conceived in a storm of conflict, he was not a personal witness to the first revolution. Still, its excesses had shocked many of the French intelligentsia, including Saint-Simon, who forty years Comte's senior was to become his mentor. Given these and subsequent events, it is not difficult to understand Comte's lifelong quest for order.

Although a child of the aftermath of the first revolution, Comte was also to witness the almost cyclical change in nineteenth-century French rule. During his life, the political organization of the country took the form of two short-lived early *republics* with a nominally democratic structure, two Napoleonic *empires,* and an extended period of return to *royalist* rule.

In 1804 Bonaparte was crowned emperor. He built an empire through conquest before his fall from political and military grace. He was exiled to Elba in 1814 and returned to a brief hundred days of glory commencing in March of 1815 and ending with his defeat at the Battle of Waterloo in Belgium that June. The first Napoleonic empire was followed by the restoration of the kingdom of France under the House of Bourbon (1814–1848). During this period, a rapidly moving industrialization began to supplant local cottage industries with an emerging factory system. A growing working class came to form crude unions and reacted to the misery of their lives through violent protest. Reactive Bourbon repression set the stage for the Revolution of 1848 (de Sauvigny, 1966: 250–260).

The forces of the revolution consisted as usual of the laboring poor in the streets and the disaffected industrialists, financiers, and other bourgeoisie behind the scenes. The Second Republic came to pass in 1848, and Bonaparte's nephew, Napoleon III, was elected president. His ambitions quickly proved to be somewhat lofty. With the heavy financial support of the nouveaux riches, Louis Napoleon staged a coup. As had been the case with his uncle, he was the beneficiary of a pledge to improve prosperity through nation building under benign and necessary autocratic rule. In control of the state, he authorized national plebescites to rewrite the constitution and declare himself emperor. Given the chaos of the era, he won both. In 1852, five years before the death of Auguste Comte, Napoleon III became sovereign of the Second Empire.

# The Enlightenment and Comtean Assumptions

It is within the stream of eighteenth-century thought that we find the unlikely roots of Comtean positive sociology. The prevailing intellectual vision of that time has been termed the Enlightenment. Its ideals included progress and rationalism, learning and science, skepticism and empiricism. Its philosophers were to wed the Newtonian conception of lawful and predictable natural order with a belief in the inherent perfectability of human nature and a utopian image of social order.[2]

Certain Enlightenment thinkers were notorious for critical philosophies seen by other intellectuals (including Comte) to have planted the seeds of political revolution. Montesquieu (1689–1755), for example, held in *The Spirit of Laws* that the distribution of power is essential to freedom and that a system of laws is necessary to ensure that neither the state nor any organized segment of society becomes tyrannical. Rousseau (1712–1788) argued that human nature is neither selfish nor cruel and that laws that assume so are the regressive product of a repressive government. He forcefully concluded (see Chapter 9) that the social contract was to make sovereign power contingent on the consent of the governed.

Comte was impressed more by thinkers not identified strongly with the revolutionary implications of the social contract. One such thinker was Turgot (a minister for Louis XVI), who believed that society, culture, and their material manifestations (such as art, science, education, industry) progressively evolve toward higher plateaus. Later, it was Condorcet who expanded the theme of a rational person, continually perfected through the advance of science and technology. Both Turgot and Condorcet foresaw a strong role for a coming scientific elite. Finally, from the Scottish moralist Adam Smith, Comte came to the image of the nation as a marketplace. Although he specifically rejected Smith's laissez-faire dictum of an "invisible hand," Comte embraced the inherent benefits of the industrial model with its highly differentiated division of labor (Comte, 1896, Vol. 2: 194–208, originally published 1830–1842).

Given the turbulence of French history, the Enlightenment philosophes came to represent a two-edged sword. On the one hand, a positive-empirical science centered in the assumption of a rational mind gave hope to the dream of personal and societal improvement. On the other, a fervent embracing of the social contract came to be identified with the excesses of the Jacobins. *Some French intellectuals, including Comte and his master Saint-Simon, were to split off positive science from the perceived anarchistic philosophy of the contractualists. Embracing the empirical methods of the former (comparative, experimental, sensory observation), as well as its quest for laws, they repudiated the revolutionary politics of the latter.*

---

[2]An important work on the role of the Enlightenment in shaping early sociology is Irving Zeitlin's *Ideology and the Development of Sociological Theory* (1968).

One watershed experience in the intellectual life of Auguste Comte was his association with the eminent social theorist, Henri Saint-Simon. One year after the second abdication of Napoleon I, the expelled Comte left his studies in physiology at the École Polytechnique. He returned to Paris to become Saint-Simon's secretary, beginning a seven-year period of collaboration. The relationship ended acrimoniously with Comte denouncing his former teacher. The young Comte was still dissatisfied with the traditions of academic serfdom, and in this case he objected to the publishing of his essays under Saint-Simon's name. Perhaps more important was Comte's belief that his mentor was seeking the orderly and utopian reconstruction of society before a mature positive science had been developed. Nevertheless, the central ideas of his mentor proved to be central to Comte's own sociology.[3]

In 1813 Saint-Simon argued in print that the individual sciences and their many separate laws would come to be synthesized in a unitary and overarching law. (This was later repudiated by Comte [1896, Vol. 1: 17].) He further claimed that science would become the basis for a new spiritual transformation. While he called for the conversion of ethics and politics into positive sciences, Saint-Simon also believed that Christianity would soften the ravages of growing industrialism by advancing philanthropy among wealthy believers. He argued for the perfection of religion and the training of the clergy in science.

Saint-Simon's booklets also contained the "law of the three stages," in which he sought to trace the history of authoritative knowledge. Other seminal ideas advanced by this thinker included the imperative of social engineering, the necessity for a creative elite (including the industrialists), and the positive value of a nonexploitative system of stratification. To Auguste Comte fell the task of their refinement, enlargement, and systematization.

## Theoretical Content

The beginning point of Comte's somewhat turgid *The Positive Philosophy of Auguste Comte* (1896, originally published 1830–1842) was his rendition of the "law of human development." As touched on in Chapter 2, the law is that human knowledge and intelligence evolve toward a higher level. Or that such "passes successively through three different theoretical conditions: the Theological or fictitious; the Metaphysical or abstract; and the Scientific, or positive" (Comte, 1896, Vol. 1: 2). Although the positive stage represents an image of what sociology must be (an assumption), there is some potential here for a theory of knowledge (see especially, 1896, Vol. 2: 299–319).

Indeed, Comte was caught up in the struggle between the rational/scientific heirs of the Enlightenment and the ideological forces of the church and

---

[3] One excellent source on Saint-Simon is Frank Manuel's *The New World of Henri Saint-Simon* (1956).

metaphysical philosophies. He understood well that given changing social milieux, the explanation of phenomena would take radically different forms. Further, he did attempt to loosely explore underlying events and ideas, while
contending that explanation evolves first in the form of supernatural forces,
then in personified abstractions (forces inherent in all beings), and finally in the
search for natural law. Hence, Comte's conception falls clearly under the
shadow of the empirical side of the Enlightenment:

> In the final, the positive state, the mind has given over the vain search after
> Absolute notions, the origin and description of the universe, and the causes of
> phenomena, and applies itself to the study of their laws—that is their invariable
> relations of succession and resemblance. Reasoning and observation, duly com-
> bined, are the means of this knowledge. (1896, Vol. 1: 2)

Comte's crude theory of knowledge also linked the development of human thought to corresponding forms of *solidarity* in society. To be precise, he
argued for a historical connection between (1) theological knowledge and the
military basis for societal cohesion, (2) the metaphysical stage and a solidarity
founded on a legal system, and (3) the positive stage and a rising industrial
order.

For Comte, the strongest of bonds tied the dogma of the church and the
power of armed force together in a common regime. Here the cross followed
the flag, and military chiefs sought to ensure their rule by claiming religious
authority. A similar bond emerged from the simultaneous evolution of metaphysical explanation and the rise of state-sanctioned law. Comte believed that
legal systems are conceived as an expression of natural law, thereby reaffirming
the power of the sovereign. However, expressing his faith in the rising bourgeoisie, Comte held that in the positive stage science and industry will join to
produce a universal order based on benevolence (1896, Vol. 2: 328–333).

Comte also attempted something of a crude evolutionary theory of scientific knowledge. Little more than a taxonomy, his division of the sciences
included the *inorganic* (astronomy, physics, and chemistry) and the *organic*
(physiology and sociology). Ironically, just as Spencer could not keep distance
between his training as an engineer and his sociology, or Freud his neurology
apart from psychoanalytic theory, so Comte combined physiology and sociology. Throughout his work, the natural science imagery of the former penetrates the latter. But whether human being, society, or knowledge, all evolve
for Comte through successive stages of progress. This especially applies to sociology, destined by Comte to become uppermost in the hierarchy of science.

The thought of Auguste Comte also contains the first of recurring attempts to divide the discipline of sociology into two major categories. These,
in turn, correspond with the evolving nature of society. For Comte, sociology
was a positive science born of the laws of *order* and *progress,* laws also evident in
the nature of society. The discipline could thus be subdivided into *social statics*

and *social dynamics.* It is within these that we find the roots of later *functionalist/systems* theories in sociology.

By social statics, Comte referred to a "theory of spontaneous order of human society." Such a spontaneous order consists of three components: individual, family, and society. At the individual level, Comte believed that:

> . . . personal instincts must give an aim and direction to our social action. All notions of public good must be based upon those of private advantage, because the former can be nothing else than that which is common to all cases of the latter. (1896, Vol. 2: 279)

In his treatment of both family and society, Comte introduced the conceptual basis for the organic division of labor. Compared to the later classic by Durkheim, Comte's attempt appears quite superficial. Nonetheless, Comte argued that the family had a natural division of labor (see Chapter 3) while society must reflect a "distribution of employments." However, he went beyond role and task specialization to argue that society evolves toward a natural inequality. Comte saw this in the subordination of ages (the old ranked above the young), as well as hierarchies of intellect and the ability to command. He proposed that in governmental affairs particularly, some were fit and some were not.

Social dynamics refers to the "theory of natural progress of human society." The movement toward a more perfected state is inherent but can be influenced by such factors as life expectancy, population growth, and the evolution of reason as evidenced in the three stages. Progress is thus in large part contingent on the succession of positive science and the decline and fall of metaphysical and fictitious knowledge and their associated forms of social organization (see above).

The concept of an emerging and universal social order is central in Comtean thought. The essence of that order is *interdependence:* the consolidation of the arts, sciences, and social institutions into a unified whole. As the laws of social life are discovered, the ability to predict and control will be perfected. It follows that a perfected social system driven by the engine of positive science will end the historical human antagonisms born of obsolete knowledge.

This ultimate system will not be confined to a single nation-state. For Comte, the emerging universal order is a "great process" founded on five distinctive elements born of the superior contributions of European civilizations. France would contribute its political and philosophical wisdom; England, its realism and utilitarianism; Italy, its aptitude for art; Spain, a sense of personal worth; and Germany, a talent for theoretical generalization (1896, Vol. 3: 413–414).

Comte did not view his as a pure theoretical system. He held that "ideas govern the world" and that intellectual anarchy is a precondition for political anarchy. The ultimate task of sociology is that of social engineering, the application of knowledge concerning a lawful social system to the problems of society. The new spirit of the times would be one of benign generosity. Within the structure of this secular religion, the industrialists would be the new priests of a new order. But the sacraments they performed would be those discovered by positive sociology.

## Critique

In many respects, the thought of Comte is more a framework of assumptions about the nature of human being, society, and science than it is a system of explanation. His work does not offer us the means of verifying or testing propositions so important to the positive science he embraced. Further, twentieth-century neopositivists (see Chapter 8) have parted company with Comte on the question of applied sociology. They would enjoin the same note of caution Comte offered to Saint-Simon. For today's "natural science sociologists," prescribing for the ills of society is (still) premature and constitutes an infringement on the necessary detachment of science. Nevertheless, Comte offered conceptions of social life that have endured in modern times.[4] The following specific points of criticism are offered not merely to identify the problematics of early positivism but to sharpen our understanding of the content of this theory.

Comte's "law of three stages" falls considerably short of a prototype for a sociology of knowledge. A theory on the social basis of knowledge demands verification by means of a systematic historical method. Comte did not tie each of his intellectual stages to the specific events and ideas of corresponding eras. Once he described his law, he was content to accept its face validity. Much of Comtean thought is a polemic in defense of science, in his day a mode of knowledge in mortal combat with the forces of religious tradition and political instability.

Furthermore, like sociologists yet to come, Comte relied heavily on imagery drawn from physics, biology, mechanics, and other domains of the natural world. It is of some interest to note that the organic conception of society, including the imagery of evolutionary progress, did not await the work of Darwin. However, Comte's "insights" based on organic and naturalistic analogies and metaphors do not constitute evidence.

Comte's early attempt to account for a division of labor makes synonymous differentiation and stratification. Although all societies reflect a division of labor, this need not be taken to reflect a natural order of dominance. For

---

[4]Of central importance to positivistic methodology, Comte emphasized the importance of measurement.

example, despite Comte's assertion to the contrary, advancing age need not bring superordination. Elders in one society may be respected and provided for, while those in another are ignored and impoverished. Also, a comparative and historical analysis demonstrates great variation among societies in the prestige, power, monetary compensation, and other rewards accorded to occupations. Some arbitrary social judgment, whether born of tradition, consensus, the influence of interest groups, or class and state coercion, may be the basis for deciding that some people or some tasks are more important than others. (Such criticisms may also apply to modern functionalist theories of stratification, within and without sociology.)

Another concern is Comte's obsession with natural order. The issue is drawn whenever those arrangements already in existence come to assume a self-evident rationalism. Then, what *is* stands legitimated as what *must be*. This naturalistic fallacy is clearly evident in Comte's claim that there is a biological (hence natural) basis for the subordination of women in the family. Again, this point may be used to address modern theories of order.

To this point, it should be clear that the thought of Auguste Comte has ideological implications. With the modern industrial societies of the Western world as our reference point, his sociology can only be judged a paragon of conservative thought. However, we should remember that Comte in his time opposed the political turbulance he attributed to a decaying aristocracy, militaristic empire builders, and believers in radical democracy. Instead, he retained a conception of necessary hierarchy in both knowledge and society but bent it to fit the design of the ascending industrial order. Abandoning the past, he hitched his star to the rising bourgeoisie. His faith in industrialism as a force for societal integration blinded him to the divisive attributes of the class system. Thus, for Auguste Comte, positive science was more than the evolution of knowledge. It was, in political terms, the basis for a more perfect societal hierarchy.

Positivism therefore has a diversity of meanings. In Comte's words, it emerges both as a lawfully ordered world and as a reaction to the "negative" (critical and revolutionary) philosophes of the Enlightenment.[5] Hence, the social antithesis of the coming industrial-positive order was the "first French Revolution." For Comte, this period was born of a Rousseau-like illusion that civil society should be measured against the standard of human freedom. He repudiated not only Rousseau but all aligned "metaphysicians" who contributed to the "violent opposition to the movement of modern civilization" (Comte, 1896, Vol. 2: 157–158). Individual welfare, argued Comte, is a function of societal development and equilibrium. Freedom is incidental to order.

---

[5] Zeitlin (1968) holds that Comtean thought represents an ideological reaction to the democratic philosophers of the Enlightenment. This is true only in part. Comte retained the Enlightenment heritage in the form of a faith in science, progress, and public education.

# ■ Herbert Spencer (1820–1903): Society as Organism

Another early sociologist who adhered strongly to an evolutionary vision of society was Herbert Spencer. Born in Derby in the Midlands of England, he was the only surviving child of William and Harriet Spencer. Spencer's health was poor in his youth, and he was educated at home by his schoolmaster father until he was 13. He then spent three years under the tutelege of one of his uncles, Thomas Spencer, a parson and reformer of the Church of England. Herbert's family was comprised of firm Dissenters, who chose not to conform to the teachings of the established state-church. They held strong political convictions, opposing the role of the state as a provider of public services (such as national education) and supported laissez-faire economics (Barnes and Becker, 1938: 664–665).

## History and Biography

After leaving the home of Thomas Spencer, young Herbert took a job as chief engineer for the London and Birmingham Railroad at the age of 17. A remarkable ability in mechanics, perfected and refined over the next decade, was to color his image of both biology and society throughout his life. While an employee of the railway, Spencer wrote his first serious essay, *On the Proper Sphere of Government,* in 1822. At the age of 28, Spencer became subeditor of *The Economist,* a London-based weekly noted for its editorial opposition to government regulation and its support of free trade. He went on to publish his first book, *Social Statics* (1892, originally published 1850), three years later. In 1853 Thomas Spencer died, making Herbert his heir. Another paternal uncle and his father later bequeathed their fortunes to him. These inheritances supported him and made possible the publication of a number of his works (Kennedy, 1978: 11–22).

The life of Herbert Spencer intersects a turbulent history of war, revolution, and the expansion of the empire. The social world of his father, mother, and uncles was one of continuous conflict with revolutionary France between 1793 and 1815. The United Kingdom emerged from the conflict with substantially enlarged colonial holdings. This acquisition of an empire on which the sun never set provided raw materials for the exploding factory system of the British economy. Wealth grew and so did its concentration. In the meantime, the political scene was clouded by the ongoing upheavals in France. In such a context, democratic conceptions of political freedom espoused by the Enlightenment philosophes came to be defined as anarchy. These events and ideas, taken as a whole, set the historical stage for the coming to power of the Tories.

In the first decade of Spencer's life, the forces of reaction repudiated the forces of revolution across the channel. The Tory party (renamed the Conservative in 1830), dispossessed the Whigs (renamed the Liberal party in 1832). On the economic front, it was a time of burgeoning industrialization and urbanization. The working class agitated for the establishment of trade unions, which were legalized within a context of unemployment among adult workers and the exploitation of child labor. However, the unions were severely limited in their influence, and many of the unemployed, especially in the rural areas, emigrated to British colonies. The Tory refusal to reform parliament led to the party's defeat in 1830.

The victorious Whigs moved to extend the vote to more of their "middle-class" constituency; however, even though the number of electors doubled, both farm and factory workers remained without suffrage. The young Spencer, at this point, joined with his Uncle Thomas in support of suffrage for the working class. The two believed that an alliance could be formed between workers and the rising industrial and commercial interests that chafed under the aristocratic bias of the Conservatives. This political marriage proved unworkable, and Herbert drifted quite literally toward the new bourgeoisie. He met one Lawrence Heyworth, a wealthy Liverpool merchant, at a political meeting. Heyworth, like the Spencers, sought to impose the ideology of the rising entrepreneurial class on the workers' movement. However, most workers proved less than satisfied with the solutions offered by self-sufficiency and laissez-faire economics. Heyworth, whose family offered a second home to Spencer, came to denounce the working class (Kennedy, 1978: 19–20).

The nineteenth century represented the zenith of an age of imperialism for Britain. During the reign of Victoria (1837–1901), the Crown Colonies were the center of frequent rebellions. Victoria resorted to the establishment of a system of self-rule in the colonies that offered some measure of local political control without severing the imperial connection. Revolts in Canada (1837), the Crimean War (1854–1856), the Indian Mutiny (1857), and war with China (1858–1860) punctuated Victoria's early rule. It was, however, the full blooming of the industrial revolution that made imperative the quest for assured sources of raw materials and new markets for manufactured goods. Such forces together with similar expansionism on the part of the French, Germans, Japanese, and other imperial powers accelerated the process of empire building in the last quarter of the century.

It should be remembered that the Age of Victoria strongly coincided with the adult life of Herbert Spencer. Perhaps more to the point, the first of his three volumes of *The Principles of Sociology* (1925–1929) was originally published between 1876 and 1896, when Disraeli as prime minister was directing overseas expansion. On the domestic front, the conditions of the English working class could fairly be described as quite desperate throughout the century. It is not difficult to understand how these events shaped the established knowledge of the era toward the ends of conservative ideology.

## Assumptions

Ironically, a work in biological science rather than philosophy or social thought came to be used in the defense of both class inequality and global colonialism. The Darwinian conception of natural selection, addressed in the *Origin of Species* (1859), was converted into a crude ideology. Termed social Darwinism, this idea system sought to legitimate a "survival of the fittest" on the societal and national level. Although Spencer came to wear the label "social Darwinist," the roots of his work, as we have seen, go deeper. The legitimation of social domination had not awaited the coming of Darwin, or Spencer for that matter. It had been sought historically in various philosophies and religions, as well as in nationalism and political chauvinism. However, the twisting of Darwinian thought brought a biological dimension to the ideology of dominance. Spencer had been a social Darwinist before Darwin (1892, originally published 1850). Nevertheless, he felt vindicated by the work of the evolutionist and defended it at length.

Another contemporary of Spencer also employed certain aspects of Darwinian thought. A pioneer in the field of genetics, Sir Francis Galton, published a number of works on heredity between 1869 and 1906. In these he attempted to demonstrate the genetic inequality of human beings. Put simply, Galton believed that specific abilities (in mathematics, art, political leadership, and so forth) were inherited; thus excellence was born far more than made. However, he did not stop here. Galton argued that the principle of genetic inequality could be applied to groups and races, a position that brought him to advocate *eugenics*. This meant that the biologically and morally best should be encouraged to procreate while the mentally and socially inferior should be hindered. Herbert Spencer had some precise views on how this hindrance might be realized.

## Theoretical Content

Spencer wed his belief in a biological basis for the triumph of the fittest with the assumption that the natural state of society is one of hierarchy. He was widely read in biology, engineering, and physical science and used such imagery to argue for a positive science. Although he published many works in philosophy, politics, and early anthropology and psychology, he is basically remembered for fledgling efforts in sociology. These include *First Principles* (1900, originally published 1862), *The Study of Sociology* (1961, originally published 1873), and the aforementioned *Principles of Sociology* (1925–1929, originally published 1876–1896).

Spencer's theory of society is splashed over these and other minor works. In it he offers a dual conception of society and a corresponding division of sociology. *Social statics* represents the institutional structure (familial, governmental, religious, industrial) and the division of labor built into such enduring patterns. *Social dynamics* refers to the ongoing evolution of the whole. In the sixth edition of *First Principles* Spencer wrote:

> On Passing from Humanity under its individual form to Humanity as socially embodied, we find the general law still more variously exemplified. The change from the homogeneous to the heterogeneous is displayed equally in the progress of civilization as a whole, and in the progress of every tribe or nation; and it is still going on with increasing rapidity. (1900: 314, originally published 1862)

For Spencer, evolution was tantamount to a natural law for the physical, biological, and social universes. In all such worlds, there exists a lawful change from the homogeneous to the heterogeneous, from the uniform to the multi-form, from the simple to the complex. Before Darwin explained the biological origin of the species by natural selection, Spencer conceived of both an individual and a societal struggle for survival in which the self-sufficient and strong would overcome. He held that society as a whole should be conceived as a special organism evolving toward higher states of perfection.

In its lowest stage, wrote Spencer, the social order is little more than a coming together of individuals having like powers and functions. While there is some division of labor based on sex roles, every woman and every man have essentially the same skills and the family is autonomous. Over time, conquest produces the massing of tribes, with governing and dominant functions passing to stronger individuals and groups. Ruling authorities, both secular and sacred, then evolve into complex hierarchies supported by their organization and a growing world of custom (1900: 280–371).

The line connecting Spencer to later sociological thought (see especially Durkheim in Chapter 5) is evidenced in his treatment of the division of labor. Once again, he remains true to his evolutionary vision and his assumptions of natural hierarchy.

> Meanwhile there has been going on a differentiation of a more familiar kind; that, namely, by which the mass of the community has been segregated into distinct classes and orders of workers. . . . The governed part has undergone a more complex development, which has resulted in that minute division of labour characterizing advanced nations. (1900: 317)

Society, argued Spencer, is *superorganic*. This is to say that it is organized as a social entity in the same way that a body is organized as a biological entity. Each grows and matures, and if unfit will decay. Accordingly, the proper state of the societal organism is one of equilibrium: among individual members, groups, and classes. Its social relationships and population size, as well as the nature of its institutions, all contribute to this state of balance. For example, supply will adjust to demand, political policy will respond to the wishes of the population, and population growth will be governed by Malthusian checks (especially, the supply of food). All such adjustments contribute to the integration of the whole. However, equilibrium does not mean peaceful coexistence, especially during the early stages of societal development. Rather, it is an uneasy and temporal condition that assumes the form of a struggle for existence.

Within the framework of this evolutionary organicism, Spencer constructed a position on militarism and industrialism. As reformulated by Franklin Giddings (in Barnes and Becker, 1938: 668), Spencer argued that the conflict inherent in the struggle for existence evolves into a more complex organizational structure: that of militarism. Militarism shapes human character, behavior, and social organization into a fitness for warfare. It further consolidates through compulsory cooperation differing individuals, groups, and societies into larger and larger entities, and through the process contributes to greater social integration. With its growing efficiency of organization, militarism makes it possible for an increasingly larger segment of the population to engage in industry and to remain at peace.

With the growth of industry and more lasting peace, human character, behavior, and the organization of society evolve into a peaceful society in which individual initiative and voluntary cooperation abound. In such a society, members can move freely and change their social relationships without damaging the integration of the society. However, the transition from militarism to industrialism and peace is not possible until all nations and races have evolved to a more perfect state of equilibrium.

From *First Principles* and *The Principles of Sociology*, we can extract Spencer's view that evolution, although ultimately lawful, is not necessarily unilinear or progressive for a given society. For evolution to prove progressive, the principle of *self-sufficiency* must be obeyed. The best sort of society, therefore, is one that institutionalizes laissez faire in all dimensions of social life. To intervene in the natural evolutionary process, to artificially impair the role of self-sufficiency in the necessary struggle for existence, is to impede progress toward human perfection. This is evident in Spencer's opposition to state education:

> If supply and demand are allowed free play in the intellectual sphere as in the economic sphere . . . it must follow that the children of the superior will be advantaged: the thrifty parents, the energetic, and those with a high sense of responsibility, will buy education for their children to a greater extent than the improvident and the idle. And if character is inherited, then the average result must be that the children of the superior will prosper and increase more than the children of the inferior. There will be a multiplication of the fittest instead of a multiplication of the unfittest. (1902: 92–93)

Spencer further qualified the conception of evolutionary progress by noting that societies may be inherently weak and subject to *dissolution*. If some individuals are unfit or less fit, it follows that some societies may also be unfit or less fit. Along these lines, Spencer believed that societal evolution might be retarded through the mixing of races. He also believed that races are differentially endowed. And finally, he argued that a preceding evolutionary stage might have an adverse impact on a succeeding one, or that a society might be inhibited in its development by surrounding nations.

# Critique

So much for the essence of Herbert Spencer's theory of society. It is an early example of sociology founded in large part on the assumptions of the order paradigm. However, unlike others we will examine, Spencer did not emphasize consensus as a basis for equilibrium. Nor did he advocate a powerful sovereign state. Equilibrium in his theory meant a naturally occurring hierarchy. In concrete terms, this means laissez-faire economics and an end to governmental meddling. Public attempts to care for the weak can only mean a less perfect society. Unbridled and unhindered self-sufficiency is in the interest of the "fit," whether individuals, groups, or nations. For Herbert Spencer, the Hobbesian nature was not to be unduly chained.

Spencer's theory is cast in the image of natural science. His work employs the language of the biological and physical worlds, as well as its "laws" to explain the societal organism. He assumed that the evolutionary process was universal and transferable. No matter how appealing such ideas were in their era, however, we can identify little evidence that society is simply superorganic. Although there may be some crudely drawn similarities between societal equilibrium and biological balance, the two do not equate. Put bluntly, evolution in the biological world was transferred by Spencer to the social world without proof. Hence, his concepts do not facilitate through research the discovery of the sociological equivalents of Darwin's fossils. It appears then that Spencer's organicism is more an analogy than an explanation of society. And an analogy remains just that: a similarity or likeness between things in some respects when those things are otherwise not the same.

At base, Spencer's organicism appears to be a form of biogenic reductionism. This is to say that the nature of a society reflects the nature of the individuals that make it up. Implicit in his pleas for noninterference, his thinly veiled racism, and his description of "primitive" societies as simple, savage, and backward is the contention that good biological stock makes for good societies. If personal traits and abilities determine society, there is in effect little place for social forces. Such an argument effectively reduces societal change to the level of individual evolution, and social institutions to a system of rewards to be conferred upon the deserving. Even peace within and between societies must logically, for Spencer, be contingent on the disappearance or control of the biologically unfit.

Spencer's sociology is quite unambiguous as an ideological system. It is an example of Victorian scholarship, conceived and written within the context of an age of imperialism and class conflict. In Spencer's thought, change is lawful, but it assumes an orderly unfolding of superior individual traits. Spencer did not believe that history had simply stopped. However, the international implications of his theory could only be that the leading nations of the era were preeminent by a natural selection. At the domestic level, those with greater wealth and power or superior education and social standing were fit. This Platonic hierarchy ignored structural inequality, inheritance, or simply good fortune. (Ironically, Spencer himself was rather generously treated as an heir.)

In the arena of social policy, Spencer's Darwinism took concrete form. He opposed not only public education but public ownership of the postal service, government-sponsored sanitation, even the improvement of harbors and light-houses. He opposed public support of the disabled, the weak, and the poor. When he visited the United States in the early 1880s, he was hailed for his con-tributions by members of the industrial elite. They, like others, found in Spencer ideological legitimation for laissez faire, social inequality, and the concentra-tion of wealth.

Spencer's privatized conceptions form the basis for an ideological system that can be termed *antisociety*. In such a system, both the liberal ideal of the public good and the critical conception of social, political, and economic egali-tarianism are lost. The State is reduced to an instrument of individual protec-tion and national defense. Personal initiative and private wealth are trusted to develop resources, provide services, and build industry. Governmental provi-sion for the general welfare is contracted sharply and left to voluntary philan-thropy. While Spencer and the cruder forms of Darwinism may be past, it is evident that the nostalgic myths of laissez faire and self-sufficiency are most contemporary.

# ■ William Graham Sumner (1840–1910): Social Darwinism

The heir apparent to the ideas of Herbert Spencer in the United States was William Graham Sumner.[6] Sumner was born in Paterson, New Jersey, the son of an immigrant mechanic from England. There is some evidence that his fa-ther was forced to leave his native land because the industrial revolution made his trade obsolete. Despite such staunch working-class origins and his family's adverse experiences, Sumner was to become an energetic defender of a body of ideas described earlier in this chapter as social Darwinism.

Sumner was educated in political economy at Yale, where he graduated in 1863. He went abroad to continue his studies, preparing for a career in the min-istry. After studying language at Geneva and Göttingen and theology at Ox-ford, Sumner returned to the United States, where he served for a brief time as an ordained Episcopalian curate. In 1872 he accepted a position as professor of social and political science at Yale. Three years later he offered one of the first classes in sociology on the continent, adopting as his text Herbert Spen-cer's *The Study of Sociology*. With this beginning, Sumner pursued a sociology marked by conservative politics, descriptive accounts of societal evolution, and the nature of normative systems.

---

[6] For two valuable biographical references, see Davie, 1963 and 1971.

## History and Biography

William Graham Sumner graduated from Yale in the midst of the Civil War, a bloody struggle for unification that grew from the rupturing of a nation divided along social, political, and economic lines. In it, the industrial North with its machine technology joined in mortal conflict with the still feudal agrarian South. With the war's conclusion, the center of industrial capitalism, complete with an urban–based factory system fueled by immigrant labor, began its shift to the United States.

In the last three decades of the nineteenth century, the corporation form of economic organization emerged as dominant in the new citadel of capitalism. In part to resolve the threat to profits represented by competition, leading corporations engineered the *combination movement*. In some cases, larger firms simply bought out competitors or drove them into bankruptcy through price wars. In other cases, robber barons engaged in industrial warfare, often resorting to armed violence and sabotage (Josephson, 1934). The development of powerful trusts in vital economic sectors gave rise to the Sherman Antitrust Act in 1890, a piece of legislation designed to thwart monopolistic restraint of trade. However, the act was more symbolic than real. Between 1897 and 1905, the combination movement saw 318 corporations gain control of over 5300 firms (Dowd, 1977: 71).

During the closing third of the century, other political events also altered the course of economic history. State regulations came to provide the appearance of control while preserving a favored market position for more powerful concerns. For example, in 1886 the Interstate Commerce Commission was born, in part a response to the demand by farmers for relief from transportation monopoly. A convincing historical case can be made that the ICC came to be controlled by the railroad industry (Kolko, 1965).

Other significant currents swept through the era of William Graham Sumner, leaving indelible impressions on his social thought. These included a continuing tide of immigrants, the growth of cities, the disappearance of the frontier, and the beginning erosion of an independent middle class. Half the population still lived on the land, but that too would pass. The society, with its developing state power, swelling corporate firms, and fragmented culture, was reshaped in the aftermath of civil war. It was a time of gaudy prosperity and economic panic, of an industrial elite marshaling the wealth to command, of working classes looking to unions to survive, and of the clashing cultures of diverse urban populations juxtaposed with the homogeneity of pastoral life. Made over into something unique and distinctively American, the center of the bourgeois revolution had crossed the Atlantic for good.

Sumner was insulated somewhat from the seamier side of conflict and the real struggle for existence. Having reached the comparative safety of the towers of Yale, he was influenced more by the works of Darwin and Spencer than by memories of his class origins. Impressed by the advances in biological science, he developed an evolutionary view of society complete with the use of biological analogies. His critics considered him dogmatic, but this did not diminish his status as a master polemicist. His early writing and classroom oratory matched all too well the turbulance of the times.

Perhaps Sumner realized that the scions of the wealthy who studied at Yale were drawn to the ideology (if not the reality) of a free market. Perhaps he did not. What is certain is that Sumner believed in the necessity of social hierarchy even more fiercely than did his advantaged students. Here he left behind his father's family, class, and circumstances. He was a high priest of the cult of individualism, a staunch defender of Spencer's noninterference, and an opponent of public welfare. For Sumner, the social world, as the natural, was an orderly creation obeying the prime direction of all life: a struggle in which the fit survive and the unfit perish.

> The sociologist is often asked if he wants to kill off certain classes of troublesome and bewildered persons. No such inference follows from any sound sociological doctrine, but it is allowed to infer, as to a great many persons and classes, that it would have been better for society and would hav nvolved no pain to them, if they had never been born. (Sumner, 1963: 25)

## Assumptions

As with Spencer, the Hobbesian view of human nature must be modified to fit the arguments of William Graham Sumner. For Hobbes, it was imperative to establish a commonwealth with sovereign power sufficient to promote and protect a rising commercial revolution from the awful power lust of an unbridled humanity. Thus, Sumner held in common with the Englishman an image of the competitive struggle for domination. However, this was a new era.

Sumner knew that the sovereign power of the Hobbesian leviathan under mercantilism had been employed historically to thwart the growth of the free market, to regulate labor, and to deny competitive opportunity to those who did not enjoy the pleasure of the crown. Although royal power had succumbed in the early nineteenth century to the new owners of property, the history of such abuses was not forgotten by the new champion of laissez faire. Moreover, the issues of public services, including education, social insurance, and aid to the poor, were widely debated during Sumner's era. For the Yale professor, the natural order of society emerged from an unfettered competition. Intrusion therein could only produce a declining civilization.

Sumner paid the obligatory homage to the positive image of science, calling for the discovery of social laws, decrying sentiment and morality, hailing fact and objectivity. Yet he, as many others of his time, was not converted by his own message. It can be argued that Sumner's work is more ideology than theory, assumption than propositions, ethnography than deductive or inductive reasoning. Yet sifting through his work, we can abstract from its sum two major variations of social Darwinism. At the societal level, Sumner envisioned an organism evolving through a social form of natural selection. At the interpersonal level, he conceived of an instinctually based, yet socially refined, system of norms. These twin positions give rise to his more specific arguments.

## Theoretical Content

Society progresses, according to Sumner, through its own evolutionary nature, in accordance with its own lawful properties toward an ever-improving ideal state. Interference in this process can only be irrational and futile, if not dangerous. In this body of social thought, the very existence of the "tough old world" confirmed the existence of "spontaneous forces" that could only in the slightest way be deflected, despite all the efforts of humankind (1950, originally published 1894). For Sumner, the organic evolution of society was immutable.

Within this often painful process of development, a struggle for existence emerges, marked by naturally occurring hardships including war, monopoly, and the conflict of classes. The social variety of natural selection requires no apology, for it is the method by which a perfect hierarchy takes shape and the unfit wither away. Sumner wrote under the influence of Spencer's principle of noninterference when he argued that social classes (especially the successful) owe not a thing to others (1978, originally published 1883). Hence, the divergent conditions of the fit and the unfit do not call for intervention. For the former student of theology, the drunkard in the gutter, the pauper without a loaf, the great masters of industry, and the millionaires have each earned their station.

Within the process of societal evolution, Sumner discerned two basic regularities: the law of population and the law of diminishing returns. Taken together, these mean that population increase is ultimately limited by the level of environmental resources and further that the labor of workers may produce more from these resources but never in proportion to population growth. From such "laws," Sumner drew two conclusions. First, overpopulation represents an often unrecognized opportunity, or "the struggle for existence and the competitions of life are intense where the pressure of population is great. This competition draws out the highest achievement" (1963: 23). However, his second point appears to contradict the first.

Sumner wrote that demography is related to political and economic structure. More precisely, he held that overpopulated societies reflect a caste system controlled by an elite and an economy featuring maximal exploitation of human and natural resources. Underpopulated societies on the other hand are typified by social mobility, self-sufficiency, economic surplus, and democracy. Sumner left no doubt as to the nature of his own society. "The United States is a new country with a sparse population and no strong neighbors. Such a state will be a democracy and a republic, and it will be free in about any sense that its people choose" (1963: 48–49).

Taken together, it appears that Sumner embraced both population density and scarcity. However, for this sociologist, as long as such are naturally occurring processes, they must (by his reasoning) each play a role in the evolution of society. Thus, the existence of population extremes confirms their necessity. With this as his premise, Sumner discovered evolutionary purpose in both.

In an examination of standards and expectations, Sumner sought to explain the normative order, and in so doing he examined the question of social control. He began in characteristic Darwinist fashion by arguing that persistent group habits and customs are shaped by (1) underlying instincts (unlearned behavior inherited from animal progenitors), all of which reflect the common motivation of self-advantage, and (2) the inherent predisposition to define behavior primarily in terms of pleasure and pain. These underlying biologically based impulses lead to behaviors that prove to be more or less adaptive.

Through trial and error, Sumner argued, human beings learn which behavior works best to maximize pleasure, minimize pain, meet instinctual needs, and fulfill the motivation of self-advantage. Those tested, widely disseminated, and recurring behavioral norms that contribute to the struggle for existence, he termed *folkways*. They are backed by weak sanctions and emotions.

Folkways do not move beyond simple attempts to meet instinctual needs; they do not pass the hedonist principle. When standards or expectations for behavior acquire ethical or philosophical content, they are then raised to another plane. Known as *mores,* such norms include the power to "make anything right." Mores set the limits for ideas, faith, and tastes and are founded on strong sanctions and sentiments. As such, they carry taboos or punishments that follow violations. Mores provide the moral basis by which a society coerces individual members. And for Sumner, they change only in accordance with the needs of the societal organism.

## Critique

Sumner's work, as that of others who resorted to a crude biological organicism, was and continues to be faulted for its naturalism, dependence on analogies, and the animation of society. Even his valuable distinction between kinds or levels of norms (folkways and mores) is tainted by *instinctivism,* a form of explanation that is tautological. This means that a phenomenon is said to exist because of inborn impulses, the existence of which is "proved" by the phenomenon itself. Thus, the evidence for Sumner's "biologically based impulses" rests only in the existence of the folkways and mores such impulses purport to explain. Along similar lines, Sumner's sociology transforms the discipline into a corollary of biology. This is a form of reductionism he shares with Herbert Spencer.

Moving on, Sumner's attempt to demonstrate a connection between demography and the political and economic organization of society is simplistic. Demographic factors must be considered when analyzing political economy, but not in isolation. If population growth is antithetical to democracy and productive of caste stratification, then more populous modern Japan should be less free (by Sumner's definition) than its prewar counterpart.

Also implicit in Sumner's position is the belief that private wealth is the measure of worth. Private wealth, he argued, is the only suitable means by which the services that give an advantage (such as education) should be provided. What then are we to make of inheritance or the social disadvantages that attach to one's birth? It would appear that for Sumner those born to wealth are fit by definition. If, by the force of Sumner's logic, the struggle for existence produces a more perfect hierarchy, shouldn't the conditions of that struggle be equally odious for all? And who then are the fit and the unfit? By Sumner's criteria, the wealthy are valued over the poor, the healthy over the sick, and by implication men over women, whites over nonwhites, and colonists over the colonized. At base, this sociology transforms inequality into a natural law.

# ■ *Bibliography*

Barnes, Harry E., and Howard Becker
1938                    *Social Thought from Lore to Science*. Vol. 1. Boston: D. C.
                        Heath.

Comte, Auguste
(1830–1842) 1896    *The Positive Philosophy of Auguste Comte*. Freely translated
                        and condensed by Harriet Martineau. 3 vols. London:
                        George Bell and Sons (Ann Arbor, Mich.: University Microfilms, 1971).
(1851–1854)          *System of Positivist Politics*. Translated by J. H. Bridges
    1875–1877           et al. 4 vols. London: Longmans.
(1852) 1958          *The Catechism of Positive Religion*. Translated by Richard
                        Congreve. London: Kegan Paul.

Davie, M. R. (Ed.)
1963                    *William Graham Sumner*. New York: Crowell.
1971                    *Sumner Today: Selected Essays*. Westport, Conn.:
                        Greenwood.

de Sauvigny, Guillaume
1966                    *The Bourbon Restoration*. Philadelphia: University of Pennsylvania Press.

Dowd, Douglas
1977                    *The Twisted Dream: Capitalist Development in the United
                        States Since 1776*. Cambridge, Mass.: Winthrop.

Ferré, Frederick
1970                    *Introduction to Positive Philosophy*. Edited with introduction
                        and revised translation by Frederick Ferré. Indianapolis:
                        Bobbs-Merrill Company.

Goodwin, Albert
1966                    *The French Revolution.* 4th rev. ed. New York: Harper &
                        Row.

Hawkins, Richmond L.
1936                    *Auguste Comte and the United States (1816–1853).* Cam-
                        bridge, Mass.: Harvard University Press.

Josephson, Matthew
1934                    *The Robber Barons: The Great American Capitalists.* New
                        York: Harcourt, Brace & World.

Kennedy, James G.
1978                    *Herbert Spencer.* Boston: G. K. Hall.

Kolko, Gabriel
1965                    *Railroads and Regulations, 1877–1916.* Princeton, N.J.:
                        Princeton University Press.

Lefebre, George
1962–1964              *The French Revolution.* Translated by Elizabeth Moss
                        Evanson. London: Routledge and Kegan Paul.

Manuel, Frank
1956                    *The New World of Henri Saint-Simon.* Cambridge, Mass.:
                        Harvard University Press.

Price, Roger
1972                    *The French Second Republic.* Ithaca, N.Y.: Cornell Univer-
                        sity Press.

Spencer, Herbert
(1850) 1892            *Social Statics.* New York: D. Appleton.
(1862) 1900            *First Principles.* 6th ed. New York: D. Appleton.
(1873) 1961            *The Study of Sociology.* Ann Arbor: University of Michi-
                        gan Press.
(1876–1896)            *The Principles of Sociology.* 3 vols. New York: D.
  1925–1929            Appleton.
1902                   *Facts and Comments.* New York: D. Appleton.

Sumner, William Graham
(1883) 1978            *What Social Classes Owe Each Other.* Caldwell, Idaho:
                        Caxton.
(1884) 1950            *The Man Vs. the State.* 2nd ed. London: Watts.
1919                   *Forgotten Man and Other Essays.* Edited by A. G. Keller.
                        Freeport, N.Y.: Books for Libraries.
1963                   *Social Darwinism: Selected Essays of William Graham
                        Sumner.* Englewood Cliffs, N.J.: Prentice-Hall.

Zeitlin, Irving
1968                   *Ideology and the Development of Sociological Theory.* En-
                        glewood Cliffs, N.J.: Prentice-Hall.

# CHAPTER 5

# ■ Functionalism

The puzzles of the order paradigm have produced other systems of theoretical explanation that focus on the bonding forces of social life. In this chapter we shall examine the *functionalist* tradition in theoretical sociology. Please be aware that there is no great gulf between the organicism we examined earlier and the functionalism we now analyze. The focus here, as earlier, centers on the conditions and relationships that are productive of continuity and cohesion, interdependence and consensus, unity and wholeness. Moreover, in the work of Durkheim and Toennies, we find the familiar strain of evolutionism. As we shall see, the former stressed the transition of society from the intimate community to the impersonal association. The latter dealt with the unfolding of an increasingly complex division of labor that strongly altered the nature of solidarity among the members of social order.

Yet there is a distinctive logic that marks the functionalist tradition, a method of analysis that need not be rooted in the organic analogy of the preceding chapter. As we argued in Chapter 3, the concept of function since Aristotle has referred to the necessary contribution made by the part to the whole. In sociology, functionalists have variously argued that stratification systems are necessary in order to get the most important work done by the best people; that the purpose of deviance and its sanctions is to identify and reinforce normative boundary lines; that prostitution functions to protect the institution of marriage by allowing for unemotional sexual involvement.

Whatever the social habit, arrangement, or phenomenon, when it is commonly found and recurring, the functionalist "logic" since Durkheim is that it must have some *social purpose* or it would not exist. Modern functionalists, such as Robert Merton, often seek to break with this teleological view. Theirs is an interest in the societal *consequences* of social phenomena, whether such consequences are intended or unintended, positive or negative.

# ■ Émile Durkheim (1858–1917): Social Integration and the Division of Labor

Émile Durkheim, whose sociology came to represent the exemplar for functionalist theory, was born in Epinal, Lorraine, not far from Strasbourg. He grew to maturity in a region of France where patriotic fervor and intense nationalism marked community life. A member of a cohesive Jewish minority, he was expected to become a rabbi like some members of his family. However, his destiny was not to study an ancient faith but to forge new knowledge.

## History and Biography

The France of the young Durkheim was a nation of contrasts. At the time of his birth, the countryside held fast in the womb of tradition. The centers of change were instead the metropolitan areas with a class structure based in large measure on the industrial factory system. Among the two million inhabitants of Paris in the 1860s, the differences among the strata were profound. Even then a city of beauty, proud of its artistic, cultural, and intellectual heritage, Paris gave hint of further turbulence in France's political winter of discontent. Here workers were ravaged by disease and poverty, fearful of unemployment or uncompensated accidents. They coexisted with large and powerful banking, industrial, and business interests and a somewhat uneasy middle class. Such forces in conflict had already surfaced domestically in a number of riots, continuing the upheaval of the French nineteenth century. (Refer to the historical section dealing with the work of Auguste Comte in Chapter 4.)

In 1870–1871 the French suffered an unexpected war and humiliating defeat at the hands of Bismarck's forces. The Prussian conquerors then called for the selection of a provisional government with which to negotiate a peace. The resultant assembly, sitting in Versailles, represented in the main large commercial interests and landowners. They sought to restore the monarchy and put an end to the nominally democratic nature of republican rule. A revolutionary city government, the Paris Commune, was quickly formed in reaction. The political leaders of the commune were no longer bound by unquestioned allegiance to the conservative influence of the church. Its leftist members quickly engaged in a bloody and protracted battle with French regulars, attempting a revolution within a war. They and their sympathizers were soon to be decimated by mass execution and deportation (Peyre, 1964). The aftershocks of such events still reverberated when the young Durkheim left family and community to attend secondary school in the Paris of 1876.

The Franco-Prussian War was followed by other squalls in the storm of

French history. During the 1870s, huge reparations were paid to Germany, and a largely republican Chamber of Deputies was elected (1876). The latter event left those favoring a monarchy out of office but not out of power. During the last quarter of the century, the growing wave of industrialization continued to build the nation's wealth and the poverty of the working class. However, it was to be a sensational charge of treason against the only Jewish member of the military general staff that brought the nation to the verge of a civil war.

In 1894 Captain Alfred Dreyfus was accused of passing information to German military attachés. A court martial determined his guilt and sentenced him to life imprisonment. However, the trial was held in secret and afterward Dreyfus continued to protest his innocence. A movement on the part of sympathizers to secure a new trial was aided when a key witness admitted to the forgery of evidence and committed suicide. The Dreyfus affair became a symbolic crusade with the army and church allied on one side and the civil libertarians and critics of militarism on the other. Dreyfus received a pardon, but the controversy did not die easily.

Other events were no less contentious. With the coming of the twentieth century, the ever-seething labor unrest took the form of a general strike carried out on May 1, 1906. In 1910 the great railroad strike brought transportation to a halt. By 1914 the Socialist party was the largest in the Chamber of Deputies. Then came the great war that decimated the French nation.

These then were the times of Émile Durkheim: political turmoil, the intensification of class struggle, revolution, anti-Semitism, military corruption, and war. Durkheim died on November 15, 1917, at the age of 59, one year after his only son fell in battle.

## Assumptions

The events of his era formed only one part of the historical crucible that shaped the thought of Durkheim. Powerful intellectual undercurrents added another dimension. After graduation from secondary school, he studied philosophy at the École Normale Supérieure in Paris, developing a passion for political and social thought and the reputation as an iconoclast. Here Durkheim began to study in the fledgling field of sociology, while frowning on some aspects of classical education. He began to develop a sense of sociology as science, an assumption he retained throughout his academic life. Almost four decades after he entered the École Normale he was to write:

> Sociology . . . does not seek to know the defunct forms of civilization in order to reconstitute them. Like any positive science, it has primarily as its object the explanation of a reality which is close to us, and which thus can affect our ideas and our behavior. (1964: 1, originally published 1912)

This citation of commitment to positive science is typical. Durkheim's sociology reveals this Comtean position as a matter of course. Yet in addition to this image of science, he was also in tune with Comte's consensual vision of normative systems and often employed organic metaphors of society. Finally, Durkheim held fast to a Hobbesian conception of human nature, in which the dangerous ability to imagine unfettered power necessitates strong forms of social control. Such assumptions clearly supported those aspects of functionalist theory that point up the disorganizing consequences of social change. As Zeitlin (1968: 234–280) observes, Durkheim's work featured a conservative ideological infrastructure, intended in part to counter the structural criticism of the socialists of his epoch.

Durkheim, like Comte before him, was heavily indebted to the ideas of Saint-Simon. If you remember, Saint-Simon argued that science could resolve political and social questions. It was science that would emerge as a new ethic, a striking moral power that would guide the construction of a new society. With this new society in place, reason could be applied to the solution of the more extreme problems of class conflict. The hierarchical nature of society would remain, but in the Platonist sense of the organism, the new order would be one of integration and stability with norms sufficient to hold in check the destructive passions that plague human nature. Undergirding this new integration would be a community of ideas.

> If Saint-Simon saw as his major task to determine what kind of moral system post-Revolutionary European society required, Durkheim viewed his own work in a similar light: to provide a secular, moral system that would bind together into a solidary social order the classes, strata and occupational groups of contemporary France. (Zeitlin, 1968: 236–237)

## Theoretical Content

Durkheim's teaching career began in 1887 with an appointment as professor of sociology and education at the University of Bordeaux. It was the first such position in France, and he remained there until 1902. At this time, he took a similar position at the Sorbonne in Paris.

While Durkheim wrote numerous essays, many of which were edited and compiled into volumes, his major works were the subject of four books. The first three, *The Division of Labor in Society, The Rules of the Sociological Method,* and *Suicide,* were published during his Bordeaux period. Also of significance during this time was the establishment and editing by Durkheim of the journal *L'Année Sociologique,* which appeared in 1886. At the Sorbonne, he wrote *The Elementary Forms of the Religious Life.* The theoretical issues in each of these distinctive works bear the stamp of the order paradigm.

In *The Division of Labor* (1933, originally published 1893), Durkheim developed a watershed work in societal unity, or more formally, *solidarity.* Here he made the case that the process of task division holds the key to the interdependence and reciprocity of members of a society. More "primitive" societies possessed a *mechanical* solidarity, a unity born of the similarity of members that held this more homogeneous community together. As societies grew to be more heterogeneous, individual members were less alike. However, the increasing task specialization that marked such complex orders meant that members of society grew more interdependent. Simply put, social relationships were strengthened by mutual need, and an *organic* solidarity prevailed.

Given the less specialized division of labor in the traditional type of society, social integration is more dependent on an effective if repressive normative system. However, in industrialized societies, such heavy social constraints come to be replaced by formal relations. For example, in modern societies Durkheim noted the existence of a system of legality with its binding agreements and its reliance on the judiciary. Predictably, when solidarity is of the organic sort, rooted essentially in the interdependence brought by a highly developed and specialized division of labor, the society reflects less integration.

Durkheim employed these two forms of solidarity to demonstrate the importance of collective forces in social life. Specifically, he sought to show that individuals are constrained by the *collective conscience,* a system of beliefs common to most members of society. This common sense of right and wrong is strongest, he argued, in traditional societies because of the similarities of members. In heterogeneous societies, the influence of this common conscience tends to decrease.

Durkheim turned to the sociology of law to demonstrate this evolution in social control. Under conditions of mechanical solidarity, he argued, the law tends to address criminal offenses through harsh and repressive sanctions. However, in the case of organic solidarity, law embodies a different form of collective conscience, with an interest more on restitution than on punishment. However, in this theoretical work, social control is a primary issue, even for organic societies. Such is clearly evident in Durkheim's analysis of crime:

> . . . the only common characteristic of crimes is that they consist . . . in acts universally disapproved of by members of each society; . . . crime shocks sentiments which, for a given social system, are found in all healthy consciences. . . . An act is criminal when it offends strong and defined states of the collective conscience. . . . Everybody is attacked; consequently, everybody opposes the attack. . . . Crime brings together upright consciences and concentrates them. (1933: 73, 80, 102)

Thus, for Durkheim, crime and deviance and the resultant punishment thereof could be understood as *functional,* as meeting the underlying need in society to reinforce moral unity and define normative boundary lines. Also evident is Durkheim's position that the criminal act is so defined by the collective conscience. Stripped of the trace of mysticism that has always plagued notions of "group mind," we are left to conclude that the nature of crime and punishment is decided by the members of a society (at least the upright). Society's norms, including those that specify criminal acts, are the product of *consensus*.

With the increasing heterogeneity of society, the growing dissimilarities of people, and the weakening of constraints, new forces of integration become operational. For Durkheim, the cohesion of the modern order could not be based on the intimate controls of primitive community or on the custom and loyalties of the vanished feudal order. Nor would military force, the church, or new contractual political arrangements suffice. Instead, Durkheim found the vision of Comte and Saint-Simon to be compelling. The new society could only be held together by industry (1933: 130–151).

Durkheim's second major work was originally published in 1895. In *The Rules of the Sociological Method* (1958), he advanced an image of sociology as science (see Chapter 3). However, in the process of making the case for a distinctive new discipline, Durkheim developed a refined conception of the collective conscience. Whereas this concept appeared to represent the beliefs of the average upright person in *The Division of Labor in Society,* in *The Rules of the Sociological Method* a new conception of restraint emerged.

In the latter Durkheim argued that through the interaction of individual minds, there evolves a collective psyche quite different from the sum of personal thought and emotion. Group standards, as well as group behavior, must be distinguished from the standards and behavior of the individual members that make up that group. It follows that social reality, including matters of normative control and group action, cannot be reduced to a psychological reality. Durkheim believed, as did Herbert Spencer (see Chapter 4), with whom he shared an organic sense of social reality, that society was more than the sum of its people. Hence, the collective conscience was not simply analogous to an enlarged Freudian superego. It was rather a system of normative constraints with an existence of its own that transcended human personality. As such, a distinctively social reality affected human behavior and ideas and could be transmitted by means of social institutions from one generation to the next.

In his next book, Durkheim rejoined the problem of human freedom. In his previous books, he had already placed profound controls on choice. In these he argued that behavior is neither a matter of will nor a function of psychological instinct; instead, it is a social product. Yet, for Durkheim, freedom was problematic in other ways. When organized in the form of movements for social change, new definitions of freedom might come to challenge moral unity and threaten the cohesiveness of society.

In *Suicide* (1957, originally published 1897), Durkheim added to this theory of social control in a rather ingenious fashion. Here he argued, with no small amount of irony, that the intensely personal and private act of taking one's life is a consequence of social forces or "facts." Some of these conditions are well outside the intimate circle of interpersonal relations or private motives often cited as the cause of death. Of course, Durkheim the sociologist did not attempt an explanation of why particular *individuals* committed suicide.

Rather, he was concerned with why certain groups were more prone to this behavior than others.

In this effort, he supported his theoretical argument by means of a statistical inquiry into the differential rates of suicide for differing segments of the population of Europe. He demonstrated with some success that external social facts could account for the variations in these rates. His typology remains a classic means of understanding suicide.

1. Where group integration is weak, a form of suicide termed *egoistic* prevails. For example, Durkheim argued that the unmarried and those of the Protestant faith represented poorer cohesion and higher suicide rates.

2. In a demonstration of the negative consequences of social change, Durkheim held that suicide increases with a breakdown in norms (anomie). Hence, in both periods of economic depression and periods of prosperity, the rates of *anomic* suicide rise. Ironically, either social state may lead people to question traditional norms or disrupt established social relationships. This interpretation reveals Durkheim's underlying conception of human nature. He believed that the members of society need socal constraints, a trusted and ongoing normative system and strong social institutions, to hold in check their aspirations. Robert Browning wrote that our reach must exceed our grasp, "or what's a heaven for?" For Durkheim, Browning's paradise had quite a different meaning.

3. Ironically, too much social cohesion may also lead to an increased suicide rate. *Altruistic* suicide may occur when social conditions reflect extreme devotion to a group and its cause, as when a soldier sacrifices for comrades.

In the last of his major books, Durkheim investigated *The Elementary Forms of the Religious Life* (1964, originally published 1912). In it, he used secondary sources to analyze the place of religion in the social life of an Australian aboriginal tribe, the Arunta. Durkheim saw the Arunta as representing a simple social order, with a mechanical form of solidarity. Hence, he believed it possible to isolate the most fundamental functions of religion.

Totemism among the Arunta was interpreted by Durkheim as the most basic of religious systems. It is founded on the conception of a sacred spiritual force that gives life to the totem (which may be a plant, animal, or some natural object). The same force is the basis for moral unity and punishments for the violations of taboos, or the most important of society's norms. In their social life, the Arunta drew a hard and fast line between the world of the spirit and the world of the profane. Clearly stated, they saw the secular world as reflecting a dull, if necessary, division of labor and rigid adherence to norms. However, when the Arunta gathered for sacred rituals, a transition occurred. Joy and contagious euphoria were forthcoming.

Durkheim's explanation of the role of religion for the Arunta tribe was consistently functionalist. This is evident in his belief that the distinction between the sacred and profane as well as the social functions attributed to religion are *universal*. Please note that Durkheim was no longer talking specifically about the Arunta and totemism. Rather, he was talking about all societies and all religions.

Given the teleological nature of functionalism, Durkheim believed that the religion of the totem, like all religions, reflects the needs of society. Moreover, he saw dogma and practice as the consequences of social life. Therefore, *the sacred world is a social product*. Gods, rituals, taboos, and precepts are not created by some supernatural force but are the creations of humankind. Religion exists because it offers prestige and prominence to believers, undergirds the normative order, and offers explanations for the unexplainable. And above all, sacred symbols are shared collectively, thereby unifying believers into a single moral community.

## Critique

Émile Durkheim contributed greatly to both theoretical sociology and the methods of social science. He was clearly a leader in the development of theory and its integration with empirical research. He pioneered in the establishment of a distinctive academic niche for the discipline of sociology by arguing convincingly that the social world is both real and unique. However, as with all systems of thought, a critical examination is in order.

Durkheim's conception of the collective conscience is vague enough to draw fire from critics. If by this he meant a social psyche or group mind floating somehow in social space independent of actors, then Durkheim's break with psychology may have left him trapped in a form of mysticism. However, the sociological worth of the collective conscience appears to be found in other meanings now commonly termed culture, normative systems, and values.

It should be remembered that Durkheim believed that society has a reality *sui generis* (of its own kind). He further believed in the existence of *social facts*, which are external to individuals and restraining of behavior. Although these are truisms for most sociologists who conceive of society in macro terms today, Durkheim was at war in his time with psychological and other reductionists. This led him at times to draw a rigid line between social and psychological facts, between society and the minds of its members. Hence there is little room in this theoretical system for interpretation or voluntarism on the part of actors. Weber and other pluralists (see Chapter 9) would criticize this as an overly deterministic view of human nature.

To the extent that societal change is an issue for Durkheim, it appears as unilinear and evolutionary. Societies move by means of an increasingly intricate and interdependent division of labor from traditional to modern, from mechanical to organic solidarity. Critics would note that change is instead dialectic and multilinear and its nature is regressive or revolutionary. However, Durkheim's continuing focus on constraint and control leaves little theoretical room for explaining change. If social institutions, practices, and customs are explained by referring to the purposes they meet, then all that exists, exists by necessity. Further, if existing norms are the product of a generally shared social consensus, then change can only be defined as a form of *deviance* on the part of those who are the products of faulty socialization. Given the logic of functionalism, change is problematic because it threatens the cohesiveness of social order.

At an ideological level, Durkheimian functionalism is inherently conservative. Within its boundaries, institutions become superordinate, acquiring a life of their own. Whatever exists is somehow fitted into the pattern of the whole. Such an explanatory system, however inadvertently, imposes the face of legitimacy on the existing order. Correspondingly, Durkheim viewed individual rights including dissent as potentially dangerous, and freedom as a frequent disguise for the egoism that threatens social integration.

Durkheimian thought tends to redefine the inequality in society from that of a problem requiring change to a functional requisite of social life. All strata are portrayed as sharing a common interest in the organic whole. Politically, such views are quite compatible with nationalism, while in economic terms a hierarchy of classes is legitimated. In a like vein, Durkheim saw the growth of a privately owned industrial system as a unifying force. Critics, then and now, see it as a means of concentrating wealth and power, therefore divisive.

Durkheim, like Saint-Simon before him, foresaw a coming meritocracy. In such an integrated society, scientists and industrialists would lead, not because of their power but because they would possess greater knowledge. Plato's guardians were no longer the philosophers, but the role is identical. Simply put, Durkheim's utopia offers the tranquility of conformity in a world yearning for new beginnings. Rousseau's critique is appropriate here: There is peace in dungeons.

# ■ Ferdinand Toennies (1855–1936): *Gemeinschaft* and *Gesellschaft*

Ferdinand Toennies[1] was born in Germany in Schleswig-Holstein. His early years were spent first on a well-to-do farm and later in a small town. His

---

[1] Insights on the life and times of Ferdinand Toennies can be drawn from Oberschall, 1965, and Solomon, 1936. Rudolph Heberle, the son-in-law of Toennies, also published various works seeking to elucidate the theory and the man.

mother's devoutly Lutheran family included a number of clergy. Although Toennies would come to be considered an agnostic by most believers, he grew before his death to believe in a universal religious faith that would reconcile the divisions that plagued humankind.

Some would no doubt characterize Toennies's early experiences as provincial. He developed a pastoral *Weltanschauung,* complete with the patriotism that often follows when the loyalties to tradition and the small community are projected to the broader concerns of the nation. He was the product of a distinctive form of social life that left an abiding sense of integration: in nature, in the interaction of people, in the ways of culture, and ultimately in all social life. Despite extensive travel, Toennies lived his entire life in the region of his birth. But his sojourns to various universities and the cosmopolitan capitals of Europe juxtaposed urban and rural life and the contrasting forms of solidarity represented by each.

The resources of his family made it possible for Toennies to pursue his academic training to an advanced level. He entered the University of Strasbourg in 1872 and, after transferring to several other institutions, took his Ph.D. in philology from the University of Tübingen. After continuing his postdoctoral studies at the University of Berlin, Toennies traveled to London. It was here that he took substantial interest in the work of Thomas Hobbes, and then began work on the masterpiece *Community and Society* (*Gemeinschaft und Gesellschaft*) (1963). After its original publication in 1887, Toennies edited two books on the work of Hobbes that were published in 1889. He authored his own work on this political philosopher in 1896.

Along with Max Weber, Georg Simmel, and Werner Sombart, Toennies founded the German Sociological Society, serving as its president from 1909 to 1933. He contributed heavily to the professional literature, largely without benefit of a university position. Toennies did accept a chair at the University of Kiel, which he held from 1913 to 1916. He returned here to teach sociology as professor emeritus from 1921 to 1933.

## History and Biography

Toennies's life intersected the history of his nation at critical junctures. In his youth came the unification of Germany under Otto von Bismarck. This notorious political figure came to power as minister of the Prussian king, William I, in 1863. It was Bismarck who promptly declared to parliament that the great issues of the day were to be solved not by majority vote and speeches but by "blood and iron." In 1864 the control of the region of Toennies's birth (Schleswig-Holstein) sparked war between the two leading German states (Austria and Prussia) on the one side and Denmark on the other. Successful in this venture, Bismarck then turned on Austria in 1866 and unified the German states in part through a war with France in 1870 (refer to the times of Émile Durkheim in the previous section).

When Toennies entered the University of Strasbourg at the age of 17, Bismarck was waging a domestic war on the growing socialist movement. The strategy of the hour was to support both repressive legislation aimed at the radicals and social insurance programs designed to pacify their followers. Bismarck began to harden, however, and finally when he pushed for more anti-socialist legislation and an end to universal suffrage in Germany, he was dismissed by William II in 1890.

In the wider sphere of social life, a number of forces were at play. The population of Germany grew rapidly from some 40 million in 1871 to over 65 million on the eve of the First World War. During this era, the German colonial empire was expanding as was its navy, while the army was among the most powerful of the world. It was within this context of the Bismarckian attempt to unify through the sword, of industrialization and population growth, and of a growing external empire that Ferdinand Toennies wrote of the social origins of solidarity and the Hobbesian problem of order.

However, World War I resulted in the defeat of Germany and the loss of its colonies. The Treaty of Versailles stripped these possessions, as well as foreign investments, the merchant marine, and over 10 percent of its European land area. So began an economic decline compounded by postwar inflation and the ravaging of the middle class. By 1932 over 6 million Germans were unemployed and another 15 million were on relief. Such events, together with the emergence of strong ideological currents of betrayal and racism, set the historical stage for the rise of national socialism. Toennies had sought to support and defend the German cause during the First World War. However, he strongly and openly opposed the rise of nazism. Predictably, the old scholar was dismissed from his post at Kiel in 1933 and subsequently died in 1936.

## Assumptions

The political philosophy of Thomas Hobbes left an indelible mark on the work of Toennies. Yet that mark is both subtle and complex. On the one hand, Toennies held that the integration of modern industrial societies depends in large measure on the power of Hobbes's political commonwealth. On the other, he argued that an earlier form of society was united by means of a naturally occurring organicism that subjected individual wills to that of the group. As we shall see, the conception of will is crucial to the thought of Ferdinand Toennies. And although he approached this subject from the vantage point of the ideal type, *will* was for this theorist a real force, not an abstraction. Toennies has emerged as something of a romantic, drawn to an earlier, more pastoral conception of social life based on a more congenial type of human nature. However, it was the evolution toward the "reasonable" and "individualistic" side of will, with its expression in the impersonal bonds of industrial society, that shaped his theoretical sociology.

Toennies's assumptions about the discipline followed the positive conception of science that prevailed in his day. He divided sociology into three distinctive areas: (1) a pure form consisting of central conceptions that form an integral system, (2) an "applied" form in which pure theory is used deductively to explain societal development,[2] and (3) an empirically based approach to social research. Throughout *Community and Society,* he moved back and forth from theoretical conceptualization to the findings of social research.

## Theoretical Content

The more significant writings of Ferdinand Toennies emerged during his youth and in many respects detailed the decline of an old order and the rise of a new one. The analysis that follows is based on the classic he wrote in response to such conditions, *Community and Society (Gemeinschaft und Gesellschaft).* As we shall see, he preferred the more binding social relationships of traditional society. His work has endured, however, because it moves beyond romantic nostalgia. It reflects in a striking fashion the great division between folk and urban society; between the intimate relationships of family, kin, and community and the impersonal alliances born of modern polity, economic exchange, and state power. This portrayal of two worlds of human existence still strikes a responsive chord.

In this system of social thought, social reality consists of various social entities existing at different levels of abstraction. These include the *interpersonal relationship,* the *corporate groups* that act through representatives (such as officers), and the broad *collectivities* that transcend and subsume lower level groups and relationships (such as nations and classes). All such entities, and the forms they assume, are the product of differing manifestations of human *will.*

The conception of will in the thought of Toennies is both central and difficult. In a general sense, it refers to voluntary and meaningful purpose. Yet a closer examination reveals two distinctive dimensions analyzed by Toennies through the prism of a Weberian ideal type. The *Wesenville,* or natural will, drives those actions that are engaged in for their intrinsic worth or their own sake. It is the basis for unconditional emotional bonding and a reverence for tradition. The *Kurville* refers to the human propensity toward a reasoned selection among alternatives. Thus, the action of rational choice is willed because it is instrumental in achieving ends.

These types of will are expressed in two contrasting forms of social life. The foundation of the *Gemeinschaft* or "community" is the *Wesenville.* Conceptualized at the societal level, the *Gemeinschaft* consists of social relationships of an intimate or primary sort, such as those of family, club, or religious order. Predictably, the type of law that prevails in such an order will be that based on the informal codes of family and kin, and social control will be left to consen-

---

[2]It should be evident that Toennies did not primarily mean by "applied" sociology an attempt to build policies and programs.

sus, custom, and religious precept. Wealth is centered in the land, the individual is subordinate to the collectivity, and the central institutions are those of the family, small village, and town. Remember that the relationships, sentiments, and rules of the *Gemeinschaft* are willed for their own sake.

However, given the momentous changes of his era, Toennies acknowledged the ascension of the *Gesellschaft*. The creation of the rational will, "society," represents the more impersonal means-to-an-end forms of social relationships. These are marked by the purposes of exchange and reasoned calculation. At the group level, *Gesellschaft* relationships are exemplified in business or professional associations. At the societal level, the state and the economy of industrial capitalism supplant the centrality of the family, kin, and village. Law is a matter of formal contracts, both civil and criminal, secured by legislation and specifying the rights and responsibilities of individuals to individuals and members to the commonwealth. Public opinion and the conventional wisdom replace heritage, articles of faith, and "natural" consensus as informal means of social control.

Within the *Gemeinschaft* form of social order, a homogeneity of view, the ties of kinship, a common language, and a sense of place are the basis for an organic unity. Alliances are based on closeness and mutual aid, while authority is personal and often paternalistic. Authority is commonly fixed in the elder, the master, the patriarch. For the *Gesellschaft,* the identity born of community surrenders to the anonymity of mass society. The emerging industrial order with its burgeoning cities and centralized power is held in one piece by artificial bonds. Such bonds tend to be more malleable; they come and go, disintegrate and reform as the needs of the state, bureaucracy, business, or workplace change. Here, social relationships are based on special needs, class interests, and personal ambition. The connectedness of society is a matter of interlocking positions of status. This formal structure supplants the more natural coming-together of like-minded persons who gain emotional sustenance from sharing a common moral universe.

*Gemeinschaft* and *Gesellschaft,* for Toennies, represented more than differences in social relationships or societies. They were also separate poles on a continuum of change. Yet this inevitable evolution with its industrialism, its commonwealth, and its population redistribution could not help but tear the fabric of human relations. Within his era, Toennies witnessed the cutting off of goods and services from the common production of the community where members were bound by common purpose. Rather, economic exchange became a function of the impersonal market. And with the rise of a multiplicity of "publics" in the heterogeneous social order, the threat to equilibrium was self-evident.

## Critique

Toennies made an ingenious usage of his distinction between community and society. By means of these ideal types, he assessed social change, the predominant forms of total societies, and the nature of the social entities within society. However, as with all such types, we should remember that the attributes will be exaggerated. Toennies readily acknowledged that the ascendance of the *Kurville* did not mean the extinction of the *Wesenville*. Thus, even the predominantly *Gesellschaft* order could be seen to retain some of the more intimate relations. Going a step further, Pappenheim (1968), who took his cue from Toennies, noted the ironic attempts to construct pseudo-*Gemeinschafts* in the modern depersonalized society. Fraternity *brothers,* sorority *sisters,* corporation *families, warm-hearted* banks represent a few examples to seize upon a perceived death of community.

Despite the lingering appeal of this taxonomy, it might be argued that Toennies advanced an oversimplified view of social life. Perhaps this is more a criticism of the exaggeration of attributes implicit in the methodology of the ideal type. Nevertheless, it is worth remembering that the multiple nuances of society and the entities that comprise it defy stark and contrasting description.

More important are criticisms of the cardinal standing of the "will" in Toennies's system of thought. In one sense, his emphasis on purposeful action brings this conception quite close to the Weberian sense of minded behavior (see Chapter 10). Yet Toennies ascribed to this concept something more than the human ability to attach meaning to action. By "will" he sought to identify a more or less independent basis for the establishment of social order. Still, it is difficult to investigate this force, which for Toennies was the basis for all interaction, all relationships, and the major forms of society. In effect, he converted an unverifiable assumption into a tautological theoretical proposition.

In terms of its ideological implications, this work in theoretical sociology represents a conservative repudiation of the problems of the industrial revolution. While Toennies's interest in the fragmentation of society led him to examine carefully the works of Hobbes, he stopped short of embracing that philosopher's solution. Given the choice, he would not exchange the natural culture of humankind for the equilibrium ensured by the sovereign state. Movement into the *Gesellschaft* was inevitable, not desirable. However, for Toennies, the solution to disorder, egoism, and mechanical associations was not to be found in the erection of a new order.

The sociology of Ferdinand Toennies represents a humanist critique of modernization, a critique in which the central problem is change. This is abundantly clear in his little-known work on the life and teachings of Karl Marx (1974, originally published 1921). Despite his respect for Marxist thought, Toennies clearly divorced his own work from a system-specific critique of the capitalist mode of production. For Toennies, the problems Marx attributed to the form of economic order that dominated their era were to be explained in different ways. His was rather a theoretical assault on the impersonalization of the *Gesellschaft culture,* and he faulted Marx for ignoring moral will, for refusing to "appeal to the moral consciousness of the laborer, much less that of the capitalist, in order to improve or even to abolish those conditions" (1974: 156).

Stated simply, Toennies believed that the morally bonding aspects of the

*Gemeinschaft* could give to capitalism a human face (1974: 143–163). Although drawn to Marx's portrayal of the trader or merchant whose bargaining was intended solely to maximize profit, Toennies made of this huckster a metaphor for the ethical bankruptcy of the unchecked *Gesellschaft*. The trader "wants to obtain 'advantage' merely by means of repeated exchange, that is . . . to harvest the fruits of labor without having performed the labor" (1974: 151). This, however, was a problem of moral consciousness, not the structure of capitalism.

Unlike Marx, Toennies held that capital and labor need not be separate and in conflict, that entrepreneurs and managers add value to what is produced, that factory systems under capitalism may be organized along humane and cooperative lines. He was convinced that the destructive properties of both the capitalist system and its associated bureaucracy could be checked by the resurgence of the natural will. His models of social relationships within hierarchies were the old guilds and crafts with their *Gemeinschaft*-like ties among master, artisan, and apprentice. Hence the utopian vision of Ferdinand Toennies was not rooted in the Marxist society of tomorrow. For this thinker, the future could be found in the past.

# ■ Robert K. Merton (b. 1910): Anomie Revisited

The contemporary functionalist Robert K. Merton developed his early conceptions of theoretical sociology at Harvard, within the historical and intellectual milieux shared by his contemporaries Talcott Parsons (Chapter 7) and George Homans (Chapter 8). One of his earliest and more enduring arguments was formed in the essay "Social Structure and Anomie" (1938), written and published during the Great Depression in the United States. The distress of this period appears to have forged a solid tradition of order that shaped the Harvard mind, a tradition that Merton did not leave behind when he joined the sociology faculty at Columbia University. However, he was to modify somewhat the optimistic assessment of equilibrium that pervades that theoretical sociology founded on the order paradigm.

Merton (1983) credits the then young Talcott Parsons as an important mentor along with another grand theorist of systems, Pitirim Sorokin. And, as did Parsons, Merton also came under the influence of the biochemist L. J. Henderson (see Chapter 7). For several decades, Merton collaborated with Paul Lazarsfeld, a sociologist whose major interests were community disorganization and the loss of autonomy. However, it is to the French "master at a distance," Émile Durkheim, that Merton expressed his greatest debt and rightly so.

## Assumptions

Stated succinctly, Merton's image of human nature is centered in the Hobbesian/Durkheimian problem of unrealistic expectations, while his image of society reflects more an interest in balance than in change. Such images are expressed theoretically in questions of social control, specifically, the relationship between expectations of success and opportunities for success. (We shall explore these shortly.) Moreover, Merton was to qualify the societal vision of functional unity and inherent progress attributable to most order theorists.

As to his conception of sociology and its theory, Merton departed markedly from the macro-level approach of Parsons and others. He came to view theory as the development of *middle-range* propositions. Thus, instead of constructing grand and abstract theories of society, theorists were advised to explain a restricted set of social phenomena. These modest explanations were then to be verified through empirical research and then perhaps systematized into theoretical systems of broader scope and content. Implicit, then, are Merton's assumptions on the integrated nature of society, the need to control the victims of false expectations, and the positivist nature of sociology.

## Theoretical Content

Merton's first seminal work was in the form of a theoretical piece, "Social Structure and Anomie," published in the *American Sociological Review* (1938). In it, he sought an explanation for deviant behavior through an explication and refinement of Durkheim's conception of anomie. It is not our purpose to include in this book on theories of *society* the more specialized forms of theoretical sociology. However, this explanation of deviance is centered first of all at the societal level. Please recall that Merton, as had his historical mentor, wrote in a context of crisis and change. And, as did Durkheim, Merton focused on deviance as a consequence of structural disorganization.

In this classification of anomic deviance, Merton explored the relationship between cultural goals and the structural means to achieve those goals. For this sociologist, when success *goals* were universally imposed on the members of society while the *means* to achieve them were restricted for some members, deviance could be expected on a broad scale. As evident in the following schemata, it is the type of consistency or inconsistency between goals and means that leads to either conformity or to one of the four "types" of anomic deviance. (See Figure 5.1.)

From Merton's scheme we can understand that the *conformist* internalizes the common success goals but also has access to the approved means to realize the goals. For the other relationships, a condition of goals–means dysjunction exists. The *innovator* role manifests the adoption of disvalued means (for example, theft) to realize success. The *ritualist* follows the rules obsessively but

**Figure 5.1** Robert Merton's Classification
of Anomic Deviance

| GOALS | MEANS | ROLE BEHAVIOR |
|-------|-------|---------------|
| + | + | Conformist |
| + | − | Innovator |
| − | + | Ritualist |
| − | − | Retreatist |
| ± | ± | Rebel |

loses sight of the overall goals (for example, the inflexible bureaucrat). The *retreatist* abandons both success goals and the means to realize them (for example, the drug addict). The *rebel* rejects both the traditional goals and means, but envisions new ones as the basis for a new social order. It should be stressed that Merton saw deviance not in terms of personality types but as *role responses* to different forms of dysjunction.

Merton's theoretical contribution to the field of deviance serves as a window to his later efforts to construct a system of functional analysis. Here he demonstrated his proclivity for intensive study of a more limited theoretical puzzle. Yet it is obvious that he sought to explain the puzzle of deviance in the conceptual language of sociology. Like Durkheim, Merton avoided pathological interpretations based on either biological or psychological variables.

In this theoretical matrix, actors in a social system are constrained by happenings in the broader sphere of society. Deviant roles are not created by willful intent or intimate experiences. They occur as patterned responses to a breakdown between universal expectations (to be successful) and the availability of approved methods to achieve those ends. Or in Merton's words, when a society professes that every office boy can become president, while the avenues to such aspirations are socially limited, the stage is set for deviance on a broad scale.

As with other order theorists, Merton came to focus in his later work on the social consequences of patterned, predictable, and recurring phenomena (such as societies, cultures, organizations, and groups). He also conceived of elements within larger wholes in terms of their contribution to the adjustment of a given system (Merton, 1968: 104). However, clearly evident in this early work in the theory of deviance are distinctive properties that were carried throughout his career.

First of all, Merton focused on a more *modest* theoretical problem (in this case, that of deviance). Second, his argument held that cultural ideals might *in unintended fashion* serve as a source of unexpected role behavior. And finally, he noted that many are not afforded the legitimate means to reach universal goals. Thus, he intimated that not all existing practices contribute to the positive integration of the total society.

By 1949 it was obvious that Merton would attempt to make over functionalism. And in so doing, he came to modify the central premises of this theoretical system (1968: 73–138). Please understand that traditional functionalism, whether contained in the organicism of the nineteenth century, or early cultural anthropology, or the emerging systems approach in sociology (see Chapter 7), conceived of society and culture in terms of unified wholes. Therefore, all customs, practices, and arrangements were seen to contribute to the integration of the existing order. Merton took issue, arguing instead that such a tightly drawn conception might be useful to understand more homogeneous and smaller societies but that the complex and heterogeneous order seldom reflects such perfect integration. For Merton, findings about the tightly knit and traditional society could not be uncritically generalized to all societies.

Traditional functionalism also holds that whatever exists at a structural or cultural level serves a positive function, a socially necessary purpose, or else it would not exist. Merton was again to demur, arguing that the consequences of existing social practices are not uniform for society. Thus, practices might be positive, negative, or irrelevant for the social order in question. For example, it might be argued that paying less for women's work has positive functions for the employers paying their salary and for some men who are paid more to do comparable work. However, the practice might prove to be *dysfunctional* not only for women but for a society in which poverty is rapidly becoming feminized.

In a slightly different vein, Merton theorized that certain rituals or practices have *no* important consequences for an existing social order. Such may be mere holdovers from history. For example, groups such as the Women's Christian Temperance Union are today merely shells of once powerful social movements. Hence, this organization might be considered *nonfunctional* for the society at large.

Finally, traditional functionalism also embraces the fallacy of *indispensability* or absolute necessity. Every part that exists in a societal or cultural system is seen as essential and representing the only alternative. For Merton, however, alternative practices, customs, and forms are often viable. Changing the part, therefore, does not presage the collapse of the whole, and certain parts of a societal system can be eliminated or modified. Building upon this *reformulation of functionalism* as a system of analysis, Merton offered other points of distinction.

First of all, it is not enough to analyze the *manifest* or apparent functions of social elements. Modern functionalism must explore the *latent* or hidden consequences of these repetitive and enduring patterns. For example, one might argue that poverty is *manifestly dysfunctional* for society (as well as the poor) for a number of obvious reasons. However, if we explore the latent consequences of poverty, we might find a number of hidden benefits and beneficiaries.

Such an approach is evident in an essay by an urban sociologist who does not favor poverty but seeks to explore its "positive functions" (Gans, 1972). Some of these "benefits" are:

1. Poverty ensures the "dirty" work is done through maintaining a class of people to fill the menial, temporary, dead-end jobs.

2. Poverty creates jobs for such people as welfare workers, criminal justice personnel, and pawnshop owners (among others).

3. The poor can be identified and used as scapegoats for alleged or actual deviance to define and uphold dominant norms.

4. The needy, particularly those disabled or otherwise incapacitated, allow us to evidence pity, compassion, and charity toward the "less fortunate" (as long as they are truly needy and deserving).

5. Those in want help the affluent through enhancement of their self-image (knowing one is better off than others), and by means of their systematic exclusion from competition for the better jobs. They also provide a purpose for philanthropic organizations and the bureaucracy designed to help them.

6. The poor have historically built civilizations through slave labor, and through their poetry and music (jazz, blues, spirituals, and "country") have enriched the lives of the nonpoor.

7. Finally, the poor absorb the costs of progress (as with urban renewal) and share disproportionately in the costs of welfare.

Second, functional analysis can be carried out at various levels. One might examine the total society or culture, or opt to study less general but enduring formal organizations (such as bureaucracies), or perhaps even family units. Each such example reflects a different plateau within social order.

Third, Merton also sought to reconcile social determinism and individual volition (Stinchcombe, 1975). He did so by arguing that the motivated actor selects from among institutionalized patterns of choice. In effect he acknowledged that the human condition does not revolve on a changeless normative axis. Everywhere, human beings confront conditions of ambivalence where the rules are often in conflict.

Fourth, early organicists often conceived of society as a self-correcting system, evolving toward perfection. Merton, while not abandoning the emphasis on adaptation, considered this a myth. Societies contain incongruities and contradictions, ambiguities and confusion. In his revision of functionalism, Merton sought to make its logic fit the old nemesis of change.

Fifth, Merton's multifaceted conception of function introduced a sociological form of trade-off or net balance. By considering both the (positive) functions and (negative) dysfunctions of social practices, it is possible to appreciate, if not resolve, the complexities of social life.

Sixth, the contributions of this sociologist to theories of the "middle range" can be found in works on deviance, bureaucratic life, mass communication, professional socialization, and other substantive issues. Some of his more important conceptions include the reference group and the self-fulfilling prophecy. By means of the former, he accounted for the relationship between group orientation and self-appraisal. Through the latter, he demonstrated that a widely publicized and believed social prediction may contribute to the very behavior that confirms the prophecy.

## Critique

The theoretical sociology of Robert K. Merton is best conceptualized as a form of *neofunctionalism* developed in response to the criticisms often leveled at its logical base. However, this effort leaves many substantive points untouched, while several of its reforms raise new questions.

To begin, Merton's work may be an attempt to reconcile the irreconcilable. For example, the effort to accommodate change occurs in a theoretical matrix primarily concerned with adjustment and order. This means that such theory can conceive of change only in the limited sense of tempering or eliminating certain dysfunctional parts of the whole, a process that leaves the overall societal system intact. It is clear that Merton's revision of functionalism does not address change at the societal or institutional level. His focus was on adjustments that are consistent with the existing nature of the social system. Thus the underlying dilemma of functionalist (as well as organicist and systems) theory remains untouched. In creating a portrait of order, societal and cultural patterns emerge as systems of mutually reinforcing elements. Substantive social change, specifically in the form of new institutions, is simply unexplained. It can only represent, as it did in Merton's early sociology, a process pushed by those trapped in deviant roles.

There are other examples of the union of opposites. Merton sought to soften the Durkheimian image of the social actor as a passive respondent to impersonal and external forces. And he also acknowledged, as we have seen, the troublesome ambiguities of social life. However, these are *qualifications* of functionalism, not basic departures from its cardinal premises. Merton has not succeeded in freeing the actor from the subjugation of society. Nor have his concessions to societal ambivalence altered an emphasis on a well-integrated (if not perfectly integrated) normative order.

We should also recall that theoretical systems are, by definition, given to *explanation*. Merton's reformulation of functionalism has rendered it a form of *analysis*. Whether this is a blessing or a curse depends upon one's assumptions about sociology. As a system of explanation, functionalism seeks to answer the "why" of existing patterns by showing their purposes as well as their necessary consequences for the system as a whole. However, Merton's reformulations (including the concept of dysfunction) encourage us to analyze the consequences of social practices while selectively rejecting their necessity or positive value. And this introduces an important problem. Traditional functionalists do have an answer, albeit a recurring one, for *why* a social or cultural phenomenon exists: *It is necessary for the whole; it contributes to the adaptation of society.* Merton's logic, however, cannot account for *why* a dysfunctional element exists and still remain functionalist logic.

Finally, whatever the intentions or beliefs of its makers, functionalism lends itself to a conservative ideology. This is because the issues of conflict, inequality, state coercion, and other sources of disharmony and change simply do not fit the logic of this theory. Through purging functionalism of those premises that have drawn critical fire, Merton's efforts may have created a more perfect conservatism. In the final (functionalist) analysis, he has cast society as a system that adapts and survives irrespective of some mistakes, normative ambiguity, and human volition.

Here the criticisms of functionalist thought are blunted in part through the forging of a *conceptual elasticity.* Functions become dysfunctions, the positive becomes negative, and society survives and adapts through trade-offs. By such means, social systems of whatever range become less rigid, more able to adapt while remaining the same.

# ■ *Bibliography*

Durkheim, Émile
(1893) 1933          *The Division of Labor in Society.* Translated by George Simpson. New York: Macmillan.
(1895) 1958          *The Rules of the Sociological Method.* Edited by George E. A. Catlin. Glencoe, Ill.: The Free Press.
(1897) 1957          *Suicide: A Study in Sociology.* Glencoe, Ill.: The Free Press.
(1912) 1964          *The Elementary Forms of the Religious Life.* New York: Humanities Press.

Gans, Herbert
1972          "The Positive Functions of Poverty." *American Journal of Sociology* 78:275–289.

Merton, Robert K.
1938          "Social Structure and Anomie." *American Sociological Review* 3:672–682.
1968          *Social Theory and Social Structure.* New York: The Free Press.
1976          *Sociological Ambivalence and Other Essays.* New York: The Free Press.

1983 "Robert K. Merton: An Autobiographical Sketch." In George Ritzer, *Sociological Theory*, pp. 228–229. New York: Alfred A. Knopf.

Oberschall, Anthony
1965 *Empirical Social Research in Germany, 1898–1914.* New York: Humanities Press.

Peyre, Henri
1964 "Durkheim: The Man, His Time, and His Intellectual Background." In Kurt H. Wolff (Ed.), *Essays on Sociology and Philosophy*. New York: Harper & Row.

Pappenheim, Fritz
1968 *The Alienation of Modern Man.* New York: Monthly Review Press.

Solomon, Albert
1936 "In Memoriam Ferdinand Toennies (1855–1936.)" *Social Research* 3:348–363.

Stinchcombe, A.
1975 "Merton's Theory of Social Structure." In Louis Coser (Ed.), *The Idea of Social Structure: Papers in Honor of Robert K. Merton*. New York: Harcourt Brace Jovanovich.

Toennies, Ferdinand
(1887) 1963 *Community and Society (Gemeinschaft und Gesellschaft).* Translated and edited by Charles P. Loomis. New York: Harper & Row.
(1896) 1925 *Thomas Hobbes: Leben und Lehre.* Stuttgart: Fromman.
1905 "The Present Problems of Social Structure." *American Journal of Sociology* 10:569–588.
1909 *Custom: An Essay on Social Codes.* New York: The Free Press.
(1921) 1974 *Karl Marx: His Life and Teachings.* Translated by Charles P. Loomis and Ingeborg Paulus. East Lansing, Mich.: Michigan State University Press.

Toennies, Ferdinand (Ed.)
(1889) 1928a *Behemoth: Or, the Long Parliament by Thomas Hobbes.* Cambridge, England: Cambridge University Press.
(1889) 1928b *The Elements of Law, Natural and Politic.* Cambridge, England: Cambridge University Press.

Zeitlin, Irving
1968 *Ideology and the Development of Sociological Theory.* Englewood Cliffs, N.J.: Prentice-Hall.

# CHAPTER *6*

# ■ The Politics of Order

It can be convincingly argued that all social thought is political and that formal theoretical systems are no exception. As we have discovered, sociological explanations that grapple with the puzzles of order routinely manifest a conservative ideology. This conclusion is supported by the recurrence of major themes. To be specific, the integration of society is presented as a natural condition, norms are legitimated by the fact of their existence, and social control is portrayed as essential to harnessing the wayward bent of the human spirit. Societies are seen as self-adjusting organisms or systems. Individual transgressions are defined as deviance, not resistance, and institutional change is cast as disorganization, not reorganization.

In the works to be examined in this chapter, the issues of politics are not confined to the ideological infrastructure of theoretical systems. For the Italian Elitists, power and its organization represent the overarching puzzle of social life. Hence we will discover in Gaetano Mosca's ruling class, in Vilfredo Pareto's early systematism, and in Robert Michels' "iron law of oligarchy," mandates for the domination of society by an elite of command.

## ■ Gaetano Mosca (1858–1941): The Ruling Class

Gaetano Mosca did not develop a grand theory of society as a system as did his contemporary Vilfredo Pareto. However, within a more narrowly drawn political sociology, Mosca's work demonstrates the form of systemic logic that is quite compatible with the order paradigm. Born in Palermo on the Mediterranean island of Sicily, west of the Italian peninsula, Mosca took his

**91**

law degree in 1881 at the age of 23. His homeland was not immune from the strife and upheaval of nineteenth-century Italian history. But it was the specific conditions of Sicilian history that contributed to a strongly developed ideological stance, as we shall soon discover.[1]

## History and Biography

The Sicily of Gaetano Mosca featured a geographical isolation well matched on the social, political, and economic fronts by a tendency to face the past. It is not enough to say that in the Sicily of this era, time stood still. Rather, for this detached island, the clock appeared to run backward. At a period when the events of the mainland featured a halting (compared to Britain and France) bourgeois revolution, Sicily remained structurally, culturally, and psychologically apart. While those on the peninsula struggled to resolve the conflicting demands of laissez-faire economics, public services by the state, and parliamentary democracy, Sicily remained an entrenched feudal order.

Poorly developed, the Sicilian agrarian economy yielded a meager subsistence for most of its inhabitants. On the cultural side, a strong suspicion of the outside world, of institutional authority, and of remote central government dominated the customs of power. Influence and rule were interpreted in personal terms. The ruling lords of medieval Europe had passed, but their political descendants remained in Sicily in the form of powerful dons who, through vendetta, terror, and a code of silence, formed a shadow government.

As we note later in an examination of Pareto's milieu, the industrial development and relative prosperity of northern Italy did not reach the southern regions, whose inhabitants suffered from the concentration of land ownership and the corresponding abuse of state power. Of course, the central problem of representative government is that some may be represented more than others. In nineteenth-century Italy and Sicily, this problem was compounded politically by restrictions on suffrage and economically by the concentration of wealth. For the south, and even more so for Sicily, the problems of poverty and tyranny were too entrenched to be resolved through the vote or by means of voices in parliament. It was within the web of such events that Gaetano Mosca nurtured his formal conceptions of power.

The intellectual forces that molded Mosca included first of all the ever-present apparition of Machiavelli, whose somewhat cynical image of humanity found clear expression in the writings of the Sicilian. Second, Mosca's criticism of democratic positions came to be molded by the historian Taine. And finally, Mosca came to embrace both rational philosophy and the lawful certainty of

---

[1] Important general references on Mosca include Meisel, 1965, and Burnham, 1943.

order in the social universe. In such matters, he acknowledged a debt to Saint-Simon (see Chapter 4), attributing to the French philosopher as well his inspiration for a theory of politics.

As we shall see, Mosca embraced Saint-Simon's dual conception of power. The ability to control others, to create and enforce the binding decisions of organized societies, is found in two complementary orders. One of these is the material, the other the intellectual/moral. Those authorities that control the means of economic production, together with those that speak with ideological force and legitimacy, constitute a *ruling class*.

Mosca demonstrated antipathy toward his era's experiment with democracy in his first major work, *On the Theory of Governments and Parliamentary Governments* published in 1884. However, it was in his book *The Ruling Class* (1939, originally published 1896) that Mosca developed a basic theoretical system that he held throughout his life. His conception of power was acted out politically as he was elected in 1908 to the Chamber of Deputies as a conservative. In 1912 he voted against the expansion of suffrage and became a senator seven years later. Mosca's theory came to be hailed by some fascist intellectuals because of its criticism of majority politics. However, his early guarded sympathies toward Mussolini's experiment faded in later life.

## Assumptions

Mosca's assumptions concerning human nature, society, and science can be gleaned from our discussion to this point. His image of human nature bore the indelible mark of Machiavelli, who held that the human animal responds well only to organized forces and coercion. As Zeitlin argues (1968: 196–197), Mosca held that a struggle for *preeminence* is a universal law of human psychology and thus a feature of all societies. Despite an apparent affinity to its central logic, the Sicilian specifically rejected social Darwinism.

Ironically, Mosca broke with Pareto on the question of a reformation of society. Like most of the early European positivists including Pareto, Mosca assumed that society in its natural form reflects a hierarchy. However, with Comte, Saint-Simon, and others, Mosca believed that the application of social science could be beneficial. Also consistent with the positivist tradition, both early and modern, Mosca's vision of science called for certainty and inductive reasoning.

## Theoretical Content

Mosca's theoretical system can be succinctly presented. To begin, his ruling class is a political class, not an economic one. So too are the ruled. Thus, the world of power invariably represents those with authority and those who obey, with control always residing with a well-organized minority.

At base, the various political ideologies represent little more than ideological legitimation. Democracy, socialism, and liberalism may have dissimilar content, but they are all formulae for political control by a ruling class. For Mosca, each idea system matches the prevaling conditions of the historical period in which it arises, appealing to the specific expectations of the ruled. Thus, the subject classes in different epochs and places are exposed to the political tranquilizers that all rationalize the control of society by an elite. These in turn become fundamental for the creation of a consensus among the ruled, a consensus that is only an illusion. It should be apparent that Mosca's "political formulae" represent the basis for Pareto's later and more ambitious taxonomy of derivations.

Although the existence of a ruling class is constant through history, Mosca argued that this political phenomenon assumes different forms. The *aristocratic* ruling class maintains control across generations through the passage of power to descendants. In this form, power flows *autocratically* from top to bottom. In a *democracy,* the ruling circles absorb from below the more able members of the subjugated class. Hence the flow of authority allows some upward movement from the masses, a political process known as *liberalism.*

It should be clear from the preceding paragraph that Mosca's early work strongly influenced Pareto's selection of the internal components of his systemic theory. Mosca's ruling class, although not subject to a full-blown systems theory, described the process Pareto came to call the circulation of the elite. Moreover, his "law" of constancy (in this case the universality in all political systems of a ruling class) is a common feature of systems thought. However, it is an early conception of *equilibrium* that clearly marks the systems logic of Mosca's work.

In this theoretical system, the structure of the ruling class is two-tiered, with the official government presiding over the remaining organized political interests. The natural state of the ruling class is one of equilibrium born of *countervailing power.* By means of this divergency of authority, and the checks and balances it represents, the rising of an elite within the elite is prevented and the self-negation of government is forestalled. One coterie within the ruling class holds primacy in the economic sector, another rules through religious authority, still another controls secular power, and a final dominates the means of military force. Whatever their position, members of the ruling class have superior intellectual, material, and moral qualities.

Mosca the lawyer argued that such a balance of ruling forces typically gives rise to *judicial defense,* that is, a government based on formal law. Through law there emerges an aura of justice and a respect for moral order within society. He also held that an open ruling class is advantaged compared to a closed one. The former is more apt to acquire a moral legitimacy, a sense of popular justice.

## Critique

Mosca's conception of political domination remains thought provoking in at least two major ways. First, although he presaged certain of Pareto's assumptions and theoretical conceptions, he avoided the use of instincts and sentiments to account for social order. With the notable exception of his belief in the universal struggle for preeminence that is productive of a ruling class, Mosca's language and conceptualization are strongly sociological. Also important was his rejection of a monolithic ruling class in favor of a structure of countervailing power. As we will see later, an analytic division by function of the ruling class appears in the conflict theory of C. Wright Mills (see Chapter 16). However, Mills entertained quite different assumptions about human nature, society, and science and assigned a theoretical role to social change.

For his part, Mosca failed to examine a possible economic basis for a ruling class and the class system. He also argued the universality of a ruling class without presenting compelling historical or comparative evidence bearing on his proposition. And his focus on a pinnacle of power, then as now, gave rise to a *conspiratorial* interpretation of power founded in plots, cabals, and collusion on the part of dominant minorities in service of their own interests. His work neither reflects nor inspires the comparative analysis of political structures as they arise under specific socioeconomic conditions.

A consensus of political, economic, and social views for other order theorists (such as Durkheim and Parsons) is expressive of the popular will. For Mosca (and later Pareto), consensus is a myth called into being by political ideologies, the content of which varies with the particular value system in effect in society. An alternative to his approach is to view ideologies as reflections of institutional structure. As such, they are seen to reside more in the organization of society and less in the Machiavellian tendencies of rulers to seek legitimacy.

## ■ Vilfredo Pareto (1848–1923): The Circulation of the Elite

Vilfredo Pareto[2] was born in Paris in 1848, the year of the revolution that brought the fall of the House of Bourbon and the rise of Louis Napoleon (refer to Chapter 4 and the historical era of Auguste Comte). Pareto's father was an Italian nobleman and political exile, and his mother was French. With the issuance of a general amnesty, the family returned to Italy in 1868. Vilfredo graduated from the Polytechnic Institute in Turin with a degree in engineering. He

---

[2] Biographical information as well as a sense of Pareto's era can be found in Finer, 1966; Lopreato, 1965; and Stark, 1964.

first worked for two Italian railways and then served as general superintendent of iron mines owned by a bank in Florence.

Pareto's contributions to sociology were matched by his early efforts in the field of economics. He was greatly influenced by the works of Leon Walras on economic equilibrium and, in a personal meeting with the Swiss academician, succeeded in demonstrating his command of Walras's work. In 1893 Walras resigned from the University of Lausanne, and Pareto became his successor. Five years later, he became heir to a sizable fortune and through the remainder of his life left Switzerland only rarely.

We can identify two major turning points in the intellectual life of Pareto. Over time, the engineer-economist became convinced of the limitations of narrowly drawn conceptions of economic systems and advanced the need for a general theory of society. So inspired, in 1902–1903 he published *The Socialist Systems* and some years later added to a long list of publications his *General Treatise on Sociology* (1915). A refined and reorganized version of the latter was published in 1935 under the title *The Mind and Society*. Throughout his writing career, the thrust of Pareto's work was toward an equilibrium model of society. His conception of the social system came to be highly influential at Harvard University, particularly in the work of Talcott Parsons and George Homans (see Chapters 7 and 8).

Another watershed in the life of Pareto was more clearly political and ideological. In his youth he was swayed by the democratic and humanitarian ethic. He opposed the authority of the church and the ready resort to military force that swept European history. However, Pareto's early sentiments were to change. In the last decade of the nineteenth century, he wrote scores of articles calling for the reorganization of society along the lines of laissez-faire economics. In the current of Italian politics, the ideals of democracy came to assume a socialist face. Pareto fiercely retained his "liberal" conception of free trade, while repudiating political equality.

Before the publication of *The Socialist Systems*, Pareto had decided that his own prior reasoning in support of political liberty was more emotional than rational. Both this work and his later *Treatise* were to contain polemical assaults on democratic structure and ideology. Pareto drew fire from his critics who labeled him variously the "Karl Marx of the bourgeoisie" and the "Marx of fascism." One of his admirers was Benito Mussolini, who offered him a seat in the Italian senate shortly before Pareto's death in 1923.

## History and Biography

A brief sketch of the historical milieu in which Pareto's life was shaped will bring us back to a familiar theme: Sociological theories of order were typically a conservative response to conditions of disorder. In the nineteenth century, Italy (like European society in general) was divided and fragmented. With the fall of Bonaparte in the early years of the era, the French Bourbons and the

Austrian emperor came to rule various republics and duchies in Italy, with Pope Pius VII regaining the Papal States. Hence the specter of foreign domination coexisted with the division of the nation, a separation that inhibited the commercial interests of the rising bourgeoisie.

This was a time for the formation of shadowy organizations predicated on political resistance, which succeeded in touching off popular rebellions throughout the nation. New leaders were to appear, such as Mazzini, Gioberti, and Garibaldi, each of whom sought to unite Italy through a half century of fire and blood. One year after Pareto graduated from the Polytechnic Institute in Turin, Rome became the capital of a newly unified Kingdom of Italy. However, there proved to be more to unification than lines drawn on maps.

Divisions in the new Italy were as always political, economic, and social. However, these conformed to some extent with the major geographical regions of the country. In the north, modernization had taken the form of political bureaucratization and industrial development. The largely agrarian south featured widespread poverty, misery, and illiteracy. The forces of the right, based in the more affluent north, controlled the kingdom until 1876. Its panaceas of free trade, unequal taxation, a balanced budget, and an austere attitude toward public work expenditures alienated large segments of the population. Riding the tide of disaffection, the predominantly southern political left swept to a parliamentary victory. Although promising progressive taxation, public services, and wider suffrage, the liberal government ruled by patronage and corruption until the First World War.

Some industrial development in Italy was evident in the latter part of the nineteenth century, particularly in textiles. However, the level of that development lagged behind other European states such as France and England. In the south, the larger owners successfully opposed the land reform desperately wanted by the peasants. Laws calling for compulsory education were not implemented, taxation remained regressive, and the governmental bureaucracy remained bloated and ineffective. Popular insurrections flourished, the intellectuals became disaffected, and liberal democratic ideals withered in the dust of economic stagnation. On October 28, 1922, Benito Mussolini marched on Rome.

Within a short time, the vision of peace gave way to the glorification of war. The interests of the owning class were preserved under a system of centralized state control while the dream of political enfranchisement succumbed to one-party rule. The diversity of unions, minority groups, and political opposition collapsed under the press of nationalism. Together, these conditions marked the advent of the iron fist of Italian fascism.

## Assumptions

Pareto's theory, written in the positivist tradition, fits almost too well the ideal type that is the order paradigm. To begin, he assumed sociology to be an empirical discipline, meant to follow the methodological lead of the natural sciences. He called for the establishment of the "logico-experimental" method by which investigation would be based solely on experience and observation. Moreover, the construction of his theory, particularly its major terms, reflected his view of order in the universe. Pareto believed that the highest form of human organization is the social system. It logically follows that the natural state of society is one of dynamic equilibrium.

In some important ways, Pareto was influenced by the works of Comte and Spencer (see Chapter 4). He embraced Spencer's position on noninterference (especially as it applied to laissez-faire economics). The concepts of greater differentiation and interrelationships developed by both Spencer and Durkheim appear to have also informed the work of the Italian, especially his early sociology. However, by the time his *Treatise* was published (1915), Pareto was to condemn Spencer and Comte along two lines. First, he rejected the earlier positivists for their lack of scientific sophistication. Second, he faulted their vision of evolutionary progress.

It must be admitted that Pareto's conception of the social system was quite mature when compared with the efforts of his contemporaries. He drew on his engineering background to substitute a mechanical image (system) for a biological one (organism). Of crucial importance was Pareto's conception of society as a system of elements or variables in a state of reciprocal and mutual interdependence. His systemic explanation of how a society works, and its interpenetration with the minds of its members, rendered organicism quite crude in comparison. However, Pareto's intellectual break with Spencer and Comte went beyond the question of sophistication.

Pareto imagined in the work of his intellectual ancestors the unacceptable tainting of the Enlightenment philosophes. In the *Treatise* he called for the abandonment of the ideal of unilinear progress, a principle he had discerned in the evolutionary conceptions of his predecessors. As we have seen, neither Comte nor Spencer assumed the perfectability of human nature. They held fast to the Hobbesian conception of the antisocial being saved from mutual destruction only through reason. However, Pareto went beyond Hobbes. When the promise of progress in his native Italy fell far short of fruition, he was drawn to perhaps the starkest portrait of human nature in Western philosophy, that of Niccolo Machiavelli.

In an attempt to end his exile at the hands of the Medici conquerors of his native Florence, Machiavelli (1469–1527) wrote *The Prince*. In it, he argued that the ordinary sentiments of humankind are those of greed and selfishness. In concrete terms, those who are subject to political authority are without gratitude, honesty, and courage. The subject population by nature is unable to resist the passions of the moment and will violate both principles and the rights of others. At an intellectual level, there is no creative thought but only the imitation of authority. It is this imitation of authority, together with the desire for self-preservation, that represents the only hope for human redemption.

Machiavelli did not specify precisely how those in power came to avoid the disaster of such a nature. However, he found in the despicable condition of the subject population a mandate for political action. He wrote that rulers are required to employ means that are beyond the pale of personal morality. These include a mastery of legal forms of social control but may also include deception, brute force, and the evaluation of all strategies by means of the ultimate end to which they are put. Therefore, the ruler is advised to give the appearance of virtue, piety, and thrift, thus behaving as the *fox*. Or when necessary, the ruler must resort to power and cruelty as does the *lion*. In the words of Machiavelli, it is "safer to be feared than loved." The power of such imagery had a striking impact on Vilfredo Pareto, as we shall soon discover.

One final point is in order. As we suggested earlier in the case of Auguste Comte, it is not necessary to conclude that the events of his era somehow converted Pareto from democrat to elitist. The ideological alliance between economic "liberalism" (then laissez-faire capitalism) and democracy was weak throughout the turbulence of eighteenth- and nineteenth-century Europe. It was inconceivable to the new owners of property that the fading aristocracy should retain its political privilege. It was also unacceptable that the crown heads continue to use their power to grant economic charters only to those persons and firms that enjoyed royal pleasure. Adam Smith's *Wealth of Nations* became the manifesto of the rising bourgeoisie simply because it called for laissez-faire economics. This meant in effect an end to the mercantile system whereby the crown frequently conferred monopoly status on favored enterprises.

Calls for bourgeois democracy in this historical context did *not* mean universal suffrage, political representation of the whole people, or the recognition of common rights in governmental affairs. Ultimately, it meant state assurance of a free economic order whereby the demands of the marketplace would determine what should be produced, who should produce it, how it should be produced, and how the production should be distributed. Of course, the new owners would be the definers and executives of the "will of the market."

For Pareto, when disenfranchised workers and peasants pressed for land reform, union organization, and public works, democracy had been carried too far. In the situation of his times, the Italian (like Comte and Spencer before him) was a laissez-faire revolutionary. However, he perceived little economic gain and great turmoil to be had should political freedom be expanded. Indeed, before Mussolini's rise to power, the bourgeois agenda was under serious attack by the adherents of an alternative: democratic socialism. Given such conditions, Pareto's "antidemocratic" shift, as seen in his turn to the heritage of Machiavelli, represented a logical step, not a dramatic conversion.

## Theoretical Content

With an understanding of the historical antecedents and the assumptions that informed Pareto's knowledge in mind, we can now turn to his theory proper.

We have compiled his "propositions" from the major works mentioned earlier, *The Socialist Systems* and *The Mind and Society*. Two volumes of selections from Pareto's *Treatise* edited by Joseph Lopreato (1965) and the work on Pareto by S. E. Finer (1966) are also important references.

The general logic of Pareto's work follows from his conception of society as a systematic whole made up of interdependent parts. He argued forcefully that the introduction of change at any point affecting any part will necessarily produce change in other parts, as well as in the total system. Forces within society work to maintain the existing form of social organization and to ensure that change is orderly and compatible with the nature of the social system. Hence, for Pareto, change is not conceived in terms of dramatic institutional response. To the contrary, action and reaction within the system represent a process of *maintaining* order in the presence of threats. As with homeostasis in physiology, the components of society compensate automatically for alterations or strain in the external environment.

The relationships among variables in Pareto's system are not unilateral. As a rule, relationships involve *reciprocal dependence*. For this reason Pareto rejected the traditional conception of cause and effect as both one-sided and simplistic. He believed that the association of social variables could be best understood as *functional,* but he appears to have employed a mathematical conception of function. By this we mean that the state of the variable depends on and changes with another (or other) variable(s). In a quantitative sense, fluctuations in the system can best be conceived as correlational, as a matter of the degree of relative correspondence. This is different from Durkheimian functionalism, where the focus is on the purposes of social practices.

For Pareto, the most important elements of a social system are those that are universal, that is, found in all systems. These constant elements tend to be regular and uniform and to demonstrate continuity over time. He argued that the *identification* and *measurement* of the constant components that comprise the social system represent sociology's reason for being.

Turning his attention to the members of society, Pareto held that human action within the system can be classified as either *logical* or *nonlogical*. Logical action occurs when a preponderance of rigorous evidence is employed by the actor to assess (1) whether an end can be realistically achieved, and if so, (2) what the best means are to reach that goal. Influenced heavily by Machiavelli, Pareto argued that logical action is unusual (confined typically to such rational behavior as economic and scientific conduct). Rather, it is nonlogical action, reflective of underlying human sentiments or innate instincts, that dominates the range of human behavior. Pareto did not separate human action from the social system. Rather, he incorporated both the logical and nonlogical within its internal dynamics.

Pareto held that systemic equilibrium is a consequence of the constancies of external conditions and internal elements. External conditions consist of two major categories: the impact upon society by its natural environment (geography) and the influences represented by other systems or by the same system at an earlier historical stage. Internal elements can be classified into principal types. These are *economic interests, residues, derivations, social stratification,* and *the circulation of the elite*. For Pareto, economic interests represent logical action directed toward the maximization of satisfaction. He did *not* consider this internal element of value in the understanding of the social system.

Another internal element consists of nonlogical actions that are manifestations of underlying mental or psychic states or sentiments. Termed *residues,* such manifestations correspond with innate dispositions that appear to be bioinstinctual in essence. At the individual level, residues seem synonymous with drives or basic impulses that ordinarily culminate in social interaction. Such an interpretation has to be inferred from Pareto's classification of residues as well as his general usage of the concept.

Pareto identified 51 residues and combined them into six distinct classes: (1) *combinations,* or the impulse to form associations and categories of things, events, and ideas; (2) *persistence of aggregates,* or the impulse to preserve abstractions, symbols, and social relationships over time; (3) *sentiments through exterior acts,* or the impulse to express powerful underlying emotions through religious rituals, political agitation, and so forth; (4) *sociability,* or the impulse to impose uniform standards of behavior to realize popularity, prestige, and standing; (5) *integrity of personality,* or the impulse to preserve the personality; and (6) *sexuality,* or the impulse toward all sexually related action.

*Derivations* constitute the next constant and internal element of social systems. Derivations are a form of nonlogical action. And just as residues are manifestations of sentiments, so too are derivations manifestations of residues. Derivations are in effect ideologies or "pseudo-logical" defenses that are subject to further classification. These are *assertions, appeals to authority, claims that are in accordance with prevailing sentiments or the conventional wisdom,* and *verbal proofs that employ ambiguity, abstractions, and analogies in lieu of hard evidence.*

It is crucial at this juncture to make note of Pareto's theoretical intent. By means of his residues and derivations, he sought not only to identify constant elements of the social system but to construct a basis for criticizing rival theories that did not measure up to his "logico-experimental" conception of science. Thus, for Pareto, both the social system and his theoretical attempts to explain it were based on logical action. Alternative theories, especially those that seemed to offer an alternative vision of society, were dismissed as mere "derivations," ideologies masquerading as science. They sought legitimacy through assertion, authority, "what everybody knows," and verbal obtuseness.

For Pareto, still another constant element found in all social systems is *social stratification.* By such, Pareto meant that residues are differentially distributed among individuals, groups, and classes in society. Such a state of affairs, when combined with real moral, intellectual, and physical differences, represents the basis for inequality. This fundamental component of society means that all theories of political democracy, classlessness, and mass govern-

ment are contradicted by the systemic imperative of social stratification. Therefore, egalitarian conceptions of society can be nothing more than derivations
(unfounded ideologies) used by ruling circles to control the lower strata.

The final internal element for Pareto is the *circulation of the elite*. History,
he argued, is the "cemetery of aristocracies." By this he sought to show that
although stratification is a part of the natural order of things, the composition
of its elite circles does not remain unchanged. According to Pareto, those on
the top often resort to measures of repression that sustain them for long periods. However, sooner or later the "more fit" members of the subject classes
will demand their place. If they are not assimilated into the existing elite, then
the historical stage is set for the revolution or coup d'état.

As expected, Pareto found specific residues at the base of the circulation
of the elite. These are the residues of *combinations* and *persistence*. Combination
residues are the basis for grand schemes of political and financial empire building, or the bringing together of state power and the interests of economic enterprise. The elite act in the style of Machiavelli's *foxes,* and although they are
willing to innovate and assume risks, they prefer deception to force.

Persistence residues, on the other hand, dominate a contending body of
elite. For Pareto, these were Machiavelli's *lions* with their strong and enduring
attachment to family, class, country, and other traditional social relationships.
Here we find the patriots and nationalists who fear neither the use of violence
nor the raw exercise of power. Pareto's world saw the predominance of foxes.
Soon, he predicted, the day of the lion would dawn.

## Critique

As mentioned earlier, Vilfredo Pareto's conception of the social system was
strongly to influence the early work of the leading American systematist, Talcott Parsons. This is true in part because the Italian succeeded in freeing the
functionalist image of society and the vision of positive science from the simplistic organicism of other theories of order. His conception of systemic interdependence (which includes the relationship between human action and the
external environment), the role of nonlogical action in both society and science, and the search for constants in the social universe proved to be enduring
contributions. And for some, his insistence on cutting off utopian visions from
explanations of how a society really works has been preserved. Clearly, however, discernable problems emerge from a critical analysis of this form of systems theory.

To begin, the *construction* of Pareto's theory presents problems. He failed
to implement his stated ideals of logical induction and disciplined observation
(his so-called logico-experimental method). Instead, he settled for a classification scheme, a multilayered taxonomy of systemic elements and subelements.
Second, despite an insistence on precision, Pareto's major concepts are often

poorly defined. This is especially true in the case of residues, which represent the fulcrum of his theory. However, this central concept can be faulted on more serious grounds than those of definitional ambiguity.

By use of the term *residues,* Pareto sought to explain the emergence of the social system in terms of drives or impulses that are the reflections of underlying sentiments or instincts. His logic is flawed in two important ways. In terms of *level of abstraction,* Pareto's residues represent a form of *behavioral reductionism* while the innate predispositions they supposedly manifest cannot be studied at all. Ultimately, Pareto turned to instincts to account for society and in so doing fell into a tautology. This circular reasoning can be expressed in the following: Why do human beings seek popularity and differential prestige (actions that for Pareto represent the residue of sociability)? Because of an underlying and innate sentiment. How do we know such a sentiment exists? Because human beings seek popularity and differential prestige.

Furthermore, Pareto's insistence that inequality is constant and that systems are universally governed by an elite falls victim to the *naturalistic fallacy* that commonly plagues order theories. The existence of an elite does not prove its universal necessity. Also of crucial importance is the fact that such assertions do not allow us to assess the *differential degree* of elite dominance among systems.

It is also true that Pareto's "circulation of the elite" (in true Machiavellian style) assigns little importance to the role of mass movements in history. Instead, the system, ultimately rooted in nonlogical action, stands as an immutable order. Because it is founded on changeless instincts, Pareto's conservative society lies beyond the pale of revolution or planned intervention. For this sociologist, the vision of humanistic change was merely an illusion by which the cycles of elite domination may be disguised for a brief historical moment.

Pareto, as noted, was quite sensitive to the ideological implications of alternative theories. However, there is no evidence that he understood the political nature of his own thought. Turning the language of this theory against him, Pareto's social system is perhaps a derivation (ideology). As we have seen, the ideological content of his work was not lost on the architects of Mussolini's new order.

# ■ Robert Michels (1876–1936): The Iron Law of Oligarchy

"Who says organization says oligarchy." Thus wrote the German sociologist Robert Michels in his magnum opus, *Political Parties* (1966, originally published 1911). And by this conclusion he identified the victor in the struggle between the egalitarian ideals in democratically conceived movements and the organizational structures designed to implement those ideals. For Michels, the phrase "democratic organization" tends toward a contradiction in terms.

The sociology of Robert Michels is a study in ambivalence. On the one hand, he was taken early in his life with forms of trade union socialism and developed an affinity for democratic government and ideology. He also came to share Max Weber's pluralist concern with the structural dangers of large-scale organizations. These concerns are clear in *Political Parties*. Yet there were other forces at work in the life and time of Robert Michels.

A careful reading of *Political Parties* reveals the kernel of *antidemocratic* themes in Michels, as well as a strong corollary to Mosca's law of constancy. Just as Mosca argued the inevitability of ruling class dominance in all political systems, so did Michels argue that even democratically conceived organizations are bound to be dominated by their leadership. And when further contrasted with Pareto's circulation of the elite, the "iron law" of Michels can be fairly said to complement the conservative political sociology of the Italians (who adopted him in more ways than one). But once again, we begin at the beginning.

## History and Biography

Robert Michels[3] was born in Cologne, a member of a wealthy and socially prominent family. He attended the gymnasium in Berlin, a secondary school that prepared the well-to-do to enter university. The young Michels served in the military and then studied in England, Paris, Munich, and Leipzig before entering the University of Halle in 1898. He defended his dissertation two years later and became a lecturer first at the University of Marburg and later at the University of Turin (where he was a close colleague of Gaetano Mosca).

While at Marburg, Michels became a socialist and then an active member of the Social Democratic party in Germany. Although he left the S.D.P. in 1907, he joined the Italian Socialist party while serving as a lecturer at the University of Turin. He also resigned from this organization, but his socialist views meant that he was to be spurned by German universities. However, it was none other than Max Weber (see Chapter 10) who noted the promise of Michels and over time encouraged his writing and intellectual labor.

After 1904 Michels was influenced by a number of noted *syndicalists*, including George Sorel. Syndicalism was both a theory and movement, originating in France, under which all means of production and distribution would be brought under the control of federations of labor unions. Although a number of direct methods might be employed to achieve that end, the foremost was to be the general strike. (Whether implemented or not, the very myth of the

---

[3] General references employed in this section include Linz, 1968; Lipset, 1966; and Zeitlin, 1968.

strike would serve to unify working people and offer them some sense of power.) Michels saw not only in syndicalism but also in the work of Marx and Proudhon ideas that might spur on the trade unions in particular and the European socialist movement in general. However, his early infatuation with syndicalism was to fall to the Machiavellian-inspired assumptions of the Italian intelligentsia, as we shall see.

Born during the Bismarckian era (Michels was 16 when the stern minister was dismissed by William II), Robert Michels knew a Germany of rapid industrialization, population growth, and colonial expansion. The conditions of the German workers were harsh, and socialist ideology found fertile soil within the trade unions and the Social Democratic party. Yet his own conditions of privilege rendered Michels somewhat the outsider, a rebel to his class who sought meaning in political life. When he confronted the wide gulf between a workers' ideology that called for revolution and the often timid policies of worker-based organizations, he grew frustrated. And when he witnessed the parliamentary maneuvers and quest for dominance within leadership factions, he became convinced that organizations were inherently oligarchical.

Michels broke with Weber, apparently over the issue of the latter's support for the German war effort, and became increasingly tied to Italy, his adopted nation. However, since 1907 Michels had been influenced by the far more conservative and Machiavellian Italian tradition (including the ideas of Mosca and Pareto). This not only had an impact on his major theoretical effort but combined with his disenchantment with socialism, it resulted in a later interlude with the fascist vision of Benito Mussolini. In 1928 Michels accepted a position at the University of Perugia (offered by none other than Il Duce). Robert Michels did not live to see the failure of Italian fascism. In 1936 the expatriate died in Rome.

## Assumptions

The assumptions on human nature that underlie much of the work of Michels are not purely Machiavellian. On at least one issue, Michels had something in common with Rousseau (see Chapter 9). Each believed that the masses have the potential to learn, or in the words of Michels: "Every proletarian of average intelligence, given the necessary means, could acquire a university degree with the same facility as does the average bourgeois" (1966: 300). Yet Michels was far less sanguine concerning the *existing* state of the masses. Simply put, he thought the mass to be incompetent, a condition "almost universal throughout the domains of political life" (1966: 112).

Michels assumed political ignorance on the part of the masses, who are motivated only by egoism and worsening conditions. And even within the "organized mass of the labor parties," Michels found an "immense need for direction and guidance" (1966: 85–89). Citing proof of the "organic weakness of the mass," he held that when "deprived of their leaders in time of action, they abandon the field of battle in disordered flight; they seem to have no power of *instinctive reorganization*" (1966: 90; italics added). And finally, Michels observed a *cult of veneration* among the masses, who believe their leaders belong to a "higher order of humanity" (1966: 93).

As to the nature of society, Michels centered his vision in organizational necessity. To begin, Michels believed that under all circumstances, *direct* forms of democracy cannot work because of the *size* of national populations (1966: 65–66). When this "technical impossibility" is combined with the incompetence of the masses, the only way that work can be accomplished is through organizations. And within those organizations Michels found the clash of interests among leaders and cadres who struggle to maintain themselves and lose sight of their true reason for being.

In *Political Parties,* the vision of human science waffles between a Marxist conception of historical materialism (see Chapter 14) and the universalist explanations common to the work of Pareto and Mosca. However, when Michels purported to discover a "law" of oligarchy that existed independent of specific historical conditions and social systems, he came down on the side of positivism and the Italians.

Michels also tended toward "group mind" forms of explanation, such as that evidenced in the *crowd* of Gustave Le Bon. Michels concerned himself with the "exceptionally bold, energetic and adroit" leaders who "dominate crowds" and the masses who need to "pay adoring worship" to those who inculcate their ideals (1966: 64–65).

> In the object of such adoration, megalomania is apt to ensue. The immeasurable presumption, . . . sometimes found in modern popular leaders, is not dependent solely on their being self-made men, but also upon the atmosphere of adulation in which they live and breathe. This overweening self-esteem on the part of the leaders diffuses a powerful suggestive influence, whereby the masses are confirmed in their admiration for their leaders, and it thus proves a source of enhanced power. (1966: 97)

And yet it is not a pure psychology that distinguishes the work of Michels. To the contrary, it is within the *pattern of relationships involving organizational needs, those who lead, and those who follow that we find the inevitability of oligarchy.*

## Theoretical Content

In his examination of parties and unions, Michels focused on organizational processes. These he viewed as virtual imperatives. To be specific, organizations measure success by growth, and growth makes the sovereignty of the membership increasingly impractical. As organizations grow, the problems of communication and quick decision making increase. Administrative tasks and duties increase in both size and complexity, necessitating a more specialized division of labor (1966: 70–77). Looking expressly at the party, Michels termed it a "fighting organization," and as such, it must employ effective tactics. These include the ability to quickly *mobilize* the membership and form necessary *alliances* (1966: 78–80).

For Michels, the political party has many properties in common with the state. The modern party, like the modern state, seeks to *widen its base* in terms of membership and financial support. Also like the state, the party relies on a complex *bureaucracy* to rationally and efficiently administer party affairs through its specialized administrative units. However, for this theorist (as for Weber), a bureaucracy is a bureaucracy. "It comes to assume the form of an endless screw. It grows ever less and less compatible with the general welfare" (1966: 189).

Now, at the level of the state, this means that its bureaucratic structure will serve the interests of politically dominant classes. But even within socialist parties, there will emerge hierarchy, the suppression of individuals, status seeking, and a narrowness of purpose. And just as the state bureaucracies lose touch with the general welfare, so even do socialist party bureaucracies grow isolated from their wider ideals (1966: 188–202).

Ironically enough, Michels argued that social-democratic, working-class parties (emerging under capitalism) are doomed to *embourgeoisement*. First of all, as the party grows it will attract not merely proletarians but a petty bourgeoisie, including proprietors, independent artisans, property owners, students, and members of some liberal professions. Further, the labor organization itself will create a new petty bourgeois level of paid party workers who abandon manual work for more mental forms. These processes cannot fail but transform a party of workers into a party of greater privilege for some.

These organizational imperatives do not stand in isolation. They command the emergence of skilled leaders who both respond to the party or union structure and shape it to their personal or psychological interests. Nor are leaders the only players on the stage. They enter into a reciprocal relationship with the masses who follow. The attributes of leadership and mass, within the context of organizational necessity, further ensure the coming of Michels' contradiction (between the nature of organizations and the nature of democracy).

As previously noted, Michels observed the masses to be incompetent, mired in apathy and requiring guidance. Hence they see little relationship between public affairs and private interests. Ideological struggles, as well as contests over tactics, are not only misunderstood by the rank and file but "leave them altogether cold" (1966: 86). Another attribute of the working class is the *petty bourgeois* ideal: Simply put, proletarians routinely desire the same rewards enjoyed by those in a higher stratum. And finally, Michels argued that the working class itself is commonly divided along hierarchical lines. Thus emerge subclasses who pursue their own interests (as with union versus nonunion, or trade versus industrial unions). All such conditions bode ill for socialist forms of democracy.

Michels also argued that leaders who develop organizational skills become convinced of their indispensability. Such convictions are supported in part through interaction with the masses. For their part, those who follow are sincerely grateful to those they perceive to belong to a superior order. Gratitude breeds reelection, which contributes to organizational *stability*, but at the expense of political choice (1966: 92–97). Also crucial to leadership are the qualities of *oratory* and *writing*. Now on the one hand these would appear to flourish under democratic orders, and Michels so acknowledged. However, he also held that the masses are prone to a superficial attachment to the style of a spoken or written argument rather than its substance (1966: 98–106).

Given this interlocking state of affairs, leaders (and often followers) grow to confuse the leader's personal standing with that of the party (Le parti c'est moi). In the final analysis, there can only be a widening gulf between those who lead and those who follow. Those in command lose their sense of class solidarity, and the proletarian "captains" are split off from "common soldiers" (1966: 109). If the gap is negatively defined from below (as when the struggles among leaders for power become public), then the party may face a revolt. However such revolts are inevitably suppressed. And in the words of Michels: "The natural and normal development of the organization will impress upon the most revolutionary of parties an indelible stamp of conservatism" (1966: 171). Hence, the *iron law of oligarchy*.

## Critique

Robert Michels, by theoretical definition, considered organizations to be inherently antidemocratic. And he extended his argument to bureaucracies and the state. Although his work points up the tensions that abound in organizational structure, it is neither system precise nor historically specific. In the absence of comparative studies (Michels did not study other forms of party organization), we are left to conclude from this theory that there are no significant differences among organizations or states in regard to their domination by an elite.

If we concede that elites often operate under the guise of democracy, does this in itself mean that all organizations are created unequal, or that they are unequal in the same ways? There are also other questions to be directed to Michels. Is the fact of leadership incompatible with democracy? Is the practice of direct democracy by an informed public (organized locally to deal with matters of general policy) truly unrealistic?

Perhaps most important, is the true measure of democracy contained within organizational/bureaucratic life itself—or is human freedom a larger issue? As with Weber's bureaucracy, the organizational oligarchy of Michels looms as a central and unavoidable threat to freedom. But both give insufficient attention to the kinds of societies within which organizations rise, ignoring their polity, their economy, their customs, and their history. Similarly, both also downplay the truth that organizations with similar internal structures may be directed toward vastly different ends. Perhaps it is within this larger sphere of reality and purpose that the question of democracy must be joined.

As with Pareto, the ideological transformation of Robert Michels from social democrat to a supporter of Mussolini was not so wide as some believe. If direct democracy is impossible and organizations are doomed to oligarchy, then one alternative is the advent of the *charismatic* leader of substance who can reach the masses directly (Lipset, 1966). Combined with Michels' views on the woeful abilities of the masses (a reality if not an inevitability) and his non-specific conception of systems and history, the universality of oligarchy can be easily transformed. *Political Parties* was intended in part to expose oligarchy so that its dangers to democracy might be minimized. However, if both the nature of the mass and the nature of organizations contradict the nature of democracy, then one might be driven to conclude that democracy is only an illusion. Ultimately, then, in the battle between pluralist and Machiavellian visions for the intellectual soul of Robert Michels, Machiavelli won.

# ■ *Bibliography*

Buckley, W.
1967             *Sociology and Modern Systems Theory.* Englewood Cliffs, N.J.: Prentice-Hall.

Burnham, James
1943             "Mosca: The Theory of the Ruling Class." In James Burnham (Ed.), *The Machiavellians: Defenders of Freedom,* pp. 79–115. New York: John Day.

Finer, Samuel Edward
1966             *Vilfredo Pareto: 1848–1923: Sociological Writings.* Translated by Derick Mirfin. Totowa, N.J.: Rowman and Littlefield.

Linz, Juan
1968             "Robert Michels." In *The International Encyclopedia of the Social Sciences.* New York: Macmillan Company and The Free Press.

Lipset, Seymour M.
(1954) 1960     *Political Man: The Social Bases of Politics.* Garden City, N.Y.: Doubleday.
1966             Introduction. In *Robert Michels, Political Parties,* pp. 15–19. New York: The Free Press.

Lopreato, Joseph
1965             *Vilfredo Pareto: Selections from His Treatise.* 2 vols. New York: Crowell Collier.

Meisel, James H. (Ed.)
1958                    *The Myth of the Ruling Class: Gaetano Mosca and the Elite.*
                        Ann Arbor: University of Michigan Press.
1965                    *Pareto and Mosca.* Englewood Cliffs, N.J.: Prentice-Hall.

Michels, Robert
(1911) 1966             *Political Parties: A Sociological Study of the Oligarchical Ten-
                        dencies of Modern Democracy.* Translated by Eden and Cedar
                        Paul. Introduction by Seymour M. Lipset. New York:
                        The Free Press.

Mosca, Gaetano
(1896) 1939             *The Ruling Class.* New York: McGraw-Hill.
(1932) 1958             "The Final Version of the Theory of the Ruling Class." In
                        James H. Meisel (Ed.), *The Myth of the Ruling Class:
                        Gaetano Mosca and the "Elite,"* pp. 382–391. Ann Arbor:
                        University of Michigan Press.

Pareto, Vilfredo
1935                    *The Mind and Society.* Edited by Arthur Livingston. New
                        York: Harcourt Brace Jovanovich.
1968                    *Rise and Fall of Elites.* Totowa, N.J.: The Bedminister
                        Press.

Stark, Warner
1964                    "In Search of the True Pareto." In James H. Meisel (Ed.),
                        *Pareto and Mosca.* Englewood Cliffs, N.J.: Prentice-Hall.

Zeitlin, Irving
1968                    "Robert Michels." In *Ideology and the Development of So-
                        ciological Theory,* pp. 218–233. Englewood Cliffs, N.J.:
                        Prentice-Hall.

# CHAPTER *7*

---

# ■ Systematism

A final category of the theories of society founded in the order paradigm is here termed *systematism*. At the onset we should realize that the term *system* is not confined to the discipline of sociology. To cite only a few examples: In astronomy, the solar system commonly refers to the interrelationships of the sun and all the bodies in space that revolve around it. In biology, the term may refer to the body as an integrated whole, or to a number of body organs that work together to perform an essential function (as with the circulatory system). In the world of computers, a systems analyst must understand the interconnections between and among hardware (the physical parts of the computer and its peripheral equipment) and software (programs that instruct the computer). It is the logic of dynamic connectedness and consequences that ties these and countless other forms of "systems" theories together.

As with our earlier attempts to understand organicism and functionalism in theoretical sociology, we find that systems theories also address the puzzles of balance and equilibrium, of cohesion and integration, of the interconnections and interdependence of parts and their relationship to the whole. However, systems theories in sociology are seen by their proponents to be distinctive in ways that can be specified. (We shall argue in due course that such distinctions are not truly so clear-cut.)

In this chapter, we will focus on that theoretical sociology which considers society to *be*, as opposed to simply *resemble*, a system. Those who construct systems theory commonly claim to reject both the organic *analogy* (society is like an organism) and the real organicism that gives to society a biological life of its own. They also seek to avoid the teleological attributes of functionalism by which each social practice is presumed to meet, in purposeful fashion, some real and observable need *within* society. For systems theorists, social practices have consequences all right, but consequences for the overall *maintenance* of a real social system.

At the societal level, systemacists argue that institutions, patterns, customs, and other social practices represent dynamically related elements of a larger and complex form of social organization. From this premise, it follows that changes in any part of the system have far-ranging if subtle implications for the whole. Systemacists also hold that the major imperatives, the "laws" that drive a system, are those of dynamic equilibrium and survival. Depending on the particular theory, systems emerge at different *levels* (civilizations, societies, institutions may each be conceived as a system). Some systems will be theoretically conceived as closed (to external input); others will be conceived as open. Within the larger system, subsystems may be seen to operate and their organization and integration presented in the language of the theory. Strains or crises may also be identified because they threaten the equilibrium or survival of the system (Wilson, 1983: 79–81).

Actually, our survey of systems theories based on the assumptions of the order paradigm began in Chapter 6 with the vanguard work of Vilfredo Pareto. That discussion sets the stage now for a consideration of the *action* theory of Talcott Parsons, an approach that views the social actor as both rational and voluntaristic on the one hand, and as a member of a system on the other. Finally, we will examine the *process* kind of systems theory evident in the work of Amitai Etzioni. Here, the system is presented as an ongoing interactive process among structural components that are constantly changing (Buckley, 1967: 18–19).

# ■ Talcott Parsons (1902–1979): Social System and Social Action

The major theoretical line of the order tradition now passes from the Europeans to the American sociologist Talcott Parsons. Born in Colorado at the turn of the century, Parsons graduated from Amherst College with a major in biology. He was a graduate student at the London School of Economics, where his sociology was well complemented by his study under the renowned functionalist anthropologist Bronislaw Malinowski. Later, while at Heidelberg, Parsons came to be influenced by the thought of Max Weber. Here he took his Ph.D. in sociology and economics, defending his dissertation on the treatment of capitalism in the theoretical systems of Max Weber and Werner Sombart. After a year as instructor of economics at Amherst, Parsons joined the faculty of sociology at Harvard University in 1927.

## History and Biography

Talcott Parsons returned from study abroad during the Roaring Twenties. For many, it appeared to be a time of growing prosperity, an era of limitless opportunity. However, in important ways this was a decade of the bizarre and the banal. The postwar problems of unemployment and inflation were superimposed on a social order suffering from runaway urbanization, the resurgence of the Ku Klux Klan, and the rise of Al Capone. Herbert Hoover had declared in 1922 that American business enterprise was no longer plagued by the win at any price philosophy. Bruce Barton's popular book *The Man Nobody Knows: A Discovery of the Real Jesus* was published in 1925 and praised the Nazarene as the founder of modern free enterprise. Shares of stock could be bought for 10 percent cash and the buyer's good credit (Baritz, 1970).

During the twenties, a pair of courtroom dramas electrified the nation and came to symbolize the politics of the times. One focused on a trial for murder and banditry of two Italian immigrants, Nicola Sacco and Bartolomeo Vanzetti. However, the criminal charges were transformed by the prosecution (Frankfurter, 1927: 409–432). The defendants were required to testify concerning their political beliefs (they were socialist and pacifist), and the real charge appeared to be their flight to Mexico to avoid the draft. With the "red scare" raging, a verdict of guilty was reached on July 14, 1921. Despite a six-year attempt by civil libertarians to secure a new trial, Sacco and Vanzetti were executed in the summer of 1927.

In that same summer, in the small and sleepy town of Dayton, Tennessee, the "Scopes Monkey Trial" was the stage on which the deep conflict between science and fundamentalist religion was joined. Clarence Darrow, as defense attorney, and William Jennings Bryan, as prosecutor, played out their roles in a clash of the sacred and the secular, urbanism and folk society. Scopes, the erstwhile teacher of evolutionary theory, lost and was fined $100. But the symbolic victory went to Darrow and the changing times (Allen, 1925). Then, two years after the execution of Sacco and Vanzetti, the Scopes Trial, and the move of Talcott Parsons to Harvard, the show business newspaper *Variety* signaled the beginning of a long economic nightmare for the United States with a headline: "Wall Street Lays an Egg!"

On October 24, 1929, a financial collapse began on the New York Stock Exchange. As reported by the *New York Times* the next day, "the most disastrous decline in the biggest and broadest stock market in history" was temporarily repelled by "five of the country's most influential bankers." However, the reprieve was short-lived. On October 29, the crash became irrevocable. The loss on issues of the exchange was estimated at between eight and nine billion dollars.

When the dramatic shock wave of the crash had subsided somewhat, the more pervasive gyrations of an economic system gone out of control became apparent. Unemployment began a terrifying upward spiral. In March 1929, the estimates of joblessness ranged from 3.25 to 4 million. A year later, some four or five months after the Wall Street debacle, those estimates had doubled. By March 1932, the range was reported at 11.25 to 12.5 million people unemployed, and a year later the Congress of Industrial Organization estimated that the number had grown to 16 million. In 1931 the Soviet Union, in need of skilled workers for industrial development, advertised for 6,000 American workers to move to the Soviet Union and accept pay in rubles. Over 100,000 applications were received (*Business Week,* October 7, 1931).

The circles of tragedy rippled throughout much of the society. Hoovervilles, as the shanty towns for the homeless were called, blighted the urban landscape. Farmers, who had begun to suffer earlier in the twenties, saw the total collapse of the marketplace and the ruin of crops and livestock. Forced migration and widespread starvation stalked the land.

> The roads of the West and Southwest teem with hungry hitchhikers. The campfires of the homeless are seen along every railroad track. I saw men, women, and children walking over hard roads. Most of them were tenant farmers who had lost their all in the late slump in wheat and cotton. Between Clarksville and Russellville, Arkansas, I picked up a family. The woman was hugging a dead chicken under a ragged coat. When I asked her where she procured the fowl, first she told me she had found it dead in the road, and then added in grim humor, "They promised me a chicken in the pot, and now I got mine." (Ameringer, cited in Perdue, 1974: 53)

It was within this context that the administration of Franklin Delano Roosevelt came to power. The programs of the New Deal were subsequently conceived and implemented to restore the economic order. It was also during the Great Depression, when the very core of society faced disintegration, that Talcott Parsons developed and published his first major work, *The Structure of Social Action* (1937).

## Assumptions

We need not speculate about the thought that influenced Parsons, either in his assumptions about human nature, society, and science or in his theoretical orientation. He identified them early (1937: v). They included three Europeans who played crucial roles in the early development of sociology: Émile Durkheim, Vilfredo Pareto, and Max Weber. The remaining figure was British economist Alfred Marshall.

From Pareto and Durkheim came the inspiration for Parsons' theoretical structure that presents an overarching and unified social system. Society thus becomes a holistic entity driven toward an equilibrium of parts. Societal elements are interdependent and adjustive, meeting always the needs of the system. From Weber, Parsons drew the concept of social action to develop his own framework for explaining how actors come to interpret their situation. However, it was Pareto's conception of the mutual interpenetration of human action and other systemic elements that most clearly informed Parsons' efforts to construct a macrosociological theory of systems in the positivist tradition.

Finally, Parsons used the work of Marshall to develop his model of the demand economy and the necessary equilibrium of the free market. He was then to relate the economic system to the solidarity of the broader societal order. In Parsonian theory, the free economic system adds to the cohesion of society by means of contracts, the definition of property rights, and the establishment of relationships between employers and employees.

## Theoretical Content

Throughout his long career, Talcott Parsons was a prolific contributor to the sociological literature. His interests ranged far and wide. Within the general framework of his grand theory of society, he dealt with subsystems, roles, the normative order, and the interpretation of situations by social actors. At differing times, he explored the issues of medical sociology, the social development of personality, political extremism, the university, and kinship. However, we shall be concerned here only with the broader sweep of Parsons' theory. Such can be distilled from his seminal works: *The Structure of Social Action* (1937), *The Social System* (1951), *Towards a General Theory of Action* (with Edward Shils, 1951), *Social Structure and Personality* (1964), and *The System of Modern Societies* (1971).

Overall, Parsons developed a theoretical system centered conceptually in equilibrium, evolutionary universalities, and the identification of properties that are common to all societies. In his theory, societal evolution parallels biological evolution, with modern societies evidencing greater "generalized adaptive capacity" than earlier ones (1971: 2–3). Thus, society is no less a system than are its biological and natural counterparts. For Parsons, social systems have moved historically toward greater adaptation (adjustments that maintain the systemic order), differentiation (the specialization of social institutions and the division of labor), upgrading (greater freedom from want), inclusion (normative diversity), and value generalization (values that are more reflective of the needs of an increasingly complex system).

Parsons entertained the Weberian focus on *social action*. (See Chapter 10.) However, his theory rejects the essentially voluntaristic image of the actor advanced by Weber in favor of the more systemic and deterministic view of Pareto.

> The fundamental starting point is the concept of social systems of action. The *inter*action of individual actors, that is, takes place under such conditions that it is possible to treat such a process of interaction as a system in the scientific sense and subject it to the same order of theoretical analysis which has been successfully applied to other types of systems in other sciences. (1951: 3)

Hence, Parsonian theory abandons the Weberian view of minded actors seeking to define their social universe. Instead, as for Pareto, social action or interaction is a system that responds to other interdependent conditions. Here the systemic focus on stability and order is extended into various analyses of *roles* and their contribution to social control. A good part of *The Social System,* as well as other of Parsons' contributions to the literature, deals with this central puzzle (see especially pages 301–306).

The heart of this theoretical attempt is its dual conceptualization of system. At the highest level, Parsons developed a *general system of action* that features four divisions, including the *general social system.* At a lower level, he divided the social system into four distinctive subsystems. Beginning with the general system, we find its four components to include the *behavioral-organic, personality, cultural,* and *social* systems (Parsons and Shils, 1951: 4–29). Each of these four component systems meets one of the *functional prerequisites* that must be satisfied for any living system to survive.

The functional prerequisite for the behavioral-organic system is *adaptation.* Action for this system involves the means by which living beings process information via the central nervous system and interact behaviorally with the physical environment. The functional prerequisite for the personality system is *goal attainment.* Action for this component system is conceptualized as the motivation behind gratification. (This view of personality bears a strong similarity to the psychoanalytic theory of Sigmund Freud. Indeed, Parsons' systemic conceptions of personality made him a frequent contributor to psychiatric and psychological journals.)

Moving on, the functional prerequisite for the cultural system is *pattern maintenance.* Action here refers to the decoding of the symbolic meanings that constitute human traditions, customs, and the learned ways of life. Culturally influenced action ensures systemic continuity over time. And finally, the functional prerequisite of the social system is *integration.* Action for this component system includes the coordination of individuals and groups and the bonding of members of society by means of normative constraints.

If we focus specifically on the fourth component of the social system (repetitiously called the social system), we find that Parsons identified the following subsystems (1971: 10–28). First is the *societal community,* the core subsystem that is composed structurally of *norms* that "define the obligations of loyalty" to the society for its actors (1971: 12). Matters of loyalty, however, are not matters of law. Second, we find the *pattern maintenance* or *fiduciary* subsystem composed of *values* that legitimate the culture and impose moral obligations on actors. Next comes the *polity* subsystem made up of powerful collectivities that interpret the sanctioned norms that are binding on society (such as the courts) or that enforce the sanctions for violations of norms (such as the police). Finally, Parsons presents the *economy* subsystem of the social system, composed of the practical, rational, and technological *roles* that allow the actor to effectively adapt to the environment. Practical and rational role action is regulated by the institutions of the contract (binding agreements upheld by the power of the state) and property (both definitions and rights).

It logically follows that the component systems that make up the general system of action are interrelated. They do not exist in isolation; rather, the general system reflects *interpenetration.* For example, the personality reflects the internalization of social norms and cultural values. And the memory of the biological organism stores the rules and expectations, the customs and moral standards of these systems (1971: 5–6). Furthermore, the component systems that make up the general system of action share zones of overlapping effect. For Parsons, the Freudian superego has much in common with Durkheim's collective conscience. Both, he argued, refer to a common ground between the personality, social, and cultural systems (1964: 17–33).

In response to the frequent criticism that his systems were grand abstractions devoid of content, Parsons sought to *historically* ground his conception of societal evolution. In *The System of Modern Societies,* he identified the stages of systemic development in Western history. (Ironically, "the" system referred to here is Western civilization.)

In his "premodern foundations of modern societies," Parsons explored early Christianity, drawing the conclusion that the Christian church was the first crucible for Western culture. The next evolutionary step of consequence he discovered in Rome, most notably in its highly developed system of law. Medieval society gave witness to the decline of tribalism and the rise of feudalism, to be followed by the differentiated and interdependent division of labor that marked the European system. During this process, feudal institutions came to be replaced by early capitalism with some growing centralization of political power. Then came the Renaissance and the development of secular culture within the framework of a still vibrant religious order. And finally, Parsons held that the last premodern stage was the Reformation. During this period, the priesthood began to lose its exclusive entitlement to the keys to the kingdom, an event that signaled the advent of individualism (1971: 29–49).

Parsons termed the next major era the "first crystallization of the modern system." It was centered in the European northwest (England, France, and Holland), which saw the centralization of a form of state power and the establishment of mercantile capitalism. One noteworthy development here was the coming of a pluralist political system in England (1971: 50–70).

The next evolutionary era, for Parsons, is the Age of Revolutions. During this time, the industrial revolution featured the expansion of financial markets, while the democratic revolution saw the spreading of the differentiation of rule by the people throughout Western Europe. Its values, for Parsons, were symbolized in the watchwords of the French Revolution: *Liberté, Egalité, Fraternité.*

The final evolutionary era, for Parsons, is founded in the emergence of what he termed the "new lead society." He argued that the promise of the industrial and democratic revolutions could not be realized in Europe because of its aristocratic, stratified, and monarchal traditions. Primarily because of the lack of such restrictions, together with its educational revolution and political pluralism, the "new lead society" is for Parsons none other than the United States. It is here in his native land that Parsons located the highest form of general adaptation, the embodiment of the evolutionary principle that drives systems and systemic theories (1971: 71–85).

## Critique

It might be argued that the prodigious, sometimes controversial, and always mind-boggling nature of Parsons' theoretical efforts has earned him his standing as a major contemporary American theorist. He discerned in all of its variety, human life as an interconnected whole. He sought to match this system with a theory constructed in like manner. If nothing else, his efforts have been heuristic, forcing even his critics to impart a rigor to their own social analysis. Indeed, Parsons served as antagonist for both C. Wright Mills (see Chapter 16) and Alvin Gouldner (Chapter 18), among a multitude of others. Although there is some polemic among his critics, Parsons' theory does evidence serious problems.

Parsons' theory of society is plagued by an absence of clarity. His work abounds with ambiguities in both semantics and syntax. As regards semantics, he was inconsistent or at least imprecise in the definitions of core terms. For example, *pattern maintenance* is variously defined as the primary function of the cultural subsystem of the general system of action, a subsystem of the social system, and a primary function of that same subsystem (1971: 6, 11). As to syntax, the folklore of sociology is replete with tales of erstwhile professors of English trying to figure out the unique sequencing of Parsons' words.

In a related sense, the societal theory of Parsons demonstrates an absence of empirical referents. There are simply few, if any, clearly defined terms that allow for measurement and verification (Zetterberg, 1966: 21–29). This is ironic because Parsons committed to the image of science advanced by Zetterberg, that of a deductive and testable science. However, he failed to deliver. In more esoteric terms, Parsons split off positivism from functionalism and embraced the latter.

As with other theorists who address the puzzle of order, Parsons was infatuated with the biological analogy. As we have demonstrated, he did not distance his work from that of the earlier organicists and functionalists. Although he replaced the organic metaphor with a mechanical-cybernetics one, an analogy remains an analogy. In his attempt to marshal evidence for his systemic theory of society, Parsons, like his predecessors, conceptualized change as a form of societally based natural selection. He held that modern societies (like modern species) exist because they represent the ability to adapt. History is thus a glorious march to the present.

This conception of unilinear and selective development can be questioned on several grounds. First of all, there is a serious tautological error in Parsons' reasoning. The existence of modern societies is explained in terms of their evolutionary adaptation, while the evidence for the adaptation is found in their existence. A second flaw is the selectivity of the historical support gathered to explain the evolution of society. If modern societies develop in unilinear fashion, what are we to make of the widespread regression during the so-called dark ages? Parsons did not show how and why one society evolves, becomes complex, and survives while another fails to adapt and declines. To the contrary, his evolving civilization conveniently jumps around geographically from one European nation to another and finally crosses the Atlantic.

Parsons claimed to have developed a universal theory of action. Accordingly, his conception of development supposedly applies to all *modern* orders. Quite aside from the ethnocentric (if not imperialist) use of the value-laden term *modern,* his theory remains ideologically rooted in a Western sense of civilization, the U.S. model of a nation-state, and the capitalist form of economic system. Such are clearly evident in his views on institutional structure, the nature of the market, and especially stratification. For example:

1. ". . . modern society requires a differentiation of individual statuses from diffuse background solidarities" (1971: 14). (*Translation:* Social class doesn't matter much any more in Western societies. A meritocracy has taken shape in which it's not who you know but what you know.)

2. "With no presumption that every individual or collective unit that participates will be equally productive, special rewards for the economically more productive units thus become necessary" (1971: 119).

3. "By our definition, a citizen exercises power when he casts his vote because the aggregate of votes bindingly determines the electoral outcome" (1971: 17).

4. "Hence, practical rationality is regulated mainly by institutional norms, above all the institutions of property and contract which have other bases of sanction" (1971: 18). (Parsons' analysis is heavily influenced by Émile Durkheim's views of property and contract in *The Division of Labor in Society*.)

Those sensitive to the ideological infrastructure of theoretical systems further criticize Parsons' Depression-era *Structure of Social Action* (1937) as an apology for capitalism at its darkest hour.

> Parsons' shortcoming, therefore, was not that he failed to engage problems of contemporary relevance but that he continued to view them from the standpoint of an American optimism. Because he saw them from this optimistic standpoint, he one-sidedly emphasized the adaptability of the status quo, considering the ways in which it was open to change rather than the manner in which its own characteristics were inducing the disorder and resisting adaptation to it. (Gouldner, 1970: 147)

Finally, today's pluralists who more studiously follow Max Weber's voluntaristic concept of human nature will find Parsons' systems overly deterministic. Conflict thinkers on the other hand will note the theoretical absence of coercion both within and between societies. Both camps would tend to agree with Oberschall's observation (1973) that serious social change within Parsonian theory can only be conceptualized as a form of deviance, as a breakdown of social control.

# ■ Amitai Etzioni (b. 1929): The Active Society

We conclude our survey of the systematists in theoretical sociology with an overview of the work of Amitai Werner Etzioni. Born on January 4, 1929, in Cologne, Germany, Etzioni was to escape the Holocaust and find his way to a conflict-ridden region in the Middle East claimed to this day by Arab and Jew. As we shall soon discover, Etzioni's early biography is distinctive by reason of his life and study in the fledgling state of Israel,[1] a nation he cites as a prototype in his major theoretical effort, *The Active Society* (1968: viii). He received his B.A. in 1954 and his M.A. two years later from Hebrew University in Jerusalem. He was awarded a Ph.D. by the University of California at Berkeley in 1958. His academic career features a tenure as professor and chair of the Department of Sociology at Columbia University and membership in its Institute of War and Peace Studies.

## History and Biography

Just as the United States concretely represents the evolutionary zenith for Talcott Parsons, so does Israel represent the exemplar of Amitai Etzioni's active society. This nation-state was recognized by the United Nations in 1948 after a bitter struggle to establish a Jewish homeland in the geographical region called Palestine by both the ancient Greeks and contemporary Palestinian Arabs. The historical land base consists of only some 9,000 square miles, bounded by Lebanon on the north, the Sinai desert that separates Egypt and Asia on the south, the Mediterranean Sea on the west, and Jordan on the east.

In the twelfth century B.C. the Hebrew legions who had fled from Egypt under Moses invaded, presaging the coming of the Kingdom of Israel. In the centuries that followed, the "promised land" was conquered by the Babylonians and the Romans, became a part of the Byzantine Empire, and experienced the rise of Islam in the seventh century A.D. During these and later periods, most Jews were scattered from Palestine. Thus, prior to the momentous events of the twentieth century, what was to become Israel had been home for centuries to the Palestinian Arabs.

The vision of a Jewish return to Palestine and the establishment of a homeland was cultivated in political terms by a late nineteenth-century movement headed by one Theodor Hertzl. The movement, as well as the ideology calling for the creation and advancement of a Jewish national state, came to be

---

[1] Etzioni's first publication was *A Diary of a Commando Soldier* (1952).

known as Zionism.[2] Since the sixteenth century, Palestine had been under the control of the Ottoman Empire, and attempts by Hertzl and the Zionist movement to gain sanction from the Islamic Turks for a large-scale immigration into the region were not successful. However, Turkey was on the losing side of the First World War, and the victorious British came to control Palestine.

Under the ensuing British mandate, sympathy for the Zionist movement was institutionalized in the form of official support for Jewish settlers interested in the establishment of a national homeland. In 1917 there were some 56,000 Jews in Palestine and more than 90 percent of the population was Arab. By 1931 the number of Jews had reached over 174,000 and by 1936, 324,000. This immigration of Jews was prompted first by pogroms in Europe, then by the rise of the Nazis in the 1930s.

The progression of events was interrupted somewhat by the Second World War. However, in the postwar period, political organizations in Palestine sought to establish a national state. (Some were clearly committed to the tactics of terror. One example was the blowing up of the King David Hotel in Jerusalem by the Zionist group called the Irgun.) The British authorities were then faced with a continuing flood of immigrants, increasing violence, and world sympathy following the discovery of Nazi death camps. Perhaps they also realized that a new state of Israel would be fashioned on the Western model given the European origins of many of the settlers. At any rate, the British abandoned the mandate.

From the Arab side, the largely ignored victims of these historical events were the indigenous Palestinians. Although many fled their homeland after 1948, the remainder continued to live under what they perceived to be conditions of occupation and subjugation. In a historical context of Israeli military, political, cultural, and geographical expansion, a series of bloody wars between Israel and its Arab neighbors shook the land. Today, the conflict continues.[3]

## Assumptions

Sociological theories of order commonly reflect a focus on social equilibrium and control. Such concerns are somewhat predictable given a historical epoch of serious turbulence, combined with biographical factors that suggest strong sympathy to a beleaguered status quo. Etzioni's theory is no exception.

Etzioni developed his theoretical system in response to an order puzzle of long standing in sociology. It is described by him as a "continued increase in

---

[2] There is of course a place of Zion. It is a hill in Jerusalem, a city holy to Moslem, Christian, and Jew, the site of the ancient temple of David.

[3] Informative general references include Said, 1979, and Smith, 1972.

. . . technology . . . which poses a growing challenge to . . . human values" (1968: vii). W. F. Ogburn described this phenomenon in 1928 as "cultural lag."

The solution to this (and other threats to order) for Etzioni is the *active society*. By definition, an active society is one in which members seek self-control and reassert the primacy of values over technology. It is a social state in which responsiveness to changing membership and ongoing self-transformation abound.

The image of human nature that prevails in this theory is that of an ambiguous existentialism that centers self-mastery in the sphere of social action. By this we mean that Etzioni seeks to replace purely individual control and personal responsibility with that of "taking charge." However, taking charge is possible only through acting in concert with the group. In isolation, the person is passive and ineffective. Etzioni also argued that the "activation of the social potential and . . . the establishment of social order are 'unnatural' in that their introduction and maintenance require continual effort" (1968: 95). (It is this assumption that underscores Etzioni's break with Rousseau and Marx, who held to the "naturalness" of social cooperation and community.) Although Etzioni was a bit slippery here, he was constructing a case for social control, as we shall see.

The vision of society that undergirds this theoretical system is captured in modern and classical examples. As mentioned earlier, Etzioni has cited Israel and, to a lesser extent, the Scandinavian societies as contemporary approximations of the active society. Looking to the past, he cited the Greek city-state in terms of the importance ascribed to political thought and action on the part of the citizenry. In a manner reminiscent of Plato's Republic, Etzioni also has embraced intellectual pursuit as a major feature of his active system.

Etzioni's conception of sociology is also clear. He has attempted the construction of a macrosociological theory, the major purpose of which is to provide societal guidance (1968: 110–111). In the tradition of Saint-Simon, Comte, and others, he has advanced a theory of systemic process and organization, social control, and societal transformation.

## Theoretical Content

Etzioni's explanation of societal order commenced with the identification of three basic social bonds by which social relationships emerge: normative, utilitarian, and coercive. In the normative relationship, actors playing their roles share common values and norms. In the utilitarian relationship, only instrumental or means-to-an-end interests make for a bond. And finally, the coercive relationship is bonded by violence or threat.

Moving to a higher level of abstraction, Etzioni identified collectivities and societies as the most important macroscopic units. The collectivity is his basic unit of analysis. It refers to such entities as classes, races, and strong ethnic, religious, or other categories with an overarching cohesion not founded in face-to-face interaction. These large-scale units are comprised of smaller member-units united in loyalty by common norms and a network of leaders. For their part, the leaders do not often interact on an interpersonal level. These large-scale cohesive units, despite ecological dispersion and the absence of personal interaction on the part of members, are still the basis for consensus formation.

In Etzioni's view, a society is a *supracollectivity* that features the same cohesive processes as do collectivities. However, this macroscopic unit is broader in scope and despite its ecological diffusion has more "integrative mechanisms" such as the state and its various agencies.

The cohesive collectivity, again Etzioni's central unit, may not effectively interact either directly or symbolically. Interaction is more apt to occur via institutions or *organizations* (as when leaders of different religious groups arrange joint services). For this theory, a collectivity without formal organization is passive.

Organizations, in turn, are the basis for the social control of collectivities and societies. Organizations are classified in the same way as social relationships. They can be normative (as with religious and educational organizations), utilitarian (as with factories), and coercive (as with prisons). Hence, each class of organization is distinctive by reason of its form of exacting conformity from members.

Etzioni has further argued that a society without a state is analogous to a collectivity without organization: *passive.* The state is a supraorganization that reflects hierarchy, a division of labor among levels and units of government, and authority. The state can also mobilize widespread action through downward political control.

*It follows from the logic of this theory that the active society is a processual system, featuring the downward control of organizations at various levels and the upward-flowing consensus formation of cohesive units.* In other words, Etzioni's ideal society will synthesize the consensus building touted in democratic ideology and the organizational features of state-dominated societies. By such processes, social actors are free to mobilize, press their interests, and seek power in concert with others. The state, for its part, will be changing from one point in time to the next as it responds to organized group efforts. It will still retain the structural power to plan and decide (1968: 94–129).

Infusing Etzioni's active society is a cybernetic conception of control. *Cybernetics* refers to the comparative study of the human nervous system and sophisticated electronic calculating machines in order to better understand the functions of the brain. Etzioni uses the term primarily as a metaphor to describe and analyze the political functioning of the nerve center of command at the upper level of organizations including the state.

For the energized system that is society, the prime cybernetic factor is knowledge. Knowledge is seen to be *processed* by a controlling elite, but at a broader level knowledge is the energy force that drives the active society. It is the basis for consciousness and action among the population. A second important cybernetic element is decision making. Historically, decision making has been based on one of three models: (1) *rational* understanding of alternative, large-scale courses of action; (2) *incrementalism,* or choosing policies that differ only to a limited degree from those already in place; and (3) *mixed scanning* or a combination of the first two. Etzioni holds that mixed scanning prevails in the active society as leaders take moderate steps toward macro goals (1968: 249–309).

Finally, Etzioni addressed the implementation of decisions through power: the ability to push through change despite opposition. Of course, power conflicts with freedom. However, this theorist has argued that the constantly revised, consensually validated norms that flow from the democratic processes of the active society will reduce reliance on coercive control.

## Critique

Etzioni's theory of society is well hidden. This is due in part to his attempts to lightly touch all the bases, not merely in sociology but in philosophy and humanist psychology as well. He has a disconcerting tendency to use analytic constructs (such as alienation) as simple adjectives or "pop" descriptions of the passive society. Even the term *cybernetics,* which portrays society as a system of energy, is more a metaphor than an explanation. However, the term does convey the imagery of constant feedback, decision, and cerebral-like action for this processual system.

In another vein, Etzioni shares with the early Parsons an effort to combine Weberian voluntarism with the determinism of the social system. And like Parsons, he resolves the dilemma by making systemic determinism and control the center of his theory. Etzioni's thought leaves little room for a conception of personal freedom. As was the case for Durkheim, personal freedom is problematic. However, for Durkheim individualism meant egoism. For Etzioni, individualism left untouched by group organization and control can only mean passivism.

That systems may facilitate or thwart the realization of human needs poses little controversy for most sociologists. However, Etzioni has constructed a strongly benign vision of organizations, including the state. This he seeks to qualify by proposing the precondition of *enlightened* consensus, the hallmark, of course, of Western democratic ideology. However, few modern states fail to be labeled democratic by their defenders, no matter how entrenched their hierarchies.

The active society theoretically is not supposed to rely on coercive state power; it is open, by definition, to *all who are enlightened and organized.* In a broader sense, then, the ideological infrastructure of this theory offers support to "selective" democracies, whose elite traditionally argue that subject populations either choose not to participate politically or that they are not ready.

Finally, Etzioni's emphasis on the role of an elite is also subject to question. By "elite" he means a role and not a status ranking. Hence he argues that those who play the role are not necessarily superior, nor do they form a ruling class. Finally, the elite of the active society are to be open to the society at large, a vision reminiscent of Parsons' adherence to a form of meritocracy.

Etzioni clearly makes the case that the active society is not to be governed by a self-replenishing elite who rule through access to the networks of hereditary privilege. However, despite often heroic dodging, he has not avoided the major controversy endemic to all who propose the necessity of an elite. Whether conceived in terms of temporary role or continuous status, whether founded on merit or birth, whether open or closed, elite conceptions of rule leave unresolved the dilemma of concentrated power. Indeed, the active society reproduces in another guise the contradiction of hierarchical democracy. Within Etzioni's processual system, the direct expression of popular will appears limited, whereas the consideration of class domination of the state is missing altogether.

# ■ *Bibliography*

Allen, Leslie H.
1925     *Bryan and Darrow at Dayton.* New York: Arthur Lee and Company.

Baritz, Loren
1970     *The Culture of the Twenties.* Indianapolis: Bobbs-Merrill Company.

Barton, Bruce
1925     *The Man Nobody Knows: A Discovery of the Real Jesus.* Indianapolis: Bobbs-Merrill Company.

Buckley, W.
1967     *Sociology and Modern Systems Theory.* Englewood Cliffs, N.J.: Prentice-Hall.

Etzioni, Amitai
1952     *A Diary of a Commando Soldier.* Jerusalem: Achiasof.
1968     *The Active Society.* New York: The Free Press.
1971     *Comparative Analysis of Complex Organizations.* New York: The Free Press.
1973     *Genetic Fix: The Next Technological Revolution.* New York: Macmillan.

Frankfurter, Felix
1927     "The Case of Sacco and Vanzetti." *The Atlantic Monthly* 89:409–432.

Gouldner, Alvin
1970                *The Coming Crisis of Western Sociology.* New York: Basic
                   Books.

Oberschall, Anthony
1973                *Social Conflict and Social Movements.* Englewood Cliffs,
                   N.J.: Prentice-Hall.

Parsons, Talcott
1937                *The Structure of Social Action.* Glencoe, Ill.: The Free
                   Press.
1951                *The Social System.* Glencoe, Ill.: The Free Press.
1964                *Social Structure and Personality.* New York: The Free Press.
1971                *The System of Modern Societies.* Englewood Cliffs, N.J.:
                   Prentice-Hall.

Parsons, Talcott, and Edward A. Shils (Eds.)
1951                *Toward a General Theory of Action.* Cambridge, Mass.:
                   Harvard University Press.

Perdue, William D.
1974                "The Great Depression and the Interpretation of Social
                   Phenomena." Unpublished Ph.D. diss., Washington State
                   University.

Said, Edward
1979                *The Question of Palestine.* New York: Times Books.

Smith, Sir George Adam
1972                *The Historical Geography of the Holy Land.* Gloucester,
                   Mass.: P. Smith.

Stark, Warner
1964                "In Search of the True Pareto." In James H. Meisel (Ed.),
                   *Pareto and Mosca.* Englewood Cliffs, N.J.: Prentice-Hall.

Wilson, John
1983                *Social Theory.* Englewood Cliffs, N.J.: Prentice-Hall.

Zetterberg, Hans L.
1966                *On Theory and Verification in Sociology.* Totowa, N.J.: The
                   Bedminster Press.

*CHAPTER 8*

---

# ■ Modern Positivism: New Causal Theory and Social Exchange

To this point our attempts to unravel the various sociological theories of order permit one important conclusion. With the exception of Robert Merton's middle-range explanations, all of our exemplars operate at a macrosociological level. Early in this chapter we shall take leave of such grand conceptions of societal systems and organisms. We shall focus instead on a restricted and tighter conception of the social world. If our earlier theorists seemed prone to study the forests, modern positivists are content to examine the trees. However, the particular neopositivist theory termed social exchange has more recently been moved to a macrosociological level, as we shall see.

## ■ Neopositivism

One of the distinctive attributes of order sociology is its emphasis on positive science. Commencing with Comte, exemplars of the order tradition condemned as conjectural all "nonscientific" attempts to explain society. A new temper of mind was advocated, one that assumed experience to be the basis for truth, systematic research to be the source of evidence, and predictability and control as much features of society as properties of the natural world.

As we have seen, early nineteenth-century disciples of order were often openly polemical. On the one side, they were locked in a struggle with religion, metaphysics, and undisciplined philosophies. On the other, they inveighed against the turbulence of their times. Saint-Simon, Comte, Spencer, and others made use of the language and imagery of science to engage in open ideological warfare. However, they were unconvincing in their efforts to answer the question What makes a society possible?

With Durkheim's effort, order theory assumed a growing sophistication. And despite its strongly polemical nature, Pareto's initial effort at conceptualizing society as a system laid the groundwork for Parsons and Etzioni. However, while all of these masters stressed the importance of positive science, each conceived of the social order as an overarching set of connected elements or arrangements that formed a functional whole. However, for some practitioners of contemporary "positive" sociology, the problem of society is not the crux of scientific inquiry at all. Rather, the task of social science is seen to be the causal explanation of social behavior.

Modern positivism, variously known as neopositivism or logical positivism or logical empiricism, does not refer to a development in twentieth-century sociology. Rather, it is a philosophical movement that more or less formally began in Vienna in the 1920s. As such it became a way of analyzing the nature of science, in effect answering the question What ought science to be? As we shall see, the influence of neopositivism spread through Europe and then to the United States. It came to shape the development not only of the natural but the human sciences, including sociology.

A number of philosophers and mathematicians, including Moritz Schlick and Rudolph Carnap, founded the Vienna circle. The thinkers of the circle sought to integrate rationalism and empiricism. Historically, these two philosophical systems were in conflict, each obeying a different master. For the former, authority was to be found in reason. For the latter, the source of knowledge was in experience and observation. However, from the days of the circle, the two were to be sides of the same coin.

In the late 1930s, Carnap accepted a position at the University of Chicago. Here he worked with a number of pragmatist philosophers, including C. W. Morris. Somewhat late in the history of the movement, American pragmatism added a third philosophical dimension to neopositivism. Here the value of knowledge was judged in terms of practical results.[1]

The properties or components of logical positivism can be briefly described. As we argued in Chapter 3, the positive image of science makes the strongest possible case for *clarity*. Only those propositions that reflect precision, an absence of ambiguity, can be tested scientifically. Further, scientific theory is recognizable by its *logical structure*. Some positivists argue that adequate logic is evident when theory can be rendered in axiomatic form. (See the box on p. 16.)

Given the emphasis on clarity and logical structure, it follows that the precision of *mathematical logic* would appeal strongly to the advocates of this philosophy. In this, members of the circle and others of like mind were strongly influenced by the monumental *Principia Mathematica* by Alfred North Whitehead and Bertrand Russell (1910–1913).

---

[1] Important general references on neopositivism include Ayer, 1958 and 1959; Kolakowski, 1968; and Kraft, 1953.

Modern positivism is also noted for its insistence that theoretical statements be subject to *verification* through research. Verification is in turn dependent on *operational definitions* for important theoretical terms. This means that the operation for measuring important concepts must be clearly stipulated. For example, intelligence can be defined as that which is measured by intelligence tests.

Neopositivism also obeys the rule of *phenomenalism*. That is, there can be no knowledge save that of those facts, experiences, or circumstances that are apparent to the senses. Given this property together with the component of verifiability, the position of neopositivists on ethics is predictable. Because ethical statements cannot be verified in a factual world, they are without meaning and hence outside the realm of science. (This does not mean that scientists obey no professional code but that scientific theory and research are advanced by ethically neutral "role players.")

A final component of neopositivism is the *indivisibility of science*. This means there are no different sorts of science (human, social, natural, or so forth). Scientific disciplines meet the foregoing criteria or they do not qualify. Period.

Modern positive philosophy has sparked continuing debate in American sociology. Ironically, it can be said to have had more of an impact on methodology than on theory. In other words, the issues of how research should be done often take precedence over the task of explanation. Thus, positive sociology is identifiable today by an empirical interest in observation and the collection of data and the subjection of that data to quantitative (statistical) analysis.

The properties of clarity and certainty are reflected in a commitment to precise measurement on the part of today's sociologists who work in the positivist mode. As briefly noted in Chapter 2, this has led to conceptualizing the relationships of the social world in terms of variables that can be easily quantified.

Given what we know to this point, it should come as no surprise to find that positive sociology is often drawn to a lower range. This means that the micro-level relationships of social behavior will be rigorously examined for two purposes. First of all, understanding such relationships introduces the possibility of predicting and controlling future events. Second, modern positivists hope to find regularities and patterns in the smaller world of social behavior that tell them how the society works at a higher level of abstraction.

# ■ Mathematics in Sociological Theory

It is difficult at best to select theoretical systems that conform to the criteria of neopositivism. At first glance it might appear that those sociological theories that seek to incorporate the language of mathematics would have an inside track. Indeed, the precision of mathematical logic together with its impressive history in the natural sciences would seem to support this view. However, despite the development of sophisticated statistical methods widely used in its empirical research, the discipline of sociology has advanced not a single comprehensive theory that purports to explain social phenomena in truly mathematical terms.

This is not to say that mathematical language and reasoning are absent in sociological explanations. For example, one sociologist whose work we shall examine later in this chapter remains an exemplar of *new causal theory*. Peter Blau's efforts (with Otis Duncan) to explain intergenerational mobility in the American occupational structure begin with deriving simple statistical correlations among five variables. Simply put, Blau and Duncan were interested in finding out the causes behind upward or downward job mobility from one generation to the next (Blau and Duncan, 1967).

In a sample of 20,000 American male workers aged 20 to 64, Blau and Duncan looked at the variables of present occupational status, first-job status, education, father's occupational status, and father's education. They then determined the salient statistical correlations. However, these sociologists were well aware that correlation is not causation. Simply because two or more conditions with quantifiable properties vary together, we are not allowed to infer that one produces the other. In order to overcome this barrier to causal inference, Blau and Duncan proceeded to *order* their correlations. This means that some variables logically preceded in time other variables with which they were strongly correlated.

Blau and Duncan then constructed a *causal model* in the form of a path diagram. While a replica of that diagram does not concern us here, it is important to note that they used it to theoretically explain occupational mobility. For example, the model shows that the variables of father's education and occupation precede in time the worker's education, occupation, and first-job status. Given this temporal priority, together with the strong statistical correlations between the occupational and educational status of fathers and sons, a *causal relationship* may be inferred.

Blau and Duncan are of some concern to sociological theory for two reasons. First, their work is strongly representative of contemporary positive sociology. Although causal models and path diagrams can become quite complex, employing an ever-increasing number of variables, the logic of causal inference remains the same. Second, these sociologists do employ sociological data. In so doing they avoid the temptation to create mathematical models that are detached from the empirical world (Massarik, 1965: 17–18).

Model building is quite popular in the sociological literature today. It has emerged from the growing discovery of statistical relationships among variables. Still, serious questions about the *theoretical* value of the Blau/Duncan prototype of neopositive sociology can be raised. For one, the purpose of theory is to *explain*. In the contemporary sociological literature, causal models are ultimately based on sophisticated devices for statistical *analysis* of data.

More to the point, what we see today is a rush to find more relationships and a corresponding call for more sophisticated models to handle them. Thus far, despite substantial computer technology, new causal analysis has not led to a theoretical synthesis. Perhaps that point resides in the future. Or perhaps the quest for relationships among fragmented pieces of the social world has become a de facto substitute for theory. At any rate, the attempt to connect theory and the research process continues to be the legacy of the neopositive tradition in sociology.

At this point we shall turn away from our brief discussion of new causal theory to examine two theoretical systems we believe to be exemplars of neopositive sociology. As we shall see, both share to an important extent the assumptions of the order paradigm concerning human nature, the nature of society, and the nature of science. They also reflect the more precise properties of the philosophical movement known as logical positivism. Perhaps of greatest importance, these theories break with the functionalist/systems conceptualization of society and social organizations. Commonly called theories of *exchange,* they center instead on the behavior of people.

Social exchange theories are founded on a simple premise: quid pro quo, or an exchange of equivalents. In short, when people in an economic transaction give something up they expect something in return. Whereas this elementary principle of economics refers to an exchange of goods and services, the interactions of people manifest the same process. Thus, that which is traded might be affection, respect, or some other commodity. However, the bartering conception is the basic point of departure for the explanation of all social interaction.

# ■ George C. Homans (b. 1910): Psychological Reciprocity and the New Economic Man

The sociologist who first constructed a theory of social exchange was George Caspar Homans.[2] Homans began his graduate training in the Harvard Business School in the early 1930s. Like Talcott Parsons before him he found something of a haven from the surrounding storm of the Great Depression. While at Harvard, the young Homans worked with the biochemist Lawrence

---

[2] A brief autobiographical sketch of Homans can be found in Ritzer, 1983: 240–241.

Henderson (whose influence Parsons was to acknowledge in his *Structure of Social Action* published in 1937). Perhaps more striking was Homans' early association with the noted industrial psychologist Elton Mayo.


## History and Biography

Elton Mayo was the originator of the human relations approach to the organization of the workplace. This can best be understood as an alternative to Frederic Taylor's scientific management. Taylor, who began as a consultant to Bethlehem Steel in 1898, argued that the improvement of worker productivity was dependent on making the workers indistinguishable from the machinery they operated.

Mayo, holding a more Durkheimian conception of society, held that the loss of traditional values and norms (anomie) is the basis of industrial strife. In such a context, working people are devoid of a sense of personal worth. The solution to organizational and personal disharmony is the training of an administrative elite. These leaders will then seek to humanize the workplace through such devices as therapeutic counseling and the enhancement of the working environment.

In 1927 Mayo initiated the famous studies of industrial social psychology at the Western Electric Company's Hawthorne Works in Chicago. These were to continue into the early 1940s, centering on such problems as output and lighting, the informal norms that workers institute to protect themselves from speedups, and therapeutic depth interviews with disgruntled employees.

Of crucial importance to the later career of George Homans was the microsociological thrust of the Hawthorne studies. The focus was heavily on the personal relations among workers and their responses to a changing environment. The Mayo researchers were studying workplace *behavior,* not the structure of complex organizations.[3]

This focus on the shaping of behavior in intimate settings of social interaction was to stay with Homans. However, another relationship with a different Harvard professor proved to have an even more profound impact. After returning from a tour in the Navy during World War II, Homans assumed a position on the faculty of Harvard. Here he fell under the spell of the master of operant conditioning, the psychologist B. F. Skinner.

It was Skinner who argued, on the basis of animal experiments, that learning was a consequence of the reinforcement of random or emitted behavior. For example, when a laboratory pigeon pecks the proper key(s), it is rewarded with food. Thus reinforced, the behavior will be repeated. In Skinner's view, it is unnecessary to resort to unseen and intangible thinking operations

---

[3]Two excellent works on Mayo are Rose, 1975, and Urwick, 1960.

to explain learning. Subjective concepts such as consciousness and creative thought could therefore be dismissed. This focus on overt, tangible, and objective behavior is rightly conceived as *behaviorism*.

Skinner saw in his experiments the basic process by which human learning took place. As we shall soon discover, George Homans went one step beyond. He saw in Skinner's behaviorism the key to unraveling the puzzles of human society.

## Assumptions

Homans shares with psychological behaviorists a hedonistic conception of human nature. This means that the objective of human action is to maximize pleasure and minimize pain. Moreover, Homans argued that no matter how complex societal or cultural organization, such human inventions reflect no conscious intent on the part of their makers. These and the learning processes by which they are built are not unique but the expression of the same underlying nature. Thus, Homans came to construct his explanations of social behavior on a foundation of individual human beings sharing membership in a common species.

This tendency to see an underlying universality and uniformity in both society and culture is Homans' way of "bringing men back in" (Homans, 1964). It reflects both Skinner's behaviorism and the biological conceptions of L. J. Henderson. Homans was determined to build a small social world and install the behavior of people at its center.

Of course the behavior at base is always that of exchange. And the human image underlying exchange is that of the new economic man. By "new economic man," Homans means that no matter what the nature of the rewards, it is in the nature of the species to seek a profit. However, old economic conceptions of reward and punishment are not adequate to explain such exchange.

Homans has sought to establish a new conception of economic exchange that does not embrace an "antisocial and materialistic" image of human nature. He has done this by asserting that one person's reward might be a punishment for another. For example, one might seek to maximize pleasure through altruism, another through selfishness. But however the reward is defined, each wants to come out ahead on the deal. It is human nature to want to receive more than (or at least as much as) we give (Homans, 1961: 79–80).

As for the nature of society, Homans has worked at two levels of abstraction. In his first major work, *The Human Group* (1950), he assumed that the small human group is a microcosm of the society at large. Therefore, its functions and underlying structure represent a window to the larger order. When properly understood, the relationships of the group will explain corresponding relationships in seemingly more complex forms of social organization.

The second major work of George Homans was published in 1961 and revised in 1974. In *Social Behavior,* he argued that small groups can be theoretically replaced by propositions derived from the study of animal behavior. In this stage of his development, Homans' conversion to psychological behaviorism was complete. For him, all human action is learned or shaped by differential reinforcement of simple behaviors that occur initially as if by chance.

Homans clearly retains an orderly conception of society. However, the nature of equilibrium and harmony is not to be found in social institutions, in custom, or in the vastness of civilizations. It is rather to be found in the predictable and unvarying principles of social exchange. To master these is to be able to control behavior (and hence society) by design.[4]

Homans makes explicit his image of science or, more formally, his assumptions about the nature of sociological theory. In *The Human Group,* he constructed his theory inductively. That is, he used studies of small groups to derive more general theoretical propositions that could be generalized beyond the case under study. (The inductive approach, moving from the particular to the general, is quite common among theoretically inclined positivists today. An example would be the new causal theory discussed earlier.) However, in *Social Behavior,* Homans argued that the final logical form of theory must be deductive; that is, its structure must be axiomatic (see Zetterberg in Chapter 2). The deductive requirement is that specific or particular propositions must be deduced from more general ones (Homans, 1967).

The method of explanation employed by Homans is quite predictable given his position to this point. While stressing the importance of causal relationships, he never fails to find the causal nexus in exchange behavior. For example, Homans looked historically at the relationship between the price rise of the sixteenth century and the enclosure movement that eliminated common lands (Homans, 1969: 18–20).

Homans did not explain this relationship structurally, that is, as an outcome of the rise of private property in the emerging capitalist economy. Rather he argued that the causal relationship (between price rise and enclosure) can best be explained in the sense of landlords seeking the reward of monetary gain. Remember, for Homans landlords are not unique. They do not play structurally determined roles. They are just plain people obeying an unvarying psychological law.

It should be clear by now that Homans departs radically from Émile Durkheim's conception of sociological science. Social phenomena, for Homans, are not truly unique; they have no nature apart from the exchange of rewards and punishments, which is the basis for human interaction. Therefore, the principles of psychological behaviorism can and should be used to explain sociological issues. In a nutshell, Homans argues that sociology is a corollary of psychology.

---

[4] For a behavioristic view of society, read B. F. Skinner's *Walden Two* (1948).

## Theoretical Content

As evident in our treatment of the assumptions underlying the work of Homans, it is necessary to examine his formal theory in two phases of development. In *The Human Group,* we find a microfunctionalist explanation of human behavior. By this Homans meant that the small group is a systemic whole consisting of interdependent components. Each of these parts contributes to the equilibrium and maintenance of the whole. Remember that for Homans, studying small groups or systems is a means of investigating and understanding larger systems, whether societies or civilizations.

Homans sought to build his theory on principles inferred or induced from five already completed studies of group behavior. In one of these, the relationships and work habits of a group of fourteen employees of the Hawthorne plant of Western Electric had been closely studied. Homans analyzed this study of worker behavior in the bank wiring room to find how this group functioned.

The workers in question had been pulled from their usual jobs and placed in a special workroom for a period of seven months. Their pay was determined by a piecework system that replaced their regular wages. It was believed that this system would increase productivity by providing the opportunity for higher individual and group rewards. However, this expectation was not realized.

The group instead formed their own normative system, group-shared expectations as to what constituted a fair day's work. This amounted to the wiring of two telephone banks. Those who violated these norms came to be considered deviants. Those who did not do their share were defined as "chiselers," while those who worked beyond the norm were "rate-busters." Those who violated the norms of unity by speaking negatively about coworkers were "squealers." Such deviants were brought in line through the use of sanctions. For example, labels such as "slave" and "speed king" augmented the practice of "binging." The latter was the use of a hit on the upper arm.

The original researchers had done a basically descriptive study of concern to managers interested in increasing worker productivity. However, looking at the study in his own way, Homans found a small system complete with roles, norms, and corresponding conceptions of deviance. He went through the same procedure with studies of other groups in other settings, refining a more general theory.

Despite his efforts, praised by Robert Merton for one, Homans came to believe that functionalism did not really explain groups or societies (Homans, 1974: 5–6). This approach had some success in describing and classifying observations, but it could not explain the formation and operations of group behavior. By the late 1950s, Homans abandoned functionalism or a microsystems approach and began to construct a theory of social exchange.

In his second phase, Homans found in behavioral psychology the explanatory power thought to be missing from functionalist theory. With behavioral psychology wedded to the simple view of economic exchange discussed earlier,

Homans was ready to theoretically explain social phenomena in psychological terms. His propositions of social exchange are simple modifications of Skinnerian principles.

In *Social Behavior,* Homans presented five theoretical propositions:

1. *The success proposition* holds that "For all actions taken by persons, the more often a particular action of a person is rewarded, the more likely the person is to perform that action" (Homans, 1974: 16).

   *Translation:* The meaning of this proposition is self-evident. We repeat in the future those behaviors for which we have been rewarded in the past.

2. *The stimulus proposition* holds that "If in the past the occurrence of a particular stimulus, or set of stimuli, has been the occasion on which a person's action has been rewarded, then the more similar the present stimuli are to the past ones, the more likely the person is to perform the action, or some similar action, now" (Homans, 1974: 22–23).

   *Translation:* This proposition allows for a bit of complexity to enter the learning situation. Specifically, it introduces the phenomenon of stimulus and response generalization. For example, if a student has been rewarded in the past for posing discussion questions in a sociology course, this person might respond by repeating that behavior in a history class. However, he or she might substitute a similar response, such as directing questions to the professor.

3. *The value proposition* holds that "The more valuable to a person is the result of his action, the more likely he is to perform the action" (Homans, 1974: 25).

   *Translation:* Not all rewards are created equal. We are more likely to perform actions that bring what to us are the greater rewards.

4. *The deprivation-satiation proposition* holds that "The more often in the recent past a person has received a particular reward, the less valuable any further unit of that reward becomes for him" (Homans, 1974: 29).

   *Translation:* Rewards can get old. We are not as interested in food when we are not hungry as we are when we *are* hungry (food is a terrific reward if one is starving).

5. *The aggression-approval proposition* comes in two parts. The first holds that "When a person's action does not receive the reward he expected, or receives punishment he did not expect, he will be angry; he becomes more likely to perform aggressive behavior" (Homans, 1974: 37).

   *Translation:* We get mad and are likely to act it out when we do not get the reward we thought we would or if we get punishment we did not anticipate.

   The second part of this proposition holds that "When a person's action receives the reward he expected, especially a greater reward than he expected, or does not receive punishment he expected, he will be pleased; he becomes more likely to perform approving behavior, and the results of such behavior become more valuable to him" (Homans, 1974: 39).

*Translation:* If we come out even or make a profit (especially a big one) in our social exchanges or if we avoid an expected loss, we will more probably demonstrate our approval to others. The consequences of our approval behavior assume greater value. For example, if we are praised by a supervisor beyond our expectations, we will be more apt to show our approval, perhaps by working harder. The work itself then becomes of greater value to us.

## Critique

Consistent with the imagery of behavioral sociology, Homans has based his theory of exchange on the view of a rational profit maximizer seeking to enhance reward and avoid punishment. The exchange relationship thus exhibits properties quite analogous to those of Exxon Corporation. Indeed, Homans would argue that this and all other forms of social organization consist simply of the behaviors of people, melded together in search of a distributive justice in which each person is out for his or her share. In sum, all organizations, systems, and societies obey at their root the principles of exchange. They differ only in what is defined as reward or punishment.

Homans' theory can be praised as an interdisciplinary effort that attempts to bring together explanations and research within and without sociology. His early work was an exercise in inductive theory construction while *Social Behavior* demonstrates the nature of deduction. Perhaps of greater significance is the part played by Homans' variety of exchange theory in defining the boundary lines of sociology. For critics today, this theoretical system is an example of what sociology is not. Put succinctly, in *The Human Group,* Homans eliminated society. Still dissatisfied, he proceeded in *Social Behavior* to eliminate most groups. The exchange in this, his major work, occurs between "person and other," the functional equivalents of Skinner's pigeons.

As we noted earlier, the later sociology of George Homans rests on the psychology of B. F. Skinner and more precisely his principles of behaviorism. It is safe to say that many psychologists and most sociologists find operant conditioning a simplistic, therefore unsatisfactory, explanation for human behavior. The learning of human language is a case in point.

Noam Chomsky, the noted linquist at MIT, has demonstrated that children quite spontaneously and creatively arrange and use their vocabulary to convey original meanings (1975). Such a finding presents serious problems for behaviorists, who believe that language is learned through reinforcement of the "right" words and subsequent patterns of stimulus and response generalization. While we do reinforce language responses, this in itself is insufficient to explain the original properties of language development. The theoretical focus, then, must shift to the cognitive factors that have no place in behaviorist theory.

Of crucial importance is the point that Skinner's (hence Homans') principles are based on studies of animal behavior. Serious questions can be raised about whether such findings can be generalized, even to animals outside the laboratory. (For example, how do animals learn in a more natural habitat?) Of course psychological behaviorists are interested in talking about *human* behavior, not the pigeon, rodent, or chimpanzee population.

As the gap between Homo sapiens and other species is apparently sizable, behaviorists are perhaps compelled to ignore the cognitive factor that might reside at the center of those differences. However, Homans converts the gap into a chasm. He seeks to generalize principles based on animal studies ultimately to the entire range of societies, cultures, and civilizations.

Ignoring the cognitive factor is consistent with behaviorism because this system of thought features the theoretical elimination of the subjective world of meaning, emotion, and consciousness. Homans, however, is unsuccessful in avoiding such conceptions. He finds it necessary to employ such notions as "pleased" and "anger" in his own theoretical system.

Homans insists that human culture and social structures are all reducible to the exchange behavior of their constituent actors. He fails, however, to explain the enormous variety in such large-scale phenomena. Holding fast to the view that behavior is learned everywhere in the same way does not explain the enormous differences in *what* is learned. Nor does Homans explain how a person (or more to the point a group or a people) comes to believe that radically different things constitute reward or punishment. Is there no role for culture and social institutions at least in the differential definition of rewards?

Much of what has been written to this point constitutes in part a critique of Homans' level of abstraction. Other order theorists might well join Talcott Parsons, who argued that Homans has not shown how behavioral psychology explains large-scale systems; he has only declared that he has done so (Parsons, 1964: 216–220).

Another point of criticism centers on the nature of deductive logic. Homans' major premise is that all human action is learned or shaped by differential reinforcement of simple behaviors that occur initially as if by chance. If this premise is inadequate or wrong, then all propositions that follow are inadequate or wrong no matter how logically elegant they may be.

A final set of problems is ideological in nature. It has to do with the relationship between Homans' theory and the larger social, political, and economic context. We will begin by noting that Homans broke ranks with the functionalists because he was dissatisfied with the explanatory power of that tradition. Yet he has chosen to reduce his sociology to the lowest level, centering on profit seeking in a dyadic exchange. It is interesting to note what he has retained by so doing.

Remember that in *The Human Group* Homans sought to explain the behavior of workers in the bank wiring room in terms of a microsystem, complete with norms, deviance, and negative sanctions. He later decided he was not explaining anything, only describing the interactions in question. Had Homans considered the position of workers in the factory in the sense of a power analysis, he might not have been so unhappy with the explanations he drew. For starters he might have noted that these workers were most probably not dumb. Accordingly, they would realize the interest of their managers in increased productivity. If earnings based on piecework were to increase that productivity in the experiment, then piecework might well have been instituted at the plant level.

Working people have their reasons to fear piecework and other "merit systems." They set worker against worker in a competitive struggle for existence. Perhaps the view that workers who produce more should be paid more is appealing if you are young, healthy, and plan to move on. However, if you are older, not so healthy, or looking to stay on, having to be a rate-buster every day is not appealing. Piecework can too easily become a management tool. From the worker's side, it destroys solidarity and establishes a pecking order to be used in layoffs. This is quite important because the Hawthorne Works of Western Electric was not unionized and the minimal security of seniority could not be guaranteed by a labor contract.

The Mayo researchers, including George Homans, might have considered such matters had they held different assumptions about human nature, the nature of society, and the nature of science. For example, from the conflict vantage point, they might have critically examined the role of the worker in the factory system of production. But then the plant might not have been open to their research. From the pluralist side, Homans might later have interpreted the world of work from the standpoint of the employee, but that would have required a place in his system of explanation for subjective factors.

Homans did neither of these things. Although repudiating Parsons, Durkheim, and other functionalists, he did not abandon either their emphasis on an objective social world or their determinism. Nor did he take leave of an orderly conception of societies and science. Thus, he continued to embrace the status quo while continuing the quest for prediction and control. In other words, Homans did not exchange paradigms. He simply moved to a lower plane in the same one.

A last ideological point centers around Homans' professed wish to show that sociology is individualistic and not collectivist. In this, he has aspired to defend his interpretation of the Western intellectual tradition: The nature of individuals determines the nature of society (1962: 7–24). Yet, although Homans has installed the individual as his theoretical focus, he apparently confuses this with the meaning of individualism in Western thought. That conception most certainly has a place for volition in human behavior. Psychological behaviorism, on the other hand, is a rigidly deterministic system of thought.[5] Ironically, Homans' theoretical system leaves the human actor more subject to external contingencies than the functionalists ever dreamed.[6]

---

[5] For a behaviorist critique of free choice, see B. F. Skinner's *Beyond Freedom and Dignity* (1971).

[6] We need not infer Homans' position from that of Skinner. Homans branded choice an "illusion," arguing that individual behavior is "absolutely determined" (Homans, 1967: 10).

# ■ Peter Blau (b. 1918): Exchange at a Higher Level

In an earlier section, we introduced Peter Blau as an exemplar of new causal theory. At that point we contended that his examination (with Otis Duncan) of the U.S. stratification system is representative of the contemporary positivist approach to inductive theory building in American sociology. However, Blau is best known for other theoretical contributions.

In 1964 Peter Blau published his *Exchange and Power in Social Life*. In it he attempted to break off social behavior from the Skinnerian assumptions that marked the work of George Homans. Blau tried to do this by placing exchange outside the narrow confines of direct and interpersonal reciprocity. Thus, his effort pushed the theoretical center of the tradition to a higher plateau.

Contrary to the position of George Homans, Blau's conception made peace with the functionalists and others who entertain a sociology of larger scale. In so doing, it is possible that he left the exchange tradition altogether. One thing is certain. Peter Blau's most recent work in the *macrostructural* tradition is most certainly centered on larger social structures. As such, it represents a substantial theoretical departure from both social exchange and new causal theory.

## History and Biography

Peter Blau was born in Vienna in 1918 and emigrated to the United States in 1939. He quickly became an American citizen and went on to serve in the army during the Second World War, opposing the forces of fascism that had seized control in his native land. After the war he received his Ph.D. from Columbia University in 1952 and began to distinguish himself as an authority on complex organizations.

The historical context in early twentieth century Austria featured the beginning and end of the First Republic (1918–1938). The republic signaled an end to the Hapsburg monarchy, a dynasty that dated back to the thirteenth century. Prior to the Austrian involvement in the First World War, the twentieth century had brought a continuation of the ethnic and nationalistic conflicts that marked the prior history of the monarchy. Vienna, the seat of the imperial government, had become perhaps the intellectual and cultural center of Europe. Its cosmopolitan nature contrasted sharply with the customs and conditions of rural/small-town Austria. In the prewar period, the unity of the state was preserved by means of a military dictatorship.[7]

---

[7]Important references on Austrian history include Gehl, 1963; May, 1951; and Mitrany, 1936.

Austria fought on the side of the Central Powers during World War I and by the end of that conflict domestic conditions had become intolerable. Disenchantment with the war had grown following the peace signed with Russia after the successful Bolshevik Revolution. The national minorities used the disorder to press for autonomy or secession. Declines in food production, strikes, and blockade, together with the gathering strength of socialist revolutionaries, marked the decline and fall of the Hapsburgs. Faced with the defeat of the Central Powers without and nationalist movements toward independence within, Charles I surrendered public rule on Armistice Day, 1918.

Under the terms of the Treaty of St. Germain, the newly declared Austrian republic was reduced to a land area the size of Maine and a predominantly German-speaking population of some seven million. During the next two decades, the nation was split along political lines. The largest and strongest party was the Christian Democrats, who controlled parliament between 1922 and 1938.

The Christian Democrats represented the small landowners, tradespeople, and others of the middle class. They were opposed by the Social Democrats who controlled the municipal government of Vienna. While this city survived the war to become a remarkable example of social welfare, public housing, and education, Vienna was isolated geographically and culturally from its already shrunken rural base. In the context of the Great Depression, urban unemployment and poverty rose and the Christian Socialist chancellor, Engelbert Dollfuss, established a fascist government in 1933.

Dollfuss sent troops into Vienna to destroy the Social Democrats and their trade unions in 1934. His success encouraged those Austrians who favored *Anschluss,* a political union with Germany, by then under the reign of the National Socialists led by Adolf Hitler. On the outside, fascist propaganda from both the Nazis and their Italian ally Mussolini called for unification. On the inside, the Austrian economy continued in a state of collapse. In 1938 the Nazi army occupied Austria, and the nation became a part of the German Reich.

The grim consequences of disorder in Austria, the defense of his newly adopted nation in the "good war," and education in American universities represent mileposts in the life of Peter Blau. Taken together, they form some context for his theoretical system.

## Assumptions

In some major respects, the works of Blau considered here conform with the assumptions of the order paradigm. At the human level, we will see that Blau in 1964 presented the imagery of a rational seeker of rewards who establishes social relationships on the basis of reciprocating responses from others. Consistent with the behaviorist position examined earlier, Blau did not view the inner social psychological or subjective processes as important. While we will see a modification of his position on the reciprocity of social behavior, Blau today continues to criticize the theoretical interest in subjectivity.

While repudiating the subjective side, Blau in 1964 shared with many of the pluralist tradition (see next section) the assumption that society is built from the inside out. For him, social structure evolved and emerged from exchange relations. Yet unlike Homans, to Blau reciprocity was more than interpersonal. It also involved the exchanges between groups and large-scale organizations. As we shall explore in some detail, the basis for such transactions at the higher levels was identified by Blau as *value consensus*. This view of broad popular agreement on ideas and things of worth is distinctive of the order paradigm.

In 1975 Blau edited and published *Approaches to the Study of Social Structure,* one of a number of examples of his theoretical evolution toward a *macrostructural* conception of society. As our examination of his theoretical system will confirm, Blau rejects a cultural image of society as well as a psychological one. He continues to focus on power and stratification but addresses these almost exclusively at a societal plateau. His overarching image is adopted from Durkheim's organic solidarity. Thus, social order is born of a complex and interdependent division of labor in the heterogeneous society.

Blau's assumptions concerning the nature of science have also undergone something of a transformation over time. His modern classic on exchange and power seeks to explain social behavior and social structure by focusing on the connection or form of *mediation* between the two. Thus the large-scale focus of functionalism is wed to the microsociology of social exchange.

Given what we know concerning Blau's contemporary vision of society, it follows that his assumptions about the nature of science will reject the cultural focus of functionalism (see Parsons in Chapter 7). It also follows that subjective theories that focus on the inner world of social actors have little place. Blau lately has been on the leading edge of a Durkheimian renaissance that must be seen in part as a reaction to the current popularity of microsociological theories and research. This image of sociological science is deterministic, but the search for causal explanation is far removed from the "person and other" of George C. Homans.

## Theoretical Content

In our attempt to understand Blau's earlier work, our point of departure is his *Exchange and Power in Social Life* (1964). According to Blau, social bonds or associations are contingent on rewards that may be either extrinsic (money, goods, etc.) or intrinsic (love, respect, etc.). However, whereas Homans was interested in the balanced relationship that reflected a "distributive justice," Blau considered the imbalanced association. When one member of the exchange relationship gets more than his or her share, *power differentials* emerge.

In Blau's theory, those with unmet needs (that is, those who are short on rewards to exchange with others) are power dependent. In approaching power, Blau prefers the definition of Weber who argued that the powerful are those who are able to impose their will on others (Blau, 1964: 117). Thus, in the imbalanced exchange relationship, the have-not or have-less parties have no choice but to rely on force, look elsewhere, do without, or subordinate themselves, giving those with control over them "credit" for present or future services. Blau further argues that power is a form of impersonal restraint, as opposed to responses of approval or disapproval that are more personal in nature. The former occurs more frequently in modern, complex societies.

In his explanation of emergent group formation, Blau holds that *differentiation* occurs through the medium of exchange. By this he means that those with rewards to give assume power and those without become followers. Thus he accounts for status and role differences. However, Blau recognizes that a group cannot be truly *integrated* on the basis of leadership alone. Group solidarity is enhanced when leaders take a number of important steps to affirm the worth of those with fewer rewards. They do this through readily admitting their shortcomings, delegating authority, and in general proving themselves human. In short, those with power lead only insofar as they avoid outright tyranny.

Blau also seeks to explain established as opposed to emergent social organizations. These are brought into being to realize an agenda of objectives. Examples include political parties established to win elections and industrial corporations existing to manufacture goods and make a profit. In these, leadership and subjugation are built into the very structure of the organization. However, for Blau differentiation (whether emergent or structural) sows the seeds for discord and change.

Thus far it appears that Blau centers on primary or face-to-face exchange. However, he moves to a higher level of analysis by noting that direct social interaction between or among entire societies or communities seldom occurs. Most exchange is therefore indirect. Members of a society share rewards and punishments indirectly and impersonally through a "common medium." Actually, there appear to be two such "media," namely, norms and values.

The medium of exchange between the group or organization and the individual is the normative consensus that exists in collective life. Thus, members of society receive approval or reward from others when they conform to this consensus and disapproval when they do not. The collectivity, whether group, organization, or society, also benefits because conformity produces a great measure of solidarity.

Now while this appears to be consistent with the position of George Homans, further examination reveals a crucial difference. Remember that Blau holds that the nature of social exchange is *indirect*. An example of what he means is in order. In modern, complex societies the enterprise of charity may be privately organized. In the United States, the United Way is a case in point. This formal appeal actually supplants direct and personal forms of giving.

Thus we seldom "see" the beneficiaries, let alone receive the reward of their personal approval. However, givers may be rewarded or punished through the medium of the "normative system for giving." One is expected to conform, and failure to do so may result in the withholding of approval from coworkers or superiors.

*Value consensus* is another medium of exchange for Blau. Unlike the normative consensus, agreement on values is the medium whereby collectivities in society engage in social exchange. More accurately, as Blau develops a typology of different values, they represent *media* of exchange.

*Particularistic* values constitute the medium through which group or collective unity is created, thus supplanting solidarity based purely on personal bonds. Examples would include Republicanism, feminism, nationalism, and so forth. Such values obviously serve to identify members of the in-group and out-group and set the stage for some opposition among groups within society.

*Universalistic* values enable members of a society to judge achievement on the part of members. Such are the basis for status rewards that in turn determine the nature of the prevailing system of stratification. Universalistic values are thus the medium through which a society ranks its members. Perhaps the leading example in the United States would be material success.

*Legitimating* values represent the medium through which the exercise of power is sanctioned. These are the basis of authority, and examples might include respect for the office and democratic conceptions of the state (such as the values underlying the Bill of Rights).

Finally, *oppositional* values represent the medium of change. By such means, new ideals (such as cooperation in a competitive system, pacifism in a warfare state) allow for the spreading wide of dissent far in excess of what might be expected if exchange were only based on interpersonal contact.

In his more recent theoretical efforts (1975a, 1975b, 1977, 1980), Blau has evolved beyond social exchange as an identifiable theoretical system. This is by no means a radical change. It is quite evident in his work on exchange and power that this theorist was poised to leave the academic home of the behaviorists (if indeed he was ever a resident). At any rate, the later Blau asserts clearly his Durkheimian interest in the *macrostructure* of society.

By social structure, Blau refers to population distributions among various sorts of social positions. Social positions determine the role relations and interactions of people in society. Examples of social positions include such things as class, race, sex, and age. Simply put, these positions define social structure. For Blau, the proper theoretical task of sociology is to explain these positions and the differentiation they represent (who has power and who does not, who ranks where in the stratification system, who plays what role in the division of labor). Other theoretical concerns about social positions include their interrelationships, the conditions that determine them, and their implications (Blau, 1975b: 222).

Blau notes that societies may reflect a sameness of the population. However, modern and complex societies typically reflect a population distributed among heterogeneous positions (without ranking) or among positions of in-equality (with ranking). Well-integrated societies often reflect a sameness of the population. However, the heterogeneity of modern society makes integration difficult.

Modern societies are not doomed to disintegration, however. Given the multiplicity of groups, the members of a society may come to be a part of many collectivities and organizations. Members also hold more than one status posi-tion. It is possible in this context of structural diversity that the in-group/out-group distinction will break down. Thus Blau, in his later sociology, offers more a vision than a theory of society. In it, he creates order from diversity.

## Critique

There is some good news concerning Peter Blau's theoretical efforts. Taken as a whole, he most certainly pushes social exchange beyond the limitations of psy-chological behaviorism. Some might observe that he has gone too far. Even in his earlier work, Blau appeared to twist exchange theory somewhat out of shape. However, he was determined to retain a place in sociology for social structure, for large-scale collectivities, and for groups a bit more complex than "person and other."

Blau also attempted to show that human exchange is seldom direct and that rewards have to be defined in a large-scale social context (such as norma-tive systems and value consensus). And he attempted through the explanation of social differentiation and oppositional values to resolve the old nemesis of order theories: the problem of social change.

Behavioral sociologists, working closer to the Homans tradition, would be compelled to argue that Blau did more than bend exchange theory. Indeed it appears that exchange often becomes a metaphor for interaction. In his de-fense, Blau would probably prefer to be right than consistent. However, attempting to merge theoretical systems that operate on different levels of ab-straction (in this case, Durkheim and Homans) might be expected to draw some fire. The Durkheimian side is seeking to explain society in terms of social facts, and its focus is on institutions, values, norms, and the larger issues of social life. Homans and his heirs believe that the reinforcement of behavior ulti-mately makes a society possible. The gap between these traditions is quite large.

From the functionalist side, Blau appears to discount the role of deviance or nonconformity in the integration of society. Since Durkheim, functionalists have argued that the identification and punishment of deviants have defined the moral boundary lines of society. Thus without some deviance (too much would be a threat to social order), the norms would suffer from definitional confusion. For example, the theft of property underscores its value in society, rape defines the importance of sexual consent, and homicide defines the sanctity of human life.

Those who seek to find the seeds of society in human consciousness will, of course, not be content with Peter Blau's theory. The argument that the social reality is constructed by actors who share a common world of meaning is a serious one. But it is largely ignored here.

From the conflict side, Blau seems to focus too heavily on various threats to consensus. While he recognizes that those with rewards may behave in coercive fashion, he does not inquire critically of the system that makes classes or an elite of power. Simply put, Blau fails to examine such concerns as the role of the state or the rise of the modern corporation. It follows that his conceptions of power and inequality are specific neither to social systems nor history.

The diversity apparent in Blau's work is evidence of an ongoing attempt to perfect his explanation of society. (This also makes him something of a moving target.) However, it is important to observe that despite shifts in theoretical focus, he remains relatively constant in one respect. Whether we focus on new causal theory, exchange and power, or macrostructuralism, all reflect the influence of positive philosophy and an essential tie to the underlying assumptions of the order paradigm.

# ■ *Bibliography*

Ayer, Alfred
1958            *The Foundations of Empirical Knowledge.* New York: Macmillan.
1959            *Logical Positivism.* Glencoe, Ill.: The Free Press.

Blau, Peter
1964            *Exchange and Power in Social Life.* New York: John Wiley & Sons.
1975a           "Parallels and Contrasts in Structural Inquiries." In Peter Blau (Ed.), *Approaches to the Study of Social Structure,* pp. 1–20. New York: The Free Press.
1975b           "Parameters of Social Structure." In Peter Blau (Ed.), *Approaches to the Study of Social Structure,* pp. 220–253. New York: The Free Press.
1977            *Inequality and Heterogeneity: A Primitive Theory of Social Structure.* New York: The Free Press.
1980            "A Fable About Social Structure." *Social Forces* 58:777–788.

Blau, Peter M., and Otis Dudley Duncan
1967            *The American Occupational Structure.* New York: John Wiley & Sons.

Chomsky, Noam
1975            *Reflections on Language*. New York: Pantheon.

Gehl, Jurgen
1963            *Austria, Germany and the Anschluss, 1931–1938*. London: Oxford University Press.

Homans, George C.
1950            *The Human Group*. New York: Harcourt, Brace.
1961            *Social Behavior: Its Elementary Forms*. New York: Harcourt, Brace & World.
1962            *Sentiments and Activities*. New York: The Free Press.
1964            "Bring Men Back In." *American Sociological Review* 29:809–818.
1967            *The Nature of Social Science*. New York: Harcourt, Brace & World.
1969            "The Sociological Relevance of Behaviorism." In Robert Burgess and Don Bushell (Eds.), *Behavioral Sociology*. New York: Columbia University Press.
1974            *Social Behavior: Its Elementary Forms*. Rev. ed. New York: Harcourt Brace Jovanovich.
1984            *Coming to My Senses: The Autobiography of a Sociologist*. New Brunswick, N.J.: Transaction Books.

Kolakowski, Leszek
1968            *The Alienation of Reason: A History of Positivist Thought*. Garden City, N.Y.: Doubleday.

Kraft, Victor
1953            *The Vienna Circle*. New York: Greenwood.

Massarik, Fred
1965            "Magic, Models, Man and the Culture of Mathematics." In F. Massarik and P. Ratoosh (Eds.), *Mathematical Explorations in Behavioral Science*, pp. 7–21. Homewood, Ill.: Richard D. Irwin.

May, A. J.
1951            *Hapsburg Monarchy, 1867–1916*. Cambridge, Mass.: Harvard University Press.

Mitrany, David
1936            *The Effect of the War in Southeastern Europe*. New Haven, Conn.: Yale University Press.

Parsons, Talcott
1964            "Levels of Organization and the Mediation of Social Interaction." *Sociological Inquiry* 34:207–220.

Ritzer, George
1983            *Contemporary Sociological Theory*. New York: Alfred A. Knopf.

Rose, Michael
1975                    *Industrial Behavior.* London: Penguin Books.

Skinner, B. F.
1948                    *Walden Two.* New York: Macmillan.
1971                    *Beyond Freedom and Dignity.* New York: Alfred A. Knopf.

Urwick, Lyndall F.
1960                    *The Life and Work of Elton Mayo.* London: Urwick.

Whitehead, Alfred North, and Bertrand Russell
1925                    *Principia Mathematica.* 2nd ed. Cambridge, England: Cam-
                       bridge University Press.

# ■ The Eye of the Beholder

# CHAPTER 9

# ■ The Pluralist Paradigm

In this chapter we shall explore a second paradigm or model that has guided the development of a distinctive body of sociological theory. As should be evident by now, the term *theory* is somewhat loosely used (in sociology as well as in the broader society). Moreover, as revealed in our earlier chapters, many theoreticians have contributed more in the way of assumptions than propositions. Be that as it may, models help us understand sociologists and sociological theory.

Recall for a moment the essential images or parts that constitute a paradigm in sociology. One concerns what the theorist assumes to be the nature of human being. The second concerns underlying assumptions about the nature of society. And the third has to do with preconceptions about what sociology as a discipline or, more formally, a theoretical science is supposed to be. Not all of these images or visions are made explicit in various systems of thought. Some have to be logically inferred. However, they exist at the pretheoretical level, always shaping the formal explanations that follow.

Remember also what we mean by a sociology of knowledge. The assumptions all of us hold about human nature, society, science, and other concerns are not founded in instinct. Rather, they reflect in some important ways our experiences. Experience in turn is not a simple matter of home, family, school, friends, and other close-at-hand encounters. In addition to these primary forces, we are shaped by the larger sphere of society: its institutions, culture, movements; and the way its systems of stratification, power, and ideas are organized. All of these of course bear the imprint of a particular historical era.

Now consider for a moment what these simple social observations mean for knowledge itself. Our cardinal premise is that knowledge is a human product. Does this mean that we should know something about the "truth maker's" biography? To some extent, yes. But more importantly, we should know something about the historical conditions that mark a society at the time knowledge is created. History, of course, deals with the life of a people at particular times, in particular places. More formally, it represents both *material* and *ideational* dimensions. These dimensions refer respectively to the major events and the prevailing ideas of the times.

Considering our argument thus far, we can identify the point at which "critical mass" can be expected for the sociology of knowledge. This point is the interface of history and biography. Or as we suggested earlier, it is the nexus joining the life of the person and the life of a people. Simply put, knowledge is context bound. It is created or formed in a particular time and space. It follows that this contextual place must be understood if we are to comprehend how a particular system of thought comes into being. As sociological theories constitute systems of thought, and as sociologists are human, it follows that *theory and its underlying assumptions* can also be placed in historical/biographical context.

Now that we are somewhat reoriented, we can turn to the task at hand. The second major tradition in sociology follows what we choose to call the *pluralist* paradigm. Think for a moment about this term. Quite literally it means "more than one." Earlier we argued that order theorists think in terms of the social properties that unify a society into an overarching system, a functional whole. Pluralist sociologists are on a somewhat different wavelength. Their assumptions, which in turn influence the theory they develop, recognize that modern societies often consist of divergent groups with different interests. People and groups are not the same; they vary in terms of power and influence, customs and tradition, wealth and standing. Yet, for the pluralists, this diversity is not in and of itself a disintegrating force.

As we noted in the previous section, many order theorists deal with the issue of diversity, usually signifying it by means of terms like *heterogeneity* or *complexity*. However, these differences are ordinarily presented as a barrier to stability, a threat to social control. When the logic of an order theory like Durkheimian functionalism encounters disorder (as with deviance), an attempt is made to show how a response to such disorder (such as punishment) actually works to the benefit of the total society (or system). For pluralist sociologists, some disorder (including some forms of deviance) is an ordinary condition of complex, heterogeneous nation-states. Rather than viewing such divergency as a problem, the pluralists see differences in values, norms, customs, and standing as a normal and implicitly desirable state. Thus too much order and conformity become problems in themselves.

Whatever the nature of the paradigm, theories retain certain properties in common. They feature logically interrelated concepts that show the relationships between ideas. These relationships make up a system of explanation or, less formally, a set of answers to the question "Why?" Like those in the previous section, the theories that follow in subsequent chapters will address societal puzzles rather than more specialized issues (such as crime, stratification, bureaucracies, and so forth).

The pluralist theories seek to answer a different collection of puzzles, however. Once again, we can present these in the form of representative questions: What are the forms of diversity evident in the heterogeneous society? How and in what fashion do people make their groups, organizations, and society? What role does the world of consciousness, meaning, and symbols play in human behavior? How does that subjective world both shape and react to external forces? How and in what manner do people define their social reality? What part do the reactions of others play in forming the human self-concept or behavior?

A review of pluralist theories in sociology will follow in due course. At this point we are interested in the major elements of the pluralist paradigm. In short, we want to know the common assumptions that underlie this specific body of sociological explanations. As we trace such assumptions through conceptions about human nature, society, and social science, we will once again employ the devices of exemplars and ideal types.

Remember that exemplars are thinkers whose arguments clearly and representatively develop the imagery of the paradigm. The imagery that we identify and discuss will assume the form of an ideal type, a typical description that unifies a category of related cases. Paradigms, as we construct them, are made up of such idealized imagery. Taken as a whole, they can be thought of as ideal types.

# ■ The Kantian Conception of Human Nature

As usual, we shall begin our construction of the paradigm in question by analyzing its assumptions concerning human nature. Our exemplar for this purpose will be the eighteenth-century philosopher, Immanuel Kant.[1]

Kant (1724–1804) was born, lived, and died at the age of 80 in Königsberg in that part of Europe then known as East Prussia. He was reared by a father who made a living as a saddler and by a devoutly Lutheran mother who strongly hoped that Kant would enter the ministry. However, while at the University of Königsberg, he turned to the study of philosophy, mathematics, and Newtonian physics. By the time he graduated in 1740, Kant was committed to pursuing a doctorate in philosophy.

Kant's family was not one of means. Both his mother and father died several years after his graduation, and Kant supported himself through tutoring. Given these conditions of poverty, he was unable to take his doctorate until 1755. For the next 15 years he worked at a small library. Finally, in 1770, Kant

---

[1] The major works of Kant that inform our discussion are listed in the bibliography. Important general references include Cassirer, 1981, and Beck, 1969.

became a professor of philosophy at the University of Königsberg. He never married, and there appears to be no record that he ever traveled out of East Prussia. Given this inauspicious background, it must have seemed that a man who did not assume an academic position until he was 46 years of age would have little to offer the philosophical world. However, in the next three decades, Immanuel Kant was to stand that world on end. The University of Königsberg became a leading center of philosophical thought and education.

Before we examine Kant's formal philosophy, let us briefly preview his underlying conception of human nature. Kant believed that people possess a gregarious nature best actualized in congenial relations with others. He also believed in self-sufficiency and competition. The natural state of human being is thus one of conflict between positive and negative impulses. Or in the words of Kant, "Man wishes concord; but nature knows better what is good for his species and she will have discord. . . . The natural . . . antagonism from which so many evils arise does yet at the same time impel him to new exertion of his powers" (1891: 11–12). At first glance this appears to be a paradox if not an outright contradiction. However, this assumption of the *divided human nature* came to influence other philosophical systems as well as later sociological theories.

Kant expressed his reverence for two dimensions of reality, the "starry sky above" and the "moral law within." These symbolize the thrust of his philosophical system. The starry sky above is a part of the world of appearances and as such can be studied scientifically. However, the moral law within represents a different reality to be approached by a system of ethics. As we shall see, whether the issue is science or ethics, Kantian philosophy is distinctive by reason of its focus on the nature of the human mind.

Kant's philosophical system was developed in reaction to those currents that came to shape the positive sociology discussed in the previous section. On the continent of Europe, philosophers like Descartes, Spinoza, and Leibnitz had advanced rationalism, which found authority in reason. The rationalist movement came to enshrine deduction as the basis of systematic knowledge. As we have noted, deduction is strongly featured in the contemporary work of the sociologists Zetterberg (Chapter 2) and Homans (Chapter 8).

A second philosophical movement was that of British empiricism. This system found truth not in the certainties of reason but rather in sensory experience. Reason is thus confined by perception. The mind, according to the empiricist John Locke, is not a crucible of innate ideas but rather a tabula rasa, an erased tablet written upon purely by experience. Kant, dissatisfied with the extremes of both rationalism and empiricism, was to develop a third major philosophy, that of idealism. In 1781, at the age of 57, he published his classic, *Critique of Pure Reason* (1950, originally published 1781).

In his first *Critique,* Kant distinguished between *noumena,* or things in themselves, and *phenomena,* or things as they appear to an active human mind. Science and most knowledge are not to focus on noumena or ultimate realities but rather on phenomena or appearances. While this emphasis on the world of appearances might appear heavily empirical at first glance, Kant went beyond the empiricist emphasis on sensory experience.

Kant argued that the *human mind imposes order on the chaos of appearances*. Human beings cannot understand phenomena simply on the basis of isolated sensory stimuli. The mind creates meaning holistically, from the parts of our experience. For example, we cannot truly know a constellation by perceiving its component parts as a disconnected series of stars. We impose relationships through the synthesizing attributes of human reason. However, science is restricted to the world of appearances. It follows that science cannot deal with noumena or ultimate realities even though philosophically they may exist.

To return to the starry skies above, the scientific astronomer may impose order through synthesizing the data. In so doing he or she employs innate categories of the mind (such as space and time) that detect existing patterns and relationships. Thus the movements of celestial bodies reveal an orderly rather than a random nature. However, the cognitive means to recognize this order is inborn. For Kant, all of this meant that the human mind has the innate capacity to form a priori principles in advance of sensory experience.

In *Critique of Practical Reason* (1949, originally published 1788), Kant made arguments that underlie several pluralist theories in sociology. First, he held that rationality is the basis of human action and that this property is distinctive to the human species alone because lower animals act from instinct. Further, while Homo sapiens is an animal who must contend with impulses, as a rational being he or she can also respond to categorical ethical imperatives. Finally and most important, the value of the individual is absolute. Kant argued that one must act toward self or others as if it were an end, never a means. It should be clear that there is a vast gap between Kantian philosophy and the sociological theories of exchange considered in Chapter 8.

Kant proceeded in his *Critique of Judgment* (1957, originally published 1790) to expand the human consciousness even beyond the scope of the rationalists. Here he held that the beautiful or aesthetic is in the mind of the beholder. Hence, there is a level of cognition evident in aesthetic judgment that stands above sensory form and content. It reflects a property of imagination, an element of harmony, a world of contemplative pleasure. This world of imagination transcends not only sensory experience but conception and is thus often inexpressible.

In other works, Kant explored a philosophy of law and the nature of the state. Again, his focus was the individual, but not the somewhat mindless object that is the center of psychological and social behaviorism. Kant's individualism is in the spirit of the Enlightenment, wherein personal freedom is a natural right.

Kant's conception of state and society logically follows his image of human nature with its self-sufficiency and congenial interaction. The ideal society features private property and the maximization of individual freedom. The state is necessary, a practical device to reconcile conflicts born of competition and the ownership of property. For Kant, the state conforms to the Western model of representative democracy. It functions to regulate the discord that is essential to the full development of the human species and to prevent repression.

Kantian thought is the cornerstone of a philosophical system known as idealism, the major tenet of which is that there is no reality apart from the perceiving mind. This tradition with Kant at its head was to have enormous impact on subsequent German scholarship. This included, as we shall see in the next chapter, the works of the important pluralist sociologists Max Weber and Georg Simmel. For Kant, the truly distinctive aspect of human nature was not the physical or biological being. Rather, it was the spirit, rooted in a mental world of ideas that set the species apart. As a physical being, one is subject to the laws of nature discovered in science. But as a spiritual being, one is free, rational, purposive, and creative. For those influenced by Kant, a human discipline such as sociology could never conform to the strong determinism of the natural sciences. It must instead maintain a prominent place for human volition, choice, and will. This perhaps above all is the Kantian legacy to pluralist sociology.

# ■ Jean-Jacques Rousseau and *Du Contrat Social*

Jean-Jacques Rousseau[2] was another eighteenth-century thinker whose works strongly shaped the scholarship of later eras. Unlike Immanuel Kant, whose philosophy he influenced, Rousseau centered on the political organization of society. His *social contract* constitutes a formula for reconciling the conflicting demands of the polity on one side and established authority on the other. The portrait he painted of social order is one of contrasting interests: between rulers and ruled, free will and law, the body politic and "sectional associations" (groups or organizations with special concerns). Accordingly, he represents well the pluralist image of society.

Rousseau (1712–1778) was born in Geneva, the son of Isaac Rousseau and Suzanne Bernard. His father was a watchmaker, and his mother was the niece of a Calvinist minister. While he was to spend most of his adult life in France, his political writings made him a philosophical exile in the turbulence of that society. Given this disaffection, Rousseau throughout his life considered himself a citizen of Geneva.

The affinity Rousseau felt for the place of his birth is appropriate, for it was during his childhood that he developed both an insatiable appetite for learning and the crucial ideals that shaped his works. Rousseau's mother died a

---

[2]The specific works of Rousseau that inform our summary are listed in the bibliography. A crucial general reference is Cassirer, 1963 (originally published 1932).

short time after his birth, and his father filled his early years with a vast expanse of reading. This regimen, together with political and religious discussion in workers' organizations as well as his father's shop, constituted a program of self-education.

Rousseau's self-education was more than reading and conversation. His father was a skilled worker, and his family lived in the lower city of Geneva. (The upper city was home for the wealthy owners of property.) Jean-Jacques' personal understanding of inequality was no doubt influenced by an event that occurred when he was but 10. In 1722 Isaac Rousseau had to leave Geneva following a quarrel with one of the city's prominent families. Young Rousseau was placed in the home of a minister only to return to Geneva two years later.

After a period of apprenticeship as an engraver, Rousseau left Geneva at the age of 16 and found his way to Annecy in Savoy, France. He took with him a mature taste for literature and the ideals from the "lower city" that constituted an enduring political legacy. These included beliefs in the sovereignty of the whole people, the necessity of recurrent popular assemblies, the subjugation of taxation to a vote of the people, and a distrust of the concentration of power.

Between 1728 and 1740, Rousseau lived off and on with one Mme de Warens, who although 15 years his senior became his mistress. These were years of study for a young man who, unlike the other Enlightenment philosophers, had no formal education. He studied mathematics and the natural sciences, taught himself musical theory and composition, and composed an original scheme of musical notation. Armed with this system and a draft of a comedy, he left Savoy for Paris in 1742.

In Paris, Rousseau was to find neither fame nor fortune but common obscurity. However, by the end of the decade, he published his first notable effort, a *Discourse on the Sciences and the Arts*. His essay was founded on two arguments that marked much of his later philosophy. The first of these was that people are born in a state of liberty. The second was that the sciences, letters, and arts are means of degrading the human spirit, to condition for slavery a creature originally free. Or as Rousseau was to write in his later masterpiece *The Social Contract* (1961, originally published 1762), "Man was born free, and he is everywhere in chains." As we shall soon see, Rousseau was to devote much of his philosophy to how rational beings might control the external forces of social order.

Rousseau, the self-educated son of a watchmaker, did indulge in a Calvinist disdain for luxury. However, there was more to his political philosophy. In subsequent works he centered on the problem of social inequality. Luxuries for Rousseau symbolized that inequality. Moreover, he held that the letters, sciences, and arts were often the source of ideas and products that separated human beings, both from one another and their nature. They became devices employed by monarchs and the wealthy to concentrate political power and material substance. In the wake of inequality came the idleness of the rich and the enslavement of a free people.

Rousseau's continuing attacks on luxury and privilege impelled him to repudiate the music of the aristocracy and to sell the more valuable of his possessions. Embroiled in controversy, he found himself a target of police surveillance. He wrote his *Discourse on the Origins of Inequality,* published in 1755, and left Paris shortly thereafter for Montmorency to begin work on *The Social Contract.* These two works form the core of his political philosophy.

In his second discourse, Rousseau argued that while unequal in talents, human beings in ancient societies lived in a state of equality. By this he meant they existed in isolation, not subject to the control of rulers. This primitive stage was followed by a period of simple communities. Here the companionship of others yielded friendship and enmity, harmony and turbulence, good and evil. However, the technology to develop agriculture, together with the invention of iron, laid the basis for yet a third developmental state. No longer nomadic, possessing the means of simple machines and destructive weapons, the human animal began to divide the land. Within communities, those who acquired more land sought to expand and then looked to laws to protect their holdings. At the intersocietal level, the stage was set for large-scale conflict. Human society had moved from its ancient origins of equality to a state of perennial war.

There is a strong egalitarian basis in Rousseau's writings. This, coupled with his critique of luxury, the wealthy, and European monarchies, might suggest that his thought more appropriately fits the conflict paradigm.[3] However, a careful reading of Rousseau's works reveals an important distinction between his position and that of later critics of inequality (such as Marx and Engels). As we shall see in the next section, conflict thinkers do not ordinarily assume that the consequences of class divisions can be resolved through guarantees of political liberty.

It is true enough that Rousseau was no reactionary, holding a romantic yearning for a return to the original state of nature. It is also true that he had harsh words for the divisions born of private property. Still, the crucial question remains Rousseau's vision of society. Whatever his sentiments toward the historical origins of stratification, Rousseau accepted inequality as a fait accompli. His problem therefore was not one of a new economic order in which the fruits of production would be more equitably shared. Rather, his question was how to establish public controls on unavoidable and irreversible private privilege. Inequality is an evil, but one that can be harnessed through rational human action.

In *The Social Contract* Rousseau chose to emphasize the differences in the conditions of life as differences in authority. Put simply, he asked how one person or group can *justly* decide for others. Or, on the other hand, how can the weak be protected from the strong, the few from the many, the citizen from the

---

[3]The position that Rousseau and the other Enlightenment philosophers were the precursors of later Marxist thought is consistent with this view. See Zeitlin, 1968: 23–29.

official, the individual from the state? To such enigmas, Rousseau advanced a *political* solution, that of the covenant.

Rousseau's conception of the covenant or contract hinges on the issue of *legitimate authority*. Members of society are under no compunction to obey simply on the basis of power, for this would mean that authority is no more than a natural birthright of the strongest. For Rousseau, such thinking converts power into a simple proposition of force or coercion. After all, as he noted, the pistol is a form of power. Might, whether that of thieves or monarchs, does not make right.

What then is the nature of the contract between figures or institutions of authority and the people? Rousseau's answer began with his argument that freedom is a natural right. Hence, the denunciation of freedom is the violation of one's humanity. It follows that any contract that bestows absolute power on one party denies the nature of the other. When applied to the topic of government, Rousseau's logic means that one-sided political authority is tyranny.

For Rousseau, human existence was fraught with paradoxes. These were not, however, beyond negotiation. The members of a society are born free and equal. Yet the nature of society is one of irreversible inequality. These oppositional forces can be reconciled only when each individual freely accepts the law. The law in turn protects the interests of the weak as well as the strong, the poor along with the rich, the common and the uncommon. Law is hence the supreme contractual solution to the paradox of free will and societal restraint. As such, it is not rooted in the birthright of the aristocracy or the power of the state. Rather, it is founded in the sovereignty of citizens who may change governments as the right of free people.

Rousseau's contract is a political solution that seeks to reconcile free and purposive action on the individual side with the necessity of societal controls. Those with less property or privilege still retain standing as a party to the social covenant. Given such standing, governments and societies have no choice but to be tolerant of diversity, including all religious opinions.

For Rousseau, the contract was the solution to the injustice of inequality he had addressed in his earlier writings. It was the specific device by which a form of political equality could be substituted for what he saw as an unobtainable economic equality. The covenant would ensure the protection of common interests, respect for the ultimate authority of the people, and therefore protection from the private authority of the wealthy. The contractual standing of the lesser classes would be used to introduce such reforms as public education and state-provided services. These in turn would be financed through inheritance taxes as well as levies on the luxuries of the wealthy.

Thus for Rousseau, the contract becomes a freely embraced social bond that transcends the differences between rich and poor, individuals and associations, the rulers and the ruled. It is the means by which collective life is advanced and free will preserved. Rousseau's image of society is at base a divided one. It portrays society as a place where rational and purposive actors surrender their freedom, if only provisionally, to a collectivity of political equals. The contractual order is a state wherein the general will of the body politic coexists with "sectional associations" so numerous that one cannot dominate the others. It is a society of turbulent harmony, of willful bondage, of antagonistic cooperation. Today, such imagery is representative of the vision of social life that undergirds the various pluralist theories in sociology.

# ■ The Pluralist Image of Human Science

To this point we have addressed Immanuel Kant's image of human nature and Jean-Jacques Rousseau's vision of society. Taken together such ideal types present the view of a rational, free, and purposeful actor contracting with others in a society of diverse individuals and varied interest groups. Now we can turn to the final paradigmatic element: the pluralist conception of human science.

As we have argued earlier, sociologists have historically advanced contrasting images of theoretical science. In a sense such imagery constitutes an answer to an implicit question: What is the nature of systems of sociological explanation? We might recall that sociological theories of order stress the importance of certainty, determinism, lawful relationships, and prediction. Pluralist theories are based on quite different assumptions about the nature of scientific explanation. As we might expect, such preconceptions should be reasonably in line with the Kantian position on human consciousness and meaning, and Rousseau's concern with political freedom and sovereignty. It follows that the pluralist paradigm will offer a far softer image of science than its order counterpart.

## Max Weber and Interpretative Sociology

Recall for a moment our earlier effort to portray the image of science that prevails in the order paradigm. There we abandoned for a period the broader puzzle of society to focus on the narrower topic of the family. According to Auguste Comte (whose sociology bears little relationship to modern neopositivism), male dominance can be found in all societies and is hence an expression of scientific law. At that time we were not really interested in Comte's work on the family because he did very little of it. The purpose was rather to demonstrate how a small slice of his point of view demonstrates a search for lawful relationships.

Now let us turn to another sociologist whose work (unlike Comte's) has had great impact on the field. Max Weber was also disinterested in a formal study of the family. However, we can pull from his writings a few remarks that demonstrate his assumptions about the way in which explanations should be drawn. As a bonus, the following passages also deal with the theoretical idea of the "status group." This concept was crucial for Weber and for later pluralist theory. As we shall discover in the following chapter, it is quite consistent with the imagery of society drawn by Jean-Jacques Rousseau.

> . . . submission to fashion also exists among men in America to a degree un-known in Germany. . . . This submission decides . . . that he will be treated as a gentleman . . . such is important for his employment chances in "swank" estab-lishments, and above all, for social intercourse and marriage with "esteemed" families. . . . Within a status circle there is the question of intermarriage: the interest of the families in the monopolization of potential bridegrooms is at least of equal importance and is parallel to the interest in the monopolization of daughters. The daughters of the circle must be provided for. (Weber, in Miller, 1967: 50, 53)

From this passage, we can draw some insight on how Max Weber ap-proached the task of theoretical explanation. In his discussion of fashion and marriage, this theorist *interpreted* how status circles confer upon their members (or would-be members) ideas of "correct behavior." He held that submitting to the dictates of fashion in a rather slavish manner was to do the "right thing." Yet this was not a *universal pattern*. Weber knew that the status honor born of old and established family ties was not found in the United States as in Europe. Hence would-be gentlemen without titles or respectable "old family" standing could only demonstrate their status through a code of rigid behavior, including appropriate manners, a style of dress, belonging to the right clubs, attending the proper schools, and so forth.

Now it might be interesting to note that dressing for success has not passed from the scene, especially in the offices of corporate America. But be-fore we are lost in fashion let us examine Weber's second point. In order to en-hance the standing of the status group, a form of *endogamy* was practiced. Thus, insisting that members marry within the group was a means of restrict-ing access and maintaining the honor that comes with exclusivity. In Weber's day, it was quite common to find newly rich American families seeking to marry off their sons and daughters to members of the European nobility.

Weber would argue today that fraternities and sororities, country clubs, and the Daughters of the American Revolution also represent status groups. They too would seek to enhance the honor of belonging to them through maintaining some sense of exclusivity. However, whether then or now, the con-ception of the status group is central to the Weberian tradition. It is one means by which the differentiation of society is analyzed. While the family unit is somewhat tangential to Weber's sociology, he used it here to illustrate a broader point: Status groups representing varying degrees of social honor form a part of what we have termed the pluralist society.

Let us return to the central issue: Weber's conception of human science. If we examine his work carefully we will note that he approached sociology in both a historical and comparative manner. This is not as evident in the brief passage above as it is in the broader scope of his work. But even here we see references to how American status groups operate. In addition, the role of fashion in this country is compared to German society. Elsewhere in Weber's sociology, he sought to explain the social, political, religious, educational, and economic organization of society through a careful study of history.

Yet it is the *way* in which Weber approached his subject matter that interests us. He built his theory of status groups (and indeed his entire theoretical structure) by a distinctive method of interpretation. Weberian sociology is distinctive by reason of its style of inquiry and its focus on the world of ideas (idealism). In his attempt to understand the social relationship, Weber sought to *reduce history to the mind of individual actors*. In other words, through getting inside the subjective world of meaning, he hoped to understand how people both interpret and construct the institutions, patterns, and customs that constitute the social reality. More simply put, Weber approached history by means of *experiments of the imagination*.

Weber was not interested in behavior per se but in social conduct. By *conduct* he meant that behavior to which the actor attaches subjective meaning while orienting it to the conduct of others. This attempt to comprehend the social relationship through "getting inside" is commonly known in the discipline as *verstehen* (understanding). When combined with a command of both the events and ideas of history, Weber had a powerful system by which to explain the social world.

Later we shall examine one of Weber's more important works in which he sought to explain the impact of religious ideas on the development of the capitalist economic system. At that point we shall see that he interpreted the behavior of entrepreneurs by posing an implicit question: How would a person holding certain religious convictions (the Protestant work ethic) behave in an economic sense? More specifically, how would people sharing such beliefs orient their behavior toward one another, and what sort of economic system would they construct through their social action? As Weber could not talk with historical figures long dead, he sought to infer their motivations by asking himself how they would respond to the dominant ideas of their era.

Following this line of reasoning, we might note that Weber made no claim to have personally observed or interviewed the American nouveau riche, who are the subject of the preceding passage. How was he then able to explain such "status circles"? Weber did not tell us but his work does. One implicit question is: How would young men seeking to acquire or maintain a reputation as gentlemen behave in the absence of a clearly established hereditary nobility? The explicit answer is: through a slavish conformity to fashion. A second hidden inquiry is: How can members of a status group maintain their honor? And once again, one answer is quite clearly stated: through requiring that offspring marry within the group.

Throughout his sociology, Max Weber was to develop systems of explanation that remained constant to the Kantian image of human nature. Remember that Kant emphasized the importance of consciousness and meaning to the human existence and installed appearances or phenomena as the subject matter of the sciences. Weber also came to give the world of ideas preeminence over the world of objective events. Stated simply, this philosophy (idealism) holds that any object "out there" is only a perception, a reflection, or a concept that takes shape in the human mind. *A human science therefore must seek to know how people define conditions, events, and things. It follows that ideas about things are more important than the things themselves.*

Two other assumptions about the nature of sociological science can also be attributed to Max Weber. The first has to do with the importance of classification. Weber attempted to systematize his ideas and advance his explanations through clarifying and categorizing major analytic and descriptive terms. We shall examine a number of these at a later time. However, the ideal type represents an example of Weber's use of classification to construct theory. Earlier we defined the ideal type as a clear form or category that "purifies" important aspects of the social world. For example, Weber identified ideal types of authority (traditional, charismatic, and legal-rational). These types do not exist in unadulterated form in the real world, but through identifying ideal properties, we can better analyze the social bases of the right to command (see Chapter 10).

Weber's image of science included another important dimension, a separation of personal evaluations from logical and empirical truth. Commonly referred to as a value-free sociology or ethical neutrality, this approach attempts to place judgments about what *ought to be* apart from *what is*. (Modern positivism appears to bear Weber's legacy in this respect even more than contemporary pluralist sociology.) However, his version of ethical neutrality was not intended to mean that a scientist should not have to worry about the nature or consequences of his or her work. Weber was instead seeking to distance sociology from the ghosts of people like Comte, Spencer, and Marx. These he viewed as more prophets and polemicists than sociologists.

Modern conflict theorists, joined by more than a few pluralists, mounted an attack on the notion of value-free sociology in the 1960s. They complained that the values sociology is supposed to be free of are typically only those that question the existing order. The argument that ethical neutrality is a guise for conservative politics continues today as a point of controversy. However, the idea that Weber was simply seeking to defend a pure science or wrap himself in the German flag is beside the point.

As we have demonstrated for theories of order, explanatory systems do have ideological properties. When a theory addresses the functional unity of society, change is conceived as a threat to the system. This position has obvious political implications irrespective of what one might believe about one's personal politics.

While all would agree with Weber that values are no substitute for good logic and relevant evidence, that position really does not address the controversy. The question is not one of conscious, personal bias but rather the ideological implications of one's assumptions. In other words, ideas about what is good science (or bad), as well as the nature of human being or society, are inherent in the paradigms on which theory is founded. Thus, at the very least, the sociologist's assumptions may predispose him or her toward certain issues and close off others. For example, if one assumes that a society is founded on consensus, one will not construct a theory that prominently features a ruling class.

How then can we resolve the controversy? While human thought, including sociology, cannot break free of assumptions, human beings can recognize their nature. It is in this sense that "value-free" sociology can be criticized as unobtainable, yet found useful in enhancing a more mature and reflective discipline.

## Symbolic Interaction

Pluralist assumptions on the nature of sociological theory do not end with the work of Max Weber. Despite his emphasis on the world of ideas and the interpretation of history from the vantage point of the actor, Weber focused on the larger questions of social order. In other words, though Weber stressed the importance of the subjective world, he did not develop a micro-level social psychology. Later American sociologists were to assume a philosophy of science founded in idealism. However, they broke with Weber's interest in such large-scale concerns as religion, the economy, and power politics. Their theory featured a smaller and intimate world that sought the explanation of society in the processes of interpersonal action.

Let us return to our example of the family. The following excerpt shows quite clearly how a focus on the world of human consciousness need not be limited to the historical problems of interest to Weber.

> A congenial family life is the immemorial type of group unity, and the source of many of the terms—such as brotherhood, kindness, and the like—which describe it. The members become merged by intimate association into a whole, wherein each age and sex participates in its own way. Each lives in imaginative contact with the minds of others, and finds in them the dwelling-place of his social self, of his affections, ambitions, resentments, and standards of right and wrong. (Cooley, Angell, and Can, 1933: 61)

Charles Horton Cooley, the author of the above quotation, was an early and influential exponent of a tradition in sociology later termed *symbolic interaction*. Certain of the properties that distinguish this theoretical system can be gleaned from a careful examination of his form of interpretative sociology. For

Cooley and others, social life revolves around two circles of influence: primary and secondary groups. Secondary associations represent the influence on personal development from such sources as crowds, communities, corporations, and nations. However, the more important human groupings are typically small and intimate and represent some sense of permanence. Examples include the "home, spontaneous play group, and the old fashioned neighborhood" (Cooley et al., 1933: 210).

This distinction is quite simple. Nevertheless, it is crucial to our understanding of the pluralist conception of the nature of human science. Notice that groups for Cooley and his colleagues are categorized on the basis of their proximity in time, space, and social influence to the individual. Thus, Cooley and those who follow his lead turn the Weberian interest in broader societal issues on end. Simply put, while Weber was concerned with the actor on the stage of history, Cooley's play was a much smaller production.

Symbolic interaction is a body of ideas and specialized analytical tools that focus on an *intimate interpretation* of social relationships. Its major concepts center on the process by which a person explores and discovers the distinctive nature of his or her own mind while also relating to the world of others who share a common social space. This system attempts explanation through pointing out the importance of images, signs, and representations to human interaction. This is to say that people share with others a universe of abstract symbols. These symbols stand in for both the subjective world of thought and feeling and the objective world of concrete things. Of course, the clearest example of a symbolic system is language. However, nonverbal symbols such as gestures, body position, voice inflection, glances, and so forth may convey subtle but powerful meaning as well.

Consistent with the visions of human and societal nature discussed earlier in this chapter, interactionists seek to understand the intimate social relationship through an analysis of *self-consciousness*. The ability to stand as somehow separate, not only from the surrounding environment but even from one's own body and sensations, is unique to the species. For example, we have the ability to transform who we are into an object of study. Thus we consider "self" as a distinctive entity. We learn through association with others and through the experience of events to endow our person with an identity, a character, and a sense of being.

Not only does the self grow and acquire meaning through social interaction; this measure of our person can be placed in time. Accordingly, we have a sense of the past, present, and future. Social being becomes in part a matter of what we have been, what we are now, and what we plan to be tomorrow. When combined with an active and purposeful image of human nature, the "self in time" concept means that we can reflect on the past and build our future. More concretely, we can establish goals and shape our behavior toward those objectives. As interaction has no end in life, so the self is in a constant process of becoming.

Crucial to interactionist theory is the concept of *social reality*. Two essential features distinguish this sociological approach to what is real. One has to do with the origin of all social relationships, including society. The second addresses the role played by social definitions in decisions about what is authentic, actual, and true.

In the first regard, interactionist theory explains a reality that is socially *constructed*. This means that through purposeful encounters with others, relationships are constantly formed, shaped, and changed. Society, as a network of social relationships, is thus conceived as a process, not a product. As to the second feature, the social reality we construct is in essence a matter of *definition*. This means that there is no truth apart from the meaning attached to phenomena by the actors on the social stage. An example of a socially defined reality is found by one sociologist in witchcraft.

Do witches exist? An interactionist would argue that they were real in the mind of the religious members of the Massachusetts Bay Colony. As such they found a place of prominence in the world of the Puritans, often with tragic consequences.

> Ann Cole had once been "a person of serious piety" . . . but one day she was "taken with very strange fits" and began to perform remarkable feats like speaking in Dutch, a language she presumably did not know. When her fits had abated, she admitted that she had made a covenant with the Devil and had sealed the bargain by permitting him to have "frequent carnal knowledge of her." It goes without saying that Mrs. Cole was promptly hanged. (Erikson, 1966: 194)[4]

Now interactionists do not necessarily believe in the objective existence of witches or witchcraft. However, that is quite beside the point. The Puritans had constructed a social reality in which the definition of witchcraft played a central role. And the only way to understand that reality is to enter it on its own terms. Or in a play on the dictum of W. I. Thomas (see Chapter 12), if the Puritans defined witchcraft as real, it was real in its consequences.

As we shall examine in some detail in Chapter 12, sociologists at the University of Chicago in the 1920s and 1930s established the groundwork for symbolic interaction. Given what we have stated thus far, it should come as no surprise to find that they were seriously at odds with other conceptions of science. Their emphasis on subjective definitions separated them from the philosophical movement of neopositivism. And as that movement represented well the philosophy of the natural sciences, the estrangement of the interactionists from the scientific community was severe. Perhaps most controversial was their rejection of *determinism* and thus the abandonment of the search for social *laws*.

During this period, interactionists also took issue with the prevailing ex-

---

[4] While Erikson's work has interactionist implications, he owes a major debt to Durkheim. Simply put, he argued that witch trials identified the deviants in a theocratic society. This served the function of normative "boundary maintenance" for the Massachusetts Bay Colony.

planations of behavior offered up by psychological behaviorism and biological instinctivism. These systems of thought were found wanting because both denied the supremely social nature of human conduct. The first transformed the person into a mere set of responses to environmental stimuli. The latter made human behavior into an essentially unlearned and reflexive form of automatic conduct.

The interactionists argued that there was more to the richness and often unpredictable nature of human conduct than could be accounted for by instinct and reinforcement. While respecting the role of environmental forces, these scholars chose to theoretically embrace a decidedly antideterminist view. For them, what people are and do could not be understood as an unvarying consequence of external societal, cultural, or psychological forces. Nor could a satisfactory explanation be found in innate biological impulses. Instead, human actors bring a decidedly willful and creative interpretation to the parts they play. There remain too many variations in human interaction, too great a place for interpretation and deviation for social behavior to be simply dismissed as passive and imprisoned (Blumer, 1966). Thus, while the determinists embraced causation, predictability, and order, interactionists celebrated volition, creativity, and change.

In summary, the interactionist conception of science foreshadows a theoretical structure equipped to explain through entering the subjective world of meaning. That world is formed through interpersonal conduct in a typically intimate setting. Or more formally, interactionist theory frequently takes shape as a microsociological system of thought operating at a low level of abstraction. Thus, the purpose of human theoretical science is to explain a society as a web of interacting members who share a common world of symbols by which they interpret the "world out there."

In effect, sociology must show how society is created from the inside out. Given this mission, the determinism, quest for certainty, and focus on objective variables are left to positive science. In this softer side of theory, interactionists argue that major concepts can only guide or direct us toward an enriched sense of understanding. Consider our often-used phrase, human science. While various positive theorists would choose to italicize *science,* interactionists would underscore *human.*

# ■ Assumptions of the Pluralist Paradigm

Putting Weber and the American interactionists aside for a moment, it is now possible to present the major assumptions of the pluralist paradigm. Taken as a whole, this model presents its own distinctive assumptions about human nature, the nature of society, and the nature of human science.

*Human Nature*

1. The interactionist conception of human nature is a strongly intimate one. There is great emphasis on the *private world* of the actor (Bendix, 1977: 1–10).

2. Human behavior is assumed to be *intentional and voluntary*. This does not mean that there are no outside influences. For example, we may play one role in the presence of one person and yet another role when we are with somebody else. Still, the pluralist would argue that external conditions do not simply determine our behavior. In a basic sense, people know what they are doing. We act with purpose and our conduct reflects a contemplated design (Berger, 1963: 125–126).

3. As can be gleaned from the thought of Rousseau, *freedom* and a sociopolitical system that ensures it will be crucial for pluralist theory. However, for Rousseau and many pluralist thinkers, this freedom is primarily individual and personal rather than collective. Thus, members of society remain sovereign parties to the social contract. The right of the person to speak her mind, or to be all she can be, is an example of personal freedom. The concept of collective freedom (more in keeping with the conflict paradigm) stresses the welfare of the whole. For example, freedom does not exist unless all are free from want.

4. Human nature reflects an abiding dualism; it is both sociable and self-assertive.

*Nature of Society*

1. Society ultimately is a social reality, a state of consciousness based on the shared ideas and meanings of its members. Thus, society does not exist outside but rather *inside*. Its essence is the subjective world of definitions and perceptions that we create through contact with others.

2. The cornerstone of a society is reciprocity—not in the sense of the sharing of rewards stressed by theories of social exchange but in the sense of orientation to others. If each member of a group behaves on the basis of what others are thought to be doing or thinking, the relationship is reciprocal (Freund, 1969: 118–123).

3. The meaning of reciprocal relationships, symbols, and conceptions of self must be understood as part of a bigger picture. Failure to achieve this leaves the study of human conduct at a psychological level. For example, while human beings create culture, they do not *recreate* it from scratch each time they interact. Guidance is provided by larger patterns of meaning such as customs, laws, and ideas. This point was driven home by Max Weber when he held that Protestant ideals are crucial to understanding the motivations for enterpreneurial behavior.

4. The broader institutional patterns of a society (such as the state, religion, education, the economy, the family) can best be conceived as an *organization of roles* that are interpreted and shaped by human action.

Order and conflict sociologists also employ the concept of role. However, they are more deterministic than the pluralists. While interactionists understand that roles are not invented anew by each member of a society, they would stress that role content varies and is subject to reinterpretation. Hence, what it means to be a woman can be redefined over time.

5. People do not share the same world of meanings. The pluralist view is one of a heterogeneous society representing perhaps many cultures and certainly more than a few interest groups. Though members of most groups will share the most important meanings that hold a society together, they may disagree on customs and the choice of life-style. Also, not all groups will have the same influence or power.

It is crucial to note that pluralist theories do not assume a conflict of classes in society (at least not to the extent that the conflict tradition does). Nor do they embrace the value consensus of the order paradigm. The pluralist vision of society is rather one of the ongoing opposition of *interest groups* and the *clash of cultures*. Tolerance and diversity are embraced, and forms of social control such as law are viewed with ambivalence. On the one side, law can be an instrument of arbitrary state power and the means by which the interests of dominant groups (not a dominant class) are advanced. On the other side, law, when it is the expression of a freely developed social contract, can be the means of reform.

6. This vision of ambivalence toward the law is quite consistent with the larger pluralist vision. The nature of society is one of an abiding dualism, an *antagonistic cooperation*. At one level we see the rise and fall of competing interests and the battle of organizations. At another level we find a general commitment to the order born of the social contract. One faction, no matter how influential for the historical moment, does not realize total and continuous control. It is checked by countervailing organizations and the sovereign right of people to dissolve their covenants, if the state persists in the unjust support of one group over others. Thus, the idealized pluralist portrait is one of a *balance of power,* where force is checked by force, and tyranny is eliminated by means of the covenant.

### The Nature of Science

1. The truly distinctive thing about people and their relationships evolves from their ability to think, to create a world of ideas and attach meaning to human conduct. Thus, for the pluralist paradigm, the philosophy of idealism is the basis for human science. Put simply, no object has meaning apart from a perceiving mind. The "stuff" of theory, its major concepts and logical linkages, must conform to this subjective imperative.

2. Human action has a strongly *unpredictable* quality to it. Thus, the explanations and methods of social science cannot be founded on concepts such as determinism, laws, or even statistical probability. Theories based on the pluralist paradigm ordinarily seek to explain the multiple realities of the social world (Freund, 1969: 37–47). However, this does not mean that pluralists habitually reject any sort of scientific generalization.

As a case in point, Weber distinctly rejected both nomothetic and idiographic conceptions of history. Whereas the former holds that the course of history follows general laws (cycles, linear progress, dialectical change), the latter conceives of history as unique and specific events. For example, the nomothetic approach would seek to find the general law or laws underlying all revolutions. On the other hand, the idiographic method would center on one unique case such as the Chinese Revolution.

Weber believed that similar events may share common analytic properties and that these together form an ideal type. Thus, he sought to resolve the nomothetic/idiographic controversy by arguing that phenomena are not unique but representative of such general analytic categories. Hence, the understanding of a specific phenomenon (such as the Chinese Revolution) is possible only if referred to the larger classification (such as all revolutions). Weber's use of the ideal type constitutes a kind of generalization. However, this remains quite apart from the quest for laws.

3. The primary unit of sociological investigation is the individual. The target of theory (and research) is consciousness, and consciousness is a property of the person (Freund, 1969: 112).

4. Sociological theory will not answer the question why in an absolute fashion. Nor will theory be constructed to valiantly resist falsification. Systems of thought will enhance our understanding of interpersonal action and the social construction of reality. This will be done through the discovery of ideas that heighten our awareness of how social actors interpret and make the empirical world about them. Given this assumption, it follows that pluralist theories will give rise to qualitative rather than quantitative research.

The paradigmatic elements, assumptions, and ideal types that together comprise the pluralist paradigm are outlined in schematic form in Figure 9.1.

---

**Figure 9.1**   The Pluralist Paradigm

| PARADIGMATIC ELEMENTS | ASSUMPTIONS | IDEAL TYPES |
|---|---|---|
| Image of human nature | Intentional, active, voluntary, rational | Kant's consciousness |
| Image of society | Antagonistic cooperation, state of mind, shared meanings, constructed from the inside out | Rousseau's social contract |
| Image of science | Philosophical idealism, unpredictability of human action, "getting inside," qualitative | Weber's *verstehen* |

# ■ *Bibliography*

Beck, Lewis White
1969        *Early German Philosophy: Kant and His Predecessors.* Cambridge, Mass.: Harvard University Press.

Bendix, Reinhard
1977        *Max Weber.* Berkeley: University of California Press.

Berger, Peter
1963        *Invitation to Sociology.* Garden City, N.Y.: Doubleday.

Blumer, Herbert
1966        "Sociological Implications of the Thought of George Herbert Mead." *American Journal of Sociology* 71:535–548.

Cassirer, Ernst
(1932) 1963        *The Quest of Jean-Jacques Rousseau.* Translated and edited by Peter Gay. Bloomington: University of Indiana Press.
1981        *Kant's Life and Thought.* Translated by James Haden. New Haven, Conn.: Yale University Press.

Cooley, Charles H., Robert C. Angell, and Lowell J. Can
1933        *Introductory Sociology.* New York: Charles Scribner's Sons.

Erikson, Kai T.
1966        *Wayward Puritans: A Study in the Sociology of Deviance.* New York: John Wiley & Sons.

Freund, Julian
1969        *The Sociology of Max Weber.* New York: Random House.

Kant, Immanuel
(1781) 1950        *Immanuel Kant's Critique of Pure Reason.* Translated by N. K. Smith. New York: Humanities Press.
(1783) 1951        *Prolegomena to Any Future Metaphysics.* New York: Liberal Arts.
(1784–1795) 1891  *Kant's Principles of Politics, Including His Essay "On Perpetual Peace."* Edited and translated by W. Hastie. Edinburgh: Clark.
(1788) 1949        *Critique of Practical Reason and Other Writings in Moral Philosophy.* Translated and edited by Lewis White Beck. Chicago: University of Chicago Press.
(1790) 1957        *The Critique of Judgment.* Translated by James Creed Meredith. Oxford, England: Clarendon Press.

Miller, S. M. (Ed.)
1967        *Max Weber.* New York: Thomas Y. Crowell.

Rousseau, Jean-Jacques
(1750–1755) 1964  *The First and Second Discourses.* Edited by Roger D. and Judith R. Masters. New York: St. Martin's Press.

(1762) 1961        *The Social Contract.* London: Dent.
1962              *Political Writings.* 2 vols. Edited by C. V. Vaughn. New York: John Wiley & Sons.

Zeitlin, Irving
1968              *Ideology and the Development of Sociological Theory.* Englewood Cliffs, N.J.: Prentice-Hall.

# CHAPTER 10

# ■ Divergent Interests

Guided by an understanding of the assumptions that comprise the pluralist paradigm, we turn to the first group of theories that reflect this imagery. The major figures to follow present their explanations of the distinctive puzzles of meaning, social action, and divergent interests. While all pluralists are concerned with how human beings define and shape their social world, the scope of that universe varies greatly. The two Europeans analyzed in this chapter are considered together because their work constitutes a point of departure for the major theoretical tributaries of the paradigm. The first is Max Weber, whose insistence that sociology is properly concerned with individuals often gave way to a historical and comparative sociology. The second is Georg Simmel, whose work greatly informed the American sociologists at the University of Chicago who laid the groundwork for symbolic interaction.

## ■ Max Weber (1864–1920): Religion and Power

Max Weber[1] was born in 1864 in the Germany of Otto von Bismarck. He was the son of a devoutly religious mother and a father trained in law who came to occupy a somewhat important political position. For the first 29 years of his life, Weber lived primarily at home, which became a gathering place for noted

---

[1] Biographical and historical materials relating to the sociology of Max Weber, unless otherwise noted, are synthesized from the books of Bendix (1977), Freund (1969), and Coser (1977).

politicians and intellectuals. He attended the universities of Heidelberg, Berlin, and Göttingen before passing his examination in law in 1886.

## History and Biography

Calvinist theology, with its stern emphasis on piety, self-denial, and a strong sense of duty, was an important influence in the lives of Weber's maternal ancestors. Both his mother and sister took their religious heritage seriously. The young Weber was to witness Protestant precepts put into action at home. While these experiences did not make of him a true believer, he was later to develop a strong scholarly interest in the social and historical nature of religion. On the paternal side, Weber's father replaced the asceticism of Protestant dogma with a taste for material indulgence. His was a bureaucratic state of mind, exhibiting a taste for order, rational authority, and a reluctance to criticize the status quo.

In 1889 Weber received his Ph.D. from the University of Berlin, defending his thesis entitled *A Contribution to the History of Medieval Business Organizations*. This effort represented a formal signal of an enduring interest in the economic organization of society. In it he examined the legal principles that dictated how the profits and risks of a business are shared by joint owners.

Subsequently, Weber worked at a frantic pace, engaged both as a lecturer at the University of Berlin and as a lawyer. He suffered a collapse in 1897, one year after assuming a professorship at the University of Heidelberg and shortly following the death of his father. He recovered well enough to visit the United States in 1904 and read a paper at a scholarly meeting held in conjunction with the World's Fair at St. Louis, Missouri. Weber was strongly impressed with what he interpreted as Protestant virtues at work in the economic life of the American people. Back at Heidelberg in 1905, he published perhaps his best known work: *The Protestant Ethic and the Spirit of Capitalism* (1930, originally published 1904–1905), which we shall examine at a later point.

Weber's prodigious scholarly output continued through the first decade of the twentieth century and into the second. During this period he helped found the German Sociological Society (1910) and published his work on several world religions. With the onset of the First World War in 1914, he volunteered for service. Given his history of poor health, Weber was not assigned a combat role but was placed instead in charge of hospitals in the Heidelberg area.

A strong nationalist, Weber at first supported the war though he later openly criticized the German leadership. He continued a vigorous pace after the conflict, combining renewed scholarship in the sociology of religion with varied political activities. He contributed to the writing of a new German constitution, wrote newspaper articles, and spoke to student and academic groups on social reform. His major work *Economy and Society* (1968, originally published 1922) was unfinished at the time of his death on June 14, 1920.

Weber's personal biography cannot be separated from the broader events of history. He lived during an era that saw the unification of Germany under Bismarck, a leader who ruled by means of a synthesis of militarism, autocratic state power, and a system of social insurance. The last program offered some support to the working class in the event of sickness, accident, or old age, thus undercutting the German socialist movement.[2]

Weber's era gave evidence of the growth of state power in other ways. He witnessed an expanding bureaucracy with its administrative units and civil service system (even university professors were civil servants). He saw the continuing rise of industrial capitalism with its growing technology, specialized division of labor, and clear chain of command. This growth of the industrial economy and the formalization of state power signaled the weakening of the influential landowning class (the Junkers) and their claim to aristocratic privilege. In their stead came a newly rich industrial elite. Simultaneously, the burgeoning factory system was busily transforming rural agriculture laborers into an urban working class. Finally, Weber's historical epoch was marked by the rivalry and conflict of the great European powers, culminating as we noted earlier in the devastation of World War I.

## Assumptions

History consists not simply of material events but of the stream of ideas. Weber's period was a high point in the massive German intellectual tradition. Historical scholarship in particular was impressive, investigating at length the great differences among the ideas and values of different people. This continuing inquiry into the role of human consciousness and the place of ideas in the behavior of historical actors shaped the knowledge of the day, including the theoretical system of Max Weber.

As noted in Chapter 9, this interest in the world of ideas did not emerge during Weber's era. Perhaps the most influential philosopher of the eighteenth century, Immanuel Kant argued that human being is more than a matter of a physical body inhabiting a material world. It is also embodied in a spiritual/mental nature existing in a world of ideas. For Kant's intellectual heirs, then, the mind is not subject to the laws that govern the natural universe. Rather, human action is purposive, willful, and not simply "caused" by outside forces. It follows therefore that the methods of the natural sciences cannot be used to understand social behavior and human society. This splitting of natural and social science is especially clear in the work of the historian Wilhelm Dilthey (1833–1911). Taking a position that is clearly reflected in the work of Weber, Dilthey argued that to understand history is to first comprehend the meanings given to the social world by the historical actor.

---

[2] You may review the events of the Bismarckian era in our discussion of Ferdinand Toennies in Chapter 5.

The *historical idealism* that appears in the sociology of Weber and others was a logical outgrowth of the intellectual currents of the age. For those of this tradition, there was no inconsistency in conceptualizing such disciplines as sociology, history, and economics at what appears to be a micro level, while studying social institutions and organizations by means of historical research. Nevertheless, the blend of minded action and macroscale issues so crucial to Weber has not indelibly stamped all pluralist theory. For some modern pluralists, sociological theory and research have been directed along the lines of small-scale processes. (See especially Chapter 12.) For others, the Weberian interest in the higher order of society remains paramount.

## Theoretical Content

Max Weber's point of theoretical departure is thus twin born. It is also something else. The historical idealism that Weber brought to sociology separated his thought from that of his intellectual "antagonists at a distance" (Durkheim and Marx). While each had fundamentally different answers to the question of what makes a society possible, they both believed in a macrosociological reality. On the other hand, Weber's adherence to what he termed "individualist" methods constituted an attempt to eliminate all collectivist ideas from causal standing in sociology. He did not deny the reality of such things as groups and collectivities. It was his intention, however, to understand them as mere conglomerations of individuals (Weber, 1968: 8, 13).[3] Such a position clearly serves to distance Weber from both functionalism and class conflict as explanations of society.

For those who do not understand the Kantian legacy and the reverence for larger-scale historical issues among the historians of Weber's age, there is an abiding tension or inconsistency between his conception of the discipline and his choice of problems. On the one side, Weber seemed to be embracing individual meanings and motives. On the other, he wrote volumes on such topics as the bureaucratization of power, the forms of authority, and the class, party, and status divisions in society. His interest in religion was global, historical, and comparative, and one of his major works examined the relationship between the ideals of Protestantism and those of capitalism.

Weber's choice of problems has led some of his intellectual descendants to argue that he sought causal explanations at the level of social-structural conditions. Roth, a leading Weberian scholar, declared that the master's work on *Economy and Society* was an "empirical comparison of social structure and normative order in world-historical depth" (1968: xxvii). Given these interpreta-

---

[3] You might remember that the elimination of the collective was also an express desire of the behaviorist George Homans.

tions, yet another problem emerges. Those who focus purely on Weber's choice of issues may fail to comprehend the connection between his sociology and later narrowly drawn theories of the pluralist paradigm (such as symbolic interaction and phenomenology).

How then are we to resolve this dilemma? Given the apparent gap between definition of the field and the level at which he actually worked, perhaps we should conclude that Weber was simply forgetful. On the other hand, perhaps he had two heads, a kind of intellectual schizophrenia. Or perhaps there is truly *no* connection between Weber and other microsociological systems of thought. However, if we draw these conclusions, we will miss a very important point. In fact, we might miss Weber and the tradition of historical idealism altogether.

## SOCIOLOGY AND SOCIAL ACTION

Most misconceptions or incomplete understandings of Weber's work center on *what* he concluded (about religion, ideology, rationalism, authority, and so forth). What we should focus on is *how* he drew those conclusions. Now, Weber's scale is large, and his research is historical. However, he understood such structural and normative phenomena to be the products of the meaningful acts of individuals oriented, if you recall, toward the conduct of others. Let us return to his distinctive definition of sociology: "that science which aims at the interpretative understanding of social conduct (action) and thus at the explanation of its causes, its course, and its effect" (Weber, in Miller, 1967: 18).

The core concept in Weber's theoretical sociology is *social action.* Social action does not refer simply to behavior in groups. Action is social only under two related conditions. First, people draw subjective meaning from the ideas that prevail in their world of experience. Second, action acquires social meaning when the actor considers the behavior of others and is directed by their expectations. In other words, thought, cognition, and orientation to others are crucial to all forms of social conduct.

Given the foregoing, it should come as little surprise to find that Weber created an ideal typology of social action.[4] He began with *traditional action,* a form of conduct that can be best conceived as ritualistic obedience to prevailing customs. *Affectional action* refers to emotionally shaped behavior such as sexual gratification or aggression. Most important for Weber were *rational goal-oriented action* and *rational value-oriented action.* The latter refers to conduct that conforms to the political, religious, or other value convictions of the individual. Unlike traditional action, this type is not a blind response to custom. However, the purest form of rational action is that directed toward clearly defined objectives. It is identifiable by a weighing of possibilities and consequences. As we shall see, rational action is the cornerstone of Weberian thought.

---

[4] This explication of social action is drawn from Weber's *Basic Concepts in Sociology* (1962).

With some understanding of Weber's definition of sociology and his typology of social action to guide us, let us return to our original puzzle. Despite what his microsociological focus might suggest, Weber was not concerned with the interpersonal processes by which ideas and ideals are transmitted. Later interactionists, especially those from the University of Chicago, were to closely examine this social-psychological level. Weber instead used his conception of social action to explore history. Yet it was his belief that people made history, not the other way around. In other words, the past, present, and future course of human societies obey no internal laws that negate the role of reason.

The guiding question for Weber thus becomes clear: How do historical actors through these different types of social conduct make their societies and the various organizations or institutions? In seeking an answer, Weber imagined the inner world, and its specific powers of motive and interpretation. He concluded that although larger structural and systemic factors are operational, they cannot explain in and of themselves the puzzles of history. In order to understand this principle, let us turn to a specific example.

THE PROTESTANT ETHIC

In his monumental *The Protestant Ethic and the Spirit of Capitalism* (1930, originally published 1904–1905), Weber pursued his continuing debate with the ghost of Karl Marx. Marx had argued that religious values as well as other forms of culture follow major structural forces, chief among which is the economic mode of production. Particularly, Marx had held that the Protestant Reformation with its new reliance on individualism was a consequence of the rise of the capitalist system. Weber, through systematic comparative sociology, sought to demonstrate the inverse. He attempted to show that the presence or absence of a religious ethic (that of Protestantism) was the "cause" of a mature capitalism.

Weber's theoretical explanation of the rise of capitalism featured a historical study of the socioeconomic conditions that prevailed in China and India. He argued that taken as a whole, the purely structural, objective, and material conditions present in these still feudal societies should have been conducive to the rise of capitalism. However, the ethical systems of Confucianism and Taoism in China and Karma in India were not.

Confucianism teaches a reverence for the past, centering in worship of ancestors, a respect for literary as opposed to technical education, and the necessity of adjustment to the existing order. Taoism was likewise founded on traditional social action, and its teachings emphasize the realization of an inner state of harmony. The Hindu religion for its part teaches that behavior in one of the successive states of existence determines the fate of the soul in the next. Hence, the teaching of the "transmigration of souls" connects logically with a reverence for all life forms. However, the faith also embraces adherence to the unalterable caste system, position in which is determined by birth. If Weber were to employ contemporary language, he would argue that the prevailing religious systems in these societies are not "pro development." By a similar procedure, Weber attempted to show that Roman Catholicism also forestalled the rise of a mature capitalism.

In those nations of the West that had developed a mature capitalism, Weber detected a decidedly different ethical system. He argued that the ideals of Protestantism (exemplified in John Calvin's dark doctrines) favor and encourage the behaviors that built the capitalist system. Calvin taught that an ascetic life filled with hard work and prosperity is a mark of God's favor. He also taught that some souls are elected at birth for salvation, some others for damnation. For most, their religious destiny is in their own hands.

Now to this point it appears clear that Weber was attributing major explanatory power for the rise of an economic system to the religious factor. (He was careful to say this was not the only factor.) Others might say that his focus was cultural as well as historical and comparative. These concerns appear quite large in scale. What then has happened to his microsociology? How do individuals, the conscious mind, and especially rational social action fit into his theoretical system?

Let us recall two things about Weber's sociology. First of all, ideas such as those of Protestantism do not simply float around outside the person but are rather to be found within. Second, while Weber dealt with such apparently grand ideas as the Protestant ethic and the spirit of capitalism, there is something distinctive about his approach. Simply put, *he placed between Protestant doctrine and capitalist virtues the conscious, thoughtful, rational historical actor.* The contact point is the individual mind and the subjective meaning that it constructs.

Returning to the Protestant ethic we can now understand *how* Weber constructed his theory. Given that self-denial, toil, and prosperity are doctrinal imperatives; given also that some souls are doomed already; given further that material success is a measure of God's favor, how would rational believers calculating the foreseeable consequences of their actions conduct themselves? To answer these questions Weber projected himself inside the historical actor (*verstehen*). From this vantage point he explained the rise of capitalism. It was clear to him that the Protestant believer would work hard and acquire wealth (as long as it was not enjoyed). This might at least confirm to the prosperous ones that they were not doomed (else why would God waste favor?). Furthermore, wealth and self-denial could only translate into investment capital. The ethically correct businessperson would then rationally plow the money back into the business. As for those who labored, the virtuous worker would serve his or her employer dutifully.

We should be careful to understand Weber's theoretical line. The Protestant ethic here becomes a motivation for an economic order. *Therefore, early capitalism was at base a system of economically based, rational social action.* Capitalist behavior (entrepreneurial enterprise) acquired its spiritual meaning and therefore its being from Protestant virtues. Members of the Christian faith before the Reformation had been taught that poverty and suffering were signs of faith while the accumulation of wealth was met with suspicion. After all, Jesus of Nazareth had taught that it was easier for a camel to go through the eye of a needle than for a rich man to enter the kingdom of God. However, Protestantism offered a new interpretation. Prosperity was in. The Protestant God, it appears, was a capitalist.

One final word of caution is in order. Weber's problem has been to explain the *rise* of capitalism. This system once in place does not have to be recreated by every actor or by each succeeding generation. It becomes, in Weber's terms, "an immense cosmos" that mandates conformity on the part of those locked into a system of market relationships. For Weber, however, capitalism was not the evolutionary product of the societal organism as some nineteenth-century order theorists might have been compelled to argue. Nor was it the consequence of the dialectical forces of contradiction that Marx discerned. Capitalism was instead the rational product of the rational Western mind, provided ethical legitimation by a religion that measured piety in terms of hard work, prosperity, and asceticism.

LEGITIMACY AND AUTHORITY

If Weber's interest in religion reflected in part a maternal influence, perhaps his concern with forms of power and authority were in part a legacy from his father. Be that as it may, his inquiry into the puzzles of political sociology continue to inform modern thought.

Weber defined power rather simply as "the possibility of imposing one's will upon the behavior of other persons" (1954: 323). He saw power as permeating social relationships. However, Weber held that forms of social influence are distinctive by virtue of their source. For example, one important type of power comes from the mutuality of interests between organizations and individuals who control resources and others who need them. While a powerful central bank can impose conditions for the granting of credit, other members of the banking system may not be forced to become debtors. If they do so, it is out of a sense of their own interests. However, Weber was not primarily interested in a conception of power based on the mutuality of interests. Instead, he focused on the established kinds of *authority* that legitimate both command and obedience (Bendix, 1977: 285–297).

Once again Weber employed the ideal type. His intention was not simply to identify the pure characteristics of authority as a tool or method of historical analysis. Rather, his purpose was to identify the differences in the social basis for power relationships. Weber was fascinated with the arrangements by which some ruled and others were ruled, some controlled and others submitted, some led and others followed even when obedience was neither willed nor self-serving. This emphasis on the social basis of authority is encapsulated in Weber's concept of legitimacy. By *legitimacy,* he meant that authority is not based simply on force and coercion, though these may play their part. The issue instead is the conversion of power into justifiable rule. In other words, why do people believe it to be their duty to submit to an often authoritarian domination?

For Weber, there were three pure types of legitimate authority.[5] The first involves command and obedience grounded in charisma. Weber defined *charisma* as "a certain quality of an individual personality by virtue of which he is set apart from ordinary men and treated as endowed with supernatural, superhuman, or at least specifically exceptional powers or qualities" (1967: 77). In this case, domination rests with those such as prophets, mystics, the shaman or magician. The evidence for charismatic authority may occasionally reside with certain signs, proofs, or miracles, but its *legitimacy* goes beyond such things. For true believers, it is grounded in a sense of mission or duty that sweeps away personal interest and individual sovereignty.

Under *traditional authority*, the grounds of legitimacy rest with a legacy of power. By this Weber meant that control is transmitted from one generation to another. Here, rule is not based on miracles or a sense of mission. Nor does it reside in the ability to convince and sway the masses. Rather, obedience is due the traditional position of those such as kings or chiefs. While rules may be a part of tradition, this mode of authority rests on loyalty to the person, not the ritual of laws and procedures. Those who wear the mantle of this pure type of command may be dependent on the past, but they are not its prisoners.

Weber's final type demonstrates again his infatuation with the calculating mind and the products of its creation in Western societies. Authority here is grounded on a *rational* basis exemplified by a system of laws. Under legal authority, those who rule retain legitimacy only insofar as they function politically in a lawful manner. In the Western nation-state, a legally constituted person or body (president, parliament, legislature) exercises authority through officials (bureaucrats, civil servants). Those subject to this form of domination might be termed citizens. They submit neither through a sense of mission and devotion nor through a reverence for tradition. They obey out of respect for rational law.

## THE BUREAUCRACY

Weber's identification with the rational-legal type of authority led him to examine the bureaucratic forms that often administer such rule. In his work, he related the rise of the bureaucracy to the technological growth of the industrial revolution. And the economic center for this revolution was Western capitalism. Why the rise of the bureaucracy? Because for Weber it represented the most rational and efficient means of meeting the needs of this complex and orderly economy.

The bureaucracy is an organization of official functions. It operates in ac-

---

[5] The following discussion is based on Weber's *Theory of Social and Economic Organization* (1957: 324–365, originally published 1922).

cordance with obligatory rules and regulations now called in the vernacular, "standard operating procedures." Every bureaucratic actor knows what is required in the way of job performance. However, this desire for an orderly process may give rise to an entanglement of regulations today termed "red tape." Most people have experienced problems at one time or another because their situation does not conform to bureaucratic rules.

The bureaucracy also reflects a specialized division of labor. Faced with the complexities of administration in the heterogeneous society, the rational drive toward efficiency compels the breaking up of tasks into smaller parts. People assigned to complete one specialized duty are not responsible for other facets; nor are they responsible for the whole. In contemporary parlance the operational phrase is "that's not my department."

The structure of the bureaucracy also evidences a hierarchy or a clear chain of command. Offices and duties are arranged accordingly. People working in this setting know who they are accountable to and what they are expected to do. However, supervisors in one area do not necessarily have authority in another. This is because bureaucratic authority is impersonal. It is founded on rules and obligations that are typically formalized in writing.

Weber also described distinguishing properties of bureaucratic work. He noted that such workers have supposedly demonstrated their competence and may be required to secure technical training to qualify for their position. Hence a principle of merit (often measured by experience and examination) is to replace judgments made on traditional or emotional grounds. However, bureaucrats own neither their positions nor the means of production. This means that such workers have no independent economic position apart from the organization. (Here Weber seemed to employ the Marxist analysis of the working class under capitalism to describe the bureaucracy.)

Despite Weber's conviction that the bureaucracy is indispensable in a rationally organized society, he viewed this form of legal authority with ambivalence. On the one hand, he considered it as essential to administration. On the other, Weber feared that the bureaucracy would come to "strangle opportunities for private profit" (Weber, in Bendix, 1977: 461). (Such concerns still are heard in capitalist societies long after Weber's death.) He also saw in the bureaucracy a clear and present danger to human freedom:

> It is horrible to think that the world could one day be filled with nothing but those little cogs, little men clinging to little jobs and striving toward bigger ones—a state of affairs which is to be seen once more . . . playing an ever-increasing part in the spirit of our present administrative system. . . . This passion for bureaucracy . . . is enough to drive one to despair. It is as if in politics . . . we were deliberately to become men who need "order" and nothing but order. (Weber, in Bendix, 1977: 464)

## CLASS, STATUS, AND PARTY

Max Weber's theoretical system includes a final important dimension. Given his interest in the social bases for authority, it should come as no surprise to find a strong interest in political and other forms of stratification. Somewhat consistent with Rousseau's societal imagery, and in opposition to that of Plato, Weber did not assume a consensual basis for existing social hierarchies. However, his thought was even more distant from the Marxist vision of class domination. Weber instead developed a triadic conception of inequality (1946: 180–195, originally published 1906–1924).

The first form of stratification is that of *economic inequality,* represented by the simultaneous existence of *classes* in society. For Weber, class meant a group of people sharing the same economic interests. He disagreed with Marx who had defined class in terms of relationship to the means of production (owning or working). For his part, Weber was interested in the economic component (defined in terms of goods and opportunities for income) and its causal relationship to life chances. Marx had argued that the exploitation of the worker under capitalism is structural. That is, it is built into the very organization of the system. However, for Weber the working class is distinctive by reason of its competitive disadvantage in the market.

Simply put, for Weber class situation is the same thing as market situation. This means that class position is a consequence of the goods or skills one might exchange for income. While Weber agreed with Marx that a major distinction can be drawn between those who hold property and those who do not, his emphasis was different. The issue was not the property system but the *unequal distribution of opportunity* within that system. Thus, there is a clear distinction between these two conceptions of class. The Weberian usage implicitly allows for the improvement of one's market situation (more goods, more pay for labor, etc.) and the subsequent improvement of life chances. (Workers, for example, may form unions or political parties in service of their interests.) This can be contrasted with Marx, who offered a devastating structural critique of the class order (see Chapter 15).

We should not conclude that Weber was a champion of the capitalist system and the sweeping rationalization on which it was founded. He was also clearly not a critic. He approached both capitalism and its rationalist base with a studied ambivalence. Rational social action emphasizes the calculation, the weighing of alternatives, and the abiding interest in predicting outcomes so evident in modern capitalist society. On the other hand, Weber held that its ascendance has introduced the widely experienced problems of bureaucratic despotism. For its part, the capitalist order yields advantages to the owners of property and converts such societies into markets where passion, enchantment, and personal loyalty have little place.

Yet, in the final analysis, Weber acceded to the relative merits of capitalism and the process of competition on which it is based. Socialism, he argued, will lead only to greater reliance on ever-growing numbers of bureaucrats, hence a stronger threat to purposive human action (1968: 220–225, originally published 1922). As to competition, Weber defined it as a "formally peaceful endeavor to obtain the power of disposition over opportunities which are coveted also by others" (1968: 26). Further, he held that competition is the basis for the growing rationalization of action and the selection of "superior personal qualities" (1962). While he had a dark view of the soulless Western world and its dominant economic forms, his vision of the future was blacker still. He was, with Hamlet, better fit to bear existing ills than flee to others unknown and uncharted.

Weber was not content to explain only the economic form of stratification. In his early studies of farm labor and the stock exchange in Germany, he developed the construct *status group*. By means of this he attempted to show the nature of *social inequality* based on rank or position. This conception was often used in German society to signify the social origins of marriage partners. It was the basis for making judgments that one or the other had married within or without his or her status "community," or perhaps beneath or above it. (Remember Weber's treatment of marriage and status in America from the preceding chapter.)

For this theorist, social position could be differentiated from either political power or economic control as the basis for inequality. Status groups form hierarchies based on honor, esteem, and a distinctive life-style. Weber used the concept to refer to such groups as the traditional land-owning aristocracy, the American nouveau riche, Jewish believers in a chosen people, or even farm workers and slaves, who enjoyed considerably less prestige.

Weber was still not through. His concern with authority led him to an examination of *political inequality*. The major analytic construct for this form of stratification is the *party*. This he conceived as group organization for the sake of influence. Parties, Weber argued, live "in a house of power." Now less we misunderstand, Weber did not refer merely to Democrats, Republicans, Liberals, Tories, and the like. Such are parties, of course, and they do exist in that house of power known as the state. However, such organizations may exist at any level where the purpose is to realize "their own will in a communal action even against the resistance of others who are participating in the action" (1946: 180, originally published 1906–1924). The actions of the party are typically planned and goal-directed, hence *rational*. Whether state power, or something less grandiose, the ability to force others to consent against their will may be valued for its own sake.

## Critique

Max Weber remains a striking figure in the discipline, representing, as Marx and Durkheim, one of sociology's holy (or unholy) trinity. The range of his interests, the uniqueness of his method, and the perceptiveness of his analysis marked not only his conceptual scheme but that of large numbers of later scholars. As always there remain points at issue, and the identification of these should improve our understanding.

We have coined the term *historical idealism* to clarify how Weber went about the construction of his theoretical system. While interesting, the combination of a comparative sociology and experiments of the mind introduces some problems. Simply put, the state of mind or consciousness (and the ensuing social action) that Weber sought to understand is not close at hand. His projection into the subjective world of action was over great expanses of time and space. This empathy at a distance magnifies the dilemma faced by all of those who seek to enter the conscious world of another. How can those with a certain temper of mind, a specific state of consciousness, alter that so as to see the world as others see it? In Weber's case, how could his rational mind fathom the impact of different idea systems on the motivations of such historical actors as the Chinese and followers of the Hindu religion?

We remarked earlier that Weber's thought has been typified as a debate with the ghost of Marx. It was also a rather clear repudiation of the specter of Émile Durkheim. Weber believed that society, values, and organizations are ultimately states of mind. While sharply at variance on most issues, Durkheim and Marx agreed on one thing. The social world represents a state of being. It has its own reality, independent of the definitions and perceptions of those abiding within. From these perspectives, Weber's sociology comes dangerously close to psychological explanation.

Weber's work has led some to observe that types of social action (such as rational/legal) become institutionalized in the form of such things as religious ideologies and bureaucratic structures. While there are macro-level issues and implications in his comparative approach, social actions remain narrowly focused and are not treated as independent of individual minds. As Julian Freund (1969: 19) argued, for example, Weber's rationality and other ideal types are the "by-product of the activity of a certain type of [person], who may or may not transmit it to the rest of humanity. More precisely, it relates to the meaning which those men attach to their activities." By means of such a vision, Weber defined his sociology as a search for motivational chains of explanation. Durkheim would no doubt have viewed Weber's methods as reductionist.

Weber's attempts to steer a course away from collectivist theories that rely on historical or societal determinism were clearly stated. He believed in neither the evolutionary laws of the organicists nor the revolutionary laws in theories of conflict. History is not the maker; it is made. This position, however, introduces a troublesome question, that of *historicism*. By this is meant the claim that all historical events are unique. They reflect no broader pattern and no regularities, and their properties cannot be generalized to like phenomena. Weber, you may recall, attempted to resolve this problem by means of the ideal type. He argued that what is true for one phenomenon is probably true for others of the same type. However, when history becomes an extension of the minds of its makers, it would appear to constantly shift, change, and reform. In sum, it becomes a series of unique experiences that do not conform to general laws. We can only conclude that generalization was less important for Weber than for theorists working in the order and conflict traditions.

A final set of criticisms concerns the ideological properties of Weber's theory. With Rousseau, he envisioned a society of competing interests where the delicate balance could be upset and reestablished by the actions of individuals, parties, classes, or status groups. This is a liberal view of social order at variance with the contrasting imagery of both consensus and coercion. Weber, however, held out little hope for reform. He understood the problems of the Western world but remained its prisoner. This is ironic because he ascribed great force and significance to the human mind but he did not trust its potential for good. Perhaps the ideological basis for his pessimism was a conviction that there is no exit from the existing order.

# ■ Georg Simmel (1858–1918): Forms, Types, and Interaction

The German philosopher and sociologist Georg Simmel juxtaposed, as did his contemporary Max Weber, a microsociological conception of the discipline with an interest in the larger domains of history, culture, and structure. He also held in common with Weber an aversion to the organicism of Comte and Spencer, though this particular critique did not emerge until his work matured. However, Simmel's theory is distinctive from Weber's in at least two important ways. First, the scope of Simmel's issues did not parallel the historical and comparative sweep of his colleague. Second, Simmel viewed society as a *web of interactions*. Such interactions among individuals come to represent patterned associations, the *forms* of which constitute the subject matter of sociology.

## History and Biography

Georg Simmel[6] was born a Berliner in 1858. His parents were Jewish, but his father became a Roman Catholic and his mother a Lutheran by faith. Simmel was baptized into the Lutheran church, but he later abandoned such beliefs while retaining an intellectual interest in religion. Fortunately for Simmel, his family was prosperous. His father, who had been a businessman, died leaving the young Simmel a substantial inheritance. He was never wealthy but managed to sustain himself even though denied a professorship until very late in his life.

Simmel studied at the University of Berlin, concentrating in history and philosophy. He received his doctorate in philosophy in 1881, defending a dissertation entitled *The Nature of Matter According to Kant's Physical Monadology*. This work won Simmel a prize and led to a subsequent work on Kantian phi-

---

[6]Important general references on Simmel and his times include Wolff, 1964; Coser, 1956; and Weingartner, 1962.

losophy, which met the requirements of his *habilitation*.[7] In 1885 he became a *Privatdozent* at Berlin, an unsalaried lecturer supported by student fees. Though somewhat an academic outcast then and throughout his later career, Simmel was distinguished as a lecturer and teacher. He offered classes in a broad range of topics, including philosophy, logic, and sociology, attracting a large following of students and intellectuals.

At the age of 43, Simmel was given an honorary professorship at the University of Berlin. While no longer a lowly lecturer, his rank still did not allow him to participate in the academic mainstream. This exclusion can be somewhat explained in terms of his partial break with the German intellectual tradition (evidenced in a frequent preoccupation with microsociology). However, the ugly visage of anti-Semitism also blighted his historical period. Despite his continuing rejection by the academic elite at Berlin, Simmel was not deterred from advancing his scholarship.

The eclecticism of Simmel most probably contributed to his disrepute. His work in sociology was sandwiched between more numerous publications in philosophy, and his career also featured a number of intellectual forays into the arts. Distinctive too was the breadth of the audience Simmel sought to reach. Many of his publications were to be found in nonscholarly sources. However, his contributions to the fledgling human science of sociology were significant and lasting. They earned him the open regard of Ferdinand Toennies and the esteem of Max Weber. Émile Durkheim published one of his pieces in *L'Année Sociologique*. Albion Small (the first editor of the *American Journal of Sociology* at the University of Chicago) did likewise with a number of Simmel's articles (1896, 1897–1898, 1902, 1904). And as we mentioned earlier, Simmel joined with Toennies and Weber in the founding of the German Sociological Society in 1910.

Simmel, perhaps more than Weber, represents the precise intellectual link between German idealist-based sociology and the symbolic interactionism that was to flourish at the University of Chicago under the primary direction of Robert Park. (We take up Park in Chapter 12.) This was only one aspect of an international reputation that saw many of his publications translated into other languages. Despite all of this Simmel remained an outsider until at the age of 56, he secured a full professorship at the University of Strassburg. The year, however, was 1914, and his students were to soon go to war. The defeat of Germany came four years later. So did the death of Georg Simmel, who died of cancer of the liver in 1918.

Simmel, like Weber and Toennies, matured during the era of Bismarck, who as you may recall was the chancellor of Germany under William I. A better understanding of the times may be had by reviewing the historical overview that prefaces the theoretical systems of Toennies and Weber. Our purposes here

---

[7] Habilitation in this specific sense refers to the requirements to be met by those who wish to be qualified to teach in German universities.

will be served by a brief foray into the major events and intellectual currents that informed the sociology of Simmel.

After the defeat of France in 1870 (see the historical preface to the sociology of Émile Durkheim in Chapter 5), Berlin as well as the newly unified German Reich underwent important economic, political, and social changes. Demographically, the nation witnessed both rapid population growth and the concomitant urbanization that comes with industrial and commercial development. In the early decades of the nineteenth century, some 80 percent of the German citizenry lived in rural areas. By the end of the century, the distribution was reversed. Now, some 80 percent lived in the cities.

The frenzied development of business, industry, and finance in Germany between 1870 and 1914 overtook and surpassed the French and the English before the outbreak of the First World War. Such a belated revolution brought into prominence a new bourgeoisie. However, the newly ascendant economic elite were not to seize immediate political control. While their interests were well represented in Parliament, the old Prussian aristocracy in concert with the landowning Junkers continued to hold the lion's share of state power. They exercised their influence through their positions in the court of the kaiser, but most especally in the chancellery of Bismarck. The political scenario in Simmel's Germany was therefore one of contradiction. Under Bismarck, insider power was authoritarian and vested in the hands of an old elite. This anachronistic state structure survived his dismissal in 1890. On the outside was the new capitalist class in charge of an industrial empire too easily turned to the ends of war.

The struggle for political representation left the growing working class disenfranchised. Their parties and unions were the subject of persecution and their right to vote severely limited. In the context of burgeoning industrial production and the growth of a centralized banking system, in the setting of the new authoritarian state, organized workers resisted their roles as cogs in the well-oiled machine that was the German Reich. Hence, a struggle of classes represented yet another form of opposition that marked the era of Simmel.

## Assumptions

Dominant ideas are also a part of the undercurrent of forces that shape formal systems of thought. Simmel's intellectual progenitors included others than the omnipresent Kant, though a modified form of this master's thought is indispensable for Simmel's theory. As we shall shortly see, Simmel approached sociology by means of a quasi-dialectic method. His tendency to center on the forces of opposition and repulsion in society must have been influenced by Marx and Hegel. However, we shall refer to Simmel's method as *dualistic* in order to clearly distinguish his conception of conflict from the class-based version in Marxist thought.

When Simmel argued that human nature is dualistic, he joined somewhat the imagery reflected in Rousseau's ambivalent vision of the essence of the species. Such dualism, he argued, is evident in all sociological relationships. Hence "concord, harmony, coefficacy, which are unquestionably held to be socializing forces, must nevertheless be interspersed with distance, competition, repulsion, in order to yield the actual configuration of society" (Simmel, 1964: 315). Simmel did not stop here. He went on to identify other forms of contention. Specifically, the organizational patterns of society remain vital only if they are disturbed by individualistic and irregular forces. At the interpersonal level, intimate relationships remain close only when there are periods of absence and distance. Even a "lie" in the form of restricting information about oneself to another may be the integrating basis for a social relationship.

This dualism is suggestive of conflict and contradiction. However, it is far removed from the dialectic forces that mark the structural world of conflict sociologists working in the Marxist tradition. Examine the foregoing examples closely. Although Simmel's focus was on the apparent clash of opposing forces, the consequences of such conflict are the purification and strengthening of ongoing relationships, whether at the societal or individual level. Unlike Marx, Simmel did not envision a material dialectic in which the conflict of classes produces a new social order.

However crucial the dualistic conception, the major intellectual influence for Simmel was Immanuel Kant. He agreed with Kant (and repudiated the empiricism so crucial to modern positivism) by holding that the world of experience has no inherent order. Rather, order and knowledge about it must be created by the mind. And if you recall, this created knowledge is shaped by a priori mental categories such as space and time. This analytical approach is the foundation for Simmel's later separation of *form* from *content* in sociology.

For Simmel, content could be any phenomena or experience. However, form refers to the pattern, the structure, or the organization given to the content by the human mind. For example, history is not merely a description of well-ordered events unfolding according to some natural law. The events and ideas of history acquire their being and their meaning from the historical actor. At another level, the historian also imparts form when he or she selectively creates the coherence of the historical record.

## Theoretical Content

For Simmel,[8] the science of sociology seeks explanation neither in individual action nor divine gift. He defined both the field and the scope of his theory

---

[8]Perhaps the best single volume containing the works of Simmel is that edited and translated by Kurt Wolff (Simmel, 1964). However, a quartet of *American Journal of Sociology* articles (1896, 1897–98, 1902, and 1904) also inform this review.

clearly: "If the concept of 'society' is taken in its most general sense, it refers to the psychological interaction among individual human beings" (1964: 9). Even transient interactions, should they become more intense and continue over time, build what is known as society. Finally, the ultimate structures that constitute the social order (such as the state, family, church, classes) are best conceived as "crystallized" interactions based on common interests. However, he argued, sociologists should not confine their inquiry to these "large social formations."

Simmel's microsociology is often reflected in his choice of issues. One of the clearest of these is his work on the "secret society." By means of this analysis, Simmel attempted to demonstrate that much of social interaction is based on incomplete information and distorted understanding. Because human beings do not fully know each other, we react and respond to fragments and cues. The work of Charles Horton Cooley and many contemporary interactionists to be reviewed in subsequent chapters closely complements Simmel's observations on the social meaning of "secrets."

Simmel also proposed that the distinctive analysis afforded by sociology allows the logical connection of seemingly different events. For example, Simmel argued that the study of contagion (specifically, the sweeping changes in mood) in a theater audience has implications for criminology. The individual in such a context may lose his or her ordinary values and restrictions of mood and be carried into forms of otherwise atypical behavior with no sense of regret or guilt. Likewise, members of a mass may perform criminal acts that transcend the individual's ordinary barriers of conscience (1964: 13–16).

INTERACTIVE PATTERNS AND
SOCIAL LAWS

Sociology, Simmel argued, is not a superscience subordinating the fields of history, economics, politics, anthropology, and psychology beneath it. However, the phenomena of concern to these disciplines are grounded in a "purely sociological structure." History, for example, is not the product of "great men" (a clear reference to Carlyle); nor is it subject to the laws of historical materialism (again, the apparition of Marx). Rather, historical changes reflect underlying changes in "sociological forms." In other words, the great movements and changes that mark the epochs of history follow transformations in the *elements* or atoms of society. These elements in their most basic sense are the ways individuals and groups behave one toward the other (Simmel, 1964: 16).

This theoretical aproach is crucial because it demonstrates clearly Simmel's conception of laws or regularities in history. He held that historical laws cannot be proven and in that sense whatever has happened in the life of a people can be considered unique. However, sociology is about *social* regularities that specify the recurring forms of interpersonal behavior. Such patterns are not bound by time or space; thus they do not vary with the specific conditions of history. Simmel's "comparative" analysis of history did not focus on the broad forces, movements, and ideals of great and sweeping epochs. He sought rather to contrast vastly different phenomena only to discover the common *processes* by which members through interaction make their social reality. Simmel did not share the positivist quest for the sociological equivalent of natural law. However, he did hold the conviction that the social forms that underlie history are everywhere the same.

It follows that while the content of social life reflects enormous variability, its forms of interaction are patterned, stable, and regular. Hence, even diverse groups share a consistency of such configurations. For example, whether one focuses on the family, the art school, a band of conspirators, or the state, all reflect such forms as superiority and subordination, competition, division of labor, and internal solidarity (1964: 21–23). Forms are never found in their ideal or pure state, however. Each societal relationship or structure is the setting for the coming together of a number of such patterns.

The most crucial of the forms conceived by Simmel reflects the patterns of superordination and subordination (1896: 167–189). By means of these he attempted to show that differentials in influence, power, and authority mark much of social life. Consistent with his approach, Simmel advanced an interpersonal explanation of the nuances of the superordinate-subordinate relationship. These include domination, authority, leadership, and even law. For example, Simmel argued that superordinates do not wish to simply determine the fate of subordinates. Rather, dominance is a case of interaction wherein the dominator is interested less in exploitation for material gain than in confirming his or her will and standing. This in turn presupposes that the dominated party has some freedom and worth, else the act of domination is without value.

Characteristically, Simmel proposed that authority is not merely one-sided coercion on the part of the superordinate. It is rather the *believer* in authority who in part transforms the ordinary into the extraordinary, who attaches an objective power to the elite personality. For Simmel, this process assumes a certain autonomy on the part of the subordinate. In like fashion, followers often define and control the nature of leadership. Hence, the master is slave and all leaders are led. And as for law, another type of the superordinate-subordinate relationship, the party in power does not behave in a purely unilateral sense. Simmel proposed that even the despot is bound by his or her decrees and that these edicts provide the basis for a claim on the part of the subject.

## ON THE SIGNIFICANCE OF GROUP SIZE

In this theoretical system, forms of interaction are heavily influenced if not determined by the size of the group. Simmel argued that numbers have great importance for social life. For example, socialism can only realize the principle of justice (in production and distribution) if the group is small. He believed with Durkheim that an increase in the size of the unit requires a complex division of labor and a resulting specialization. This in turn makes comparisons among individual achievements and awards extraordinarily difficult.

In a similar vein, Simmel reasoned that religious sects thrive only insofar as they remain small communities, isolated within a larger society that meets certain of their economic and political needs (such as trade and military protection). Paradoxically, the larger society provides the contrast (often assuming the form of persecution) by which sect solidarity increases. And in a last example of the importance of numbers, Simmel noted that the essence of the *aristocracy* is one of smallness (1964: 87–93).

Simmel's work on group size (1902) remains influential among modern sociologists who believe that crucial processes can be understood in two- or three-person groups. In a dyad (such as a monogamous marriage), the union of the two parties is complete, and secession by either party (as with death or divorce in marriage) would destroy the unit. Thus, the nature of this group is trivial (in the sociological sense, not necessarily in the estimation of its members). However, it is also intimate in that great meanings, even secrets, may be shared. Finally, it is the destiny of the dyad to cease to exist. Although there is some dependence here compared to the maximal freedom of the unattached individual, there is little more to the relationship than its members.

With the addition of a third party, group processes undergo a fundamental change. Relationships are no longer merely direct as in the dyad. Now they are also indirect. To explain, if two are participants, one is reduced to only a spectator or intruder. Two may form alliances against the one, or the third may mediate differences between the others or seek to divide them. Harmony is difficult if not impossible. In summary, relationships in the triad are intensified by the third member and come to represent great complexity. However, they also set the stage for hierarchy and authority. To demonstrate his point, Simmel cited a proverb: "He who has one child is his slave; he who has more is their master" (1964: 141).

Simmel envisioned a supremely pluralist image of society. He centered on the processes by which society is constructed from the always expanding web of interactions. From the formation of dyads to the crucial addition of the third party, ever larger groups emerge in history. These in turn often subdivide into competing parties operating under the maxim "Who is not for me is against me." With a growth in size come the inevitable forms of inclusion and exclusion. Despite these, Simmel believed that in this societal context of opposition, there "is opportunity for a plurality of party formations, for tolerance, for mediating parties, for a whole range of subtly graded modifications" (1964: 143). Yet when this pluralism gives way to the mass movement, the darker face of history is shown. Under these conditions, individuals are reduced to the lowest group denominator. They follow the leaders with extremist temperaments. Hence for Simmel, the mass is a radical and intolerant force (1964: 122–144).[9]

If Durkheim and the functionalists stressed the impact of society on the

---

[9]Here Simmel is in agreement with Le Bon, who advanced a negative view of mass behavior in *The Crowd*.

individual, then Simmel reversed the emphasis. Still, it is his conception of the processual nature of this and other social relationships that is distinctive. Simmel held what some describe as a dialectical approach to sociology. This is shown in a variety of positions. He argued that the growth of society diminishes the individual, and hence there is a basic tension between a social order and its members (1964: 58–64). He also postulated a basic antipathy between freedom and equality, a contradiction that can be resolved only if contending parties "are dragged down to the negative level of propertylessness and powerlessness" (1964: 66). Finally, when he turned to the institutional side of the social equation, he noted that industrialization is a simultaneous source of alienation and freedom. Despite this taste for dualism and opposition, Simmel's work is grounded more in a sociological relationism than a mature dialectic, as we shall demonstrate shortly.

## THE MODERNIZATION OF CULTURE

Nowhere is Simmel's ambivalence toward social life more apparent than in his multifaceted work on modernization. Simmel's world as we have seen was caught in the forces of change. German society had been transformed, but Simmel and other critics believed a substantial price had been paid. The lines of his argument are clear. Members of society through interpersonal relations build new economic, political, and social structures. Human beings through their subjective powers of production, that is, their *individual culture,* also construct and control an *objective culture,* including such elements as the arts, the sciences, tools, and religious dogma. Ironically, both the institutions and culture of the modern industrial order then come to confront their makers, restricting their development and stifling their creative spirit. It is as if the artist through the painting of the portrait confers upon it a life and power of its own. Through this transformation, the creation becomes the idol and the creator the idolater.

The problematics of modernization run like a gossamer thread through Simmel's sociology. His work on the metropolis and mental life (1964: 409–424) bears the stamp of the accelerating urbanization of his time. It also reveals the recurring pluralist puzzle: the retention of autonomy and individuality in the face of the external forces of culture, society, and history. The modern metropolis, according to Simmel, is the context in which objective culture explodes and individual culture is threatened. It is typified by blinding and intensive stimulation that appears to overload the psyche and uproot the individual. As a protective reaction, the metropolitan personality preserves subjective life through adaptation. The major components of such adaptation are cognitive: increased intelligence and greater perception. However, this response may come at the expense of deeper emotional relationships more commonly noted in small-town or rural life.

The metropolis, of course, was the center of the exploding industrial economy. For Simmel, the growth of the money economy was enhanced by industrialization, a source of dehumanized relationships. Hence, the often complex bonds of personal responsibility are replaced by the more impersonal forms of financial obligation. The money economy produces an exaggerated independence as well as reducing questions of quality to ones of quantity. It also facilitates the growth of a rational and calculating personality at the expense of warmth and concern. However, as with the metropolis and indeed the whole of modern culture, Simmel was ambivalent about the money economy. He saw its purposive and calculating nature as closely related to other spheres, such as natural science and the rational search for knowledge.

## Critique

Our brief review does not do justice to the richness of Simmel's work. What we have explored, however, is a theoretical system that begins but does not end with the micro-level world of individual culture and social interaction. What is intriguing about Simmel is his contention that the human actor, in building a society, is also constructing the prison of objective culture. Nevertheless, as with all other theoretical systems, there remain points of criticism.

Perhaps the most disturbing point about Simmel's sociology does not reside with Simmel himself. Others have frequently used the term *dialectic* to describe his sociology. We believe that conception is misleading. Although there are many shades of meaning for the term, *dialectic* for our part is best understood as a contradiction of opposing ideas or forces (such as Hegel's thesis and antithesis) and their *continual resolution* (Hegel's synthesis).[10] While Simmel was taken with the antipathies, inconsistencies, and struggles of social life, his work did not clearly reach such resolutions. There was no synthesis, either in his ideas or (as with Marx) in the material realm of history. Put simply, Simmel was stuck.

Simmel's dilemma was not unlike Weber's. He recognized the chains of modern society but viewed them as naturally forged in human nature. Thus the autonomous person (in concert wth others) creates external structures and an objective culture that threatens both freedom and dignity. And as these outside forces grow, as they inevitably do in modern industrial societies, the tension is beyond a synthesis. While Marx located his forces of opposition in the historically specific class structure of capitalism, Simmel's contradiction was between any social order and its members. Simmel's logic inexorably transformed all modern societies into penitentiaries for lost souls.

If Simmel's approach to sociology is not best understood as dialectic, then how should it be described? To reach that conclusion, we should identify three of Simmel's fundamental presuppositions. First, social reality is in essence pro-

---

[10] For a more detailed discussion of the dialectic, see Chapter 14.

cess and movement. Second, all elements of that reality are best understood as interdependent. Finally, even the most one-sided social relationships feature some *reciprocity,* which makes even the pariah or outcast essential in unrecognized ways. As an example of the last, Simmel analyzed the "stranger" as a social type. As with all of his types (such as the poor, the spendthrift, the nobleman, and so forth), this theorist was concerned with a specific form of interaction. The stranger is not merely the powerless outsider, the perennial victim, the ceaseless wanderer. Rather, the stranger by the very fact of his or her social distance brings objectivity to the group, thereby providing fresh views and alternative visions. At another level, the stranger reminds the members of the group that a common humanity extends beyond their immediate circle.

If we consider interdependence, process, and reciprocity together, Simmel's thought emerges as a *dynamic relationism.* It is a sociology of hidden connections, unrecognized consequences, ongoing construction, and mutual dependence. In Simmel's system, society is neither a structural whole of historically determined institutions nor an organism obeying its own unfolding evolutionary laws. Rather, it is a web of interdependencies with any unity based purely on the interactions of members. It is only reasonable that Simmel's position would draw fire from both the order and conflict sides. Both see in Simmel a theoretical system in which structure and culture are rendered unreal, reduced to forms that are more psychological than sociological.

Moving to another point, those of the positivist tradition would be upset with Simmel's soft and malleable sense of social laws (founded only in the recurring forms of interaction). In fact, Simmel argued that social phenomena often have different and diverse causes. Hence, lawful relationships among isolated social variables cannot be discerned. Simmel's thought also repudiated the quest for laws of equilibrium and adaptation advanced by systems theorists, as well as those in the conflict tradition who seek to account for change at the historical level.

Finally, despite its emphasis on the purposeful creation of social life, Simmel's sociology retained an aversion to progressive change. On the one hand, his was a sociology of the silver lining. He managed to find the hidden positives, even in superordinate-subordinate relationships. To be explicit, his theoretical system conferred autonomy on the powerless, strength upon the weak, mastery on the slave, and dignity upon the degraded. This tendency often blurred the lines between his theory and that of functionalism. For example, in his treatment of the "poor" as a social type, he analyzed the reciprocal relationship between those obliged to give aid and those who rightfully take it. Although favoring state support for the poor, Simmel noted that such aid is necessary to shield the social order from attack by the dangerous classes and to protect the children of the poor from a like fate.

Taken as a whole, however, Simmel's vision of the future remained decidedly pessimistic. He held that human beings are alienated, dominated by the objects made by their own hands. However, unlike the case for Marx, such impotence is not the property of a specific social system. It is rather the inevitable consequence of a human nature bent on fashioning systems of social control that acquire their own inertia. Simmel did not deny the reality of change; rather, he stripped it of hope.

# ■ *Bibliography*

Bendix, Reinhard
1977                    *Max Weber.* Berkeley: University of California Press.

Coser, Lewis A.
1956                    *The Functions of Social Conflict.* Glencoe, Ill.: The Free
                       Press.
1977                    *Masters of Sociological Thought.* New York: Harcourt Brace
                       Jovanovich.

Dahrendorf, Rolf
1964                    "The New Germanies—Restoration, Revolution, Recon-
                       struction." *Encounter* 22 (April):46–57.

Freund, Julian
1969                    *The Sociology of Max Weber.* New York: Random House.

Miller, S. M.
1967                    *Max Weber.* New York: Thomas Y. Crowell.

Simmel, Georg
1896                    "Superiority and Subordination as Subject-Matter of So-
                       ciology." *American Journal of Sociology* 2:167–189,
                       392–415.
1897–1898              "The Persistence of Social Groups." *American Journal of
                       Sociology* 3:662–698, 829–836; 4:35–60.
(1900) 1924            "Money and Freedom." In Robert E. Park and Ernest W.
                       Burgess (Eds.), *Introduction to the Science of Sociology,*
                       pp. 552–553. Chicago: University of Chicago Press.
1902                    "The Number of Members as Determining the So-
                       ciological Form of the Group." *American Journal of
                       Sociology* 8:1–46, 158–196.
1904                    "The Sociology of Conflict." *American Journal of Sociology*
                       9:490–525, 672–689, 798–811.
1964                    *The Sociology of Georg Simmel.* Edited and translated by
                       Kurt H. Wolff. New York: The Free Press.

Weber, Marianne
1975                    *Max Weber: A Biography.* Translated and edited by Harry
                       Zohn. New York: John Wiley & Sons.

Weber, Max
(1904–1905) 1930   *The Protestant Ethic and the Spirit of Capitalism*. New York:
                    Charles Scribner's Sons.
(1906–1924) 1946   *From Max Weber: Essays in Sociology*. Translated by Hans
                    H. Gerth and C. Wright Mills. New York: Oxford Uni-
                    versity Press.
(1922a) 1957       *The Theory of Social and Economic Organization*. Translated
                    and edited by A. M. Henderson and Talcott Parsons.
                    Glencoe, Ill.: The Free Press.
(1922b) 1954       *Max Weber on Law in Economy and Society*. Translated by
                    Max Rheinstein and Edward Shils. Cambridge, Mass.:
                    Harvard University Press.
(1922c) 1968       *Economy and Society: An Outline of Interpretive Sociology*.
                    4th ed. 3 vols. Edited by Guenther Roth and Claus Wit-
                    tach and translated by E. Fischoft et al. Totowa, N.J.: The
                    Bedminster Press.
1962               *Basic Concepts in Sociology*. Translated by H. P. Secher.
                    Westport, Conn.: Greenwood.
1967               *Max Weber*. Introduction by S. M. Miller. New York:
                    Thomas Y. Crowell.

Weingartner, Rudolph H.
1962               *Experience and Culture: The Philosophy of Georg Simmel*.
                    Middletown, Conn.: Wesleyan University Press.

Wolff, Kurt H.
(1950) 1964        "Introduction." In *The Sociology of Georg Simmel*. Edited
                    and translated by Kurt H. Wolff. Glencoe, Ill.: The Free
                    Press.

# CHAPTER *11*

# ■ The Open Society: Pluralist Politics

With some understanding of European pluralism behind us, we now turn our attention to its sociological heirs in America. However, one point must be understood before we seek to unravel the particular theoretical puzzle at issue in this chapter. As is true for the order theorists we considered earlier, not all pluralists operate at the same level of abstraction. Some follow the lead of Weber, who was more concerned with the ends of the social reality than with the means by which such ends are constructed. Others, knowingly or unknowingly, work in Simmel's tradition; they focus on the interactive processes, seeking to understand the nature of social operations and development. While the latter emphasis has dominated pluralist theoretical development in the United States, the larger sweep of the former can also be discerned. The puzzle to be examined in this chapter is of this grander sort. We shall call it the *open society,* and it provides the common bridge linking the work of Ralf Dahrendorf, David Riesman, Daniel Bell, and Lewis Coser.

# ■ Ralf Dahrendorf (b. 1929): Domination and Submission

The contemporary theorist Ralf Dahrendorf describes his own work on authority as a form of "conflict" as opposed to "order" sociology. For this reason, it might appear strange to include his work under the pluralist paradigm. However, Dahrendorf conceives of only two models of society, each with a corresponding type of sociology. This text employs *three* distinctive *paradigms,* each a configuration of assumptions not only about society but also about human nature and the nature of human science. For reasons that will become apparent, Dahrendorf advances a pluralist theory of *social* conflict based on shifting interest groups. This is a problem that *presupposes* the liberal conception of an *open society*. (Remember, just because a sociologist employs the term *conflict,* this does not necessarily identify the underlying paradigm.)

## History and Biography

Ralf Dahrendorf was born on May 1, 1929, in Hamburg, Germany. His youth was marked by the rise and fall of national socialism in his native land and the struggle of the German people to reconstruct both a material base and a new social fabric in the postwar era. A precocious scholar, he received one Ph.D. from the University of Hamburg in 1952 and another from the University of London in 1956.

Between 1952 and 1954, Dahrendorf met for "discussions in a small informal group of younger sociologists from diverse countries at the London School of Economics" (1959). It was during this Thursday evening seminar that the theoretical seed which became *Class and Class Conflict in Industrial Society* was planted. The book was published in German while Dahrendorf served in his early career as an assistant, then *Privatdozent* at the University of Saarbrücken. In 1957 and 1958 he was a fellow at the Center for Advanced Study in the Behavioral Sciences at Palo Alto. The English-language version of *Class and Class Conflict in Industrial Society* was published in 1959, while Dahrendorf served as a professor at the University of Hamburg (1958–1960).

Dahrendorf served through the 1960s first at Tübingen, then Constance. He became director of the London School of Economics in 1974. His career features periods of service in the German Parliament (1969–1970) and as a trustee of the Ford Foundation (1976). A number of awards and honorary degrees mark the academic respect accorded to Dahrendorf's lifework. However, the analysis and review that follow will focus on the most important of his contributions.

## Assumptions

Dahrendorf's image of human nature is best expressed in a construct: the new "sociological man" (1968: 19–87). By way of contrast, modern economic thought features *Homo economicus,* who buys, sells, and consumes on the basis of a careful and purposive set of rational calculations. Modern psychology presents the "second being" of social science.[1] *Psychological "Man"* (at least of the Freudian ilk) is a configuration of invisible and often ambivalent motives.

---

[1] Some would take issue with Dahrendorf's depiction of psychology as "social science."

Now comes *Homo sociologicus,* constructed by Dahrendorf to represent the *bearer of socially predetermined roles.*

None of these are descriptions of real people. They are rather *scientific constructs:* systematic ideas that advance knowledge, often by showing us what to analyze or by explaining phenomena. (For example, the *atom* in physics, like *role* in sociology, is a scientific construct.) However, in pointing up that human beings are the bearers of roles, sociologists face a dilemma. And it is within that dilemma that Dahrendorf revealed his vision of human nature.

> If sociology is not to fall victim to an uncritical scientism, the attempt to sketch in some dimensions of the category of social role must not lose sight of the moral problem created by the artificiality of its model. (1968: 25)

Now what precisely is the *moral problem* stemming from an uncritical acceptance among sociologists of the construct *Homo sociologicus?* It is simply the paradox of freedom and role constraint. For Dahrendorf, "human nature is not accurately described by the principle of role conformity." Instead the gap between this "theoretically fruitful construct" (role conformity) and the idea of human nature represents "almost a contradiction" (1968: 101). For Dahrendorf, the human essence is that of "intelligible moral character" with a "claim to liberty" (1968: 86–87). The predisposition of this theorist to define liberty in the language of individual freedom and self-fulfillment is a clear expression of the pluralist conception of human nature.

Dahrendorf's *dual* image of society clearly follows that of Simmel (see Chapter 10). Briefly reviewed, his order and conflict models of society serve to divide the discipline into two contrasting camps. For sociologists in the order tradition, society is *stable,* a functional organism or an integrated system founded in consensus. It assumes its existing form because of the integration that follows the sharing of values on the part of society's members. For sociologists in Dahrendorf's depiction of the conflict tradition, society is marked by *change;* it is a moment in a historical process driven by the clash of opposing interests. Whatever stability exists is based on the coercion of the weak by those in power (1959: 157–165).

For Dahrendorf, the nature of society is one of integration *and* coercion. In his explanation of dominance and submission within social organizations, however, he assumed the "coercive nature of social structure" (1959: 165). Yet we should not read too much into Dahrendorf's theoretical language. As we shall see, his is a decidedly pluralist conception of coercion, rooted in a Weberian definition of authority. He holds further to the pluralist image of the *open society* (1968: 128) and offers forms of Rousseau's contractualism (negotiation, voting, and so forth) as means of conflict resolution.

And despite what one might expect from the title of Dahrendorf's best-known work, he clearly rejects Marxian *class conflict* by *definition.* His classes are nothing like owners and workers but rather "conflict groups" arising out of the *authority structure* of social organizations (1959: 206). Consider the following language, which transforms Marx's classes (born of structural inequality in the capitalist system) into little more than competing interest groups:

> The progressive institutionalization of the values of achievement and equality has removed many barriers which for Marx were associated with the concept of class. . . . [W]e can already conclude that conflict groups in modern society are likely to be rather loose aggregations combined for special purposes and within particular associations. (1959: 201–202)

Finally, we find in Dahrendorf's work a somewhat mixed vision of human science. On the one hand, he rejects the common pluralist focus on the subjective dimension of social reality. On the other, his remains a Weberian approach rooted in the macro-order of society. (This is clearly evident in his conceptualization of the authority structure of social organizations, which we will examine shortly.) True to the pluralist paradigm, Dahrendorf also remains qualitative in his conception of science. And while his work is not historically specific, he is clearly aware of the changing authority relations and the emergence of diverse interest groups over time.

Yet the pluralist bent of Dahrendorf is clear in a final crucial way. Despite his conception of *Homo sociologicus* as a bearer of roles, he joined Weber in avoiding a hard determinism.

> Sociology is about an understanding of structures . . . which make a determinate behavior regularly probable. . . . [T]he *concept of change imposes limitations on any simply causal connection of given structures and observed behavior* . . . because the relationship between norm and action, structure and behavior is of necessity tenuous. (Dahrendorf, 1979: 65–66; italics added)

## Theoretical Content

Dahrendorf began *Class and Class Conflict in Industrial Society* (1959) with a systematic critique of the Marxist theory of class. He noted that Marx only introduced the final (fifty-second) chapter of the third volume of *Capital*. Dahrendorf thus proposed to complete that crucial section entitled "The Classes." He offered his interpretation neither as conjecture nor as a Weberian "experiment of the mind." Instead, using relevant and isolated statements in the work of Marx, he sought to offer a systematic presentation of what Marx would have written about "the classes" if he had finished the manuscript (1959: 8–18).

Dahrendorf identified a number of sociological elements in the Marxist theory of class in capitalist society (1959: 18–27).[2] He then mounted a critique,

---

[2] We need not present these here as they offer little more than can be gained from a review of "the class structure" in the theoretical content of Marx in Chapter 14.

seeking to demonstrate that certain aspects of the Marxist theory of class retain promise, while others are to be rejected. On the side of promise, Marx held that structurally rooted conflict is a necessary feature of society. For Dahrendorf, the "idea of a society which produces in its structure the antagonisms that lead to its modification appears an appropriate model of the analysis of change in general" (1959: 125–126). Also important for Dahrendorf was the Marxist conception of a dominant form of conflict between two major forces. In his words, it is important to have "something like" a two-class model to understand conflict (1959: 126).

However, at this point, Dahrendorf began to take issue with Marx on conflict and its relationship to social change (1959: 126–154). For Dahrendorf, class conflict is only one form of a more general social conflict. For example, societies routinely feature bipolar clashes between races (white and nonwhite), age groups (young and old), and the sexes (men and women). He argued further that classes need not be "manifestly antagonistic groups" engaging in violent forms of struggle. Rather, they might resolve their differences through such means as strike, parliamentary debate, and negotiation (1959: 134–135).[3] Thus, while some form of change can be expected from a conflict of classes (or other groups), that change need not be revolutionary.

Dahrendorf also rejected the Marxist "property source" of classes. He argued that dividing capitalist society into owners and nonowners is archaic. Under modern industrial capitalism, "legal ownership and factual control are separated." This means that those who exercise authority (whether in the economic sphere or elsewhere) need not own the means of production. This is the crucial point in Dahrendorf's "supersedure" of Marx: Authority (instead of property) becomes the "structural determinant of class formation and class conflict" (1959: 136). Hence, the distribution of authority is the basis for conflict and any ensuing social change. And control of the industrial economy is in itself only a special form of authority, not the basis for a ruling class.

Having distanced his work from that of Marx, Dahrendorf offered an explanation of conflict rooted in the authority structure of society (especially, industrial society). He employed Weber's conception of authority as the "probability that a command with a given specific content will be obeyed by a given group of persons" (1959: 166). And following Weber's rational-legal type, Dahrendorf argued that authority is a matter of social positions and roles, not the force of personality. Hence, the relations that matter for Dahrendorf are those of *structurally legitimated domination and subjection.* For example, in the military structure of authority, officers command enlisted people. In the corporate structure, managers command workers.

Dahrendorf holds that the particular social relations of authority always involve superordination and subordination (refer to Simmel's work in Chapter

---

[3] Here Dahrendorf deferred to Parsons' conception of latent conflicts, whereby classes can peacefully coexist. The work of Parsons is considered in Chapter 7.

10), where some are socially expected to command and others to obey. These expectations are made "legitimate" by means of their association with enduring social positions. However, authority is specific in terms of who can be ordered, as well as the spheres of control. Finally, legitimated authority is upheld by *sanctions,* including those provided by the legal system (1959: 166–167).

Although Dahrendorf acknowledges that the exercise of authority may contribute to a function needed by society as a system (Parsons again), he emphasizes the other side. For this theorist, the "ugly face" of authority means that its exercise is at the root of social conflict. Thus within all units of social organization (including state, church, industry, bureaucracy, and so forth), only two major "sides" contend in a relation of authority. These groups, one superordinate and one subordinate, hold contradictory interests. This being true, the *legitimacy* of authority on which *effective* dominance resides is perennially in jeopardy.

Dahrendorf conceives of the polity (political organization of society) in terms of Weber's *imperatively coordinated associations.* This refers to organizations or groups whose members are "by virtue of a prevailing order, subject to authority relations" (Weber, in Dahrendorf, 1959: 237). Given the variety of such associations, it is possible for the same person to be a member of more than one group and to experience different authority relations in each (1959: 167–176).

In this theoretical system, conflict is purely structural. That is, it ensues from the contradictory interests rooted in (two-tiered) hierarchical positions (of dominance and subjugation) within the associations just described. As people play the roles associated with these positions, they become adapted to this inherent conflict of interests (1959: 178–179). When these interests (which bring those with authority into conflict with those without) are not recognized, they are termed *latent.* When a collectivity of people share only latent interests and do not organize themselves, they are termed by Dahrendorf a *quasi-group.* When such opposing interests become conscious, they are termed *manifest* and the organized collectivity sharing them is called an *interest group.*

If the major form of conflict in industrial society is not confined to Marxian classes, then what is the nature of those groups locked in contention? In other words, how do real conflict groups emerge from the authority structure of organizations? To address this question, Dahrendorf employed two preliminary constructs mentioned earlier. The first is the quasi-group, or potential group which is a "community of latent interests" (1959: 180). Such associations exist at a high level of analysis (for example, one might consider a socialist community or a Christian community). Quasi-groups can be considered recruiting fields for interest groups, which are the true agents of group conflict. Interest groups are distinctive by virtue of structure, organization, goals, and specific membership. The modern political party is Dahrendorf's exemplar of an interest group.

Given certain preconditions, interest groups will emerge from quasi-groups. These include the *technical prerequisites* of founders/leaders/organizers and ideology: the *political prerequisite* of an open (nontotalitarian) society that tolerates the formation of divergent organizations; and the *social prerequisite* of effective communication and "patterned recruitment" (1959: 184–187). By patterned recruitment, Dahrendorf meant the structural (nonrandom) channeling of specific groups within "imperatively organized associations" into such interest groups.

How then does this theorist conceive of class and class conflict? For Dahrendorf, this is simply a generic phrase for the clash of interests between dominant and submissive groups. *Social class* in this theoretical system refers simply to any collectivity of people (whether organized or not) who share common interests (whether latent or manifest) because of their shared position in the authority structure of associations (1959: 238). Thus, it subsumes quasi-groups and interest groups. Defined in this way, classes are always in conflict.

What then determines the intensity of class conflict and the prospects for violence? For Dahrendorf, the intensity of class conflict decreases to the extent that (1) classes (as defined above) are free to organize; (2) class conflict is contained within an organization and not superimposed elsewhere; (3) the distribution of authority and the distribution of rewards are dissociated; and (4) classes are open. Violence decreases (1) if classes can organize, (2) if the *absolute* deprivation of rewards for the subject class gives way to *relative* deprivation, and (3) if class conflict is effectively regulated (1959: 239).

It is important to note that Dahrendorf's class conflict produces structural change, but only for the association(s) within which it occurs. *Hence, structural change in this theory does not refer to society as a whole.* The radicalness of change (within specific associational structures) is a function of the intensity of class conflict, and the suddenness of change is a function of its violence (1959: 240).

## Critique

As we have seen, Dahrendorf's work is first about models of society (order and conflict), which for him constitute a major division in sociological thought. Yet in his own theoretical attempt to explain change, Dahrendorf has moved the conception of conflict from Marx to Weber, from class to interest groups, and from relations to the means of production to authority relations. Thus, his "conflict model" of society seems to be much more compatible with what we have presented in this book as the pluralist paradigm.

Borrowing from Mannheim (see Chapter 18), Jeffers Chertok has argued for a truly dialectical interpretation of order and conflict models (something that Dahrendorf has failed to do). In Chertok's reconstruction, order and conflict visions are distinctive in their conceptualization of "time," or more specifically, history and social change. The orderist view of history assumes the preeminence of the present, with the past as its genesis and the future its continuation. The focus is on important people and events; analysis is particular rather than holistic; and historical time is reduced to "periods." Also presented is a consensual and integrative sense of social history. The latter corresponds with a tendency to confine dramatic social change to the past, allowing only for small-scale adjustments in the present and future. Such conceptions of history clearly appeal to the powerful with a vested interest in the status quo.

The truly conflictual view (largely abandoned by Dahrendorf) conceives of history as an ongoing social process, with the present order (1) emerging from a reorganization of the past and (2) containing the kernel of a strongly altered future. The focus here is on groups as moving forces and makers of history and their "positional interests and relationships." The events and ideas of history are viewed holistically across space and through time with an eye toward societal transformation. Hence, the disintegrative, destructive, and coercive features of history are manifested. And conflict is conceived as the crucible of macrostructural change. Such conceptions clearly appeal to the powerless (Chertok, 1986).

Moving to the level of formal theoretical content, certain of Dahrendorf's major constructs are also open to question. To be explicit, the concept of social class is emptied of economic content altogether (although dominant groups may use their position to gain rewards).[4] It hinges on authority and the roles associated with position in the authority structure of "imperatively coordinated associations." Given the fact of multiple associations, and multiple opportunities to play a different authority role, a real "actor" need not be consistently powerful or powerless. It follows that it is quite possible in Dahrendorf's theory for an individual to be a simultaneous member of different classes, both ruler and ruled.

In a cogent argument, Peter Weingart (1969) raised other issues. Remember that conflicting interests are defined by Dahrendorf in terms of different role expectations (stemming from different positions in the authority structure). Further, structural change ultimately means an "exchange of roles" resulting from conflict. (In other words, new personnel move into different authority positions with different role expectations.) Given this conception, Weingart wondered whether Dahrendorf truly developed a theory of social change or a theory of *social mobility*. Better stated, Dahrendorf's work is less about how social institutions (or even imperatively coordinated associations) change than it is about the moving of individuals (or wholly different interest groups) into authority positions within organizations *as they are*. Ideologically, then, Dahrendorf's theory of change is really a theory of the changing of the guard within an existing order. It is this liberal affirmation of the open society that ties this European to the American sociologists to come.

---

[4]Sociologists of all persuasions would question why Dahrendorf uses the concepts of class and class conflict at all. He declares in effect the death of classes as societal-wide groupings founded in part on the production and distribution of wealth.

# ■ David Riesman (b. 1909): Demography Is Destiny

David Riesman is the second sociologist to consider the puzzle of the open society so basic to pluralist politics. He was born the oldest son of a well-to-do Philadelphia Jewish family. His father was a prominent physician who also served as a member of the faculty of the University of Pennsylvania. Riesman became an undergraduate at Harvard, where he received a bachelor's degree in chemistry in 1931. He continued his training at Harvard Law School, and his early career was in the legal profession. Riesman served briefly as a member of a law firm in Boston, as a clerk for Supreme Court Justice Brandeis, and as a deputy assistant district attorney for the State of New York. In 1937 he took a professorship in law at the University of Buffalo. Five years later he traveled to the University of Chicago, where he became a member of the social science faculty. In 1958 he returned to his alma mater to further enhance an already distinguished academic career (Meyerson, 1979).

Although his university training and much of his early career coincided with the Great Depression, Riesman was somewhat sheltered from the night terror of that era. As might be expected, many of his early written contributions were published in various law reviews. However, even these quickly assumed a sophisticated awareness of the broader societal context in which legal systems emerge and operate. By the end of the 1940s, his interests had expanded to include individualism, opinion, and social character. These were to converge in a book that continues to attract both admiration and serious criticism in intellectual circles.

In 1950 Yale University Press published *The Lonely Crowd,* which Riesman authored with the assistance of Nathan Glazer and Reuel Denney. The book quickly became a phenomenon, attracting more interest outside than inside academic circles. Over the next two decades, two paperback editions and one revised edition were published in the United States. International editions were also printed in some 15 nations.[5] Despite a varied and impressive number of contributions to the literature, *The Lonely Crowd* and his later *Individualism Reconsidered* (1954) remain the touchstones of Riesman's sociology today.

## Assumptions

Riesman shares with Max Weber a conviction that the motivations of the human actor are crucial to the theoretical explanation of society and its properties. The subtitle of *The Lonely Crowd* is appropriately enough *A Study of the*

---

[5] A bibliography of Riesman's work appears in Gans, 1979: 319–346.

*Changing American Character.* Riesman and his co-authors defined character as "the more or less permanent socially and historically conditioned organization of an individual's drives and satisfactions—the kind of 'set' with which he approaches the world and people" (1969: 4). More specifically, *social* character refers to that aspect of character formed through the common experiences of significant social groups (1969: 4). (It appears clear that in Riesman's view one of Weber's more important works dealt with the unique "Protestant character" that "made" the economic institution of capitalism.)

Riesman shares other broad conceptions that are crucial to the sociology of Max Weber. He explicitly rejects the determinism of social institutions, believing it possible for conscious human action to manage them (1969: xxv). Yet in the ambivalent fashion so pronounced in the work of Weber and other pluralists, Riesman demonstrates a somewhat foreboding impression of the forces of modernity. One senses in his work a wistful longing for utopia, accompanied by the conviction that the Western world has lost the specific form of social character necessary to build that enlightened future. This will be evident as we review his theory and develop a subsequent critique.

Riesman also employs (in modified form) the methodology of Weber. As we shall see, he fashions an ideal typology extracted from his comparative study of history. And when Riesman juxtaposes traditional societies with those of the West, he (as Weber before him) finds their differences in the nature of their ideas, their motivations, and their view of the world. What Weber described as the rational, work-oriented, dutiful imperatives of the Protestant ethic, Riesman defined as the "superlatively efficient and impressive social character" (1969: xxxii) that had constructed the history of the West.

The pluralist heritage extends beyond Riesman's intellectual ties to individual sociologists. His conception of political power is expressed in terms of the "veto groups," by which narrow organized forces (such as corporations, labor unions, bureaucracies, and "cause-oriented" social movements) seek to "stop things conceivably inimical to its interests and, within narrower limits, to start things" (1950: 244). Such a vision of countervailing power placed Riesman in continuing opposition to the conflictual political sociology of his contemporary C. Wright Mills. While Riesman viewed veto groups as a threat to the democratic process, Mills saw the domination of society by a self-replenishing elite of power. While Riesman saw an American character eroded by mindless conformity, Mills saw an American class system in which the masses of people controlled neither their individual nor collective destiny (Riesman, 1951).

Riesman was to debate Mills in a manner reminiscent of Weber's struggle with the ideas of Marx. For example, Mills viewed the state primarily as a tool of the elite, and Riesman saw the state as an ally with any abuses of its influence due to the power of veto groups. Further, in keeping with the pluralist imagery of society, Riesman fashioned an ambivalent role for the media. He discounted Mills's claim that the mass media were ever-expanding forces of political distraction. Rather, he argued that they are, at their best, forces for tolerance and political involvement and, at their worst, purveyors of empty consumption.

For Mills, the critical issue surrounding the print and broadcast industry was ideological control. For Riesman, the media through the sameness of its message, the uniform smiles of its actors, and the blandness of its accounts is a long-term shaper of negative change in the American character.

As we have established, the political philosopher Jean-Jacques Rousseau exemplified the pluralist sense of antagonism between society and the person. His was a critique of modernity, of technological expansion, and unchecked inequality that threaten not only inner tranquility but political freedom. In his writings, he imagined a two-edged solution to this malaise. On the one hand, Rousseau's portrait was that of the autonomous and authentic citizen, armed with education, who refuses to renounce personal sovereignty. On the other hand, this sovereign being submits to the necessary demands of social order only through a fairly negotiated covenant (Featherstone, 1979).

David Riesman shares similar assumptions about human nature and the structure of society. As we shall see, he strongly adhered to Rousseau's imagery in his account of the type of social character basic to the construction of Western and American society. However, it is that quality of autonomy and freedom in both private and public life that Riesman perceived as lost. Hence, Rousseau's vision of the future became for Riesman a dream of the past.

## Theoretical Content

In a general way, Riesman's theoretical work focuses on the linkage between character and society. He postulates that every society is founded to some extent on the conformity of its members. For Riesman, the nature of that conformity varies for the simple reason that societal norms and expectations differ. Hence every society is marked by a particular form of social character on the part of the individuals that comprise it. However, at a more specific level, Riesman's work is a tale of the replacement of the nineteenth-century American social character by a contemporary alternative. This new type suffers in comparison to the old, as we shall see.

Differences in social character, that is, variations across societies in how their members conform and what they conform to, assume three distinctive types in the work of David Riesman. The first is termed *tradition-directed,* a kind of conformity in which "ritual, routine and religion" (1950: 11) predominate. People here do not seek new solutions to old problems. Although they have a sense of belonging, their range of choice is limited and they look to the past for guidance. In Weberian fashion, Riesman argued that tradition is the basis for power relations that often endure for centuries in the form of clans, castes, professions, age and sex groups, and so forth. With the exception of the Middle Ages, Western civilization has not shaped or been shaped by this character type.

The second category in the typology of social character is called *inner-*

*directed*. For Riesman, inner-directed character built Western history, its Renaissance, its Reformation, and its economic patterns of expansion, exploration, colonization, and imperialism (1950: 14–15). People in such societies are provided with a sort of internal gyroscope, quite often "implanted early in life by the elders and directed toward generalized but nonetheless inescapably destined goals" (1950: 15). Inner-directed people know a wider range of choice and all the problems that such choice entails. Character formation is here marked by less reverence for heritage, greater adaptive capability, and increasing demands on the environment.

The last pure type of social character is the *other-directed*. Although described by Alexis de Tocqueville a century before in his *Democracy in America*, Riesman saw a twentieth-century phenomenon most clearly evidenced in the urban upper middle classes of American society. Now the inner-directed social character has not been subject to a total eclipse. It survives in the "old middle class—the banker, the tradesman, the small entrepreneur, the technically oriented engineer" (1950: 21). However, Riesman argued that other direction is the character type of the new middle classes, its salaried employees, its bureaucrats, its increasingly leisured white-collar robots. The society they inhabit reveals an expanding peripheral economy in which an exploding service industry replaces jobs in traditional manufacturing, heavy industry, and agriculture. Words replace sweat, and production accedes to the new reign of consumption.

The source of direction, the locus of conformity for this new emerging type is found in the signals of contemporaries. Ever sensitive to the wishes of others; swayed and molded by the models of friends or the images of the media; dressed, educated, and nurtured for success, the other-directed person is chained by the need for approval. Here the internal gyroscope of inner direction is replaced by an external radar screen. For Riesman, the new American character is oriented neither to the future nor the past. Its clay is formed by the fashions, conventions, and tyrannies of the times.

While interesting on the face, social character is connected by Riesman's theory to demographic changes. Relying on the terminology and theory of Frank Notestein, Riesman described a population "S curve." Simply put, three phases are evident in the curve. The bottom of the S represents high rates of birth and death, and hence a phase of "high growth potential." With a decrease in the death rate (because of improvements in medicine or hygiene, for example), a population may increase rapidly. This phase is known as "transitional growth" and is represented by the middle of the S. Finally, when a population reaches the top of the curve, birth rates begin to drop (because of economic considerations, for example), and the stage of "incipient decline" is entered.

For Riesman, these population shifts require that the affected societies will bring forth a corresponding type of social character. Where there are high birth and death rates, societies will be homogeneous, feature elaborate systems of kinship, and value the past and time-honored custom. In such societies, the "tradition-directed" person will be typical. Given the transitional growth population, the society in question will be expanding, exploring, and open to revolutions in the arts, commerce, and industry. In this context, inner direction prevails. And when birth and death rates are low, with incipient population decline at hand, the society will be increasingly urban, bureaucratized, and white collar. This becomes the era of other direction. Hence for Riesman, demography is societal destiny.

## Critique

Riesman's work on the nature of conformity and the question of individualism gives rise to a number of critical issues. The first of these concerns the explanatory value of his theory. Simply put, he has not clearly explained the connection he seeks to establish between demographic and societal forces on the one hand and the ensuing types of social character on the other. Nor has he offered compelling historical evidence for this proposed correlation. Generally put, Riesman has not found lucid explanation in either the world of individuals and motivations he applauds or the grand forces of economic history and population growth he describes. Neither has he analyzed the processes by which these forces interact with the different modes of conformity represented in his typology of social character. Hence his pure forms of "direction," like the title of his major work, remain more a rich metaphor than an answer to the question "Why?"

Another point at issue is the S curve adapted by Riesman to his own work. If population growth is related to the rise of inner direction and the various revolutions that signal mastery and prosperity for people, then efforts at world population control are seriously offtrack. (In so saying, we need not embrace the views of those who seek to account for the economic and political difficulties of many nations outside the West by blaming their high birth rates.) Moreover, other serious questions can be posed about explanations that assign primacy to the demographic factor. From the order side, population change is related to the world of cultural values. From the conflict side, population growth and distribution vary with structural changes in the mode of production. In each of these alternatives, demography is more consequence than cause.

Riesman also evidences a strange ambivalence toward modernization. He is clearly uneasy with the new age of other direction. However, when he analyzes "traditional" character and societies he implicitly joins Weber. Both appear to hold that non-Western societies owe their absence of economic "development" to the fact that they are not Westernized. Both theories place great credence in a rational, risk-taking, future-oriented, and innovating view of the world that bends the environment to its will. Each (perhaps inadvertently) contributes to contemporary modernization theories which hold that "underdeveloped" societies can overcome their problems only when their people think and act like their Western counterparts. While a case can be made for efficiency of organization, history also confirms that the success of Western development has clearly associated with the colonial subjugation of traditional societies and the modern forces of neocolonialism.

When analyzed ideologically, it appears that Riesman's theory like pluralist systems in general is an example of liberal thought. His ideas celebrate diversity, reaffirm political democracy, and embrace institutional reform. Such views, together with a strong belief in personal freedom, are evident not only in Riesman's major works but in his continuing interest in educational issues. Given this quality of mind, the puzzles of society find explanation in the character of its people, which in turn reflects the openness of its institutions. When institutional arrangements are questioned, such queries remain tertiary. The existing order, with all its imperfections, remains a given.

Pluralist thought often reflects the horns of the liberal dilemma. On the one side, the present system (as all alternatives) is seen as too large or impersonal, too complex or bureaucratized, and its problems the necessary and intractable outcomes of attempts to *administer* modern societies. On the other, hope remains for a new generation of leaders or a new wave of scientists and technicians to adjust the order from within. For David Riesman, institutional rebirth awaits the second coming of the inner-directed character.

# ■ Daniel Bell (b. 1919): Beyond Ideology

Daniel Bell is the third of our contemporary Weberians who grapple with the larger issue of social order while keeping faith with the idealist tradition and the pluralist vision of society. Weber sought to account for the changing of Western civilization through the ideal of rationalization, its embodiment in the bureaucracy, and finally, the bureaucratization of institutions. As we shall see, however, Bell's system of thought implicitly stresses the rational temper of mind, although not imprisoning it within the iron cage. Bell believes that the rationalism of theoretical and technological ideas pushes the modern society on—and further, that those who hold legitimate claim to intellectual expertise will come to form a new basis of power in a changed society. Knowledge and its application thus become the means for making and shaping the social world of the future.

Daniel Bell was born in New York City in 1919, the son of Benjamin and Anna Bolotsky. He was educated at City College, where he received his B.S. in 1939, and at Columbia University, where he received his Ph.D. in 1960. As suggested by the age at which he received his doctorate, Bell came late into the academy. This is because his was a dual career. The first stage was in journalism, where he served as managing editor of the *New Leader* from 1941 to 1944, and then as labor editor for *Fortune* magazine from 1948 to 1958. Although he was an instructor in sociology at the University of Chicago between these editorships, Bell's formal academic service began at Columbia, where he was professor of sociology from 1959 to 1969. Since 1969 he has held a similar position at Harvard, and in 1980 he became a Henry Ford II Professor of Social Sciences.

## Assumptions

Bell first attracted serious attention with his edited work *The Radical Right* (1963, originally published 1955). The book was fired in the kiln of the McCarthy era, when the junior senator from Wisconsin had come to symbolize the cold politics of anticommunist hysteria.[6] Its essays sought to unravel the historical, political, and economic forces behind an era of blacklisting, ideological purges, and the withering of dissent. This and later works on the problems of modern capitalism have led some observers to place Bell's sociology within the conflict paradigm. This assessment is misleading for the reasons that follow.

In contrast to the optimism of Marx and his intellectual heirs on social being (see Chapter 14), Bell utilized what by now should be familiar pluralist imagery to describe the duality of human nature.

> But what does not vanish is the duplex nature of man himself—the murderous aggression, from primal impulse, to tear apart and destroy; and the search for order, in art and life, as the bending of will to harmonious shape. It is this ineradicable tension which defines the social world. (1973: 488)

A second distinctive pluralist assumption centers on the power of ideas in science. An early indication of this is found in Bell's essay "Marxian Socialism in the United States" written in 1949 and 1950 and published for the first time in 1952 as part of a larger compendium of articles on American socialism. In the 1967 paperback edition of the essay, Bell made his position clear. Movements to bring about the social ownership of the means of production and distribution had clearly failed in the United States. Or, forcefully put, "American socialism had become simply a notation in the archives of history" (1967: 193). Bell found the reasons for this stillbirth in *ideological rigidity*.

According to Bell, American leftist movements and parties had been historically hamstrung by a doctrinaire Marxism that argued the inevitable collapse of the capitalist system because of its structural contradictions. For example, an economy based on private property would by its very nature allow for the concentration of capital, the monopolization of state power, and the polarization of classes. Therefore, change of a revolutionary sort would take the

---

[6]For a brief survey of the Cold War and McCarthyism, see the review of C. Wright Mills in Chapter 16.

form of a struggle of classes. For Bell, this "vulgar" Marxism (at least as interpreted historically in the United States) represented a somewhat mechanical and naturalistic conception of change. Its adherents dismissed the importance of ideas in bringing about a new order. They also failed the test of pragmatism.

Bell argued that successful movements for change must be "in and of the world." By this he meant that those who seek to organize must understand the art of political compromise, an art that is often advanced at the expense of ideological purity and moral critique. As an example of pragmatic political action, he cited the American labor movement. By learning to live in and of the world, this political force realized a place for collective rights and action in a cultural context of individualism (1967: x). To have repudiated "working within the system" on ideological grounds would have made such gains impossible. In this and many other examples, Bell has clearly adhered to Weber's principle that politics is amoral, and he appropriately quoted the master to end his essay. *He who seeks the salvation of souls, his own as well as others, should not seek it along the avenue of politics.*

## Theoretical Content

While Bell has continued to write prolifically into the 1980s, three major works dominate his contributions to sociology to date. First of all, in 1960 he published *The End of Ideology.* Appropriately subtitled *On the Exhaustion of Political Ideas in the Fifties,* this book is a collection of critical essays written over a 10-year period. It is not surprising, therefore, that Bell did not here present a unified theoretical system. However, there is in the six essays that comprise Part I of *The End of Ideology* a self-described attempt at "broad theory." The springboard for this effort was Bell's contention that social theories about the United States do not fare well "due in large measure to the uncritical application of ambient ideas from European sociology to the vastly different experiences of American life" (1960: 14). It is not unfair to note that Bell's sociological antagonist was not really a European. (In fact, he is deeply indebted to Weber.) It was rather an American contemporary of the 1950s and 1960s, striving almost alone to keep alive critical sociology in the United States, who drew fire from Bell. This contemporary was C. Wright Mills (see Chapter 16).

Simply put, Bell argues that "neo-Marxist theories," including those of Mills, do not fit American society. Rather, "group interests" and "status aspirations" have instead been transformed into political action, and it is by such processes that change is to be understood. Contrary to Mills's argument in *The Power Elite* (1956) (see Chapter 16), Bell asserts there is no evidence for a small cohesive cohort of control, no compelling proof for a corporate, military, political troika of command. Mills has thus mistakenly drawn his imagery from the realities of European history. It is this alien world, Bell argues, that represents the aristocratic conceptions of honor and deference, and the homogeneity and continuity of power. The American society, by comparison, is heterogeneous, irreverent, and diverse. While there are "classes," Bell holds that the class structure cannot be used to analyze who holds power in the United States. Although he concedes the existence of wealthy and powerful groups, Bell argues that they quarrel among themselves and are forced to work inside a political system that mediates among a broad range of conflicting domestic interests and foreign-policy options.

It is within this pluralist conception of politics and the primacy of the world of ideas that Bell seeks to understand change. He believes that the "old" ideas, whether or not presented by contemporary sociologists, have played out their historical role. No understanding of American society can be had through recourse to such classical constructs as "mass or class" or through traditional institutional forms. For example, modern capitalism bears little relationship to the family-based economic system that prevailed prior to the Civil War—nor is it a system under the control of the superrich. Not only is modern corporation capitalism subject to what the economist John Kenneth Galbraith described as "countervailing power" (such as labor unions and government regulation), corporate managers do not qualify as an entrenched elite.

> Perhaps the most important fact, sociologically, about the American business community today is the insecurity of the managerial class. The corporation may have an assured continuity; its administrators have not. . . . The new class of managers, recruited from the general grab bag of middle-class life, lacks the assured sense of justification which the older class-rooted system provided. They have no property stake in the system; nor can they pass their power to their heirs. Hence the growing need of achievement as a sign of success and the importance of ideology as a means of justification. Ideology serves as a social cement, binding the business class together. (1960: 81)

Now we must be careful to keep Bell's argument straight. He assigns great importance to the power of ideas. This is evident in the argument that the achievement ethic and other related elements form an occupational ideology for the emerging business class. It is this glue that holds them together, not their class position as determined by their ownership of property. It is the Marxist tendency to view ideology as a *consequence* of the *material* nature of the prevailing mode of production (tribalism, feudalism, capitalism, socialism) that Bell opposes.

On a slightly different plane, Bell objects to the "old" radical ideas (including mass and class) that philosophically reflect historical materialism (see Chapter 14). Thus, he criticizes Mills for his structural attempt to explain the elite simply by analyzing their *position* in the organization. For Mills, managerial and other organizational behavior could be collectively predicted over time simply by analyzing position in the organization. For Bell, it is crucial to understand the ideas held by such actors.

The second of Bell's major works was published in 1973. In *The Coming of Post-Industrial Society,* he contended that the Western world is in a state of transition from the old industrial order. The postindustrial society reflects such change along five dimensions. In the *economic sphere,* the provision of services is replacing the manufacturing of goods as the dominant sector. Bell noted that in the United States more than half of both the gross national product and total employment is accounted for by the service sector (a trend that has continued unabated). Along the *occupational dimension,* Bell observed that American white-collar workers now outnumber blue-collar workers. And crucially, for his argument, the professional and technical class (scientists, technicians, engineers, teachers, and so forth) is growing rapidly. It is its members and the knowledge they command that represent the axis of the postindustrial society.

That which Bell termed the *axial principle* forms the third dimension of this new order. Whereas the integration of worker and machine is the basic imperative of industrial society, the organization of society around theoretical (as opposed to empirical) knowledge typifies the modern society. Such knowledge supposedly transforms social relationships, creating a new class structure based on the quality and quantity of expertise. On the upper tier are scientists, administrators, technologists, and those working to advance the arts, letters, and religion. In descending order, we find, respectively, the technical/semiprofessional stratum, the clerical/sales stratum, and the craftworker/semiskilled stratum.

In essence, Bell's argument is that a stratification system based on property is yielding to the fair and just hierarchy of the *meritocracy.* A class system based on knowledge, he maintains, will allow the cream to rise to the top.

> One wants entrepreneurs and innovators who can expand the amount of productive wealth for society. One wants men in political office who can govern well. The quality of life in any society is determined, in considerable measure, by the quality of leadership. A society that does not have its best men at the head of its leading institutions is a sociological and moral absurdity. (1973: 454)

In a manner reminiscent of Riesman's "inner direction" and Weber's description of rational authority, Bell described the fourth dimension of the postindustrial society. It consists of a *future orientation* manifested in the control of technology and technological assessment. The focus here is on planning, a conception that meshes well with Bell's vision of an expanded role for political management. And finally, the author identified the *decision-making component:* the creation of a new intellectual technology. By this Bell meant that through science the postindustrial society can institutionalize a systematic form of problem solving. This makes it possible to identify and replicate the procedures employed in obtaining specific results.[7]

The familiar tension in pluralist conceptions of society is evident in Bell's

---

[7] Bell followed closely here the arguments of the philosopher Friedrich Nietzsche, who in *The Will to Power* proposed that the rationalism of modern science would destroy the "unreflective spontaneity" of life.

identification of the two "modes" of postindustrial society (1973: 274–298). The *economizing mode* refers to the manner in which the new order addresses such issues as the allocation of resources, the reduction of waste, the minimization of costs, and the maximization of profit, growth, and rewards. Within this mode, costs and benefits are measured purely in economic terms, and frequently the yardstick is "individual private consumption." The *sociologizing mode* introduces a different set of concerns, those that center on the "public interest." It is, according to Bell, based on the realization that such issues as social justice, personal growth, worker satisfaction, and environmental quality demand their place in the modern society. These and other "social goods" are matters of societal rather than personal demand.

Bell of necessity has examined the role of the corporation in the new society. In the present context, he argues that corporate managers must reconcile the conflicting demands of both modes. However, in the long term corporate power will wane. This is because power is a function of resources, and these in turn are subject to change. In preindustrial society, the major resource was land; in the industrial successor, it was machines; but in the postindustrial order, the new axis is knowledge. Those who hold these resources hold power. Hence in the new society, the university and its research scientists and intellectuals will become dominant forces. They will contend with the other command center of the postindustrial order: those who occupy the "cockpit of politics" (1973: 374–378).

In his next major work, Bell moved beyond the "structural and political" nature of the postindustrial society to a cultural focus. In 1976 *The Cultural Contradictions of Capitalism* appeared and in it an exploration of "the realm of symbolic forms." More precisely, Bell followed Ernst Cassirer in defining culture as *expressive symbolism*. This includes both the arts (painting, poetry, and fiction) and religion (litany, liturgy, and ritual). Each of these seeks to "express the meanings of human existence in some imaginative form" (1976: 12).

Bell accepts Weber's argument that Protestant culture in the past provided the ethical bond that held the Western spirit and Western capitalism together. However, he proposes that in the modern era a "disjunction" has arisen between the technoeconomic structure (that focuses on the production and distribution of goods and services) and contemporary culture. Whereas the first extols efficiency, functional rationality, and organization, the second celebrates self-realization and obsessive privatism. In short, the Protestant ethic, which measured salvation by works and self-denial, has passed, and the era of the "me generation" has arrived (1976: 15–37). Hence, the basis for the "cultural contradictions of capitalism."

Yet all is not lost. In a manner consistent with his belief in the "open society" that is the United States, Bell generally sees the problem as one of the growing pains of manageable change. More specifically, he observed that we face a temporary crisis of faith.

> The real problem of *modernity* is the problem of belief. To use an unfashionable term, it is a spiritual crisis, since the new anchorages have proved illusory and

the old ones have become submerged. It is a situation which brings us back to nihilism; lacking a past or a future, there is only a void. (1976: 28–29)

In coming full circle, Bell again returns to the power of ideas in the reformulation of the cultural base. Contrary to the pessimism of Weber, he holds to the possibility of a cultural breakout that moves forward into the future. Gone forever is the asceticism and "other worldliness" of the past. However, the current hedonism with its obsessive consumption and undelayed gratification must also pass. In its stead will come an ideology that Bell has described as a "reaffirmation of liberalism."

By using the term *liberalism*, Bell expressly enjoins the political philosophy of Rousseau and other contractualists who celebrate the sovereignty and diversity of individuals. In the liberal society, pluralism prevails not only in social background and standing but in the range of respected beliefs. For Bell, as for his historical mentors, the dilemma of the social compact is never fully resolved. Each new generation must negotiate the conflict of roles between "person and citizen, individual and group." And from this process will emerge a modern compact that reflects such elements as "the reaffirmation of our past," "the recognition of the limits of resources," "the priority of needs . . . over appetites," and "agreement on a conception of equity" (1976: 277–282).

## Critique

The work of Daniel Bell strikes a responsive chord among academicians and others who seek to find the human side of sociology. In some ways his very success in articulating the social and cultural dilemmas of modern life may have detracted from the clear development of a theoretical system. Bell himself conceptualizes his work more as descriptive criticism. This, together with his eclectic interests, has been productive more of essays than truly integrated volumes. Still, there is some attempt at the explanation of the puzzle of modernization in his work. And it is such explanation that we have identified and will now critique.

Sociologists of both the order and conflict traditions would question Bell's stated opposition to a "holistic" conception of society. For this author, society consists of three distinctive and disparate realms: the technoeconomic structure, the polity, and culture. Each of these supposedly obeys different principles, and what happens in one need not directly affect the others. While the integration of society, its institutions and culture, may be imperfect, such fragmentation of spheres by Bell is dubious and inadequately explained. Capitalism, for example, is both structural reality *and* ideology, or in Bell's terms technostructure and culture. And surely the consumptive element of hedonism (a cultural malaise) follows at least in part the massive production of consumer goods and their promotion by a rich advertising industry (both aspects of the structural realm).

Bell's early aversion to the "passé" ideas of European sociology is also selective. Although he quarrels incessantly with Marx (and his presumed heirs), we have demonstrated the influence of Rousseau and Weber. (Indeed, there are many others.) The pluralist conception of human nature, society, and social science has European roots. And Bell's reaffirmation of contractual liberalism as a point of assault on the cultural contradictions of capitalism is little more than a brief resurrection of *Du Contrat Social*.

Another point of concern centers on the role of knowledge in society and social relations. Apparently, in the postindustrial society those with the power of ideas are preeminent. Now Plato advanced the conception of the philosopher king in the fourth century B.C. However, through history it appears that kings (and other ruling forces) have found it easier to employ philosophers (and scientists, technologists, and so forth) than to become philosophers.

In the modern world, knowledge is often servant to power in other ways. Today's public universities are funded by the state, while private institutions are dependent on endowments. The research programs of both are heavily dependent on the grants of government agencies and private foundations, as well as contributions and payments for services from corporations, other businesses, and individuals. Hence the agenda for the creation of knowledge, that is, the designation of the specific problems to be solved, is not constructed by academics whose only quest is "truth." These and related arguments constitute the operating principles of a "political economy of knowledge," and Bell does not tell us how or why they shall be suspended in the postindustrial society.

Bell's position on knowledge can be questioned on other grounds. He contends that the growth of the professional and technical occupations, as well as the ascendance of white-collar jobs and the increasing education of the population, confirm the preeminence of knowledge in the changing economy. There are those who disagree with this conception of the cerebral society. Harry Braverman (1974) in an exhaustive study suggested that much work has been degraded in the twentieth century. For example, most professional and technical people sell their labor for a wage. Further, wearing a white collar does not mean one is more "knowledgeable" than those wearing a blue collar, or that clerical and sales routines are more mentally demanding than factory work. Finally, most professional and technical people do not trade in the "theoretical knowledge" that Bell asserts will lead the new society.

Moving to another issue, Bell's assertions concerning corporate managers in the 1950s were and are dubious. Certainly today the upper echelons of leading corporations have a strong property interest in their organizations, with stock ownership and options representing a substantial part of their total compensation. There is, as Bell asserted, a managerial ideology just as there are other occupational ideologies. However the argument that a managerial class is united purely by common ideas and not by ownership of property is wholly unconvincing.

A final point relates to the ideological content of this theoretical system. Bell, perhaps more clearly than other sociologists, makes clear the relationship between the pluralist vision of society on the one side and liberalism on the other. His is an idea system that embraces extensive reform while clearly rejecting the transformation of the material and class structure of society. Reform instead assumes the nature of a transformation of culture, which in turn follows the expansion of the knowledge base in the postindustrial society. Further, Bell denies the power of a political elite while confirming the necessity of a social hierarchy. He argues that stratification is just when it is based on merit (defined in terms of expert knowledge) rather than property. And finally, above all, Bell remains constant to his vision of the "open society."

> The new divisions, created by the status anxieties of new middle-class groups, pose a new threat. The rancors of McCarthyism were one of its ugly excesses. However, the United States, so huge and complex that no single political boss or any single political group has ever been able to dominate it, will in time undoubtedly diminish these divisions too. This is an open society, and these anxieties are part of the price we pay for that openness. (1960: 112)

# ■ Lewis Coser (b. 1913): The Functions of Conflict

We shall close this chapter on pluralist politics with an examination of the theoretical efforts of Lewis A. Coser. A superficial analysis of this modern pluralist might suggest that Coser's explanations stem from a synthesis of several paradigms. However, while it is true that he focuses with frequency on "social conflict," it is equally true that in his theoretical system, the forces of opposition in society function to *maintain* social structure. Although this sounds like a merger of Marx and Durkheim, Coser leaves no doubt as to his intellectual debt. His is a sociology in the tradition of Georg Simmel. Nowhere is this clearer than in Coser's conception of conflict.

As we noted in the previous section, Durkheim and his heirs stress the role of value consensus in the integration of social order. Although forms of deviance (including crime) and their punishment are conceived as having certain beneficial consequences (such as defining normative boundaries), by the logic of functionalism, broad-scale conflict is socially destructive. Conversely, in Marxist social thought, an existing society of classes is destructive and requisite of change through conflict. Now despite their immense differences, the logic of both systems of thought conceives of conflict as a force that *undermines* societal structure. Simmel (and Coser) for his part conceptualized conflict as a form of *social interaction* that often serves to *found, integrate, and carry on* that structure.

Lewis A. Coser was born in Germany on November 27, 1913, the son of a Berlin banker. He attended the Sorbonne in Paris between 1934 and 1938, completing his tenure there the year before Hitler's blitzkrieg swept through

Poland touching off the Second World War. Coser emigrated to the United States, and in 1942 married Rose Laub (who was to become a worthy sociologist in her own right). Hence, the important formative experiences for Lewis Coser include the early horrors of European anti-Semitism, immigration, war, and refuge in the United States.

After a period as instructor of sociology at the University of Chicago (1948–1950), and while an instructor at Brandeis, Coser received his Ph.D. from Columbia University in 1954. He left Brandeis in 1968 to assume a position at the State University of New York at Stony Brook, where he remains as a distinguished professor of sociology. He has served as president of the American Sociological Association, the Society for the Study of Social Problems, and the Eastern Sociological Association. He is a former editor of *Modern Review* and has served in a similar capacity for *Dissent* since 1954. Coser's major works, which we shall review and critique in due course, include *The Functions of Social Conflict* (1956); *The American Communist Party: A Critical History* (with Irving Howe, 1957); *Continuities in the Study of Social Conflict* (1967); and *Greedy Institutions* (1974).

## Assumptions

The assumptions underlying the sociological thought of Lewis Coser clearly center in the pluralist model. His is a vision of human nature and society in which the essential attributes of personal freedom and sovereignty find expression in open institutions. These institutions, in turn, are accountable to those they serve. Moreover, in "modern nontotalitarian societies" (1974: 3), a segmented and heterogeneous order prevails, offering a multiplicity of choices and group affiliations to their members. Following the conceptualizations of Simmel, Coser holds that within this diverse milieu, "the individual lives at the intersection of many social circles."

The enmeshing of the social actor in this web of group affiliations means a breaking down of total loyalty to any single segment, whether the traditional spheres of family and new religious communities or the power of the state in more authoritarian societies. There is a consistent theme in Coser's work: The diverse society with its competing interests and divided loyalties faces constant threat from those who would monopolize allegiance and demand a sameness of view. In 1974 Coser referred to such forces as "greedy institutions," which are distinctive by their ability to command complete subservience. For example, those with political power are able to demand complete loyalty from "aliens" who are without roots in the society. In other cases, "greedy" families control certain members (frequently women), and similar collectives (such as the Jesuits or the Communist party) demand total allegiance from members.

Coser's interest in greedy institutions of the collective sort is evidenced in an earlier coauthored work on the American Communist party published in

1957. In it, Irving Howe and Coser traced the party's history from its "official" birth in 1919 to what the authors believed to be its effective demise in the middle 1950s. Although essentially a narrative, *The American Communist Party* identified factors related to the decline of that organization. Although the authors gave some attention to the role of the federal government in harassing the organization, especially in the 1920s, they emphasized (1) factionalism within the party, (2) "Stalinization" with its insistence on ideological purity (party over person and the myth of Soviet utopia), and (3) the purging of the party from its only base of legitimacy, the American trade unions.

The conception of theoretical science that undergirds the thought of Lewis Coser owes much to Georg Simmel. Each in his turn assumed that conflict is a process, one of several forms of social interaction (1975: 211), and constructed his theory in part upon that base. Moreover, both men believed that a macrosociological theory of grand design was too far removed from the empirical world. In this latter sense, Coser also reflects the influence of his teacher at Columbia, Robert K. Merton, who expressed his aversion to holistic theory by calling for explanatory systems of the "middle range" (see Chapter 5). Merton's sociology proved of importance to his student in yet another way. If you recall, it was Merton's particular brand of functionalism that allowed for the analysis of *unanticipated and often paradoxical consequences of social phenomena*. It is precisely this approach that Coser has followed in some of his most important work.

## Theoretical Content

In *The Functions of Social Conflict* (1956), Coser expressed his interest in recovering something of the spirit of earlier American sociology. He believed that this earlier generation would have agreed with Charles Horton Cooley, who defined conflict as "the life of society, [where] progress emerges from a struggle in which individual, class, or institution seeks to realize its own idea of good" (quoted in Coser, 1956: 20).[8] Coser explicitly rejected the sociology of Talcott Parsons as only an "extended commentary on the Hobbesian question How is social order possible?" (1956: 21). Rather than joining Parsons and other order theorists in dismissing conflict as a matter of "tension," "strain," or "malfunctioning," Coser claimed interest in its "positive" as well as its negative functions.

Coser's theoretical propositions are in actuality drawn "solely" from Georg Simmel's classic, *Conflict* (1955). In *The Functions of Social Conflict*, Coser formalized, clarified, and expanded the earlier sociology of his historical

---

[8]Cooley's theory is reviewed in Chapter 12.

mentor. He began by noting that conflict serves certain "binding" or integrative functions. Specifically, it sharpens the boundary lines that provide groups members with a distinctive identity. (Or to use the terms of William Graham Sumner, there can be no in-group without an out-group.) Recall for a moment the pluralist conception of society. While there is balance, it does not come from a consensus of values. Rather, the assumption is one of diversity and antagonism. For Coser (and Simmel), patterned antagonisms preserve the *balance of opposing forces.*

Divergent groups within the broader order also develop internal solidarity through conflict. In this reformulation of Simmel, Coser argues that "social divisions and systems of stratification" are preserved (not ultimately destroyed as with Marx) as each stratum defines its own interests and position through reciprocal antagonisms. However, in an open society where social mobility is prized, hostility for the higher classes is mingled with attraction. This emotional state was termed *ressentiment* by Simmel. Hence, rather than seeking the negation of a ruling class, those of the lower strata have a "sour grapes attitude: that which is condemned is secretly craved" (1956: 36).

Integrative conflict is also often expressed through "safety-valve" institutions and rituals. These are patterned practices, enduring over time, that allow the release of hostility and hence the maintenance of the group or social structure. Coser cites analytically diverse examples of rituals that function to "clear the air." In the first of these, a form of *socially approved conflict* may be directed toward the original source, as with the duel or other culturally limited acts of revenge. Such practices are later replaced by the power of state law in industrial societies, but each serves to prevent a widening circle of hostility.

In witchcraft and other interactions involving scapegoating, another form of safety valve is evident. Here vulnerable people or forces are blamed for the "sins," ill fortune, or difficult circumstances of the group. Conflict is *indirectly expressed toward symbolic substitutes* because the original sources are either inaccessible or powerful.

Finally, other safety valves allow for the *alteration of the means* by which conflict is expressed. For example, humor and theater may replace sword and pistol. In a related line of logic, the programming of the contemporary mass media allows for the vicarious experience of disallowed behaviors. By this means, hostility, sexual impulses, and other potentially disruptive practices and emotions are displaced and rechanneled. Although focusing on the maintenance functions of safety valves, Coser notes certain dysfunctional properties. Hence, innocent individuals or groups suffer (as with racial or religious scapegoating), and necessary social change may be slowed or denied.

Conflict, according to Coser, may be *realistic or nonrealistic.* In the former, members of groups or societies compete for specific if scarce resources and are willing to abandon one set of tactics for another. In the latter, there is no room for negotiation because members derive gratification from acts of aggression. In the first case, labor union members might work to get a larger share through strikes, slowdowns, bargaining, and legislative and/or judicial means. In the second case, Coser would argue that there is no substitute for the aggressive confrontation of the strike.

Several of the propositions Coser derives from the work of Simmel deal with hostility in more intimate social relationships. Put simply, "closeness and consequently a relatively high degree of involvement of the personality make it likely that conflict will assume greater intensity" (1956: 73). For example, members of Congress may engage in heated debate during the day and amiably converse in a social function that evening. However, when conflict occurs among family members, it is apt to be more passionate, radical, and pervasive. In the intimate relationship, little is held in reserve and the worth of the whole person is constantly at stake. It follows that societies composed of closely knit and exclusive groups and organizations will experience a more extreme form of conflict, when such erupts, than those based on a multiplicity of group memberships.

Coser discerns from Simmel a number of propositions that point up how *unexpected forms of unification* may develop among clear adversaries. In a state of warfare, antagonists are driven to types of interaction that otherwise would not exist. These may come to assume the nature of mutually binding rules of engagement or even international law. For example, banning certain forms of weapons unifies warring parties in a higher community of humanity. Once institutionalized, such norms originally conceived in conflict may become the basis for a new socialization for those with otherwise competing interests.

A similar interactive process occurs among adversarial parties within society. For example, big industry leads to big unions, the unification of worker organizations is balanced by the unification of management, and both parties develop a reciprocal structure of rules that in turn leads to a binding contract. Furthermore, a party assured of its strength will desire to deal with a unified adversary that represents "the other side." Thus, a union must have power to ensure that all members will abide by the contract ratified by a majority. Coser has also argued that organized labor needs organized employers associations so that the union does not have to bargain separately with many small interests in an industry. In this and a myriad of other ways, both competing parties "rely on a common universe of rules" (1956: 132).

As Coser interprets Simmel, conflict is ultimately a test of power. But Coser's conception of conflict is paradoxical and hence thoroughly grounded in the pluralist imagery of society. He argues that accommodation between and among various interest groups is possible only if each party understands the strength of others. Yet this understanding of the power of the antagonist can only be had through some form of conflict (preferably realistic) because no other means for testing strength is available. Ultimately, this trial of relative power is resolved by the establishment of a new state of balance. Conflict therefore is a process whereby *a succession of new equilibriums is created*. In Coser's words, the struggle of opposing forces "rather than being disruptive and dissociating may indeed be a means of balancing and hence maintaining a society as a going concern" (1956: 137).

## Critique

Although enlightening and suggestive, Coser's work raises a number of points that remain at issue. First, it is clear that his major effort is more derived than original. As he candidly admits, his is an attempt at discovering the sociology of conflict as seen by Georg Simmel. In the attempt, however, he has systematized that work and gone beyond its boundaries. Still, as with Simmel, Coser's work is process bound. Although he calls for a structural focus, conflict is dealt with as a pandemic form of interaction functioning to maintain a supremely balanced social world. It is also conceptually "positive," missing two darker yet essential properties. Let us examine these last two sentences is some detail.

In effect, Coser argues that conflict is universal and proceeds to offer so many examples at so many levels that it is impossible to refute the claim. Now on the one hand, Coser is correct. Conflict of some sort or another can be found in all societies and all social relationships. On the other hand, an obvious truism may be trivial. What Coser has failed to do is examine the historically specific structural forces that give rise to particular movements and precise types of conflict. (For example, although Marx argued that the history of the world is a history of class struggle, the nature of that struggle and the combatants therein vary with the prevailing mode of production.)

The nature of social states of equilibrium is also troublesome. In one sense, the relationship between master and slave, colonizer and colonized, powerful men and powerless women all represent conditions of balance. It appears that not all such states of equipoise are created equal. It is the ability of one side to dominate the other that is given short weight by Coser's scales. *Briefly put, in this theoretical system of conflict, the element of coercion is missing.* Coser conceives of "functional" conflict as a sort of sanitary struggle among equals that purifies the social order. Conflict ultimately threatens the equilibrium of social structures only when they are rigid.

It is the rigid social system or the "greedy" institutions that demand total allegiance for which conflict is disruptive. The open society, with its multiple group memberships, diversity, and permeable class structure, allows for the expression of hostilities and greater access to rewards and power. Such orders are able to bend rather than break, sustaining a high level of turmoil that does not threaten societal integration. Thus, in Coser's liberal theory of society, the conception of functional conflict is missing yet another element. Here, social contention is a *form of accommodation and a means of catharsis, not a force for structural change.*

# ■ *Bibliography*

Bell, Daniel
1960            *The End of Ideology.* Glencoe, Ill.: The Free Press.
1967            *Marxian Socialism in the United States.* Princeton, N.J.:
                Princeton University Press.
1973            *The Coming of Post-Industrial Society.* New York: Basic
                Books.
1976            *The Cultural Contradictions of Capitalism.* New York: Basic
                Books.

Bell, Daniel (Ed.)
1955 (1963)     *The Radical Right: The New American Right Expanded and
                Updated.* Garden City, N.Y.: Doubleday.

Bell, Daniel, and Irving Kristol (Eds.)
1981            *The Crisis in Economic Theory.* New York: Basic Books.

Braverman, Harry
1974            *Labor and Monopoly Capital: The Degradation of Work in the
                Twentieth Century.* New York: Monthly Review Press.

Chertok, Jeffers
1986            "Social Interest and Categorical Structure: Conceptions of
                History and Social Change." Unpublished monograph,
                Department of Sociology, Eastern Washington University,
                Cheney.

Coser, Lewis A.
1956            *The Functions of Social Conflict.* Glencoe, Ill.: The Free
                Press.
1965            *Georg Simmel.* Englewood Cliffs, N.J.: Prentice-Hall.
1967            *Continuities in the Study of Social Conflict.* New York: The
                Free Press.
1970            *Men of Ideas: A Sociologist's View.* New York: The Free
                Press.
1974            *Greedy Institutions.* New York: The Free Press.
1975            "Structure and Conflict." In Peter M. Blau (Ed.), *Ap-
                proaches to the Study of Social Structure,* pp. 210–219. New
                York: The Free Press.

Dahrendorf, Ralf
(1957) 1959     *Class and Class Conflict in Industrial Society.* Stanford,
                Calif.: Stanford University Press.
1968            *Essays in the Theory of Society.* Stanford, Calif.: Stanford
                University Press.
1979            *Life Chances.* Chicago: Chicago University Press.

Featherstone, Joseph
1979            "John Dewey and David Riesman: From the Lost Individ-

ual to the Lonely Crowd." In Herbert Gans et al. (Eds.), *On the Making of Americans,* pp. 3–39. Philadelphia: University of Pennsylvania Press.

Gans, Herbert, et al. (Eds.)
1979                           *On the Making of Americans.* Philadelphia: University of Pennsylvania Press.

Howe, Irving, and Lewis Coser
1957                           *The American Communist Party: A Critical History (1919–1957).* Boston: Beacon Press.

Meyerson, Martin
1979                           "Foreword." In Herbert Gans et al. (Eds.), *On the Making of Americans,* pp. vii–x. Philadelphia: University of Pennsylvania Press.

Riesman, David
(1950) 1969                    *The Lonely Crowd.* New Haven, Conn.: Yale University Press.
1951                           "White Collar: The American Middle Classes." *American Journal of Sociology* 57:513–515.
1954                           *Individualism Reconsidered.* Glencoe, Ill.: The Free Press.

Simmel, Georg
1955                           *Conflict.* Translated by Kurt H. Wolff. Glencoe, Ill.: The Free Press.

Weingart, Peter
1969                           "Beyond Parsons? A Critique of Ralf Dahrendorf's Conflict Theory." *Social Forces* 48(2):151–165.

# CHAPTER *12*

---

# ■ Symbolic Interaction

One important tradition in the history of sociology has been constructed around the most elemental and basic aspect of human social life: interaction. Although many of the acts that constitute our behavior are private, others involve mutual exchange with people. For example, the conversation that occurs between and among human beings differs from that of infrahuman species simply because it is meaningful. When we speak, we attempt to anticipate the intentions and interpretations others will attribute to our words. At the same time, we are conscious that the "others" will be doing the same. Yet our exchanges are not purely verbal. As a matter of course, we communicate by an array of body signals ranging from the clear to the subtle. When such behavior shapes, or is shaped by, the behavior of others, social interaction has occurred.

It is not enough to point up the ability of human beings to respond consciously to the acts of others. Interaction hinges on the sharing of meaning, a process that involves an intricate system of symbols. The theories we examine in this chapter stress the importance of a *symbolic universe,* a world of signs, images, and representations. Notwithstanding the vast repertoire of nonverbal symbols, symbolic interactionists in sociology generally affirm the social power of language.

Language represents both the objective properties of vocal sounds or written symbols and the subjective meaning associated with words. The human ability to employ language to create mental images of both concrete and abstract phenomena is the basis of human culture. Yet, it would be erroneous to assume that a sociological interest in language is expressed in the science of linguistics. The theories that follow do not address the study of the structure, development, and relationships of various languages. Nor are they primarily concerned with the techniques of communication or the development and employment of a vocabulary. Remember that the world of symbols is rather the *medium* of interaction. The focus remains on how people employ symbols—in reaching others, in developing conceptions of self, or in constructing a social reality.

In the preceding chapters in this section, we established the importance of philosophical idealism for the pluralist paradigm. The theories to follow in this chapter also quite logically deal with the primacy of a world of ideas. For these, the essence of reality is neither objective nor material. It originates instead in the mind of the beholder. Also to be noted is the centrality of the human actor in these systems of thought. Members of social orders are not portrayed as dwarfed and determined by massive social structures. Instead, societies, institutions, culture, and the history that marks their development are thought to be made from the inside out. Society remains, in the words of Simmel, a "web of interactions." This level of abstraction ensures for symbolic interaction a microsociological nature.

# ■ Robert E. Park (1864–1944): Human Ecology

The citadel of early symbolic interaction in the United States was the Department of Sociology at the University of Chicago. And certainly, one of the most illustrious figures at that institution was Robert Ezra Park.[1] Park's significance rests not merely with formal contributions to theory but in his linkage of European systems of thought with an early sophistication in social research.

## History and Biography

Park was born in Harveyville, Pennsylvania, on February 14, 1864, the son of a well-to-do businessman. He grew up in the town of Red Wing, located within a sparsely populated region of Minnesota. In 1887 he received a bachelor's degree in philosophy from the University of Michigan, where his chief instructor was the pragmatist John Dewey. Dewey's influence in the life of Park assumed several forms. First of all, Dewey introduced Park to Franklin Ford, with whom Park came to share a passionate interest in journalism and public opinion. More importantly, Dewey's pragmatic philosophy became a cornerstone for much of Park's later sociology. Dewey regarded the criticism of culture to be the basic function of philosophy. He believed that basic ethical and other philosophic questions could be enhanced through the widest study of the customs and inventions of human societies.

---

[1] Important biographical material on Park can be found in Turner, 1967; Matthews, 1977; and Hughes, 1969.

Dewey's conception of philosophy logically supported the worth of comparative sociology and cross-cultural inquiry. This blended well with his belief in diversity, democratic reform, and the value of free, though problem-centered thought. He believed in a "consciousness of culture" and saw social inquiry as a means toward greater understanding. However, such inquiry was to bear the stamp of methodological rigor. Dewey held that problems were to be clearly identified and that research required both a sensitivity to and constant reappraisal of the objectives and values implicit in the process. And consistent with the pragmatism evident in his view of "progressive" education, Dewey believed that the best way to know a society and its culture is through a process of intelligent, involved, and systematic problem solving. This synthesis of values, science, and philosophy was to have a clear impact on the later sociology of Robert Park.

For over a decade after his graduation from Michigan, Park served as a reporter for various newspapers in such cities as Minneapolis, New York, and Chicago. During this period he came to conceive of the urban world as a social laboratory. With reformist ideals in mind, he covered the stories of immigrant poverty and exploitation, of political machines and bosses, of the richness of the cultural mix in the metropolis. After a decade on the streets, he entered Harvard to study philosophy and some psychology. His specific intention was the scientific study of the relationship between the news media and society.

In 1899 Park received his M.A. in philosophy from Harvard, where he studied under the noted philosopher William James. It was James who argued that the world of consciousness is a "stream"; hence the mind is not best conceived as rigid and compartmentalized but as a dynamic and fluid process shaped continuously by novel experiences. This philosophical stance lent itself well to Park's emerging conception of the relationship between interaction and the inner world. It was to become fundamental to the symbolic interactionism of the "Chicago School" in the 1920s and 1930s.

Upon leaving Harvard, Park, now married and with children, went to study abroad. He attended the University of Berlin, where he received his only formal instruction in sociology through the lectures of Georg Simmel. Simmel's conception of forms of interaction was to have a clear and compelling impact on Park's later academic life. Moving on to the University of Heidelberg, where he defended his dissertation, appropriately entitled *Masse und Publikum,* Park received his Ph.D. in 1904. Afterward he returned to the United States.

The next major milestone in Park's life came when he became secretary to the Congo Reform Association. Belgium, like other colonial powers, had institutionalized a cruel and repressive regime in its African possessions. It was at this time that Park met the president of Tuskegee Institute, Booker T. Washington, who convinced Park that he should study the conditions of blacks living in the southern United States. Ever the activist, Park accepted Washington's invitation, using Tuskegee as a base while traveling the region. Over the next seven years he developed a strong interest in domestic and international race relations and wrote a series of magazine articles condemning Belgian atrocities in the Congo.

In 1914, when he was 50 years old, Robert Park accepted an invitation from W. I. Thomas to teach a course on the Negro in America at the University of Chicago. He repeated the course the next year and shortly thereafter became a member of the Chicago faculty. He brought to this institution consummate academic preparation, the skills of a journalist, and the zeal of a reformer. During the zenith of Chicago sociology, Park was a guiding force. This was reflected in his transplanting of Simmelian thought from Europe, a theoretical system that proved basic to symbolic interaction. The "Chicago School" of sociology also bore the imprint of Park's concern with minority relations and other social problems. Finally, the employment of "participant observation" as a research tactic by Chicago scholars owed much to Park's journalistic experience and methods. He left Chicago, again to travel, and then settled at Fisk, a black university in Nashville, in 1936. He died eight years later.

## Assumptions

The underlying assumptions in Park's theoretical system bear the distinctive historical imprint that marked the worlds not only of Dewey and James but of other interactionists we examine elsewhere, including Charles Horton Cooley, George Herbert Mead, and W. I. Thomas among others. Park was born the year before the ending of the great American Civil War and died a year before the Axis powers were defeated in the Second World War. However, his life was shaped more by the reformist spirit and progressive politics that marked the Midwest from the latter decades of the nineteenth century until the outbreak of the "war to end all wars." It was an era of explosive industrial growth, the urban-based factory system, and teeming cities fed by immigrants and migrants from the declining countryside. It was a time of muck, of muckrakers, and of publishers such as Hearst and Pulitzer who made fortunes by commodifying and sensationalizing despair. It was a winter of urban slums and rural blight, of child labor and industrial death and dying, of racist division and the privilege of the native born. But through it all, Park and his kindred spirits retained an optimism founded on pluralist beliefs: The abuses of their period were only temporary aberrations; the American people when educated and informed would do the right thing; and above all, the existing society held out the promise of justice.

Consistent with the pluralist image of human nature, Park held an ambivalent view of individuals. On the one hand, men and women compete and struggle. On the other, they exhibit emotional ties, ideals, and a common purpose. Although it is true that each uses the other, the one commonly joins the many in collective action to "recreate the world" (Park, 1952: 178–181). Yet Park, more than modern interactionists, reserved a place for instinct. He argued that *social distance,* a state of mind that separates groups such as races or classes by creating conceptions of social "place," does not have to be learned. Moreover, he believed that prejudice is essentially an expression of the natural disposition to maintain that social distance. However, Park also recognized that prejudice is a conservative force for the maintenance of the status quo (Park, 1950: 255–260).

As to society, Park assumed an order where antagonistic elements are bound, at least temporarily, by arrangements collectively termed "social control." Thus by means of binding norms, the members of society conform rather than give vent to their different interests. This state of equilibrium is dynamic, especially in an "open class" society (Park and Burgess, 1966: 664–665, originally published 1921). Park's conception of society is one of constantly emerging states of accommodation, in which conflict between contending parties comes to a temporary halt. Yet he defined each new plateau as a point in a progression. As a clear illustration, Park cited the turbulence of race relations in the United States. He thought such conflicts are indicators of progressive change and that the more powerless groups walk away from such struggles with a new accommodation and improved status (Park, 1950: 229–235).

Park's assumptions concerning the nature of human science logically follow from the discussion thus far. Sociology was defined as *the science of collective behavior.* However, we would miss Park's meaning should we focus on the usual meaning of the term *collective behavior.* Although Park was interested in such things as publics, crowds, and especially public opinion and the media, it is the *processual* meaning inherent in the collective forms of social life that entranced him. Such is evident in a dynamic theoretical language of stages, movement, transition, and forms of renewal. For Park (and other interactionists), the social reality is not static and timeless but changing and temporal. Its nature is not instantaneous but continuous, not that of a lanquid pool but of a current. At base, society and its means of social control are created through such processes. And for Park, as with Simmel, explanatory systems in sociology must seek to identify and clarify these essentially micro-level courses of action.

## Theoretical Content

In *Human Communities* (1952), Park pioneered with his early efforts in the field of human ecology. He conceived of the community as a "biotic" arrangement. Whether comprised of plants, other animal species, or Homo sapiens, communities share the common properties of a population distributed along territorial lines "rooted in the soil," with each constituent member or group living in a symbiotic relationship. The social community is also such a biotic order, reflecting interdependence and territoriality, which emerges from a universal struggle for existence. As with all communities, each member of society competes for position in the "spatial" order, yet each is dependent on others and the whole.

Park described the developmental change within the community by reference to the twin principles of *dominance* and *succession*. The former refers to the competitive clash among dissimilar members or groups for standing or resources. The latter refers to an orderly process through which all biotic orders develop and change. In the metropolitan community, territorial zones or areas reflect by the social conditions of their population the struggle for power. Yet, the population of such "spaces" does not remain fixed (1952: 144–155). For example, the immigrant newcomers routinely settle near the city center. City centers are typically decaying areas that are ripe for commercialization and industrialization. However, Park argued that the immigrants did not stay there. Rather they moved, over time and generations, outward through other concentric zones toward the suburbs. This is the staged movement of succession (1952: 221–225).

The principles of dominance and succession both stem from what Park (and his colleague Ernest W. Burgess) believed to be the most basic social process: *competition*. Drawing from biology, he argued that this form of interaction is universal and elementary in all natural or biotic orders. However, he identified other processes that are distinctively societal. While competition over resources and space is ongoing and impersonal, *conflict* is a conscious process intended to secure social status and the relative control associated therewith (Park and Burgess, 1966: 505–507, originally published 1921). The third process is *accommodation,* which denotes a temporary end to conflict and the support of the prevailing hierarchy through measures of social control (such as law and custom) (Park and Burgess, 1966: 664–665). Finally, comes *assimilation,* in which dissimilar people and groups share their experiences and form a truly common culture (Park and Burgess, 1966: 729–735).

A final focal concern in Park's theoretical system centers on the relationship between self and society. The conscious conceptions of distinctive identity are based in large measure on the roles played by the human actor. For Park, such roles are bound generally to one's status and specifically to one's occupation. In *Society* (1955) he argued that the origin of the self is in the responses of others to one's particular status in the social order. It therefore follows that the individual simultaneously bound by two cultures with different conceptions of status and role may possess a distorted social identity. Park employed the term *marginal man* to describe this condition. Yet in the tradition of Simmel's work on the *stranger,* Park argued that marginality provides a special vantage point from which to understand and critique arrangements taken for granted by the mainstream. And in a manner reminiscent of Dewey, Park asserted that "It is in the mind of the marginal man—where the changes and fusions of culture are going on—that we can best study the processes of civilization and progress" (1950: 356).

## Critique

Robert Park was a driving force in the development of sociology at the University of Chicago and in the formulation of the general theoretical orientation of symbolic interaction. However, as is evident in our review, Park did not break completely free from the sort of Darwinian informed organicism that shaped certain of the order theories of the previous section. This is evidenced in the primacy accorded the competitive struggle for existence and the clear preference for a progressive and evolutionary conception of social processes.

Although conflict and interdependence are both given their due, the distinguishing feature of this system of thought is its strain toward the balanced state. Not unlike Coser, social incompatibility for Park presents the opportunity to purge the present order in stages, not to make a new one. Thus social processes reflect a "natural history" of movement to higher states of integration. Such processes are evident in the following logically related examples. All reveal this theorist's faith in progress.

In Park's zones of metropolitan development, the subjugation of newcomers and other pariahs is never permanent. Rather, through succession, the marginal and outcasts move on, not simply changing residence but also status over time. In Park's analysis of social change, still another naturally occurring process is presented. This time, three stages of development are identified: widely based perceptions of injustice, the subsequent rise of social movements, and the resulting stage of accommodation at the institutional level. Finally, despite the centrality of competition in Park's thought, the ultimate victory belongs to cultural assimilation. New groups may face entrenched and unfair customs, but as neophytes (such as immigrants) grapple with the old culture, it will change its form, allowing former outcasts entrance. (Hence the dominant culture is problematic not so much for its content but for its *exclusivity*.)

In the ideological sense, the open society is as crucial to Park's theory as it is to Bell, Riesman, or Coser. Park's conceptions of new stages of accommodation and the emergence of assimilation assume a responsive power structure and a tolerance for diversity. Absent from Park's thought is the language of structurally founded coercion, the issues of stratification, and the problematics of social control. In his theory, where there is dominance, it is naturally occurring and episodic. Where there are classes, they are open. And where there is society, there is a control organization with norms, rules, and custom constantly being renegotiated by the marginal and disadvantaged.

# ■ George Herbert Mead (1863-1931): Mind, Self, and Society

George Herbert Mead is another of the original minds that shaped the theoretical development of symbolic interaction at the University of Chicago.[2]

---

[2]Important biographical and historical references to Mead include Wallace, 1967; Reck's "Introduction" in Mead, 1964; and Miller's "Introduction" in Mead, 1982.

Born in 1863 in South Hadley, Massachusetts, Mead was the son of a New England clergyman who later taught at Oberlin Theological Seminary. The young Mead was nurtured in an intellectual climate that permitted a "social gospel" interpretation of religious principles. A theology of social justice knew fertile ground at Oberlin. It was one of the first colleges to admit blacks and women, and it served as an important point on the Underground Railroad that served runaway slaves from the South. Of course, more traditional causes also flourished. The Anti-Saloon League, a bellwether organization of the temperance movement, began there (Coser, 1977: 342).

During his years at Oberlin, Mead distinguished himself as a gifted student and something of an intellectual rebel. He did not believe the traditional theological claim that the mind, as seat of the soul, has a supernatural existence independent of the body. Such a doctrine implies that spiritual perfection is somehow independent of the societal good, a view of ethics that Mead explicitly rejected throughout his academic life. After graduation from Oberlin in 1883, Mead taught school, tutored, and did railroad construction work. In 1887 he enrolled at Harvard University to seek advanced training in philosophy.

While at Harvard, Mead studied with William James and Josiah Royce, the same philosophers that were to later strongly influence Robert Park. Here Mead grappled with the Kantian and Hegelian traditions of idealism (see chapters 9 and 14, respectively) and the uniquely American philosophy of *pragmatism*. In 1888 he began a three-year period of study at Leipzig and Berlin, where he studied under the idealist historian Wilhelm Dilthey. It was Dilthey who influenced not only Mead but Weber, arguing that the understanding of individual thought requires a corresponding comprehension of the sociohistorical milieu. Also during this time, Mead came to know the work of the early psychophysiologist Wilhelm Wundt and was especially impressed by Wundt's analysis of the role of gestures in the development of language.

In 1891 Mead accepted a position in the Department of Philosophy and Psychology at the University of Michigan. That faculty also included John Dewey and Charles Horton Cooley. Encouraged and stimulated by his colleagues, Mead began to form the early scaffolding of his "social behaviorism." Cooley was to remain at Ann Arbor, but Dewey left for a new post at the University of Chicago. In 1893 Mead accepted the invitation of his friend to join the Chicago faculty in philosophy. Here he was to remain until his death in 1931.

While at the University of Chicago, Mead combined his professorial responsibilities with his interest in social reform. In keeping with the social implications of pragmatism, he joined Dewey in advocating "progressive education." Mead was also involved in the *settlement house* movement in Chicago, a forerunner of today's community centers, where the poor received educational and social services (Mills, 1966: 307–324).

Mead wrote very little for publication. However, he was a consummate lecturer, and his class notes became the basis for a number of posthumous volumes. The editing of his notes fell to certain of his students. However, the influence of Mead on Chicago sociology did not come through the professional literature. Sociologists grappling with the nature of the metropolis were not well served by the then popular Darwinian notions of competition or by ecological theory that seemed to relate the conditions of social life to the nature of the physical environment. Something else was needed, a theoretical basis for explaining the city in human form. The city, as Robert Park came to argue, is a "state of mind." It is the product of inherently *social processes*, forms of interaction that transcend the physical and artificial. It was to be the theory of the philosopher George Herbert Mead that gave voice and logic to Chicago urban sociology.

## The Chicago School

The nature and growth of symbolic interaction at the University of Chicago are not to be separated from the nature and growth of the metropolis during the era (Faris, 1967). At the turn of the century, Chicago was a thriving, bustling, expanding industrial and commercial center. Its factories swallowed up those who had in earlier generations been tied to the land. Its steel mills prospered with the ready abundance of midwestern coal and iron ore. Its location in the midst of a network of rail and waterways was natural for a transportation center. This geography, in conjunction with the ready abundance of midwestern livestock, made Chicago the center of the meat-packing industry.

The expanding economy did not benefit all. Indeed, the flood of urban prosperity at the top quickly became a trickle, drying up before reaching the bottom. Thus, Chicago became a center for many populations sharing few rewards but bearing much stigma. Its landscape was filled with immigrant neighborhoods, racial ghettos, hobo jungles, tenements, and brothels (Steffens, 1904).

Into this vast metropolitan laboratory, Chicago sociologists moved with vigor to study the underside of social life. Little attention was given to the "world of meaning" of the wealthy classes, the political elite, and the conformists. The focus was on the underclasses, the powerless, and the outsiders. Chicago scholars explored the world of delinquents, the mentally ill, hoboes, and criminals. Some were "participant observers"; others took their information from official records: police files, mental hospital records, and census data. All of these predictably confirmed the conventional wisdom: Impoverished and decaying areas of the city had higher rates of deviance.

Later interactionists were to become more aware of the social and political forces that influence both the *definition* of certain behaviors as deviant and the formal *attachment* of the deviant label by agencies of social control. However, in the early Chicago era, those deviant by convention were thought to learn behavior and self-concept through interaction with others in the cultural enclaves of outcasts and outsiders. And again, the theoretical structure for this sociology of deviance was heavily informed by the social philosophy of George Herbert Mead.

## Assumptions

Mead's assumptions on the nature of human being, society, and theoretical social science are clearly those of the pluralist paradigm. As to the first of these, he envisioned a rational, conscious, and reflective human mind in constant quest of meaning. And although centering on the role of social influence, his vision commanded a crucial place for individual freedom. Finally, a pluralist signpost is discernible in Mead's ambivalence about human nature. He held that social (i.e., cooperative) and antisocial (i.e., hostile) impulses are universals. Both are essential for all social organization (Mead, 1934: 304).

Mead's assumptions concerning the nature of society parallel the ambivalence he discerned in human impulses. He believed that those societies most highly developed and organized feature multiple and intricate relationships. In some instances such relationships are formed through common societal interests. However, conflict arises naturally through differences among groups, individuals, and even the various dimensions of the same "individual self" (Mead, 1934: 307).

On the ethical side, Mead argued that the ideal society would constantly seek the perfection of its values through a pragmatic process of redefinition based on the most advanced knowledge (1934: xxxiii). In political terms, such a society of moral beings would find "revolution incorporated in the institution of government itself" (1964: 150). However, the means of that revolution would be "legislation and amendment." At root, Mead's society is a democracy, "an open society of open selves" (Miller, in Mead, 1982: 6).

As for the nature of theoretical social science, Mead's philosophy includes a synthesis of German idealism and American pragmatism. The idealism was not nurtured purely through a reading of Kant and Hegel, or through study with Dilthey. It was advanced by Josiah Royce at Harvard. It was Royce who professed the social nature of the self and moral issues, arguing that "the individual reaches the self only by a process that implies still another self for its existence and thought" (Mead, 1964: 382). Also at Harvard, William James planted the seeds of Mead's pragmatism, later to be given water by John Dewey. For James, knowledge is an "expression of the intelligence by which animals meet the problems with which life surrounds them" (Mead, 1964: 384). Under this pragmatic test, good knowledge is not preordained but revealed through its efficacy in solving problems.

Mead's intention was to study behavior within the social process, an objective that encouraged his students to attach a subtitle to his classic. Hence the book was called *Mind, Self and Society: From the Standpoint of a Social Behaviorist*

(1934). The "social" appellation distinguishes this system of thought from the behaviorism of Mead's contemporary, John Watson, and the later work of B. F. Skinner and George Homans (see Chapter 8). In opposition to these psychological systems, Mead viewed the human mind as unique, with its higher functions having no important parallels among lower animals. This difference is clearly evidenced in the richness of linguistic systems. For Mead and later symbolic interactionists, language is the distinguishing criterion for being human.

Mead's theory is distinctive by means of its interest in the creative (as opposed to deterministic) nature of behavior and the role of contemplation and definition in experience. As to charges that such concerns are too subjective for science, Mead believed that if one's actions evoke the same response in others, then the meaning of symbols is no longer private but a *behavioral* reality that can be studied. Those phenomena that require perceivers are legitimate objects of sociological inquiry and in Mead's words: "We have returned these stolen goods to the world" (quoted in Miller's "Introduction" to Mead, 1982: 5).

## Theoretical Content

Mead's conception of *mind* is that of a "social phenomenon—arising and developing within the social process, within the empirical matrix of social interactions" (1934: 133). Not only does the mind emerge through such exchange, its nature is that of an internal process of communication grounded in the utilization of *significant symbols.* Hence, the mind is processually formed through interaction with others and self-conversation. Symbols, considered significant only when shared with others, dominate the process. For human beings, the most vital and distinctive symbolic communication is language bound. Or in Mead's words, "out of language emerges the field of mind" (1934: 133).

The conception of mind as process rather than product means that consciousness is not a simple captive of external forces. Rather, it is an active and creative force constantly changing and growing. The mind is not a box into which information and experience are indiscriminately poured. Nor does its nature simply reflect an imitation of the behavior of others or fixed responses (whether learned or instinctual) to external stimuli. The process rather is one of sifting selectively through an ongoing barrage of signals and forming "definitions of the situation."

The second component in Mead's trilogy is termed *self.* The self also "arises in social experience," can be thought of as "an object to itself," and possesses a "social structure" (Mead, 1934: 140). This suggests that individuals can conceive of their own being and convert that identity into a form of consciousness. So conceived, the self can be the recipient of both definition and emotion. Symbolic communication is of course crucial to the development of answers to the question Who am I? In consistent fashion, Mead argued that the self is best thought of as a process, and he traced its genesis developmentally.

The development of the self is dependent on learning to take the role of the other. In turn, role taking requires that we imagine how our behavior will be defined from the standpoint of others. For Mead, role taking occurs throughout the developmental process by which the self is constructed and refined. And this process consists of three distinctive phases. From a period of *imitation* without meaning for infants, through the *play-acting* world of children, and finally to the phase of the *generalized other,* the self expands, changes, becomes.

For the very young, role playing is simply a matter of doing what others do. In time, however, the child begins to play "pretend" roles such as parent, sibling, even the imaginary friend. In this course of switching identities and imaginary conversations, the self through play becomes both separate and defined. The child is learning to see a unique self from the various perspectives of other role players.

When at a later point, egocentric play gives way to the rules and "teamwork" of games, the individual learns that the behaviors of other players are somewhat fixed, impersonal, and predictable. In playing the multiple and interlocking roles of the game, and other organized endeavors, self-control emerges. Through such play, one develops and internalizes a group perspective on the self that Mead termed the "generalized other." To the extent that this collective frame of reference matures, the player becomes a social being who will demonstrate some consistency in future behavior (1934: 150–163). Thus, the "inner voice" of the generalized other continues to whisper the complex requirements of being "human."

In the lifelong context of interdependent action, two dimensions of the self emerge, are formed and reformed. In one, the individual develops an identity in *response* to the attitudes of others. Such a response emanates from the solitary individual's definition of the situation. In the other, one assumes the "organized set of attitudes of others" (1934: 175). This component of the self provides the rules for the actual response. For these dimensions, Mead employed the concepts "I" and "Me," respectively. It is the latter that comes with the internalization of the generalized other.

*Society* in Mead's system is little more than an extension of his "organized self." More precisely, the self through interaction takes on "generalized social attitudes" toward a wider environment. Such references are beyond the immediate spheres of personal relationships, intimate groups, or communities. For Mead, the institutions of society consist of "common responses" rooted in such attitudes by which "the modern civilized human individual is and feels himself to be a member not only of a certain local community or state or nation, but also of an entire given race or even civilization as a whole" (1934: 273).

In Mead's theory, both self and the society that is derived therefrom are divided. The free, active, and unique self is tempered by an externally imposed synthesis of the wishes, rules, and roles of others. Ultimately, however, his ideal society evolves—an interacting order in which the individual "I" fuses with the social "Me." In this context, the latter does not exist merely to control the former. Rather, the new self will extend to a new order. In it, the understanding of all others will enhance the uniqueness of the solitary member (1934: 273–281).

## Critique

Approached from the vantage point of the order paradigm, Mead's theory largely ignores the world of culture. Nor does his system provide a central place for value consensus and a view of society as a community of common interests. From the conflict side, Mead's thought is not founded in structural forms of explanation. Also missing is the critical edge that theories of conflict typically direct toward the organization of society. Of course, each model would question the microsociological level at which Mead constructed his system of thought. (One exception would be the modern positivists of the order paradigm. However, they would be logically prone to dismiss much of Mead's work as carrying far too much subjective baggage.) Given his microsociological nexus, Mead's thought is without understanding of large-scale global, societal, or institutional structures. His use of "structure" is limited to such concepts as the organized self, and he reduces institutions to the behavioral level of "common responses."

Other issues arise given Mead's analytic conceptions of theory and method. His emphasis on individual freedom leaves an *indeterministic* view of behavior and raises substantial questions about generalizing the findings of research based on this theoretical system. In Mead's defense, however, his interest was not in specifying the behavioral outcomes of specific forms of social interaction. Rather, the interest was in explaining the *processes* by which mind, self, and society are constructed. From Mead's perspective, such processes are universal.

In terms of its ideological implications, this system of thought exemplifies a distinctive American optimism. It embodies a progressive variety of Darwinism. Not the social Darwinism of Sumner (see Chapter 4), where the strong righteously triumph over the weak, but the Darwinism of the pragmatists, who saw an enlightened and managed evolution. They believed that through ever-widening circles of understanding and ever-perfected knowledge, free people in free societies will ultimately meet and resolve the problems of the age (Davis, 1975). Mead was both a champion of democracy and an internationalist. It is ironic that his theoretical system is so removed in conceptual level from these concerns.

# ■ Charles Horton Cooley (1864–1929): The Individual Writ Large

Although not a member of the sociology faculty at the University of Chicago, Charles Horton Cooley[3] developed a system of thought that strongly influenced symbolic interaction there and elsewhere. Born in Ann Arbor, Michigan, he was the son of a prominent lawyer who served variously as dean of the Law School at the University of Michigan, a justice of that state's supreme court, and the first chairman of the Interstate Commerce Commission. A member of an elite family, Charles had a strained and distant relationship with his father. He was somewhat shy, withdrawn, and given to introspection and fantasy. Rooted in Ann Arbor for almost all of his life, Cooley preferred a tranquil and reflective interpretation of the academic role. His was to become a much more intimate brand of sociology than that of the European pluralists who were his contemporaries.

## History and Biography

Cooley studied engineering at the University of Michigan but could muster no abiding interest in pursuing a career in the field. Rather, he received his graduate training at Michigan in economics and began to read widely in sociology. He received a Ph.D. in 1894, defending a dissertation entitled *The Theory of Transportation*. Like Robert Park, Cooley in his early work demonstrated an interest in human ecology. However, Cooley was heavily influenced by more narrowly drawn psychological positions, which we will review shortly. He synthesized his interest in mind and society in three of his most important works: *Human Nature and the Social Order* (1902), *Social Disorganization* (1909), and *Social Process* (1966, originally published 1918).

Charles Cooley took little interest in the *realpolitik* of his day, although he developed a clear ideological position that infused his work. Historically, the period following the Civil War and continuing on to the beginning of the Great Depression of 1929 was to frame his formal sociology. During the last decade of the nineteenth century, while Cooley was finishing his graduate work and beginning his academic career at Michigan, populist forces became prominent in the American Midwest. The movement featured workers, small landowners, business owners, and sympathetic intellectuals. Their professed objectives were reformist: to attack the pillars of elitism, to control the large trusts, to involve more citizens in political life, and to bring education to bear on the problems and interests of the common people.

---

[3]Important biographical and historical references to Cooley include Jandy, 1942; and Angell, 1968.

Hence, Cooley's world was penetrated by the ideology of progressive democracy and shaped by the ideals of the small community. He was sheltered, by the circumstances of his life and personality, from the rise of industrialization and the hardening of the boundary lines of class. He believed, somewhat romantically, that the best sort of human association would be found in a society protected from the greed of big business and unrestrained industrial growth. He imagined self-reliant people realizing their potential through communal harmony and participation in "town meeting" democracy. For Cooley, the open class system in American life appeared to be closing. The problem was to open it again.

Cooley's intellectual development was marked by a number of other ideas. He was well-read in the German tradition of idealism so important to the pluralist tradition. He was taken with the works of Emerson and Thoreau, whose *transcendentalism* based the search for reality on mental intuition. From Goethe, he garnered a "sense of organic unity" and from Charles Darwin the twin convictions that life is a constantly evolving creative process, with an inherent order that can be studied systematically. It was Darwin who saw the biological world as a system of interdependencies, a web of life whose parts must be explained in terms of its relationship to the whole. Cooley did not seek to convert society into a crude organism, but the unified nature of reality became his clarion call. Such is evident in his contention that "self and society are twin-born."

Cooley spent his life at Michigan, avoiding both the spotlight and frenzy that he feared would accompany appointments to urban-based universities. He developed a clear and abiding interest in the inner world, a realm he often explored through introspection and by observing the behavior of his children. Although Cooley directed the following lines toward Thoreau, they may be considered autobiographical.

> Men apparently solitary, like Thoreau, are often the best illustrations of the inseparability of thought and life from communication. No sympathetic reader of his works . . . can fail to see that he took to the woods and fields not because he lacked sociability, but precisely because his sensibilities were so keen that he needed to rest and protect them by a peculiar mode of life, and to express them by the indirect and considerate method of literature. . . . There is, in fact, a great deal of sound sociology in Thoreau. (1902: 57)

## Assumptions

Cooley's assumptions concerning human nature fall within the framework of the pluralist paradigm. Clearly, a vision of ambivalence, a portrait of duality marks his thought. On the enigmatic question of will, he argued that while people make choices these are not entirely free. The whole question of the primacy of individual will versus the power of social influence was "senseless" for

Cooley. He simply observed that human beings both influence and are influenced by others (1902: 19). In consistent fashion, Cooley unified both the sociable and "self-assertive" sides of human character. "Competition and the survival of the fittest are as righteous as kindness and cooperation, and not necessarily opposed to them: an adequate view will embrace and harmonize these diverse aspects" (1909: 35).

Cooley perceived the mind as the center of the human universe, as the definitive maker of our being. It is both an organic whole and the context for all human interaction. Thus, Cooley's supremely mental social world distinguishes his sociology from the attempts of Mead to assign primacy to social behavior. The mind, above all, is seen as modifiable, and it emerges only in relations with members of *primary groups,* one of the few theoretical constructs fully explicated by Cooley.

In *Social Organization,* Cooley answered the question What makes society possible? Early on, he appears to have dissociated himself from the specific contractualism of Rousseau that we hold to be basic to the pluralist paradigm. However, Cooley quickly reconciled his own system with that of *The Social Contract.* He argued that natural human freedom corresponds with the primary ideals of his own system and that the social contract is an expression of the "limitations these ideals encounter in seeking a larger expression" (1909: 47). However, it is not contractualism but unity born of antagonistic cooperation that is central to Cooley's vision of society.

Cooley conceived of society as a whole whose parts consist of interacting members. He rejected the Spencerian view of the societal organism as overly mechanical, but he perceived in the Darwinian model both a web of life and the promise of progress. Social process for Cooley represented a continual forming and reforming of individuals, groups, patterns, and institutions. The society that emerges is "a vast tissue of reciprocal activity, differentiated into innumerable systems" (1966: 28, originally published 1918). Those that stand the test of pragmatism through enduring over time and finding a niche in the order of things survive. Those that fail do not endure. Yet this was no laissez-faire sociology. Cooley saw no contradiction in defining a role for kindness and reform in his image of social order. He saw a basis for optimism in Darwin's selection, not a mandate for the extinction of the weak.

Given his paradoxical assumptions on human nature, it is logical that Cooley extended this view to the societal level. As we shall see, his theoretical efforts traced society to primary ideals nurtured in intimate primary groups. Thus in making the self, society is also formed. In like fashion, Cooley assumed that both the self-oriented and socially directed aspects of human nature have their counterpart in societal conflict and cooperation. Both, he argued, have their places in "our process of organic growth" (1966: 36). In a manner consistent with Coser's functions of conflict, Cooley argued that organization as a form of cooperation often emerges from selective struggle. Through contention, those most fitted for particular functions prove themselves. Through the clash of interests between labor and capital, the system is purged. Through external threat, the group learns cooperation (1966: 35–42).

Cooley's assumptions on theoretical human science were heavily influenced by early social psychology and the philosophical idealism so often connected therewith. Nowhere is this clearer than in his method of *sympathetic introspection*. Through a systematic "looking within," he sought to get in touch with inner feeling and mental states. For Cooley, sociology is something of an "artistic science," and intuition plays a rightful role in the construction of its truths. He took idealism to its extreme, holding that sociology must meet society on its own ground. Social "facts" exist purely in the imagination of individuals, and it is there where they must be analyzed.

The level of Cooley's science is logically consistent with the assumptions reviewed above. His is a microsociology heavily influenced by early social psychologists such as James Baldwin and Gabriel Tarde and the philosophy of William James. It was Baldwin who influenced Cooley's argument that "the social person is primarily a fact in the mind" and that he or she "has no existence apart from a mental whole of which all personal ideas are members" (Cooley, 1902: 90). (*Translation:* How we socially define a specific person is never purely individual. We are influenced by commonly shared social interpretations such as those of role.) Tarde provided Cooley with some insights on *imitation*, while James presented human consciousness as a stream ever-changing its course with new input.

Cooley remained consistent in his position on causation. Individuals, he argued, do not make societies nor do societies make individuals. They are "distributive and collective aspects of the same thing" (1902: 2). The individual has no existence apart from others. And there is no society not constituted of individuals. In corresponding fashion, Cooley dispensed with the nature–nurture controversy. Social and hereditary forces do not battle for dominance. They are parts of the same reality. He likewise dismissed all explanations that claim primacy for one social institution over others. No component stands over and above any other.

## Theoretical Content

The point of departure for Cooley's theory is appropriately enough his analysis of the meaning of "I." He argued that "self" can be configured by specifying those attributes called to mind when one uses the word, *I*. Those attributes include ideals, status position, role, sense of worth, and so forth. Cooley began his analysis by dividing the self into two major conceptual categories. When one has some sense of personal centrality, the self-assertive "I" is in evidence. For example, Cooley (1902: 141) cited a line from Cromwell in a poem by Lowell: "I, perchance, Am one raised up by the Almighty arm / To witness some great truth to all the world."

However, for Cooley it makes little sense to so individualize the self that it is stripped of a social nature. The social self is best conceived as reflected. It is exemplified in the well-known line "Each to each a looking glass / Reflects the other that doth pass." This looking-glass nature of the social self is revealed in three phases. First, we imagine how we appear to others. Second, we imagine others' perceptions of us. Third, we develop a set of self-directed feelings and ideas from this "mirror" held up to us by those who share our social space.

In Cooley's system, there is no great leap between the self and society. His book *Social Organization* (1909) is appropriately subtitled *A Study of the Larger Mind*. However, Cooley's society is formed in the specific context of the *primary group*. It is in these intimate settings, represented by the family, play group, and "old-fashioned neighborhood" that Cooley saw the crucible of this larger mind. This is a world of direct, face-to-face, and spontaneous relationships. Here the indispensable ideals of individual success, social unity, and freedom are born. Here succeeding generations of new barbarians are civilized. Hence the primary group is to be distinguished from the more inclusive, formal, impersonal forms of group life often bonded by self-interest.

For Cooley, the primary groups are the basis for the development and dissemination of primary ideals that are in turn integrated into the morally unified "we." Such ideals, he argued, do not exclude individuality and self-assertion. But he specifically dealt with loyalty, truth, service, kindness, lawfulness, and "natural rights." The latter include the right to labor, property, and open competition. Such ideals are "extended" into society. Thus, perfection in society can only follow perfection in its members.

The particular social order Cooley had in mind is not left to the imagination. The democratic society is the ideal, and it can only be understood as a reflection of the democratic mind. In his system, this mind predictably follows the road of progressive evolution: constantly enlarged and broadened, opened and educated. Predictably, Cooley did not disparage the masses, viewing them rather as "shrewd judges of persons" and "right in the long run." They are united in turn through the evolution of "sentiment," a "socialized feeling" embodied in such ideals as "brotherhood" (1909: 107–120).

Moving somewhat from his concern with the shaping of self, ideals, and the "larger mind," Cooley dealt with somewhat grander concepts such as class, caste, and social institutions. In his inquiry into social organization, he held that the inheritance of property is secure because it is a "means to economic stability" (1909: 229). However, he quarreled with the "inheritance of function" that often comes with the transfer of wealth from one generation to another. Although arguing that a concentration of wealth is inevitable (1909: 257), Cooley was probably the first sociologist to call explicitly for "equal opportunity" (1909: 234). It is by this process that the necessary duties of society will be performed by those who prove themselves. Although Cooley was uncomfortable with the ascendance of a capitalist class, his was not a structural theory. He believed, rather, that the integrity of the system can be maintained provided the "primary ideals" are embodied in the great owners of property. Cooley's solution to inequality was noblesse oblige.

As for institutions, Cooley portrayed these as "a definite and established phase of the public mind, not different in [their] ultimate nature from public opinion" (1909: 313). Hence they are the "mere" products of human invention, organizations that result from the direction of human thought through the ages upon particular human functions. Cooley ended as he began—with a society of the mind.

## Critique

Any substantive critique of Cooley should include a consideration of his "organic view." It was by means of this conceptualization of reality that he found support for a belief in human progress. More importantly, Cooley believed that a refusal to compartmentalize the holistic reality into cause and effect meant that he rendered the question of causal priority moot. However, saying it does not make it so.

Although perhaps not causal in the sense of a rigid determinism, Cooley assigned primacy to the shaping of the self and its social ideals within the context of the primary group. His theory predictably ignores structural and cultural factors, and it does not contain explicitly defined "independent variables" of the positivist sort. However, Cooley selected his theoretical center by arguing that underneath the apparent differences of society and culture, primary groups are essentially the same. What this means is that the *processes* of interaction whereby the self comes into its particular and general being are universal, even though the *content* of the self varies. In a related point, Cooley made claim that the self and society are twin-born. However, his theory makes clear that the self is first among equals.

This centering on the internal self leads to another issue. Despite its insights, this system of thought demonstrates a hazardous drift toward solipsism. In it, nothing appears to exist outside the human mind, and nothing is real but the self. Cooley's case is an extreme one, but philosophical idealism, when joined with an obsession with inner space and introspection, may yield an altogether imaginary world.

Finally, we come to the ideological content of Cooley's work. We need not make inferences, because his was an era in which sociology was fresh and open in its vision of the "good society." What ought to be, for Cooley, is an order featuring open classes, equal opportunity, and function based on merit. He was, above all, an American optimist who rested his beliefs in progress on an essentially benign interpretation of Darwinian thought. In concrete terms, Cooley envisioned a liberal capitalism: "The desire of possession is in itself a good thing, a phase of self-realization and a cause of social improvement. It is im-

moral or greedy only when it is without adequate control . . . when the self
realized is a narrow self" (1909: 36). And for Cooley the futurist, as the altruistic self expands, societies become democratic, and democracies unite in an
"organic international life" (1966: 265, originally published 1918).

■ **William I. Thomas (1863–1947):
The Definition of the Situation**

William Isaac Thomas,[4] another in a long line of Chicago sociologists,
was born on August 13, 1863, in a Virginia bitterly engaged in the American
Civil War. His father, Thadeous Thomas, was a dirt farmer and Methodist
minister. Yet his interest in education for himself and his family meant that he
was somewhat out of place in the social incubator of this remote region. Young
Thomas was a mountaineer through his adolescence, but his family later
moved to Knoxville, and in 1880 he entered the University of Tennessee.
There, as a student of literature and linguistics, he decided to enter academic
life and became enthusiastic about study in Germany.

After graduation, Thomas taught languages for a time at Tennessee, then
left in 1888 to study at the universities of Berlin and Göttingen. It was here that
he, like other soon-to-be-prominent sociologists, was immersed in the heavily
Kantian German intellectual tradition. In addition he cultivated a strong interest in comparative ethnography, especially as it had been used to study the cultures and communities of European peasants. Upon his return to the United
States, Thomas served for a period as a member of the English faculty at
Oberlin. However, he had grown attached to the ideas of the fledgling social
sciences, and in 1893 he entered the new graduate program in sociology at the
University of Chicago. Here he received his Ph.D. some three years later and
by this time was already instructing in the discipline. He quickly grew to
prominence and became a driving force in Chicago sociology for the next
quarter century.[5]

The most ambitious project in American sociology was initiated by
Thomas in 1908 when he received $50,000 from a wealthy Chicago heiress to
study immigration.[6] Narrowing his problem to that of the Polish community,
Thomas began a 10-year project of writing and research. During this time, he

---

[4]Important biographical and historical references to Thomas include Janowitz, 1966; Volkart,
1968; and Coser, 1977.

[5]For accounts of the historical period and especially the Chicago story, see the introductory
sections for Mead and Park earlier in this chapter.

[6]The heiress was Helen Culver, to whom the massive work *The Polish Peasant in Europe and
America* was to be dedicated.

became a transatlantic commuter, traveling back and forth to gather documentation and conduct interviews. His purpose was to study the Polish peasant in both the Old World and the tenements of Chicago. On one trip he met Florian Znaniecki, who though trained in philosophy was to make vital contributions to American sociology. Znaniecki fled to Chicago with the German invasion of Poland during the First World War. There he was to collaborate with Thomas in the publication of a watershed work in social research: *The Polish Peasant in Europe and America* (1958, originally published 1918–1921).

In 1918 a personal disaster befell Thomas. He was arrested by the FBI and charged with violation of the Mann Act (which made it illegal to transport young women across state lines for immoral purposes). The charges were dismissed, but the *Chicago Tribune* featured the story. Thomas was a social activist who did not shrink from controversy whether in his life-style or his progressive views on urban problems. And although his sociology often focused narrowly on "personal pathologies," he did not offer moralistic judgments. This proclivity put him at odds with the Chicago Vice Commission. In short, William Isaac Thomas became a symbol of liberal thought and academic notoriety who alienated elements of the Chicago power structure. Unsupported by his more retiring colleagues, Thomas was dismissed by the university's president and board of trustees. This action was "for the good of the university," a private institution born in 1892 with the aid of a large endowment—from John D. Rockefeller.

Three years later, the Chicago sociologists Robert Park and Ernest Burgess published a highly influential general textbook. In it they wrote:

> It is probably not the business of the universities to agitate reforms or to attempt directly to influence public opinion in regard to current issues. To do this is to . . . jeopardize its hard-won academic freedom. When a university takes over the function of political party or a church it ceases to perform its function as a university. (1966: 18, originally published 1921)

It is often argued that this statement reflects an interest among the scientific sociologists in distancing the discipline from the social gospel of the early Chicagoans such as Albion Small and Charles Henderson. However, the Thomas episode was also a part of the chilling context within which they wrote. Although Thomas was no master of radical thought, he was sympathetic to the plight of the immigrant poor and the urban working class. The unusual involvement of the FBI, the sensational accounts of the *Tribune,* and the summary dismissal by university trustees could not fail but send a clear message to the guardians of ideas.

For the next five years, Thomas was persona non grata in academic circles before finally landing a position at the New School for Social Research in New York City. Here he served until 1928. The remaining years of his life were spent writing outside the academy, save for the 1936–1937 academic year when he served on the faculty of Harvard. Despite it all, Thomas continued to practice his discipline. He experienced partial vindication in 1926 when a coalition of younger "scientific sociologists" organized and pushed his successful candidacy for the presidency of the American Sociological Society. William Isaac Thomas died in 1947 at the age of 84.


## Assumptions

Although keenly aware of environmental forces, Thomas assumed freedom to be a crucial property of human nature. By this logic, individuals are not simple reflections of their environment but active and purposeful beings. (As we shall see, this image is especially clear in Thomas's ideal type of the "creative person.") This view was probably influenced by the pragmatism of the age, as was his belief that the informed individual is the ultimate basis for the just society. As with others of the pluralist tradition, Thomas focused on the subjective world of consciousness, relying heavily on attitudes and definition to account for social action (Thomas and Znaniecki, 1958: 28–33, originally published 1918–1921).

As to the nature of society, Thomas assumed an antagonistic equilibrium in which broad cultural and subcultural values, as well as individual attitudes, are balanced. He stressed the always tenuous adjustment in a heterogeneous social order beset by the forces of immigration, industrialization, urbanization, and modernization. For Thomas, as with Max Weber, the fundamental component of society is *social action*. Though he dealt with the grander issues of social organization (institutions, norms, and social control), he centered his mature sociology squarely in how the human actor responds to the "total situation."

The total situation involves three components. First, there are the objective conditions, including those of enforced norms and cultural values. Second, there are both individual and group attitudes. Third, there is the "definition of the situation" by the socially influenced individual. From the last component is derived the well-known Thomas theorem—*If men define a situation as real, it is real in its consequences.* Hence, a world of meaning connects the external environment and human actions. As is true for many pluralists, Thomas sought to enter the world of the actor—to see with the eye of the beholder.

Thomas made significant contributions to the advancing of a scientific view of sociology. His is not a truly systematic form of thought, but he was an early philosopher of social science distinguished by an insistence that theory be grounded in empirical research. He advanced an early belief in lawful causality, and one of the distinctive features of *The Polish Peasant* is its attempt to explain social action through a synthesis of external values and internal attitudes. Later, Thomas came to doubt causal logic, substituting instead less deterministic inferences and probabilities. And although he pushed for the scientific elegance of the "control group," his sociology is best remembered for the softer method of the *life history* and its analysis of personal documents and oral interviews. This form of research is logically consistent with the implications of the aforementioned Thomas theorem.

## Theoretical Content

Although Thomas published widely, his most remembered work is *The Polish Peasant in Europe and America* (1958, originally published 1918–1921). In it, with co-author Florian Znaniecki, he offered explanations for personality development, social organization and disorganization, and social change. However, the threading of the massive work is accomplished by means of the theoretical relationship between value and attitude.

Thomas and Znaniecki defined "value" as "any datum having an empirical content accessible to the members of some social group and a meaning with regard to which it is or may be an object of activity" (1958: 21). "Attitude" on the other hand is "a process of individual consciousness which determines real or possible activity of the individual in the social world" (1958: 22). Put simply, the value is an external goal object to which people orient their action. Attitudes, on the other hand, are the actor's predispositions to act. More crucially, the latter represents the "individual counterpart" of the former.

The authors appeared to argue for the primacy of attitudes when they stated that values "draw all their reality, all their power to influence human life, from the social attitudes which are expressed or supposedly expressed in them" (1958: 33). However, they were not interested in simple unilateral causation. It is rather a synthesis of value and attitude in the context of the "total" situation that shapes social action. This is why actors do not respond to the same events in the same fashion.

Thomas and Znaniecki argued that attitudes can be expressed as "wishes" or desires. These include the famous (though theoretically empty) four wishes that appear to have both biogenic and sociogenic origin. They are the desires for (1) new experience, (2) recognition (including sexual attraction and social acclaim), (3) mastery or the "will to power," and (4) security. The last two are based on the instincts of hate and fear, respectively (1958: 72–73), and the first is based on "curiousity," which is described in the second volume as a "universal trait" found in "the reflex system of all higher organisms" (1958: 1859). As for recognition, sexual attraction also has implicit biogenic overtones.

All of these wishes must be fulfilled in a social context, however. This becomes the basis for social control, or in the words of Thomas and Znaniecki: As "the only medium in which wishes can be gratified," society can repress "the wishes which are irreconcilable with the welfare of the group" (1958: 73). Later in his work *The Unadjusted Girl* (1967, originally published 1923), Thomas dropped the wish for mastery and replaced it with the desire for "response" founded in the instinct of love. As we shall see, the ability of a society or community to meet, control, or modify the wishes of its members is crucial to its state of organization.

In seeking to explain the often shattering transition endured by the Polish immigrant, Thomas and Znaniecki wove explanations of both change and deviance out of the same cloth. Their theoretical point of departure stemmed from a description of the peasant community in Europe. It was represented as a cohesive form of social organization, reflecting such properties as common norms, more or less uniform socialization, and a reciprocal "harmony" of interests among the sexes. In a manner out of step with their era, Thomas and Znaniecki argued that "the greatest social efficiency is attained by a systematic collaboration of man and woman in external fields rather than by a division of tasks which limits the woman to home and children" (1958: 83).

However, in America the peasant community came to be shattered, the family divided, traditional values questioned, and individualism exalted. What follows is the familiar conflict of the generations in which "children brought with the family or added to it in America do not acquire the traditional attitude of familial solidarity, but rather American individualistic ideals, while the parents remain unchanged" (1958: 104). And as the old controls break down, deviance emerges on a wide scale.

Thomas and Znaniecki focused heavily on primary-group disorganization, especially in the families of Polish immigrants. However, their work contains the seeds of a more general theory of social change. They accomplished this through the introduction of other conceptions.

As the organization of community life begins to slip, a collective response reinforces the traditional normative boundary lines. This process is known as *social reorganization,* and it can be successful in instances where there is only random deviation on the part of a relative few. However, as the old ways are swallowed up by the new, the community is no longer able to meet the wishes of its members, and control breaks down. Then follows *social disorganization* or "a decrease of the influence of existing social rules of behavior upon individual members of the group" (1958: 1128). The authors argued, however, that it is possible to move beyond this stage. In *social reconstruction,* new institutions and normative systems can be formed. Here, the forces for change are led by an elite, a role we assume for the *creative individual.*

Thomas and Znaniecki configured certain conceptions of attitudes together with "life organization" to form ideal "character types" (1958: 1853–1857). These include the *philistine, bohemian,* and *creative individual,* each an attempt to gauge the potential for "personal evolution." Although the authors are not crystal clear on this point, it appears that such types refer to something more than personality development. It is certainly consistent with their position to argue that the prevalence of certain types play a crucial role in the nature of social change.[7] In this theoretical argument, the philistine represents rigid and fixed dispositions to act and a corresponding inability to grow. The bohemian represents an unformed character, open to all influences. Although growth is possible, stability is absent. Finally, the creative type refers to a settled and organized character, given to planned and productive change. Real personalities reflect a blend of the types, though the dominance of one or another may be evident.

It is crucial to observe how Thomas and Znaniecki in their treatment of

---

[7] This is quite similar to the logic employed by David Riesman (see Chapter 11).

social disorganization differ from Durkheim's work on anomie. Although both systems of thought focus on the breakdown of normative control, Durkheim's unit of analysis is the *larger* society. It emerges as homogeneous, integrated through a consensus of values, but threatened by the forces of change. Thomas and Znaniecki offered a different focus. For them the larger American society is heterogeneous and its dominant value system stresses individualism. Although they too portrayed the forces of disintegration, their focus is on the disorganization experienced by a traditional culture in the throes of transition. In other words, *while Durkheimian sociology would consider the problems posed by immigration for value consensus in the society as a whole, these authors inverted the problem. Their viewpoint is from inside the outcast community.*

## Critique

As reconstructed here, this theoretical effort appears to have more of a systematic nature than commonly believed. Properly understood, it is a means of understanding the shattering of a way of life from the viewpoint of those who lived in the margin. However, there are issues both technical and explanatory that should be raised. In the first case, the monumental Polish peasant suffers from a vagueness of definition that strikes key constructs such as values, attitudes, and wishes. This in part flows from the extraneous messages that inform all systems of thought. For example, the work at hand bears the imprint of Darwin, instinctivism, Durkheim, and Weber among others. It is the attempt to give such vividly different conceptions their due that distorts the theoretical language.

Despite its comparative potential, *The Polish Peasant in Europe and America* emerges as ahistorical, with few insights into the larger European or American societies. This is in part a consequence of the "life history" methodology, which reduces the life of a people to the perceptions of individual actors. And of course, a general interest in consciousness and meaning always threatens to become an incursion into psychological motivation, a problem endemic to all "theories of the mind."

The work on social disorganization and Thomas's later efforts on "maladjusted behavior"[8] raise other questions with ideological implications. In the first of these, the focus remains narrowly drawn. Hence, the disorganization analysis centers on the community, the personality, the family, and the corresponding breakdown of social control. Missing is a consideration of the institutional structure within which such disorganization worked its way. (For example, Thomas and Znaniecki studied the world of the immigrant, not the factory world that exploited immigrant labor.) Perhaps, then, the loss of fam-

---

[8] See *The Unadjusted Girl* (1967, originally published 1923) and *The Child in America* (1928).

ily and community solidarity is part of a wider system. Further, when social disorganization is blended with the "maladjustment" issue, the problem becomes one of adaptive behavior on the part of outcasts, not the substantive change of the broader system.

# ■ Herbert Blumer (b. 1900): The Interpretation of Action

Within the sociological community, Herbert Blumer is regarded as the direct link between modern symbolic interactionism and its American source: the Chicago school. More specifically, Blumer mastered, interpreted, and expanded the work of George Herbert Mead. In the process, his has been the clearest and richest statement on the assumptions that undergird the interactionist tradition. As we shall see, his own sociological passage has led him to redefine the nature of human science, a position that has yielded no small amount of controversy.

## History and Biography

Herbert George Blumer was born in St. Louis on March 7, 1900. He received a B.A. degree in 1921 and an M.A. degree in the following year, both from the University of Missouri. Aware of the burgeoning Department of Sociology at the University of Chicago, Blumer traveled north, where he was to study under the social philosopher George Herbert Mead. He received his Ph.D. in 1929 and stayed on as a member of the Chicago faculty until accepting a position as professor of sociology at the University of California at Berkeley in 1952. There he transplanted the Chicago legacy, a tradition he named *symbolic interactionism.*

Blumer's early work demonstrated a wide range of interests, including collective behavior, the mass media, social disorganization, and racial prejudice. These interests were explored within the historical context of the Great Depression. His appraisal of Thomas and Znaniecki's *The Polish Peasant* in 1939 was a serious exposition of the most ambitious research effort in early sociology. However, his lifelong task was the deciphering of the often tortuous prose of George Herbert Mead. In so doing, Blumer thrust the early Chicagoan's heuristic conceptions into the forefront of social psychology.

Although his article "Social Disorganization and Personal Disorganization" (1937) appears to be a concession to the popularity of order sociology during the 1930s, his Depression-era work bears the pluralist stamp. This was a period of movements and discontent, of threats and promises, of New Deals and old inequality. From inside the pluralist circle, Blumer focused on the world of immediate relations. He analyzed racial prejudice, the supposed links between motion pictures and mass behavior, and the ephemeral crowds, fashions, social movements, and publics of the heterogeneous society.

During World War II, Blumer served as liaison between the Bureau of Economic Warfare and the Office of War Information and as a member of the War Labor Board. Between 1945 and 1947, he was chairman of the board of arbitration for U.S. Steel (Shibutani, 1970). Such experiences gave rise to studies on morale, labor–management relations, and industrialization, adding to the range of his scholarship over the next three decades. The turbulence of the 1960s and 1970s in the United States was the background for a revitalization of Blumer's sociology in the fields of race prejudice and collective behavior.

## Assumptions

Throughout a long career, Herbert Blumer has founded his sociology on readily identifiable pluralist assumptions concerning human nature, society, and science. In respect to the first of these, his work was touched by Kantian idealism mediated through the sociology of W. I. Thomas. You should recall the Thomas theorem, commonly reduced in symbolic interactionist sociology to the phrase *definition of the situation*. This holds that situations and all objects or phenomena have no intrinsic meaning or reality apart from a conscious and reactive human mind that imposes definitions. However, the human mind (as Mead so forcefully argued) imposes meaning in a context of social interaction. And finally (showing his debt to Cooley), Blumer cited the importance of our perceptions of the real or anticipated reactions of others in self-development.

We have argued earlier that the pluralist conception of human nature stresses an active and creative approach to the social environment. This is evident in Blumer's position that people do not simply respond to external forces nor are their social behaviors informed by some genetic code. Rather, human beings construct their reality through imposing meaning and order while constantly adjusting to their interpretations of a dynamic and changing milieu. Furthermore, each actor is capable of transforming the self into an object that can be analyzed, changed, and controlled.

At a higher level, social actors interact in a concerted manner, bringing together their definitions to form complex linkages of acts. Such linkages make up "organizations, institutions, division of labor, and networks of interdependency that are moving and not static affairs" (Blumer, 1969: 50). Hence, societies and their higher-order properties have no life or reality independent of the interactions of members. The repetition of acts that center around a basic human function gives rise to a particular form of social institution. Thus society is a process, not a product. It is founded in a dynamic, conscious, and subjective world inside, not in a fixed external system.

Herbert Blumer's assumptions concerning human science were briefly reviewed in Chapter 2. Suffice it here to say that his vision of sociology does not lend itself to the imagery of positive science. Nor is he given to the grand sweep of historical inquiry into the structure of social institutions. On the one hand, he has brought into question the hallowed methods of natural science: the experiment, the isolation of variables, the necessity of measurement, the importance of both descriptive and inferential statistics. In their stead he has reared the techniques of intimate observation, often substituting the exploratory study for causal inquiry. On the other hand, Blumer's is a *social psychology* with a tightly drawn focus. Put concretely, he has analyzed *attitudes not ideology, prejudice not institutional racism, a phenomenal world not a material one*. Blumer has rooted his sociology in a Meadian world of mind, self, and society, not a Marxist one of class, power, and conflict, or a Durkheimian one of norms, consensus, and cohesion.

## Theoretical Content

Herbert Blumer's major contribution to sociological theory is his book *Symbolic Interactionism: Perspective and Method* (1969). In many respects, it is more a review of the assumptions that undergird symbolic interaction than an explanatory system. However, in some ways he has set forth a soft "theoretical scheme of human society" drawn from the social philosophy of George Herbert Mead (1966: 535). It is this scheme that deserves our attention.

For Blumer, "human beings act toward things on the basis of the meanings that things have for them." These meanings in turn follow from the interactions one has with others and are modified by a dynamic process of continuing interpretation (1969: 2). Social behavior therefore follows the interpretations given to categories of objects that make up the social world. These categories are the *physical,* as with the buildings that constitute a tangible city, the *social,* as with the roles played by urban dwellers, and the *abstract,* as with the customs that form urban culture (1969: 10). Meaning is attached to such types of objects by interacting people who actively engage and define their environment and through this process transform it into a symbolic universe.

Society itself is a symbolic universe. Its people may have a biological essence and its technology a material nature, but these objects and the countless human acts of social life must be separated out and given meaning by a conscious agent. Hence the physical, social, and abstract environments are not the objects of direct interaction. Rather, what they *symbolize* to the participant is the basis for human behavior. This "communicative process" of separating out and interpreting aspects of the environment, and attempting to match one's behavior to the definitions of others, Blumer has termed *self-indication* (1969: 80–81).

We now have the basis for understanding Blumer's major argument. To say that society is a symbolic universe is not enough. Rather, he designates society itself as symbolic interaction. What others in the conflict or order traditions term social structure, organization, and institutions, Blumer conceptualizes as *joint action*. There are of course higher-level patterns that coalesce around major social functions (such as political, economic, educational, religious, or family forms). However, these types of social "institutions" have no life of their own; nor do they constitute a preexisting environment that determines human behavior. Instead, these patterns represent nothing more than a merger of "different acts of diverse participants." Hence, society is dynamic, growing, and ever-changing. Its patterns and customs, its structure and institutions are created through the joint actions of group life. People make society; society does not make people (Blumer, 1969: 17–20).

## Critique

Herbert Blumer's conception of the voluntary person is the fountainhead from which his symbolic interactionism flows. It is basic not only to his explanation of the action basis of society but for his methodological insistence that observation and sympathetic introspection are necessary for sociological understanding. Hence his methods center in open-ended interviews, case histories, personal documents such as diaries, and participant observation. Blumer thus advances a step beyond Durkheim. Not only is society a unique and distinctive phenomenon, but it must be studied by unique and distinctive methods.

Blumer, as his mentors before him, reaffirmed through his imagery and theory the optimism of a free actor. During an era of economic calamity and world war, he advanced the argument that systems are, after all, only what those who craft them allow them to be. He studiously avoided what Dennis Wrong (1961) criticized as an "oversocialized conception" of human being in other sociological thought. If there is one abiding message in all of this, it is that sociology must decisively shun determinism.

However, while Blumer (as other Chicagoans) has reaffirmed the human element, he (and they) may also have succeeded in defining both human science and society out of existence. When institutions and social structures become nothing more than a "collectivity that engages in joint action" (1969: 17), it is impossible to speak of institutions as such at all. For example, Blumer would be compelled by his logic to argue that the interactive members of each family, each church, each political administration, each management of a business must voluntarily interpret their social reality without decisive regard for preexisting roles, norms, or ideology. It follows, that for Blumer, each group or collectivity is distinctive from all others and also that each collectivity is unique at each moment in time. Such a view of sociology effectively dispenses with generalization.

Although it might be argued that the specific pattern of interaction in families and other groups is unique in some ways, it is also true that each family does not reinvent the roles, norms, and ideologies of family life that prevail in a specific historical period in the life of a society. The same is true for individual corporations, churches, and political administrations. Each operates in a larger system with structural properties that constrain behavior. This leads to some uniformity of behavior and makes broad predictions tenable. For example, it would be compelling for Blumer's argument (and a real scoop), if Exxon's chief executive officer were to announce that the corporation was big enough and that further growth would be damaging to small, independent oil companies. However, no one really expects such a "creative" position. And the reason that we do not has to do with what we know about what drives corporation capitalism. It would appear that voluntarism, interpretation, and uniqueness have their limitations.

In Blumer's theory, society as well as science is spelled with a small *s*. If Blumer and his heirs have avoided an oversocialized conception of human nature, they have substituted an overpsychologized conception of society. This is a microsociology far removed from the wider historical concerns of the Europeans, Weber, and Simmel. It does not lend itself to the study of international and societal systems, of polity and economy, of institutions and norms, of culture and customs. To borrow from George Homans (Chapter 8), in this theoretical system, sociology has become a corollary of a voluntaristic social psychology.

Yet Blumer and others have reminded us that human actors are not robots caught up in mechanical systems beyond human comprehension or control. Sociology in the interactionist tradition makes its contribution through analyzing the processes of socialization and self-development. It contributes to an understanding of how social learning transpires. Perhaps what needs to be remembered is that *what* is learned bears some relationship to history and power. Not all interpretations are created equal.

# ■ Bibliography

Angell, Robert C.
1968                     "Charles H. Cooley." In *The International Encyclopedia of the Social Sciences,* pp. 378–383. New York: Macmillan.

Blumer, Herbert
1937                     "Social Disorganization and Personal Disorganization." *American Journal of Sociology* 42:871–877.
1966                     "Sociological Implications of the Thought of George Herbert Mead." *American Journal of Sociology* 71:535–544.

1969          *Symbolic Interactionism: Perspective and Method.* Englewood Cliffs, N.J.: Prentice-Hall.

1972          "Action vs. Interaction." *Society* 9:50–53.

1980          "Comment: Mead and Blumer: The Convergent Methodological Perspectives of Social Behaviorism and Symbolic Interactionism." *American Sociological Review* 45:409–419.

Cooley, Charles H.

1902          *Human Nature and the Social Order.* New York: Charles Scribner's Sons.

1909          *Social Organization: A Study of the Larger Mind.* New York: Charles Scribner's Sons.

(1918) 1966      *Social Process.* Carbondale: Southern Illinois University Press.

Coser, Lewis A.

1977          *Masters of Sociological Thought.* New York: Harcourt Brace Jovanovich.

Davis, Nanette J.

1975          *Sociological Constructions of Deviance.* Dubuque, Iowa: Wm. C. Brown.

Faris, Robert E. L.

1967          *Chicago Sociology 1920–1932.* San Francisco: Chandler.

Hughes, Everett C.

1969          "Robert E. Park." In T. Raison (Ed.), *The Founding Fathers of Social Science.* Harmondsworth, England: Penguin.

Jandy, Edward C.

1942          *Charles Horton Cooley: His Life and His Social Theory.* New York: Dryden Press.

Janowitz, Morris

1966          "Introduction." In W. I. Thomas, *W. I. Thomas on Social Organization and Social Personality.* Chicago: University of Chicago Press.

Matthews, Fred

1977          *Quest for American Sociology: Robert E. Park and the Chicago School.* Montreal: McGill University Press.

Mead, George Herbert

1934          *Mind, Self and Society.* Edited and with an introduction by Charles W. Morris. Chicago: University of Chicago Press.

1964          *Selected Writings.* Edited and with an introduction by Andrew J. Reck. Indianapolis: Bobbs-Merrill.

1982          *The Individual and the Social Self.* Edited and with an introduction by David L. Miller. Chicago: University of Chicago Press.

Mills, C. Wright
1964        *Sociology and Pragmatism: The Higher Learning in America.*
            Edited and with an introduction by Irving L. Horowitz.
            New York: Oxford University Press.

Park, Robert E.
1950        *Race and Culture.* Glencoe, Ill.: The Free Press.
1952        *Human Communities.* Glencoe, Ill.: The Free Press.
1955        *Society.* Glencoe, Ill.: The Free Press.

Park, Robert E., and Ernest W. Burgess
(1921) 1966     *Introduction to the Science of Sociology.* 3rd ed. Chicago:
                University of Chicago Press.

Shibutani, Tamotsu
1970        "Foreword." In Tamotsu Shibutani (Ed.), *Human Nature
            and Collective Behavior: Papers in Honor of Herbert Blumer,*
            pp. v–viii. Englewood Cliffs, N.J.: Prentice-Hall.

Steffens, Lincoln
1904        *The Shame of the Cities.* New York: McClure.

Thomas, W. I.
(1923) 1967     *The Unadjusted Girl.* New York: Harper & Row.
1937        *Primitive Behavior: An Introduction to the Social Sciences.*
            New York: McGraw-Hill.

Thomas, W. I., and Dorothy S. Thomas
1928        *The Child in America.* New York: Alfred A. Knopf.

Thomas, W. I., and Florian Znaniecki
(1918–1921) 1958  *The Polish Peasant in Europe and America.* 2nd ed. 2 vols.
            New York: Dover.

Turner, Ralph
1967        "Introduction." In Ralph H. Turner (Ed.), *Robert E. Park
            on Social Control and Collective Behavior.* Chicago: Univer-
            sity of Chicago Press.

Volkart, E. H.
1968        "W. I. Thomas." In *The International Encyclopedia of the
            Social Sciences,* pp. 1–6. New York: Macmillan.

Wallace, David
1967        "Reflections on the Education of George Herbert Mead."
            *American Journal of Sociology* 72:396–408.

Wrong, Dennis
1961        "The Oversocialized Conception of Man in Modern So-
            ciology." *American Sociological Review* 26:183–193.

# CHAPTER 13

# ■ Interpretative Sociology: The Making of Social Reality

In this chapter, we continue to explore pluralist theories that seek to unravel the puzzles of interpretation or meaning. Yet, unlike the social-psychological focus evident in the Chicago tradition, the systems of explanation to be considered here are aware of the *context* or *structure* within which interaction occurs. Although it would be inaccurate to claim that such theories are macrosociological, each acknowledges the existence of an external social reality. Thus, Alfred Schutz recognizes the controls imposed on actors by history and preexisting knowledge; Peter Berger and Harold Garfinkel acknowledge an everyday reality that once created gives order to social interaction and definition; and Erving Goffman in his mature work focuses on the *stage* for social drama, not merely the interpretations of its actors.

## ■ Alfred Schutz (1899–1959): Phenomenological Sociology

Alfred Schutz, as we shall see, sought to critically refine the sociology of Max Weber. In so doing, he wed a philosophical tradition known as *phenomenology* and sociology into a formidable synthesis. Born in Vienna in 1899, he studied law and social science at that city's university.[1] After publishing an early masterwork *The Phenomenology of the Social World* in 1932, Schutz fled his native Austria to escape the coming terror of Nazi conquest.[2] He came to the

---

[1] The biographical material that follows is drawn primarily from George Walsh's "Introduction" in Schutz's *The Phenomenology of the Social World* (1967, originally published 1932).

[2] A review of this period in Austrian history can be found in Chapter 8 in the section on Peter Blau.

United States prior to the outbreak of the Second World War to pursue a divided career. He served as an attorney practicing banking law and as a sociologist at the New School for Social Research in New York.

Schutz gave up his legal practice in 1953, choosing to teach and write about phenomenological sociology. It is perhaps ironic that his work secured widespread recognition among American sociologists only after his death in 1959. He came to augment his European sociology through a systematic study of the work of George Herbert Mead. And as Mead before him, Schutz was to live through the works of his students (such as Peter Berger, Thomas Luckmann, and Harold Garfinkel). It was their sociology that reflected well on their mentor, and in the 1960s and early 1970s the crucial works of Alfred Schutz were translated, edited, and expanded for English-speaking readers.

## Assumptions

Alfred Schutz assumed a position on human nature clearly in keeping with the pluralist tradition: Social actors create and impose order on their social world. This is to say that *voluntarism* takes precedence over determinism. However, in his elucidation of voluntary action (1967: 66–69, originally published 1932), Schutz argued that both indeterminists and determinists have cast the problem of choice fallaciously. His point was that social behavior is not a simple matter of unvarying response to antecedent "causes." Nor is it the exercise of "free will." Rather, choice is a process that engages an actor who "imaginatively runs through a series of psychic states in each of which it expands, grows richer, and changes until *the free act detaches itself from it like an overripe fruit*" (Schutz, 1967: 67, italics added).

In other words, both determinists and indeterminists assume that our options present themselves like two forks in the proverbial road. The debate then hinges on whether we are free to choose our path or whether it is in effect chosen for us by external and prior forces such as history and/or personal experience. Schutz believed that voluntary action, as it relates to the problem of choice, does not fit this image of selecting between clearly defined, fully developed goals or paths. Rather, the actor *imagines* the act and *projects* it into the future, often in multiple forms. All the while, the actor reflects upon these complex projections of future behavior that often overlap. In the process, other intentional acts are imagined, reproduced, and compared. This process continues until the act is complete. In other words, a choice is not made *before the fact* but is actively constructed *during the act* (Schutz, 1967: 67–69).

Schutz's preconceptions concerning the nature of society also fit the pluralist model. He stated explicitly that Simmel and Weber were correct in their approach to the problem of the origin of human society. He affirmed Simmel's "underlying idea . . . that all concrete social phenomena should be traced back to the modes of individual behavior and that the particular form of such modes should be understood through detailed description" (1967: 4). As for Weber,

Schutz concurred in this master's approach, which "reduces all kinds of social relationships and structures, all cultural objectifications, all realms of objective mind to the most elementary forms of individual behavior" (1967: 6). In other words, every social relationship and structure, including the most complex of social institutions and ideologies, are constituted "in the last analysis, by the action of the individual in the social world" (1967: 6).

Finally, Schutz's image of human science is pluralist, yet distinctive in important ways we have not yet explored. We should begin by noting that scientific sociology for Schutz began with the work of Max Weber. Schutz agreed with Weber that sociology must be value free, that social relationships can best be understood by means of the ideal type, and that meaningful social action is the proper subject matter of the discipline. However, Schutz did perceive recurring lapses in Weber's interpretive sociology. These begin with Weber's failure to clearly and systematically define his crucial terms, including meaning itself (1967: 5–44). Predictably, Schutz focused on the concept of meaning and sought to revise Weber by turning to the work of the phenomenologist Edmund Husserl.

Philosophical phenomenology is a method of analysis. Its adherents seek to systematically study phenomena or "that which appears." Husserl was the twentieth-century thinker at the center of this modern philosophical movement. His central contention (which came to be the foundation for Schutz's approach to sociology) was that the hard, factual data of empiricism are insufficient to build a basis for natural science. Instead, he argued that a science of sciences could only be found in the properties of *consciousness*. In simple terms, Husserl claimed that *rigorous and systematic intuition* is sufficient to grasp the essence of things (Husserl, 1931: 54–58). However, this process of recognition or insight is contingent upon the *suspension of all preconceptions of natural order*.

According to Husserl, human beings possess a "natural attitude." This is the inaccurate belief that there is an objective and preexisting order in the universe. Instead, Husserl argued (and Schutz agreed) that order is *imposed* upon reality by the actor (Husserl, 1970: 145–146, originally published 1934–1937). Transplanted to sociology, the understanding of social order (or more precisely the ordering process) is open only to those who apprehend the actor's world of consciousness, for it is within that world that order, interpretation, and intentional action originate.

Now Husserl focused on the natural sciences, but Schutz saw clear sociological implications in his analysis of science and ideas, knowledge and consciousness. To get to the essence of the conscious world, Schutz argued, phenomenological sociologists must pierce the overlapping barriers that mark complex social acts. They must rid themselves of the natural attitude in order to study it in others. They must peel away layers of behavior in order to reach those basic processes of consciousness that are everywhere the same. And when they penetrate the world as it appears, they do not find a purely subjective world of the mind. Phenomenological sociologists hold that consciousness is instead rooted in a *processual relationship* between the participant and other actors or objects. Predictably enough, the ultimate nature of that relationship centers on how actors interpret their social world.

## Theoretical Content

With some understanding of the implicit assumptions of Schutz to guide us, it is time to turn to his theoretical system. Basically put, Schutz used phenomenology to reformulate and tighten the sociology of Max Weber. His assumptions concerning human nature, society, and science are quite in line with his "mentor at a distance." However, Weber was content to sketch out the importance of social acts, the explanatory power of ideal types, and the methodological significance of *verstehen*. He then rushed on to explore the grander questions of history, ideology, and comparative social institutions. Schutz made no such leap.

In his exploration of the nature of meaning, Schutz initially explored the "stream of consciousness" (1967: 45–91, originally published 1932). He considered this a river of formless experiences, without continuity or contours. When the actor "turns inward," recognizing and reflecting on these experiences, only then are they made distinctive, discrete, and real. Hence the focus is not upon experience per se but on the interpretation of experience. This is admittedly a *selective process*. In other words, some experiences are "lost" and destined to remain "without meaning."

The *time orientation* of meaningful action is crucial to Schutz. Essentially put, goal-directed action includes the properties of both past experience and future anticipation. In other words, the actor reflects on a past or passing experience and projects it into the future as if it were already done. For example, if the experience is "taking an examination," a student gives that experience form or shape by attending to it. This is followed by imagining the process as already complete, a looking-ahead orientation Schutz described as the "future-perfect tense." (I will have completed the examination.) And with some such acts, the student actor may anticipate not only the completion of the examination but its evaluation, the place of that evaluation in a course, the place of the course in an academic career, and the place of the career in life. Hence the "meaning" of an examination may indeed be varied and complex, spanning past, present, and future time orientations.

The most valuable aspect of this system of thought emerged when Schutz employed the time orientation of action to account for the social reality. He argued that the social world is comprised of different spheres or realms. One realm is that of "directly experienced social reality," *umwelt,* which consists of the immediate relations the actor has with others. The second realm includes relations that lie outside such direct impact on the actor's perceptions but which still leave their mark on experience. These indirect relations may be with contemporaries (*mitwelt*), with predecessors (*vorwelt*) or with successors (*folgewelt*).

In the world of direct experience, the potential exists for a "face to face" relationship as another person or persons share one's community of time and space. In other words, one's experiences with others are *simultaneous,* "embracing the body of the other person as well as his consciousness" (1967: 166). In the second realm, that of indirect social experience, interaction with others assumes a "spectrum of decreasing vividness" (1967: 177). This is especially true for both future successor and past predecessor relations.

The future for Schutz obeys nothing approximating scientific law, because its inhabitants may construct quite a different social reality. Given the logic of phenomenology, a sociologist bent on understanding the future would have to somehow enter the phenomenal world of successors and explain a world yet to come. As for the past, the problem is less severe. This is because we know something of the events and ideas of eras gone by. Yet there remains the puzzle of truly understanding the social world as interpreted by actors long since dead. For example, the social world of Protestantism might have appeared quite different to earlier members of the faith than it did to Max Weber. After all, he would have had to rely on his own (then) contemporary conceptions of the meaning of Protestant thought.

It is within the relationships of indirect experience with contemporaries that Schutz saw the greatest hope for scientific study. Within this realm, the actor shares time but not space. Here the rich "we-relationship" of direct experience is replaced by a "they-relationship" in which contemporaries become anonymous. But anonymity is not simply a matter of impersonal experience. It is rather a matter of the more objective relations people have with ideal types. Put succinctly, Schutz's contemporaries are not the immediate and significant others we know *subjectively* but the remote and anonymous types we experience *objectively.*

For example, when I mail a letter certain anonymous and unknown contemporaries working for the post office can be expected to behave in certain ways. I do not know them personally; that is, I have no subjective knowledge of their personalities. Thus, I have no direct relationship with them. Instead, I know postal employees only as a "type." That type can only have an objective meaning, a meaning that will be shared by all others who interpret the type. Hence, we (objectively) know that the postal employees (a type we do not subjectively know) will deliver the mail. Remember that this and every they-relationship is indirect, at a distance, and involves a contemporary and anonymous type that can be objectively known (Schutz, 1967: 163–186).

They-relationships cover a spectrum of anonymous ideal types. Put differently, human beings can arrange indirect relationships on a scale of types that are increasingly remote. To illustrate, Schutz employed a range of examples: an absent friend, an unknown person described by someone else, a functionary (such as our earlier postal employee), and "social collectives" such as a corporation board of directors, the United States Senate, "the state," "the press," "the economy," "the working class," and so forth. Even with our friends, we know them only as an abstract type when they are not with us. If asked how their "type" will ultimately resolve a problem, for example, we can only infer on the basis of the consistency of their behavior. That is, we are denied the subjective knowledge of direct relationships and predict on the basis of a behavioral type (how people "like my friend" can be expected to act) (1967: 194–202).

No matter how remote and anonymous the world of indirect experience, Schutz agreed with Weber that the most abstract of collectivities does not "act" somehow independent of its members. For example, "every action of the state can be reduced to the actions of its functionaries, whom we can apprehend by means of personal ideal types and toward whom we can assume a they-orientation, regarding them as our contemporaries" (1967: 199). It was Schutz's conviction that sociology's promise as a "scientific" discipline increases as the ideal types of the *mitwelt* grow more anonymous and their meaning more objective. However, higher order ideal types (such as the state) are ultimately constructed of lower order personal types (such as bureaucrats).

Schutz was not content to stay on a micro level. The context within which all "we" and "they" ("direct" and "indirect") relations occur is *the life world*. For Schutz, this refers to the complete range of cultural mandates that shape human conduct. It includes the taken-for-granted "typifications" imposed on actors within their total milieu. Its components include three essentially habitual categories of action. *Knowledge of skills* is typically unquestioned and certain, such as walking. *Useful knowledge* is based on less certain, prior solutions to life puzzles, such as an intellectual orientation or even driving a car. *Knowledge of recipes* refers to a still less certain, though routine procedure for solving problems. For example, a professor may have a number of alternative methods for teaching the theory of Schutz (and will probably need them all). As we shall later see, this notion of the cultural constraints on everyday life has heavily informed the ethnomethodological tradition in sociology.

## Critique

Schutz and his disciples have demonstrated a fundamental awareness of the "natural attitude" and other elements of the conventional wisdom in social life. They accede to the existence of an external world of taken-for-granted definitions and habitual knowledge. However, phenomenological sociologists do not conceptualize that world in terms of large-scale organizations that exist independent of the minds of social actors. The world out there has no material reality, obeys no laws or principles of regularity, and is reducible ultimately to "the particular acts of individual persons, since these alone can be treated as agents in a course of subjectively understandable action" (Weber, in Schutz, 1967: 199).

Given this conception of the discipline, Schutz set out on an intricate and tortuous path. His mission was to understand in minute detail the process of meaning. Although he did not believe that the we-relationship could be studied scientifically, he nevertheless devoted a great deal of time to its analysis. And certain of his students might be forgiven for including the world of subjective, direct experience within the confines of science. Nevertheless, perhaps Schutz's microanalysis reveals more about how his gifted mind constructed meaning than about how others do the same. Hence it is possible that phenomenological sociology may tell us more about the interpretative processes of the phenomenologist than it does about the social reality.

From the conflict side, the work of Schutz and other phenomenologists is open to the Marxist critique of *false consciousness.* Put succinctly, Marx argued that members of capitalist society are quite capable of misapprehending their objective class position. As we shall see in Chapter 15, social action may be influenced by ideological forms of distortion. In Marxist terms, the class that owns and controls the material means of production also controls the knowledge and information industry. In fairness, Schutz addressed the importance of "typifications" in the life world, but he stopped considerably short of an analysis of class structure and its relationship to ideological control. Schutz and his heirs have focused on the construction of a phenomenal world, not its truth or falseness.

Finally, the present-time orientation of Alfred Schutz leaves us with two unsolved puzzles. First, simply restricting sociology as science to contemporary relations does not really solve the problem of unshared categories of interpretation. In a heterogeneous social world, people may use a virtually infinite range of experiences to understand their world. Second, the present-time premise means that no historical generalizations can be made. In other words, each generation must rediscover its own truths.

But such considerations are to some extent beside the point. The phenomenological conception of science does not seek laws in an ordered social world. Instead, its quest is to discover the universal process by which meaning is constructed.

## ■ Peter Berger (b. 1929):
## The Social Construction of Reality

Peter Ludwig Berger was born in Vienna on March 17, 1929, almost a decade before the Nazi Anschluss converted Austria into little more than a province of the German Reich.[3] He immigrated to the United States shortly after the Second World War, becoming a naturalized citizen in 1952. He attended the University of London for a year (1946), but received his B.A. degree from Wagner College before pursuing his graduate training at the New

---

[3] For a brief account of this period in Austrian history, consult the introductory remarks to the work of Peter Blau in Chapter 8.

School for Social Research in New York City. Here Berger was awarded both the M.A. (1950) and Ph.D. (1954) degrees. More importantly, he studied at the New School under the father of phenomenological sociology, Alfred Schutz.

Berger's career featured appointments at the Women's College of the University of North Carolina and the Hartford Seminary Foundation before he joined the faculty of his alma mater in 1963. Although he left the New School in 1966, it was during this period that Berger published two books that detail both his pluralist assumptions and his theoretical position on society. These were *Invitation to Sociology: A Humanistic Perspective* (1963) and *The Social Construction of Reality* (1966). Berger was joined in the latter effort by another student of Alfred Schutz, Thomas Luckmann. In later service at the City University of New York (1966–1970) and Rutgers, Berger was to refine and expand his more focused interests in the sociology of religion and political sociology. One of his later works, *The Heretical Imperative* (1977a), was nominated for an American Book Award in 1980.

## Assumptions

It is unnecessary to draw inferences or conclusions about Peter Berger's assumptions from his more formal sociology. This is because of his authorship of a provocative and lively little book intended to share a conception of the field with a wider than usual audience. In *Invitation to Sociology*, Berger revealed an intellectual orientation rooted generally in the European classics but specifically in what we have termed the pluralist paradigm. And although much of his "invitation" is merely a lucid account of the issues encountered in a good first course in sociology, other of his arguments reveal the domain assumptions that have driven his work.

Berger's image of human nature abounds with the common pluralist themes of identity, interpretation, and the conscious mind (1963: 60–61). Sociology itself is presented as a heightened form of consciousness and a "live option for the individual seeking to order the events of his own life in some meaningful fashion" (1963: 54). Such a focus on the subjective world of meaning is further evidenced in this theorist's assent to the Thomas theorem: A social situation is what its participants define it to be. Never mind that social actors may wrongheadedly interpret their reality. Berger argued that "many social situations are effectively controlled by the definitions of imbeciles" (1963: 84).

It is within the world of self-development that Berger makes clear the processual nature of being human. Thus the self is not a concrete and unbending entity that endures over space and time. To the contrary, it is a dynamic, moving, growing venture "continuously created and re-created in each social situation one enters, held together by the slender thread of memory" (1963: 106). Who one truly "is" depends on the social situation one finds oneself in— its tasks, its rules, and the responses and initiatives of others.

As did Alfred Schutz, Berger finds the issue of freedom a central one for human nature. However, in *Invitation,* he was less concerned with the phenomenological process of choice, preferring instead the insights born of existentialism. For the existentialists, "being" is a matter of assuming responsibility for one's deeds. For Berger, although boundaries are imposed on behavior by the roles we play, human beings have the ability and often the obligation to transcend these. He agrees with Sartre, who argued that to evade the agony of choice and to pretend voluntary acts are unnecessary constitutes an attempted escape from freedom, an act of "bad faith" (1963: 142–143).

As we have come to expect, assumptions about human nature quite logically lead to preconceptions about what makes a society possible. Peter Berger's portrait of society features an explicit consciousness and fear of various forms of social control. In pluralist fashion, he is disturbed by the awesome power of coercive systems of conformity. The individual in society is pictured in the center of a set of concentric circles of influence, each intended to produce a numbing sameness of action. They range downward from legal and political systems, with their formal sanctions, to the cultural controls of custom, morality, and manners, with their more informal punishments and rewards. They include the tyranny of bureaucracies, the expectations of occupations, and the human associations that most intimately touch the private life.

Class position, race, the weight of contemporary demands, and past generations, all of these and more threaten the pluralist ideals of openness and diversity. Although social behavior is not mechanically determined and all such forces are the consequence of human action, Berger clearly worries about systems of external constraint. Given the domination of his native land by one of the most brutally efficient forms of political organization in the modern era, such a theme can be easily placed in the context of history.

Berger also bares his image of science. He is critical of the positivist vision of sociology, which reduces the discipline to narrowly drawn empirical studies requiring the application of statistical techniques. These he sees as too frequently atheoretical, driven by the "publish or perish" syndrome that determines which assistant professors survive as senior faculty members (1963: 10–13). Instead, the nature of sociology for Peter Berger is embodied in Nietzsche's "art of mistrust." Its prime directive is a willingness to "see through" (1963: 30–31) the elaborate facades of what Schutz described as a "world taken for granted" (1963: 24).

Decrying the obsession with deviance and social problems among U.S. sociologists, Berger defines the field as a basic understanding of social interaction. And this crucial process is in turn best understood from the frame of reference of actors who construct widely different social systems. Accordingly, what is a "problem" to one social system may be the normal routine of things to another, and vice versa. "Loyalty and disloyalty, solidarity and deviance, are defined in contradictory terms" (1963: 37). This embracing of cultural and normative relativity is, of course, a recurring and logically consistent property of pluralist thought.

What is the essence of the sociological "invitation"? For Berger, it is to develop a consciousness that seeks to uncover

> . . . how the whole system works in the first place, what are its presuppositions, and by what means it is held together. The fundamental sociological problem is not crime but the law, not divorce but marriage, not racial discrimination but racially defined stratification, not revolution but government. (1963: 37)

Given such a charge, one might argue that sociology should be on the leading edge of fashioning alternative futures. Not so, argues Berger. Illusions about change are as much a problem as those that support the status quo. Sociology's true essence is "nonrevolutionary," one of "moderating soberness" (1963: 47).

## Theoretical Content

In *The Social Construction of Reality* (1966), we find Peter Berger's attempt to build a theory of society. Written with Thomas Luckmann, the book is "intended as a systematic treatise in the sociology of knowledge" (1966: v). However, what was attempted here is far removed from the conception of *Wissenssoziologie* explored in our introductory chapter and in the conflict section that follows. Berger and Luckmann did not conceive of knowledge as a historical product that reflects the events and ideas of the age. Nor were they concerned with the biographical world of knowledge makers through which such events and ideas are filtered. Instead, they focused on the *processes by which whatever passes for knowledge becomes real*. In other words, it is the taken-for-granted reality of the ordinary actor, not merely the formal ideas of the scientist or intellectual, that Berger and Luckmann defined as "knowledge" (1966: 1–17). And the process by which such a reality is constructed is more important than the *content* of whatever truths may be in vogue.

This concern with "everything that passes for knowledge" downplays the importance of formal or theoretical ideas that seek to discover truth, laws, or principles. For Berger and Luckmann, every participant lives in and interprets some social world. Citing the work of Schutz, they sought to explore the "commonsense world" or the "taken-for-granted typifications" that constitute the socially approved "knowledge of everyday life." With this unique conception of the sociology of knowledge in hand, they guided their inquiry into the manner in which social reality is constructed.

Berger and Luckmann held that society has a dual character. Its "reality" is both objective and subjective, and it is best understood when guidance is provided by both Durkheim and Weber. However, in the contest between the two, it is Weber who triumphs. Specifically, Berger and Luckmann were influenced by Weber's insistence that any "object" must be provided with a subjective meaning that impels action.

Although Berger and Luckmann acknowledged the existence of an orderly objective world, social order is seen as an "ongoing human production" (1966: 49). Actors produce the "self" and together they make a human environment. However, to the extent that shared patterns of behavior become *habitualized,* it becomes unnecessary for each social situation to be "defined anew, step by step" (1966: 51). Such processes of habitualization, formed through ongoing human interaction, set the stage for the emergence of institutions.

"Institutionalization," argued Berger and Luckmann, "occurs whenever there is a reciprocal typification of habitualized actions by types of actors" (1966: 51). Translated, this means that a Schutzean world of socially developed and approved "ways of doing things" acquires an existence of its own. It cannot be wished away; it is not a phantom world of the mind or a material world that somehow obeys historical laws. Institutions are produced when human beings confer upon their habits commonly accepted meanings, ordinarily embodied in routines. Such mutual understandings add a recurring quality to social exchange. In a more general sense, institutions are little more than repetitive patterns of role behavior, made through past and present human interaction. And in dialectical fashion, these institutions then confront their present makers, who perceive them (falsely) as an independent, coercive, and external fact (1966: 52–57).

Sharing with others specific goals and interlocking behaviors results in the creation of roles. Such are not "objective positions" in social structure but rather "types of actors" that share common knowledge that "makes right" a particular course of conduct. Thus, in a matrilocal society (one in which the husband establishes residence in the locale of the wife's family), an uncle may thrash an arrogant nephew as a taken-for-granted course of action. It is clear that such a typification of the role of uncle may not play well in another context. However, this and other roles are the means by which the individual participates in an objective social world of shared interpretations. "By internalizing these roles, the same world becomes subjectively real" (1966: 69).

Berger and Luckmann concluded their discussion of the objective nature of society by focusing on Max Weber's conception of *legitimation* (1966: 85–118). Given the institutional order described above, the question of its justification follows. Such legitimation occurs at various levels. At the first level, the "totality of the institutional order" must come to "make sense . . . to participants." Through this process, one fathoms the motives behind and reasons for patterned interaction. For example, participants come to know the role expectations (both their own and others) for the military order. This serves to legitimate and integrate the entire structure.

Second, passing through the institutional order must be made "subjectively meaningful" to members at a biographical level. Recalling our military example, one not only knows the norms of that institutional system, but one "knows oneself" as a member of that system. The third level of legitimation involves "explicit theories" often generated and passed on to participants by "full-time legitimators." For example, military historians may develop a specialized knowledge to explain the role of the military in international affairs.

Finally, at the fourth level, is a "symbolic universe" of legitimation that gives meaning to the institutional order. Here a world view is bestowed on the participants that justifies the system at the ultimate level. Thus, military action may be located in a "cosmological and anthropological" frame of reference. It will then be argued that war is ordained in the cosmos or that warlike behavior is inherent in human nature. Given these assumptions, peace is a function of war-making power. As examples, the motto of the Strategic Air Command is "peace is our profession," while the Department of Defense in the United States in 1984 defined peace as "permanent prehostility."

As would be expected of interpretative sociologists, Berger and Luckmann seriously explored society as subjective reality (1966: 119–173). Individuals are not born members of society; they become members. And the process begins with *internalization,* or socialization through which the outside world of meaning becomes subjectively relevant. Here, the individual "takes over" an already inhabited world. One does this by understanding (accurately or inaccurately) the subjective processes of others, processes they make manifest in their objective behavior. Through interaction, mutual identification occurs. "We not only live in the same world, we participate in each other's being" (1966: 120).

In Meadian fashion, Berger and Luckmann assessed primary socialization in social-psychological terms. For the very young, parents and parental surrogates introduce the "base-world" by which judgments of society "as it is" should be made. This internalization process begins at a concrete level with the child learning specific precepts and prohibitions. However, over time the familiar "generalized other" is formed within one's consciousness. It is an abstraction from the roles and attitudes of significant others or, simply put, the inner voice of society. The "crystallization in consciousness" of the generalized other establishes a "symmetrical relationship" between objective and subjective reality. "What is real 'outside' corresponds to what is real 'within'" (1966: 123).

Socialization also exists at the secondary level. It involves the "internalization of institutional or institution-based 'subworlds'" (1966: 127). Through secondary socialization, special knowledge, role-specific vocabularies, and tacit understandings are transmitted. This form of internalization reflects the "complexity of the division of labor and the concomitant social distribution of knowledge." Such socialization may be sharply intensified in heterogeneous societies where different subworlds compete for loyalty.

By means of socialization, a subjective reality is created and recreated throughout life. Through such internalization, the world of everyday life comes to acquire a taken-for-granted nature, yet it is not a totally placid existence. Subjective reality must be maintained, which is to say that the individual consciousness must be shielded from "threatening competing definitions." Significant others are the principals in this ongoing process of self-definition, while those less important function as a "chorus." They confirm one's subjective world through the most casual of conversations, conversations that confirm the trusted nature of social routines.

From this logic, it should be obvious that the taken-for-granted world is a powerful force. However, it is not immutable. "Transformations" can and do occur. Such a change in the subjective reality typically involves immersions in new subworlds of definitions that affect a part of one's identity. However, given a resocialization experience that mirrors the intensity of primary socialization, *alteration* can occur. A historical prototype of this would be the religious conversion. The "reality-base for resocialization is the present," and the past is reinterpreted to fit the emerging, new identity (1966: 144–150).

## Critique

Berger and Luckmann attempted a synthesis of objective and subjective "social realities," seeking to combine the sociological visions of Durkheim and Weber. In point of fact, they did not succeed. Paradigm mixing is a delicate if not impossible task because of the substantial differences in the underlying assumptions about the nature of human being, society, and sociology. To attempt a merger within the same theoretical system typically produces a "tilt" in one direction or the other. In the case of Talcott Parsons, the systems emphasis clearly overrode his Weberian respect for social action. In the case of Berger and Luckmann, the Durkheimian conception of society as a reality *sui generis* was the clear loser.

For Berger and Luckmann, society is neither unique nor truly "objective." It is fair to argue that what they argued for "legitimations" can be generalized to their total conception of objective social reality.

> What remains sociologically essential is the recognition that all symbolic universes and all legitimations are human products; their existence has its base in the lives of concrete individuals and has no empirical status apart from these lives. (1966: 118)

From the foregoing we conclude that within this theoretical system, society and its institutions do not form an objective and interdependent system. In a restatement of Husserl's "natural attitude," Berger and Luckmann maintained that any order in the social world exists only because people impose relationships and assume them to be preexisting. In an extension of this logic, the authors defined institutions as routines formed through interaction and transmitted through socialization. Such a view essentially denies the *structural reality* crucial to most order and conflict theory. Even in its treatment of objective social reality, sociology is largely reduced to social psychology.

The ideological implications of this theoretical system provide a final dimension to our critique. Let us begin by reviewing Berger and Luckmann's assertion that modern societies by and large are pluralistic. They defined this in familiar terms, citing a "shared core universe, taken for granted as such, and different partial universes coexisting in a state of mutual accommodation"

(1966: 115). Added to such hallmarks are urbanism, a highly developed division of labor, a highly differentiated social structure, a high economic surplus, and rapid social change. Interestingly enough, they added an observation reminiscent of Daniel Bell's "end of ideology." (See Chapter 11.) In the pluralist society, "outright conflict between ideologies has been replaced by varying degrees of tolerance or even cooperation" (1966: 15).

This contemporary vision of antagonistic cooperation can be augmented by the ambivalence Berger feels toward society. As we noted earlier, in *Invitation to Sociology* he focused on the problematics of social control and the need to "debunk" the conventional wisdom. Yet, in a later work (1977b: xv), he defined society as "the imposition of order upon the flux of human experience." Such order, he continued, introduces an economy into our range of choice and in so doing ensures human sanity. Berger retained his belief in freedom, in that people construct their reality, but argued that their choices are necessarily limited by the demands of the existing order (1977b: xvi–xviii).

We do not mean to imply that Berger's work reflects an ideological shift. To the contrary, he is caught on the horns of the liberal dilemma. While suspicious of the status quo, he harbors greater misgivings about structural alternatives, preferring to center his more recent works in the problems of modernity. His conception of limited freedom is more than opposition to anarchy; it is also opposition to serious change. A decade and a half beyond his *Invitation,* Berger described himself as a "conservative humanist." In so doing, he has become neither functionalist nor positivist, neither a believer in grand systems nor a social Darwinist. Instead, he has sought to reaffirm the intellectual distance between his own thought and other holistic and critical systems that gained popularity during the turbulance of the 1960s and early 1970s. As we shall see in Unit Four, these voices resurrected and expanded their own variety of humanism. However, unlike Berger and other pluralists, their search for utopian ideals drove them beyond the existing order.

# ■ Harold Garfinkel (b. 1917): Fitting In

Another intellectual descendant of Alfred Schutz at the New School for Social Research was Harold Garfinkel. This sociologist, perhaps more than any other, was to explore in minute detail the Schutzean taken-for-granted world also found in the sociology of Berger and Luckmann. Garfinkel's conception of sociology is distinctive in a second sense: What he terms *ethnomethodology* is a radical departure from most other pluralist theories, as well as other paradigmatic offerings. This has led to a storm of controversy inside the discipline, as we shall soon see.

In 1952 Garfinkel received his Ph.D. from Harvard, where he was a student of Talcott Parsons. Parsons pressed upon Garfinkel the importance of social order as well as a healthy respect for Weberian conceptions of social action. His later tutelage under Schutz at the New School was to add a phenomeno-logical dimension to Garfinkel's attempts at theory construction. It was this di-mension that proved dominant when, in the 1960s at UCLA, Garfinkel wrote his influential *Studies in Ethnomethodology* (1967).

## Assumptions

Garfinkel assumes the common pluralist image of human nature: that of social actors seeking to interpret their world. This process can best be conceived as the self-production of forms of social organization. Within the framework of interaction with others, participants seek a consistency between the world out-side and that within. More specifically, human beings seek to accomplish a *congruence* between an external moral order founded in commonly shared norms and a *practical rationality* by which everyday affairs are "made sense of" (Gar-finkel, 1967: 172–175). Interacting members "explain" their behavior and in-terpret their moral universe not as theoreticians or research specialists. Such "explanations" are rather to be found in the ordinary ways in which people practice the "art of making sense" of the real world.

The image of society that prevails in ethnomethodology is one of mul-tiple realities dynamically formed through commonplace activities. Hence, so-cial organization is not imposed by structurally "real" institutions with their own history and distinctive properties. Instead, it is made by individuals; its nature is one of ongoing accomplishment, not a finished product. For Gar-finkel, social order is negotiated in interaction with others. And, as would be expected from one who has glowingly cited the influence of Alfred Schutz, it is the taken-for-granted world of everyday life that constitutes the ethnome-thodological laboratory (1967: vii–viii).

It is the conception of human science that truly sets Garfinkel and his stu-dents apart from the sociological mainstream. He claims that through the lens of ethnomethodology, an "immense, hitherto unknown domain of social phe-nomena has been uncovered" (1967: ix). As follows from our discussion above, such phenomena are forms of social organization, which are created through a dynamic process of interpretation. This interpretation, in turn, can only be understood from the perspective of participants. The ethnomethodologist seeks to uncover the commonplace methodologies by which people make and shape their multiple social realities (1967: 10–11).

According to Garfinkel, ethnomethodological studies do not supplant standard sociological inquiries. Rather, they are "distinctive unto themselves." Nor do they offer "remedies" or applied forms of knowledge with which to address the practical actions of everyday life. Ethnomethodological studies are not in "search of humanistic arguments, nor do they engage in or encourage permissive discussions of theory" (1967: viii).

Although Garfinkel believes that practical, commonsense actions have formal properties, his sociology is based on a skepticism of the preexisting order that is taken for granted by individuals. His focus is the face-to-face world of immediate relations with others. Within this context, people seek congruence with a moral order that offers reasons and rules for social behavior.

As is the case with phenomenological sociology, Garfinkel and his heirs are preoccupied with language as the medium of interpretation. Accordingly, ordinary conversations are frequently analyzed in order to identify what is missing yet understood in this form of interaction. Finally, because ethno-methodologists are convinced of the tentative, arbitrary, and dynamic nature of a world of meaning, they "bracket" reality. Appearances are not real, even though they have real consequences.[4]

## Theoretical Content

It should be argued at the outset that ethnomethodology escapes formal defi-nition as a theoretical system. It is not truly a set of implicit explanations, much less a formal array of propositions. Ethnomethodologists are more con-cerned with how ordinary actors self-produce their social reality than why. Hence, these sociologists study the commonplace "methodologies" by which meaning is constructed and shared. This emphasis is well-hidden in Garfinkel's definition of the field, but if we wade through the verbiage we can translate.

For Garfinkel, *ethnomethodology* is used to "refer to the investigation of the rational properties of indexical expressions and other practical actions as contingent ongoing accomplishments of organized artful practices of everyday life" (1967: 11). Remember that the key to this view is that "practical socio-logical reasoning" (ethnomethodology) seeks to solve or understand the ra-tionality that is inherent in social interaction. That rationality is evident in "indexical expressions and other practical actions." In other words, people by means of their language (and behavior) are seeking to *indicate* to themselves and others the *location* of ordinary events and transactions in the wider reality. Hence the term *indexical*. Put simply, people demonstrate through their words and deeds a primary human need: the artificial imposition of order, the self-creation of patterns. Such doings (accomplishments) are organized, creative practices found in distinctively human skills (artful) rather than nature. The irony is that such a process ultimately involves giving meaning to the meaningless.

One key to understanding Garfinkel (1967: 172–175) resides in his under-standing of "rational action." Here he cited Weber for the sociological truism

---

[4]The bracketing of reality refers to the dismembering of all preexisting conceptions of "natural order." Its philosophical roots are in the works of Edmund Husserl.

that a person in "conducting his everyday affairs" can deliberate, calculate, and anticipate the consequences of various courses of action. However, Garfinkel noted that this human quality is dependent "upon the person being able to take for granted, to take under trust, a vast array of features of the social order."

The rational actor decides on the basis of facts not in evidence, inferring the properties of the iceberg from its tip only. It follows that it is the "trusted, taken for granted, background features of a person's situation, that is, the routine aspects of the situation, that permit 'rational action'" (1967: 173). Much of ethnomethodology is about making explicit the implicit (taken-for-granted) nature of social interaction. It explores the tacit (unstated) understandings that may be "left out" of language, even that of formal contracts. Thus, it is the task of ethnomethodologists to "fill in" the beneath-the-surface meanings that guide the routines of social life (1967: 173).

So far, we have the portrait of the commonplace (and rational) social actor employing indexical expressions to locate his or her behavior in a broader world of "meaning." This form of rationality is *practical* or *"sense making,"* and it appears to be manifested through the language of everyday life. On the other hand, scientists (including most other sociologists) employ a formal, more rigorous rationalism reflected in a precise and more objective language. If we extend this logic, Garfinkel would argue that when human scientists seek to discover a preexisting order, they reproduce the error of Husserl's "natural attitude." Ethnomethodologists believe that social order is "made" when people seek to align their interpretations with an *assumed* moral order.

By "assumed moral order," we mean to stress the point that anchors this approach to sociology. People define the "real world" as a "matter of objective, institutionalized" or "moral" facts (1967: 122). They then proceed, through language and other behavior, to orient their actions and meanings to that moral universe. Such a universe has no natural existence, however. Although it defines reality and is the standard by which events and ideas are judged, the moral order with its rational properties is assumed, inferred, created, and produced through an interactive process. Hence, the moral order is *perceived* by society's members as "normal courses of action—familiar scenes of everyday affairs, the world of daily life known in common with others and with others taken for granted" (1967: 35).

If there is an explanatory focus in ethnomethodology, it would appear to be found in the quest for consonance or "fitting in." This has little to do with the traditional sociological concerns of social control and conformity. Instead, the individual seeks to fit his or her circumstances into this broader moral universe. For example, Garfinkel examined the dilemma of Agnes, an hermaphrodite for whom the moral order included a "real world" of "natural, normally sexed persons." In such a dichotomized world, there was room only for *natural* males and *natural* females. Agnes sought consonance with this perceived universe, insisting that "she was, and was to be treated as, a natural, normal female" (1967: 122).

## Critique

Those who grapple with sociological theory often wish for a system of "practical" thought that deals with the "real world." Well, this is it. And although it might not be exactly what you had in mind, ethnomethodological inquiries have yielded some understanding of the tacit order of social interaction. Beyond this, those of this tradition argue on behalf of a redefinition of sociology. Given this fact, ordinary actors in the everyday world become sociologists, seeking to interpret the social reality. In turn, sociologists become ordinary actors, responding to their own sense of the moral universe, seeking to interpret the same reality.

Such a redefinition of the field, when combined with other criticisms to be explored shortly, did not go unanswered. Ethnomethodology was subjected to a rather unkind assault in the 1970s. Lewis Coser, in his 1975 presidential address to the American Sociological Association, called it trivial, subjectivist, and self-indulgent. A review of Garfinkel's *Studies in Ethnomethodology* argued that the book "elaborates very greatly points which are so commonplace that they would appear banal if stated in straightforward English" (Coleman, 1968: 130). Garfinkel and his heirs do appear able to discover layers of hidden meanings and missing "shared understandings" in the taken-for-granted world. They have also explored such burning topics as "doing walking," the "openings to telephone conversations," and "knowing when to laugh." And they are sometimes guilty of ignoring that the purpose of language is to communicate.

In fairness, much mainstream sociology can be subjected to similar criticism. Sociologists often study "meanings" that comprise the "subculture" of the "not taken-for-granted world." In fact, much of the field of deviant behavior reflects this approach. If the ethnomethodologist were to study such topics as "the jogging subculture," "obscene telephone conversations," "mood changes among the hebephrenic population," perhaps fewer eyebrows would be raised. However, given the attacks, most ethnomethodologists today are congregated in California, probably for self-defense.

Other criticisms are more substantive. Contrary to their canons, ethnomethodologists are not content to let their subjects explain in detail how they see the world. They remain the specialists in filling in the blanks or identifying the tacit understandings that guide interaction. In a similar vein, Harold Garfinkel developed a framework for studying participants, but he has not written like participants. He has employed a language strange in both semantics and syntax, and many of his descendants have followed suit. Hence, they are to be found quarreling among themselves as to the meanings their research has given to the meanings that actors give to a meaningless world. Whether this is a testimony to subjectivism, obtuse language, or a new sociology is a point of continuing debate.

Ethnomethodology has inverted traditional conceptions of science, even the softer ones that prevail in sociology. The determinate becomes indeterminate, the real unreal, and the meaningful meaningless. In a like vein, order is fiction, laws are random events, and history is lost to the present moment. The great truth of all of this for Garfinkel and his heirs is that rational actors (including sociologists who are not ethnomethodologists) act "as if" such were not true. All of us play the game of "fitting in" according to the perceived rules of the moral order. Other theorists have argued that social reality is artificially created, that organizations are self-produced, and that our own order falsely confronts us as natural. But ethnomethodology is distinctive by means of its focus on everyday events, events that form a window to hidden routines and perceived moral orders.

# ■ Erving Goffman (1922–1982): The World's a Stage

Erving Goffman was another sociologist who on the one hand focused on individuals in interaction, but on the other was aware of the "settings without," the social contexts that limit and direct such exchanges. Again, it is important to remember that the theorists examined in this chapter do not stress the importance of large-scale institutional structures. Goffman's theory, for example, is often labeled *dramaturgical* because of his predilection for theatrical metaphors. Here, the play is no dramatic epic that occurs against the backdrop of sweeping historical events. Goffman's prevailing conception of social theater is small in scale, his stage is intimate and isolated, and his actors are self-consciously mindful of the presence of others. Yet, late in his career he enlarged his drama, as we shall see.

Goffman was born a Canadian and received his B.A. degree from the University of Toronto in 1945. He attended the University of Chicago in the postwar period, receiving an M.A. in 1949 and a Ph.D. in sociology in 1953. Hence he was trained at the institution that pioneered generally in the discipline and specifically in symbolic interaction. That tradition is well evidenced in Goffman's work, particularly in the methodology he employed to make his observations of contemporary life. Yet, criticism came his way from symbolic interactionists who believed that Goffman allowed his actors too little freedom from their roles.

After receiving his doctorate, Goffman worked for three years at the National Institute of Mental Health, where he developed an abiding interest in the social world of those confined in "total institutions." He joined the faculty of the University of California at Berkeley in 1958 and published his first major work, *The Presentation of Self in Everyday Life* (1959), shortly thereafter. He conducted extensive research in the sociology of interaction, bringing out the noteworthy books *Asylums* (1961) and *Stigma* (1963).

In 1968 Goffman left Berkeley for the University of Pennsylvania, where he served for 14 years. He continued to write prolifically, using the dramaturgical theme to argue that actors on the stage of life always play to an audience. Each constantly endeavors to manage the impressions of those others who are party to shared interactions. In 1974 Goffman published *Frame Analysis,* in which he studied the organization not of society but of subjective experience. However, experiences do not appear as dissociated from existing norms and rules. In *Gender Advertisements* (1976), he investigated the manner in which advertising helps to form "masculine" and "feminine" images of role. And in his last book, *Forms of Talk* (1981), he explored again the tactics people use to control "public information" about the self. Erving Goffman died prematurely in 1982.

## Assumptions

Dramaturgical thought for Goffman evidences a number of the common pluralist images discussed throughout this section. The emphasis once again is on the minded actor, interpreting his or her experience, at once shaping and shaped through interaction with others. However, Goffman's conception of interaction is distinctive in large part because of his assumptions concerning the human essence. In his seminal work, *The Presentation of Self in Everyday Life,* he quoted the philosopher George Santayana: "Masks are arrested expressions and admirable echoes of feeling, at once faithful, discreet, and superlative." It is this conception of the mask, the *persona* behind which feeling and the unrevealed self reside, that is the plot for Goffman's theater of social life.

Throughout his writing career, Goffman held fast to the image of the con artist, the artful deceiver who seeks to "present himself in the most favorable light" (1959: 7). This is something of a twist on Cooley's "looking-glass self." Cooley believed that the self develops on the basis of one's perceptions of the perceptions of others. Goffman went a step further. He believed that human beings in interaction constantly monitor the signals they emit.

> This kind of control upon the part of the individual reinstates the symmetry of the communication process, and sets the stage for a kind of information game— a potentially infinite cycle of concealment, discovery, false revelation, and rediscovery. (1959: 8)

Now, what did Goffman assume to be the nature of society? At first blush, we might believe that individuals act to build a social world and that society is the ever-changing product of a dynamic interactive process. However, if this were true, Goffman would "fit" much more comfortably in the community of symbolic interactionists than he does. To understand Goffman's position here requires that we grasp the recurrent paradox in his work. On the one hand, he considered "social organization and social structure" (particularly in the sense of roles and norms) to be the "core matters of sociology." On the other, his work focused on the "structure of *experience* individuals have at any moment of their lives" (1974: 13, italics added). By Goffman's own admission, society is first in every way. Yet, he did not choose to study that which is first.

To use the language of the theater, Goffman was more concerned with the interpretation of roles by actors on the stage of everyday life. He did not choose to emphasize the origins of the *script* that provides the content for these roles and the standards by which performance is judged. Instead, Goffman studied how we "present." In his social drama, each actor is driven toward "engineering a convincing impression that (moral and other) standards are being realized . . . appearing always in a steady moral light, of being a socialized character . . . the sort of person who is practiced in the ways of the stage" (1959: 251). There is more than a slight resemblance here to Garfinkel's argument that individuals seek congruity with a moral order.

Goffman did not totally ignore the not-so-immediate world. But his focus was always on the consequences of that world for performance. For example, different stratification systems (such as class and caste) provide for different symbols of status. Such symbols become ritualized methods for demonstrating one's position in the social hierarchy. Status symbols are not invented; rather, they are part of a predetermined routine manipulated by those seeking to control the judgments of others.

One can find in Goffman's work a hint of how the preestablished patterns of social life emerge. He employed the term *front* to specify those regular and recurring aspects of performance that define the situation for the audience of others. Consisting of both physical setting and personal manner and appearance, the front subsumes a number of "different pattern(s) of expectation and responsive treatment for each slightly different performer and performance" (1959: 26).

In terms of the organization of society, Goffman claimed that as societies become larger and more heterogeneous, fronts become more essential. More crucially, as actors play a role, they discover that "a particular front has already been established for it" (1959: 27). Institutionalized gender fronts, for example, present a performance in which the underlying sex roles are played out. This is reflected in a variety of ways. Hence in commercial advertising, both the setting of the ads and the manner and appearance of subjects often project an image of dependency and powerlessness for women (Goffman, 1976).

Finally, Goffman's sociology reveals certain assumptions about the nature of human science. He sought to understand and explain through a perspective identified above as dramaturgical. Hence, his "sensitizing concepts" include stage, performance, front, frame, presentation, audience, and so forth. By crafting his system of thought, Goffman meant to present a "perspective from which social life can be studied, especially the kind of social life that is organized within the physical confines of a building or plant" (1959: xi).

Along with others considered in this chapter, Goffman analyzed the interaction of those who participate in the rituals and routines of everyday life. And although performances allow for some variation in personal interpretation, each is "socialized." That is, each impression given off is "molded and modified to fit into the understanding and expectations of the society in which it is presented" (1959: 35). This is a form of determinism, but for Goffman the structural forces that impinge upon the actor are small in scale and near at hand. The interacting person, with his or her wide repertoire of stage methods, remains the focus of this system of thought.

## Theoretical Content

The tie that binds Goffman's works is always some variation of *impression management*. When one enters the presence of others, each participant in the interaction that ensues looks for "sign vehicles" that suggest something about social standing, attitudes, or character. Many of these judgments are rooted in some sense of what a given situation demands of "socialized" members. Knowing this, each actor seeks to control the impressions others develop in the information exchange process. This process in turn involves two "radically different kinds of sign activity"—namely, expressions "given" and expressions "given off" (1959: 2–16). The first refers primarily to verbal symbols that convey shared information. The second centers on "more theatrical and contextual" signs by which the performers deviously attempt to influence how others define the situation.

Thus, in each social situation involving a setting and others, a *performance* is given. During performances, *routines* or "preestablished patterns" unfold that may be "played through on other occasions." Remember that when we examined Goffman's conception of the organization of the society, we introduced the term *front*. Looking at it more systematically, "front stage" is the central "region" of a performance. Through its components (physical setting and personal appearance and manner), the front allows observers to define the situation. It follows that an important part of the process of impression management is to control the "scenery" as well as things like dress and demeanor.

What do you expect, for example, from a performance that involves a surgical operation? Precisely, how should the major players be dressed? What kinds of signs do they give or give off? What would a patient expect of the operating room "scene"? What do you imagine might be going on "back stage"? If, you and others reach something of a consensus about the "front stage" of the surgical "performance," it is because such fronts have become institutionalized. Thus "collective representations" or shared interpretations about the front arise, reflecting in turn some continuity over time.

Fronts therefore allow us to deal more economically with broad categories of signals. As such, fronts are more general and abstract than specialized routines. For example, white uniforms worn in a hospital represent an abstract component of the front. Those interpreting this dress receive a sign that tasks will be performed in a sanitary and cautious manner, whether by an orderly, a nurse, or a laboratory technician. Yet, the routines of each occupation may be, or at least appear to be, much more specific.

As a social actor performs on the front stage, he presents an "idealized version of himself and his products" (1959: 48). Of course, how one behaves "backstage" may be something quite different. Hence, the surgical nurse may see the surgeon under quite different conditions than do patients. In the management of such impressions, the individual must hide some information and convey controlled appearances that vary with the audience. This is facilitated through the "segregation" of audiences. Children, for example, do not ordinarily see the "partying" behavior of their parents (1959: 34–51).

Goffman argued that social actors go to great lengths to cover up errors and other behavior that are inconsistent with the idealized self. For example, a professor may lose his or her train of thought and blunder on rather than admit it. Or, if asked a question that cannot be adequately answered, the professor may restructure the question so that it fits his or her knowledge base. Others may resort to a specialized language, not for the purpose of technical communication but to demonstrate expertise. Finally, presenting oneself in the idealized role of expert may be one tactic employed in the creation of "distance" between the performer and the "lay" audience. According to dramaturgical theory, the audience often goes along with the arts of impression management, because they wish to be party to unique performances. Indeed, members of an audience may be managing impressions of their own!

The relationship between performers and their audience represents for Goffman one type of *team*. Each is involved in a reciprocal set of behaviors. While some may appear to be major players, social theater does not involve the one-sided relationship between actors and audience found in a Broadway production. Hence in terms of the front-stage performance involving a professor and a class, the former is not the actor and the latter is not the audience. In the exercise of all routines, each participant is both audience and performer. Goffman used the term *audience* not to imply a passive onlooker but to underscore his belief that each interacting person plays to the other or others. It is even conceivable to play to an "imaginary" audience, as in "talking to yourself." This latter form of team play might get one a reputation, however.

Teams can also be conceived in other ways. They differ in terms of the frequency, intensity, and continuity of their performance. While each member of a "familiar" team uses the other as an audience, the routine may be staged more for the benefit of unfamiliar others. In such a situation, tight rules enable the team to control the definition of the situation by others in the unfamiliar audience. Both individual and team character can be staged only when the "arts of impression management" and their implicit rules are mastered (1959: 208–237).

To be precise, team members must remain *loyal, disciplined, and circumspect*. Team loyalty involves such strategies as avoiding public disagreement and identification with the audience. Team discipline means the exercise of self-control, managing the signs given off, and other performance-related behavior. Team circumspection includes but is not limited to planning the performance in advance, planning for emergency, and keeping the audience in the dark. Taken as a whole, the performers who constitute a "familiar" team enter into a "conspiracy." Each stages his or her character to prevent a disruption of the performance and knows the rules necessary to save the show.

Goffman's *The Presentation of Self in Everyday Life* includes the dramaturgical base for his later works. Two of these will suffice to demonstrate his theoretical perspective more clearly. In *Asylums* (1961), Goffman focused on the social world of the "hospital inmate." In *Stigma* (1963), he focused on the "management of spoiled identity" by the "individual who is disqualified from full social acceptance" because of some form of physical, character, or "tribal" (that is, social) defect.

The dramaturgical style is distinctive by reason of its focus on the attributes of performances played out on an intimate stage. As we have indicated, Goffman had some sense of the larger productions of life: of institutions and history, of large-scale social organization, of class and caste, of roles that transcend the immediate context. But he also sensed a play within the play, a smaller world in which each performer presents the "proper" self. This emphasis on the immediate context is clearly evidenced in *Asylums*.

The asylum for Goffman is one of a type he termed the *total institution*. The total institution represents closure and isolation. Its inhabitants are "cut off from the wider society for an appreciable period of time." Within such confines they experience "an enclosed formally administered round of life" (1961: xii). Total institutions include (1) those established to care for the indigent and harmless (such as homes for the aged or orphans); (2) those intended to care for the impaired who represent an unintended threat to the community (such as mental hospitals and tuberculosis sanatoriums); (3) those organized to protect the community from intentional danger (such as penitentiaries and POW camps); (4) those established for instrumental purposes to pursue an organizational goal (such as army barracks, ships, and boarding schools); and (5) those intended to serve as religious retreats and places of training (such as convents and monasteries) (1961: 4–5).

Goffman studied the "institutional arrangements" of the asylum that strip the person of a "prepatient" identity with its rights and liberties and supplant in its stead a new self. This new self, that of the patient, does not truly belong to the individual but is instead a property of the hospital's social system. More specifically, the patient's institutional "self" is little more than a pattern of social control (1961: 167–168).

This conversion of self, despite the "totalness" of the institution, is not complete. That is to say, patients do not simply "become" the norms and roles of the asylum. They do learn to work the system, however. The patient identifies the key players, especially members of the staff, and presents the proper self. Such a performance may include participating in therapy, acknowledging staff authority and expertise, and other strategies that demonstrate the passing of "civilian liberties." In the process, the patient may be treated more as a "normal," receive desirable work assignments, and be certified as "improving." However, "backstage," the hospital inmate holds onto a part of the prepatient self.

In *Stigma* (1963), Goffman focused on the distance between two forms of social identity, the "virtual" and the "actual." The first of these refers to real identity, and the second to expected identity. When there is a gap between these, the individual is marked or stigmatized. Stated in Goffman's language, a stigma is "a special kind of relationship between attribute and stereotype" (1963: 4). When the defect is known to interacting others (as with a physical disability), the affected person is *discredited*. When it is not immediately apparent (as with homosexuality or unemployment), the person is *discreditable*.

Given these major conceptions, Goffman analyzed the interaction between the stigmatized and others in dramaturgical terms. For the discredited, the major problem is reducing and controlling the embarrassment and often unintended psychic pain inflicted by others in an interactive situation. For the discreditable, the task is to manage impressions so that others will not find out the nature of the stigma. Such management of spoiled identity is not restricted to the more or less permanently different. Most of us, at one time or another, experience this gap between real and ideal and call out a performance to cover up.

## Critique

The works of Erving Goffman are clearly aligned with those of Garfinkel and the phenomenologists. They hold in common a refusal to impose natural conceptions of order and preordained categories and relationships on human behavior. The commitment is to a "natural inquiry" into the processes of human interaction. However, in Goffman's social world, performers have no biography, episodic encounters have no history, and the institutionalized fronts that mark social organization are not studied head-on.

The dramaturgical style is rich with insights, but its insights are somewhat stilted. This is not due to Goffman's style or logic, which is neither pretentious nor overly formal. Instead, the problem is with the scope of his social world. There is a structure here, but it is small in scale, reduced to the immediate context of the performance. In Goffman's terms, his is a near-at-hand reality with "fixed barriers to perception." And the analysis of small-scale productions, whether of everyday life or total institutions, presents an inherent dilemma. It is reflected in the detailed analysis of what can only be termed the minutia of interaction. If Goffman had been a drama critic, he would have been prone to tortuously analyze the nuances of the performances and—in the process—miss the play.

Some have accused Goffman of a cynical conception of human nature, a vivid portrayal of the con artist always on the make, living in dread of giving the show away. In a corresponding vein, Goffman's players are self-absorbed and reflective, virtually to the point of obsession. There is evidence, of course, that such egocentrism can become abundant in society. Massive amounts of energy and money can be spent in the attempt to manipulate the definition of the situation. In point of fact, entire industries may arise around impression management. At this writing, advertising sales in the United States are fast approaching an annual rate of $100 billion. Late in his career, Goffman began to recognize the logical connection between impression management and this industry. But his work on gender advertising remained more or less faithful to the dramaturgical perspective.

However, to speak of industries and forces *behind* impression management, to speak of the personality marketplace where the self becomes a commodity requires a system-specific theory. Simply put, it is quite possible that impression management, as well as the interest in studying it, is not found equally in all societies. Although this is an intellectual point, it has strong ideological implications, not merely for Goffman but for Garfinkel and others for whom the psychology in social psychology is written with a capital *P*.

There has ascended in American intellectual and popular culture an abiding interest in the "world of me." To some extent it has always been there, a reflection in part of the privatized nature of our social existence. In some of the systems of thought we have examined, this "self-interest" takes the form of an ideological solipsism. Hence the self becomes the only reality, and its states and experiences the only knowledge. *And even in those theoretical systems that focus on interaction with others, it is the individual self, first-person singular, that often remains the central point of reference.* Face-to-face sociology, intentionally or not, makes the self the center of theoretical existence. It assumes closed systems of the micro range. It overwhelms us with a virtually infinite array of signs, signals, and varied performances. Whether this "self-interest" is enlightened or not depends solely on the kinds of questions and puzzles one wishes to address. In such sociology, both history and society disappear.

# ■ Bibliography

Berger, Peter
1963     *Invitation to Sociology: A Humanist Perspective.* Garden City, N.Y.: Doubleday.
1977a     *The Heretical Imperative: Contemporary Possibilities of Religious Affirmation.* Garden City, N.Y.: Doubleday.
1977b     *Facing Up to Modernity: Excursions in Society, Politics, and Religion.* New York: Basic Books.

Berger, Peter, and Thomas Luckmann
1966     *The Social Construction of Reality.* Garden City, N.Y.: Doubleday.

Coleman, James
1968     Review of *Studies in Ethnomethodology,* by Harold Garfinkel. *American Sociological Review* 33:126–130.

Garfinkel, Harold
1967                      *Studies in Ethnomethodology.* Englewood Cliffs, N.J.:
                          Prentice-Hall.

Goffman, Erving
1959                      *The Presentation of Self in Everyday Life.* Garden City,
                          N.Y.: Anchor Books.
1961                      *Asylums: Essays on the Social Situation of Mental Patients and
                          Other Inmates.* Garden City, N.Y.: Doubleday Anchor.
1963                      *Stigma: Notes on the Management of Spoiled Identity.* En-
                          glewood Cliffs, N.J.: Prentice-Hall.
1974                      *Frame Analysis: An Essay on the Organization of Experience.*
                          Cambridge, Mass.: Harvard University Press.
1976                      *Gender Advertisements.* New York: Harper Colophon.
1981                      *Forms of Talk.* Philadelphia: University of Pennsylvania
                          Press.

Husserl, Edmund
1931                      *Ideas: General Introduction to Pure Phenomenology.* New
                          York: Macmillan.
(1934–1937) 1970          *The Crisis of European Sciences and Transcendental Phe-
                          nomenology.* Translated and with an introduction by David
                          Carr. Evanston, Ill.: Northwestern University Press.

Schutz, Alfred
(1932) 1967               *The Phenomenology of the Social World.* Evanston, Ill.:
                          Northwestern University Press.

Schutz, Alfred, and Thomas Luckmann
1973                      *The Structure of the Life World.* Evanston, Ill.: North-
                          western University Press.

# ■ Conflict and Change

# CHAPTER *14*

# ■ The Conflict Paradigm

In this chapter, we shall review the final paradigm that underlies a distinctive body of sociological theory. As do its order and pluralist counterparts, the *conflict* paradigm consists of interrelated assumptions on the nature of human being, society, and sociology as theoretical science. Again, you should recall that these assumptions are seldom made explicit by those who construct the explanatory systems we call theory. Nevertheless, they operate at a basic level, always influencing theoretical content.

As you prepare for this last assault, consider once more what is meant by a sociology of knowledge. Recall its major premise: Knowledge is context bound. In this case, the knowledge at issue is, as in earlier chapters, a total system of social thought. This includes not only the explicit theoretical explanations (developed for example by a Marx or a Mills) but the assumptions and ideological implications of such arguments. Knowledge is a product of both history and the human mind. The events and ideas of specific ages join with the life experiences of "truth makers" who in association with others, whether living or dead, make their contribution to intellectual traditions.

Now that we are again reoriented, we can consider the *conflict paradigm*. In a way the term is deceptive. As you will discover, conflict sociologists usually hold a rather benign view of human nature. And their vision of the ideal society is *not* one of continuing strife, where struggle is ceaseless and might makes right. To the contrary, conflict sociologists are routinely *utopian* thinkers who believe in human and societal perfectability. Or, in the poetic words of Alfred Lord Tennyson:

> When wealth no more shall rest in mounded heaps,
> But smit with freer light shall slowly melt
> In many streams to fatten lower lands,
> And light shall spread and man be liken man
> Thro' all the season of the golden year.

How then does the term *conflict* come to bear? For sociologists who hold conflict assumptions, "the season of the golden year" is still before us. To attain it, humankind must survive an existing winter of discontent. Hence, from this vantage point, the reality of present societies is one of structural inequality, of elites and nonelites, of masses and dominant classes. Those who hold power and wealth are seen to resort to state coercion, or ideological and other forms of social control, to hold society together. Thus the historical stage is set for conflict.

Conflict theories seek to solve a different collection of puzzles than those addressed by order and pluralist explanations. Once more, we can present these in the form of representative questions: How does the institutional organization of society (its total structure) contribute to various struggles? What is the role of the state in such conflict? How do institutions (especially those of wealth and power) compare, and how do they change through history? What role does the production of goods to meet human needs play in social relationships? How does such an objective and material world shape human behavior? In what ways does culture follow and ideology legitimate the existing structure of society? We shall explore these and other related issues in the chapters to come.

# ■ The Hegelian Conception of Human Nature

Let us once more begin at the beginning, by looking at the assumptions that constitute the conflict paradigm. The first of these have to do with human nature, and our exemplar for this purpose will be the eighteenth-century German philosopher G. W. F. Hegel.[1]

Georg Wilhelm Friedrich Hegel (1770–1831) was born in the southern Duchy of Württemberg and educated in Tübingen (1788–1793). In his youth he joined other students in a favorable response to the ideals and promises of the French Revolution. Hegel continued his education informally for the next several years, reading heavily in the philosophy of religion as he tutored the children of wealthy families. In 1801 he was appointed to the University of Jena, where he taught philosophy and began work on *Phenomenology of the Mind* (1977, originally published 1807). As Sennett notes (1981: 125), Napoleon occupied the city of Jena in 1806, forcing Hegel to flee his lodgings, carrying with him his still unfinished manuscript. (This is perhaps an appropriate start for one who was to influence greatly the still unborn Karl Marx and thereby the legacy of conflict sociology yet to come.)

---

[1] Important general references on Hegel include Collington, 1946, and Marcuse, 1941.

Hegel served briefly as a newspaper editor in Bavaria and then for nine years as the headmaster of a secondary school in Nuremberg. During this period he married and published the second work from which we glean his image of human nature, *Hegel's Science of Logic* (1951, originally published 1812–1816). He was appointed to a chair of philosophy at the University of Heidelberg in 1816 and two years later came to Berlin. By the time of his death from a cholera epidemic in 1831, he had published other major works and taken some open political positions that appear markedly conservative. Indeed, Hegel's philosophy holds that the state functions as a necessary agent of discipline and control to which the citizen should be subordinate (Marcuse, 1960: 175, originally published 1941). When this is combined with his open support of the Prussian monarchy, Hegel emerges as somewhat authoritarian.

In addition to this ideological note of caution, another point must be raised. In many ways Hegel was a philosophical child of Immanuel Kant, who, you may remember, dominated German philosophy before Hegel was born (see Chapter 9). Now Kant was an *idealist* who believed that in the world of appearances, ideas about things are more important than the things themselves. Simply put, Kant conceived of human nature in the sense of an active mind that imposes order on the chaos of appearances. Hegel was to remain a philosophical idealist and in that sense was true to Kant.

How then can an unrepentant idealist, whose work has clear authoritarian implications, be considered an exemplar for a tradition in sociology that appears so different? As we shall see, Hegel's *method* for understanding the inner world of consciousness and definition was clearly to inform the work of Marx. Although Marx and his intellectual heirs broke both with Hegel's conservatism and his idealist philosophy, they retained his image of the human essence. It is to that essence that we now turn.

In *Phenomenology of the Mind,* Hegel wrote of the master and slave as an introduction to the question of liberty (1977: 228–267). This relationship was presented as real but also as representative of a universal human nature, as we shall see. To begin, the master owns the labor of the slave and seeks to use this power to bend the "bondsman's" will and to use the slave to insulate the "lord" from the dark forces of existence. Ironically, even within this tyranny, the young Hegel discovered distinctively social attributes that can be generalized to the human spirit.

We might begin by observing a dialectic of opposites as they exist in the association of master and slave. First of all, the conditions of the one confirm and define the nature of the other. The wretchedness, the misery, and the impotence of those in bondage make possible the preeminence, the pleasure, and the power of the lord. Without the slave, and the works of slavery, what would the master possess? Without the obedience of the powerless, of what value would be the commands of the powerful? Even in this one-sided relationship, those who rule are dependent on the recognition accorded them by the ruled. So it is in all human relationships, from the most abject to the more flourishing. To fully exist, to be a whole person, requires the acknowledgment of others. This renders the human nature uniquely social.[2]

However, more implications follow from Hegel's argument. Through laboring for the master, those in bondage come to experience a growth of the spirit in spite of the harsh realities of their existence, for in protecting the master from the negative side of the struggle for existence, the slave's labor encounters nature. Although the objects of nature first appear as only forces of resistance, gradually they are transformed by the slave into something else. For Hegel, whatever is made for the use and comfort of the lord may be *appropriated,* but in a *spiritual* sense such products are not truly "owned" by the master or any other external being. Instead, the products fashioned from nature come to embody the distinctive imprint of human labor and reflect back (even on slaves) the essence of their own humanity. By this logic, what one creates remains forever one's own.

Richard Sennett has observed (1981: 128–129) that Hegel found "the birth of liberty—in the bondsman's consciousness of his work." Liberty is not so much a fixed state as a process or "journey" in which each stage negates what has gone before. At the first level, the slave finds that the only kind of freedom available for those in bondage is an inward stoicism. Here, at least, one's thoughts are one's own. But the ability to reason, often provoked by some crisis in experience, gives rise to a more critical form of thought. Now the oppressed (whose work is the source of wealth and power) become skeptical of the master's claim to "moral authority." This introduces a third state of mind, that of the dissatisfied consciousness. If the lord is no better than the slave, then bondage is a contradiction.

Hegel still dealt with this consciousness of contradiction at an inward or phenomenological level. If I am not rightly a slave, then am I not also a master? And further, am I not also dependent on others for recognition? Thus, the struggle between master and slave is played out inside. This is what Hegel meant when he claimed that each of us is both the fighter locked in battle and the struggle itself. Each is *fire and water.*

However, the quest for freedom does not end here. Given another crisis, the unhappy form of consciousness gives way to the final level, that of rational awareness. At this point, one is aware of the master and slave relationship as a property of the mind—not only one's own mind but the minds of others. In this final or absolute stage of liberty, where rational consciousness assumes a decidedly *social* dimension, the slave can act with others rather than compete with them for acknowledgment. Here emerges the young Hegel's image of a cooperative society wherein the truly rational nature is embodied in what Marx stressed as our *species being.* Now the full contradiction of bondage is apparent.

---

[2]Richard Sennett has written a particularly cogent account of Hegel's "Lordship and Bondage" in his treatise *Authority* (1981: 125–164).

Slavery by Hegel's logic may be preserved only by refusing the slave the opportunity to labor.

Hegel argued that the lordship-bondage relationship is not confined to concrete masters and slaves. Rather, its properties represent a universal for human existence. Human labor changes nature and this transformed world now holds within it the essence of the self. We now face, in the products of our own creation, what is distinctive about human nature. Expending labor to fashion a world also affirms self-existence and marks the onset of a journey toward rational consciousness. As human beings work to fashion and refashion nature, they experience the contradictions of bondage. These, as we have seen, come to change the *interpretations* given to their conditions.

Simply put, the biological Homo sapiens is also the more sociological *Homo faber* (the maker). But the maker through labor does more than create a product. He or she also embodies a movement of *perfectability* in critical reasoning. Thus perfected, the slave becomes a new person. And this is the important point: By Hegel's pure idealism, those in bondage need not displace the master or destroy the objective conditions of slavery. This may occur in history, but freedom is here defined first and foremost as a state of mind, not of being.

One final observation is in order. In Hegel's philosophical system, the inward struggle against the conditions of slave labor clearly symbolizes the many *negative forces* that arise in history to change (at least at a mental or spiritual level) the particular social relationships that gave them birth. History imposes its chains; but human reason struggles against that bondage. Therefore for the young Hegel, those conditions that constrain human reason carry within their negation the seeds of their own demise.

In "The Critique of Hegelian Philosophy" (1976, originally published 1844), Marx faulted Hegel for attempting to understand history as a product of abstract self-consciousness. In the final section of this chapter, we will see how Marx (and others) held to Hegel's logic, while transforming his subjective analysis of the world of ideas into an objective analysis of the world of things. However, it is not true to assert as some have that Marx simply turned Hegel on end. To the contrary, he credited Hegel for understanding "the self-creation of man as a process ... that he [Hegel] therefore grasps the nature of *labor* and conceives objective man ... as the result of his *own labor*" (Marx, in Connerton, 1976: 56).

However, Marx used Hegelian thought simply as a base when he argued that human nature or "real species being ... is only possible if [one] employs all [one's] *species powers*—which again is only possible through the cooperation of mankind and as a result of history" (Marx, in Connerton, 1976: 56). For Marx, authentic and self-enhancing labor can exist only when individuals work cooperatively together under *real* historical conditions of freedom. He believed that Hegel saw only the positive and ignored the negative side of labor. To put it in familiar language, Marx repudiated the Hegelian logic whereby labor alone makes the slave subjectively "free." As long as the master owns those in bondage and controls what they produce, there can be neither liberty nor humanity.

# ■ Proudhon's Vision of Society

Pierre-Joseph Proudhon[3] was a nineteenth-century socialist who both criticized the institution of private property and developed a utopian blueprint for a new society. However, if his impassioned assault on privilege won him the admiration of some believers in the social ownership of the major means of production, his anarchism alienated many others, for Proudhon argued against formal governments and challenged the very concept of state power.

Proudhon is used here as an exemplar of the conflict imagery of society. This is because his writings exemplify certain societal themes that have recurred in many formal works in conflict sociology. First, Proudhon argued that "property is theft," that those in positions of privilege do not invest their own labor but take instead a part of what the worker produces. However, he did not stop here. While some of his contemporaries (including critics such as Marx) fashioned a role for the state in societal change, Proudhon saw in the state a natural incorrigibility necessitating its termination. Now few twentieth-century conflict theories go this far, but that is not the point.

Proudhon raised the question of domination by the state and its non-responsiveness to the will of the people. For him, this is a universal law of politics. His critics, both past and present, have faulted Proudhon for his lack of historical specificity. (Marx, for example, argued that the material life of people under a particular mode of production is the real basis of the state.) Although today's conflict thinkers are seldom anarchists, many are ambivalent about the state. On the one hand, it may be seen to play at least an instrumental role in the building of a more just society. On the other, the potential for the abuse of state power by dominant groups is ever present. (Of course, Marx himself argued that under the conditions of true, classless democracy, the state would wither.)

Finally, Proudhon's thought proved to be a precursor of the more scientific socialism to come. While he logically repudiated the role of the state in the systematic building of an egalitarian order, he did not believe that such an order would spring up spontaneously once people were shed of governments. As we shall see, Proudhon's utopia presupposes both organization and planning.

Proudhon was born in Besançon, France, in 1809. His father was a cooper and brewer and his mother a peasant. The family's life was marked by long periods of poverty, and although a gifted student, Proudhon was able to continue his studies only through working as a printer's assistant. As a proofreader he assimilated much of what passed through the shop and added a store of in-

---

[3] Important biographical references include Charles Dana's introductory chapter in Proudhon's *The Solution to the Social Problem* (1927, originally published 1848) and J. A. Langlois' "His Life and Works" in Proudhon's *What Is Property?* (1845).

formation to his more formal academic training. Proudhon was almost 30 be-fore he completed his baccalaureate. He continued his studies supported in part by a scholarship for the "poor and deserving" and began to publish.

After continuing a while as a printer, Proudhon came to be employed by a trading company and was sent to Paris. Here he continued his self-education in the manner of Rousseau, immersing himself in the rich intellectual climate of the city. After the revolution of 1848, he was elected to the National Assembly and supported in oratory and writing the ill-fated programs designed to imple-ment a basic revolutionary ideal: the human right to work. He became the pub-lisher and editor of a Parisian penny daily, *Le Peuple,* and continued to press his utopian vision. In March 1849, Proudhon went to prison accused of libeling Louis-Napoleon Bonaparte, who by then had become the French chief of state. The remainder of Proudhon's life was marked by further persecution, exile, and poverty. Pierre-Joseph Proudhon died in 1865, never to experience the peace and justice he so eloquently defended.

Lewis Mumford (1962, originally published 1922) observed that since Thomas More coined the term, *utopia* has carried a dual meaning. On the one side, it stands for human folly, a vain dream of the social good that stands for-ever beyond reach. On the other, it represents the logical and hopeful conclu-sion of believers in reason and perfectability, a rational order in which the vast human potential is at last realized. Hence the Greek roots include either *eutopia,* which translates as a "good place," or *outopia,* which means "no place." And yet as the epigram at the beginning of Mumford's work notes, "A map of the world that does not include Utopia is not worth even glancing at."

The utopia of Pierre-Joseph Proudhon is perhaps both reason and folly. However, it is important to us more for what it symbolizes than for what it is. Proudhon's vision still stands as the logical extension of a sanguine belief in hu-man cooperation and excellence. However, Proudhon believed that if such a na-ture is to be realized, both the institutions of property and the state that protects it must be transcended. Consider the following:

> If I were asked to answer the following question: *What is slavery?* and I should answer in one word, *It is murder,* my meaning would be understood at once. No extended argument would be required to show that the power to take from a man his thought, his will, his personality is a power of life and death; and that to enslave a man is to kill him. Why then, to this other question: *What is prop-erty?* may I not likewise answer, *It is robbery,* without the certainty of being misunderstood? (Proudhon, 1845: 11)

To grasp Proudhon's conception of property, it is necessary to understand what he sees as its *contradictory* nature. On the one hand, property is a right of possession. On the other, its nature is that of exclusion. Hence, to the extent that some are entitled to acquire more, others are left out. Proudhon also ob-served that property may be seen as a reward for labor, and yet it is simultane-ously the negation of labor. Simply put, if one does not own and control what one produces, the labor invested is made nothing when the product is sold by others. Finally, property may be seen as a material manifestation of the human social nature when it is the product of members working in association. Yet, when property is the basis for divisions within society, such may lead to the demise of that society.

For Proudhon, the old institutions of private property are at the root of the negative side of the above contradictions. Within this system of privilege (supported in part by illusions of democracy), many find themselves excluded, their labor negated, and their society embroiled in struggle. The utopian solution of a new order is required, one in which new conceptions of property rights and economic justice will prevail. But in order to get there, the "excluded" (primarily workers) must resolve two problems. First, they must raise capital in order to be self-financing. Second, they must introduce collective ownership and the decentralization of the economy.

Proudhon's *The Solution to the Social Problem* (1927, originally published 1848) presents his answer to the first of these problems. In his society of tomorrow he proposed a "people's bank" in which credit would be provided at cost, thus eliminating interest and usury. All productive members of the community, all those engaged in trades and professions that benefit and enhance life and living, would form such a bank. The bank would, in its final form, lend not gold, silver, or currency but "exchange notes." These would entitle the "borrower" to receive from the community of lenders consumable products and services, which the borrower would repay in kind.

Within Proudhon's utopia, all productive functions would be equal. This view has two important implications. First, the hierarchy based on differential occupational prestige would disappear. Second, when equal human beings work for themselves and share in the return on their collaboration property ceases to be theft. It follows that Proudhon's conception of useful labor (together with his conception of a bank of the people) leaves the capitalist per se without value, a nonproducer looking for the ultimate deal: something for nothing.

From the foregoing we can understand what Proudhon meant by "mutualism." This is his prime principle of reciprocal and egalitarian exchange, basic to the organization of a new economic order. However, mutualism is also the key to his conception of politics. Remember that Proudhon repudiated the state as inherently tyrannical. He opposed not only the centralism of the Marxist transitional state but also the democracies that so peacefully coexist with the theft of labor. Thus in his counterpoint to Rousseau's democratic form of "social contract," Proudhon presented *The Principle of Federation* (1979, originally published 1863).

Simply put, Proudhon argued that human beings should form sovereign groups, freely associating in mutualist communities on a smaller human scale. Such groups will not exist in isolation or conflict but form pacts or alliances to maximize the free exchange of services and commodities. However, unlike other social covenants (i.e., Hobbes and Rousseau), Proudhon's federal contract rules out the transfer of political rights to either commonwealth or representative state.

In Proudhon's "federation" of communities, all citizens retain the right and obligation to voice their opinion directly. All officials in turn represent the directly expressed interests of their group or community rather than usurping the power of the people. Proudhon's vision of political society thus takes the form of the town hall, with its insistence on absolute participatory democracy, and generalizes it to the societal "alliance" at large. So organized, a community can be called free. All others are in chains. Ultimately, all societies can come to be linked in a federation of federations.

Proudhon's utopia and the political economy at its base drew heavy fire from Marx.[4] At least some of his criticism must be considered well-placed. Proudhon advanced no true theory of society, no explanation of its institutional structure. He held fast to petit bourgeois notions of individual initiative and creativity. His works were simply repudiations of centralized power, unjust hierarchies, and all systems imposed from above. In his zeal to abandon the state, he often appeared to dichotomize private welfare and public interest. And as Proudhon and Marx exchanged polemic, their differences were intensified.

Still, Proudhon's vision of society, like Marx's, was rooted in a critique of private property and the expropriation of human labor. (Such a notion found theoretical expression in Marx's theory of surplus value as we shall later see.) And as with Marx, Proudhon's thought reflects a sharp departure from Hegel's idealism. Bondage for Proudhon meant real societal conditions requiring real social change. Finally, Marx was also given to a Proudhonist "romanticism" on occasion. He saw in the Paris Commune (refer to the historical introduction to Durkheim in Chapter 5), a working-class government politically organized around the principle of the self-government of producers. Moreover, for Marx, at least during the life of the Paris Commune, the national alignment of such cooperatives represented a communism of the possible (Buber, 1960: 85–87, originally published 1949).

# ■ The Marxist Image of Human Science

To this point we have addressed Hegel's vision of human nature and Proudhon's image of society. For the first, human being is self-produced through the process of labor. Its essence is that of perfectability, liberty, and ultimately cooperation with others. For the latter, society typically fails to facilitate this cooperative nature. Instead, it is marred by the contradictions of property and the abuse of state power. Such contradiction underscores the necessity of change. Thus, in the social world of tomorrow, forms of hierarchy must disappear and mutual reciprocity must prevail. With such imagery in mind, we

---

[4]See especially *The Poverty of Philosophy* (1913, originally published 1847).

now turn to the last assumptions of the conflict paradigm: those centering on human science.

As we have argued earlier, sociologists have historically advanced contrasting images of theoretical science. In a formal sense, such assumptions answer an implicit question: What is the nature of sociological explanation? Sociological theories of order stress certainty, determinism, lawful relationships, and prediction. Pluralist theories assume philosophical idealism, the unpredictability of human action, and the importance of qualitative research that penetrates the consciousness of social actors. Conflict theories are based on quite different assumptions concerning the nature of sociological explanation. The imagery here is more often based on philosophical materialism and a holistic approach to the study of society. Conflict sociology also features historical research on institutional structure and the conflicting forces that produce social change.

Our exemplar for this discussion can be none other than Karl Marx.[5] Nevertheless, in order to introduce the conflict view of theoretical science, we will begin by drawing from the work of Marx's lifelong colleague and friend Friedrich Engels (1820–1895). As we have done for the order and pluralist traditions examined earlier, we will focus on the explanation of family life.

> Thus the social order makes family life almost impossible for the worker. In a comfortless, filthy house, hardly good enough for mere nightly shelter, ill-furnished, often neither rain-tight nor warm, a foul atmosphere filling rooms overcrowded with human beings, no domestic comfort is possible. The husband works the whole day through, perhaps the wife also and the elder children, all in different places; they meet at night and morning only, all under perpetual temptation to drink; what family life is possible under such conditions? Yet the working man cannot escape the family, and the consequence is a perpetual succession of family troubles, domestic quarrels, most demoralizing for parents and children alike. Neglect of all domestic duties, neglect of children ... is ... only too vigorously fostered by the existing institutions of society. (Engels, 1975: 424, originally published 1845)

This view of working-class family life in mid-nineteenth-century Britain is only suggestive of a rich and intricate tradition of social thought. Here Engels described the disintegration of primary group relationships. In so doing, however, he placed the question of domestic discord in a broader social context. Both for Engels and his frequent collaborator, Karl Marx, this smaller circle of intimates exists within the larger circle of an economic system. Hence, the problems that take root in that higher order cannot fail but penetrate family life. This is not a cause and effect relationship. The family for Marx and Engels is a part of the whole social structure, and its organization both reflects and reproduces the relationships of that whole. (For example, the husband is the bourgeoisie, and the wife is the proletariat.)

---

[5] Because we deal with Marx's theoretical ideas more extensively in the following chapter, we will delay an examination of his life and times.

## Historical Specificity

To grasp conflict assumptions on the nature of sociological theory, we begin with a discussion of *historical specificity*. This approach to the construction of theory is evident only if we look more broadly at Engels' work *The Condition of the Working Class in England*. Although our preceding excerpt does not make clear the kind of "existing institutions" that trouble family life, it is no secret that Engels (and Marx) had something specific in mind. Hence there is more here than a simple forging of connections between the "economic system" and more "personal" matters. For these conflict thinkers, the origin of family misery is founded in that specific way of organizing economic production known as *capitalism*.

Recall for a moment the opening words to the manifesto authored by Marx and Engels: "The history of all hitherto existing society is the history of class struggles." At first glance this does not appear very *specific* at all. Instead, it appears that struggle is *constant*. Yet for Marx and Engels, the constancy of struggle assumes different forms in different historical eras. Thus, in the antebellum South, the slave confronted the slave owner. In ancient Rome, the common plebeian contended with the patrician nobility. In the feudal period, the serf opposed the lord, and journeyman clashed with guild master. And in the capitalist era, an industrial working class stood against the owners of the major means of production and distribution (such as the factories, land, natural resources, airlines, and railroads).

Now, the common factor in all of these societies is struggle. However, the *conditions* that produced the conflict were not identical. Marx and Engels argued that for each specific historical period, the combatants were in different positions, their relationships determined by the prevailing mode of production. For example, under plantation–era slavery the domination of the bondsman was total, and a chattel standing replaced human identity. Under capitalism, the worker (unlike the slave) could sell his or her labor. But although nominally free to improve their "human capital" (skills, education, experience, and so forth), workers owned neither the fruits of their labor nor their jobs. Still, in each and every case, the oppressor faced the oppressed in a titanic struggle for existence. And within such confrontations, Marx and Engels found the engine of change.

## Contradictions and the Logic of the Dialectic

For Karl Marx, the notion of *contradiction* is crucial to the building of a theoretical system about society. At first glance, the term *contradiction* may be confused with conflict. However, whereas the latter refers to a struggle between groups (ordinarily classes), the latter encompasses the clashing of the "structural principles of system organization" (Giddens, 1979: 131–164). Simply put, social systems and social practices do not reveal the equilibrium and strain toward harmony claimed by order theorists. Instead, the inherent and expected forces within a system compete in something of a "zero-sum game" in which the realization of one negates the other.

Alvin Gouldner has referred to this inherent or structural clash as an *internal contradiction:*

> An internal contradiction is one in which a system, at any concrete level, is blocked/inhibited from conforming with one system rule because (or to the extent that) it is performing in conformity with another system rule. It is in short a "double bind." (1980: 169–170)

It follows that commitment to one systemic rule (or set of rules) produces deviance from another (or others). As both rules (or sets of rules) are "right" (as defined by the system), then followers of each are convinced of their morality. Gouldner further argued that the resolution of an internal contradiction can only be accomplished in one of two ways: Either the parties in conflict agree that some *transcendental* good will be served by introducing a new rule, or (failing this) social conflict will ensue.

For example, it is in the interest of capital to maximize profits. On the other hand, workers are entitled to a living wage. Both sides are convinced of the righteousness of their position under the rules of the capitalist system. However, one way of maximizing profit is to minimize the cost of labor. Given such a contradiction between profit and labor cost (which may be manifested in unemployment, underemployment, and poor pay), two alternatives are feasible: Either a new and higher rule comes to prevail, or each side will use force and power against the other. We may call Gouldner's rules *transcendental,* and some examples would include an appeal to the "greater welfare" or the "national interest" or the "survival of the employing corporation."

Gouldner argued that real class interests place limitations on "transcendental rules." What he failed to make clear is that an appeal to such rules as "the greater good" is often only a short-term accommodation developed in a period of crisis (for example, as when unions agree to "givebacks" and to a two-tier wage system—which offers less money and benefits to new employees—in order for their industry to remain in business or "competitive"). Hence, *structurally founded* contradictions involving class interests do not disappear because of new and higher "crisis rules." Further, it should be emphasized that a system (capitalist or otherwise) cannot permanently redefine its *cardinal* rules without a change in its essential nature.

An understanding of systemic contradictions is basic to the Marxist form of *dialectical logic.* Of course, Marx took the dialectic from Hegel. However, whereas Hegel's *thesis, antithesis, synthesis* addressed the clash of ideas, Marx applied the dialectic to the *objective relations* of the *material* world. Still, whether centered in philosophical materialism or idealism, dialectic logic challenges the "one-way" cause-effect relationships so essential to positive science (See Chapter 7). Instead, the relationship between forces or components within society is seen as reciprocal. Causation, given the logic of the dialectic, is therefore mutual and interdependent (as opposed to one-way). And it follows that a particular social phenomenon may be both cause and effect in its relations with others.

Marx sought to use the logic of the dialectic to understand the historical formation of societies. Although he broke with the conception of one-sided causation, he shared in the positivist emphasis on *lawful* relationships. He believed that the emergence of different social orders is governed by laws that exist whether people are aware of them or not (Bottomore, 1973: 38). Although we shall delay our discussion of the theoretical *content* of Marxism until the next chapter, an example of the use of the dialectic is in order.

As you recall, Marx argued that under the capitalist mode of production the relations between bourgeoisie and proletariat can only be antagonistic. By this he referred not to *individually based* conflict but to the clash inherent in their opposed social positions. However, in dialectical terms, the conditions of conflict carry within the conditions of peace. In the words of Marx: "at the same time the productive forces developing in the womb of bourgeois society create the material conditions for the solution of that antagonism." (Marx and Engels, 1968: 183)

In Marxist theory, as exploited workers become conscious of their class position and organize for change, they create a new classless reality. Again expressed dialectically, repression creates the conditions for freedom, and antagonism creates the conditions for ending antagonism. More significantly, the seeds of a new history of equality and cooperation are sown in the old history of inequality and strife. Borrowing Hegel's dialectical categories, under the capitalist mode of production, the thesis is the bourgeoisie, the antithesis is the proletariat, and the synthesis is a new classless order in which conflict ceases and the real history of humanity begins.[6]

## Historical Materialism and the Holistic Imperative

To more fully understand the Marxist form of dialectic, we must consider other of its properties. In its developed form, the Marxist dialectic is clearly centered in a materialist philosophy. In his critique of Hegel, Marx argued first of all that "a nonobjective being is a nonbeing" (1966: 182, originally published 1844). You will recall that Marx believed that Hegel (the idea-centered thinker) had transformed real human beings into little more than *abstractions of consciousness*. In Hegel's world, the ideas imposed upon reality *are* reality. But for Marx, there is a real world of social "matter" in which things are more important than ideas about things.

---

[6] We shall reserve our critique of this theoretical position for Chapter 15, when we have the total system to consider.

Stated another way, Hegel's conception of the self-creation of human being is essentially "spiritual" or, better yet, intellectual. But for Marx, the Hegelian process of self-production is *moved* from its purely intellectual base into the material framework of political economy. Human labor is no longer a source of simple spiritual development. Instead, through labor an objective world is fashioned, a world that includes wealth and social relations with other members of the species. Labor, in turn, within a historically specific system of economic production, gives shape and form to society (Bottomore, 1973: 1–10).

The crucial distinction is this: Hegel's world of the mind is diminished, and in its stead Marx raises a conception of *societal structure*. For example, the particular structure of capitalism is one of factual, material reality. Property and its ownership are real, acquisitiveness is real, exchange and competition are real, and the alienation of the worker is real. (This does not mean that Marx did not recognize the importance—and problem—of human consciousness, whether embodied in social interaction or the larger sphere of culture. This we will discover in Chapter 15.)

If the Marxist dialectic is centered in materialism, it is also anchored in history. Given the logic of the dialectic, history cannot repeat, it does not contain cycles, it does not evolve. It is governed by discoverable laws, and these laws drive a materially founded social world progressively forward. Such laws are empirically founded, yet unlike the hard sciences of physics and chemistry, they do not predict constant relationships between and among variables. Instead, the laws of history govern a "process of continuous change" (Berlin, 1963: 124). Within this historical process, conditions change from moment to moment, but each condition gives rise to its successor. Within all such *transitions* (from one state to another) the laws of history operate. In summary, historical materialism, the essence of Marxist science, quite logically gives rise to a lawful theory of change.

As we consider the Marxist exemplar to this point, it should be clear that this conception of human science features *holistic* analysis. This term has a number of important meanings, but perhaps foremost is the *connectedness* of the parts that comprise the whole of a particular social phenomenon (such as an organization, institution, society, or even world system). Such elements cannot be understood in isolation but must be considered as part of a structurally interdependent whole. And consistent with the logic of the dialectic, each component affects and is affected by others.

At first glance it appears that certain order theories, especially of the systems variety, share something in common with Marxist thought. It is true that each approach emphasizes the interdependence of social units. However, theories of order commonly assume that a consensus of members underlies societal and other systems, that whatever exists contributes to the maintenance of the whole, and that social change is a form of *disorganization*. In other words, they adopt the perspective of *system preservation*. Marxist and other conflict theories routinely emphasize the role of coercion in the integration of historical systems of inequality, ask *for whom* the existing order is maintained, and view change as a form of *reorganization*. Theirs is the perspective of *system transcendence*.

Also remember that the holistic approach does not lend itself well to the positivist language of independent and dependent variables. The conflict focus is rather on the relations between and among aspects of the whole. It is true that Marxist social thought stresses the *primacy* of the mode of economic production. However, to assert that the economic "variable" is independent is to embrace the concept of one-way causation that flies in the face of dialectic logic. (This introduces the issue of economic determinism, which we will examine in the next chapter.)

In *The German Ideology* (in Bottomore, 1973), originally published in 1845–1846, Marx made clear his holistic conception of history and society, a dialectic process that demonstrates the primacy of the economic base. He argued that the *beginning* point of such analysis is to understand the prevailing mode of production. From this base, one then explains

> ... all the different theoretical productions and forms of consciousness, religion, philosophy, ethics, etc., and traces their origins and growth, by which means the matter can of course be displayed as a whole (and consequently, also the reciprocal action of these various sides on one another). (in Bottomore, 1973: 10)

A final aspect of holistic analysis is its *time orientation*. Baumann (1976) noted that to study history holistically means to relate the society of today to both its past and its future. The seeds of the present are planted in earlier eras, and these can be uncovered only through historical research. As for the future, Marx and other modern conflict thinkers (though by no means all) have a stake in a society of tomorrow. In a clear break with Weber's conception of a value-free social science, they believe that a major purpose for understanding a society is to change it for the better. Conflict sociology today remains a haven for some futurists who hold with Bernard Shaw: "You see things; and you say, 'why?' But I dream things that never were; and I say, 'why not?'"

# ■ Assumptions of the Conflict Paradigm

It is now possible to glean from Hegel, Proudhon, and Marx the essential assumptions of the conflict paradigm. Taken as a whole, this model presents a distinctive set of images about human nature, the nature of society, and the nature of human science.

### Human Nature

1. The conflict conception of human nature is a strongly public one. There is a great emphasis on the cooperative nature of social beings.

2. Human nature is assumed to be rational and contemplative. Yet, it is in no sense independent of the historically founded structure of society.

Thus, people do not individually choose their institutional reality. For example, they do not personally and intellectually "create" a mode of production. Nor do they freely create the existing forms of state power. They do not freely choose their class and other categorical positions or the ideologies to which they are systematically exposed. For this reason, what we think is strongly related to who we are, that is, to our real position in society. People *do* possess the potential to transcend the images of ideology by means of experience, reason, and education. And on the basis of such understanding, they may organize to become a force for change.

3. Men and women become human through distinctively social activity (such as productive labor). Our humanity is discovered and confirmed in our collective attempts to shape the material world. Our essence is not subjective; we are not merely spirit, mind, or self-concept. Instead, we are real, objective, material beings.

4. Perhaps above all, human nature is perfectable.

*The Nature of Society*

1. Society ultimately is a structural reality, an institutional state of being that emerges in accordance with historical laws. Human beings routinely *interpret* that reality, sometimes correctly and sometimes falsely. However, there is a society "out there" to be discovered and understood.

2. Given the natural disposition toward a social existence, any society can be considered human only to the extent that its institutions facilitate cooperation, sharing, and the common interest. Such institutions have no sacred standing, no life of their own, and their nature is dynamic rather than static.

3. Given a society of institutionalized inequality, marked by vast differences in wealth, power, and status, the social nature of human existence is denied.

4. The unequal society is marked by inherent conflict (both overt and covert, recognized and unrecognized) between and among groups with opposing interests. The existing order carries within both the seeds of its own destruction and the embryo of its successor.

5. Given inequality, the legitimacy of social order is in question. Conformity, adaptation, and adjustment become problematic, and real structural change (toward greater equality) is mandatory. Hence, from the conflict vantage point, the society of the future fits a utopian image: Human society as human nature is perfectable.

*The Nature of Science*

1. As humans are objective beings living in a real social universe, the philosophy of materialism is the basis for human science. Put simply, thought, will, and feeling exist, but they can only be explained in terms of a material social reality. What are referred to by the pluralists as mul-

tiple social realities are best understood as multiple "perceptions" of structural reality. Thus, the stuff of theory (including major concepts and logical linkages) must conform to this objective imperative.

2. The place of history in human science is indispensable. Historical research can reveal the general laws by which societies change, as well as discern the seeds of the present order in its predecessor.

3. Human science is a quest to understand the relational properties of social order. Things like institutions, organizations, classes, and so forth cannot be studied in isolation. Because societies are structurally interrelated "wholes," they must be studied holistically.

4. Given the historical sweep and holistic thrust of conflict theories, it follows that they will be macrosociological in form. Explanations will be centered at a high level of abstraction. Given the constancy of change, the reality of contradiction, and the fact that social phenomena are frequently both cause and effect, conflict theories will often reflect the use of dialectic logic.

5. One criterion by which the practice of human science is judged is its ability to make a better world. Sociology, specifically, is not, cannot, and should not be "value free." Marx complained that philosophers are content only to *understand* a world that desperately needed *change*. Many conflict sociologists would doubtlessly agree.

The paradigmatic elements, assumptions, and ideal types that together comprise the conflict paradigm are outlined in schematic form in Figure 14.1.

---

**Figure 14.1**  The Conflict Paradigm

| PARADIGMATIC ELEMENTS | ASSUMPTIONS | IDEAL TYPES |
|---|---|---|
| Image of human nature | Maker, cooperative, rational, perfectable | Hegel's *Homo faber* |
| Image of society | Interdependent structural whole, dynamic, changing | Proudhon's federation of communities |
| Past and present | Inequality, coercion, struggle | |
| Future | Utopian, egalitarian | |
| Image of science | Philosophical materialism, historical, holistic, dialectic, applied | Marx's historical materialism |

# ■ *Bibliography*

Baumann, Zygmunt
1976                    *Towards a Critical Sociology: An Essay on Common Sense and Emancipation.* London: Routledge and Kegan Paul.

Berlin, Isaiah
1963                    *Karl Marx: His Life and Environment.* London: Oxford University Press.

Bottomore, Tom (Ed.)
1973                    *Karl Marx.* Englewood Cliffs, N.J.: Prentice-Hall.

Buber, Martin
(1949) 1960            *Paths in Utopia.* Boston: Beacon Press.

Collington, R. A.
1946                    *The Ideas of History.* Oxford: Clarendon Press.

Connerton, Paul (Ed.)
1976                    *Critical Sociology.* New York: Penguin.

Engels, Friedrich
(1845) 1975            *The Condition of the Working Class in England.* In Karl Marx and Friedrich Engels, *Collected Works,* vol. 4, pp. 297–596. New York: International Publishers.

Fromm, Erich
1966                    *Marx's Concept of Man.* New York: Frederick Ungar.

Giddens, Anthony
1979                    *Central Problems in Social Theory.* Berkeley: University of California Press.

Gouldner, Alvin W.
1980                    *The Two Marxisms.* New York: Seabury Press.

Hegel, G. W. F.
(1807) 1977            *Phenomenology of the Mind.* London: Oxford University Press.

(1812–1816) 1951 *Hegel's Science of Logic.* 2 vols. London: Allen & Unwin.

Marcuse, Herbert
(1941) 1960            *Reason and Revolution: Hegel and the Rise of Social Theory.* Boston: Beacon Press.

Marx, Karl
(1844a) 1966          "Economic and Philosophical Manuscripts." In Erich Fromm, *Marx's Concept of Man,* pp. 90–196. Translated by Tom Bottomore. New York: Frederick Ungar.
(1844b) 1976          "The Critique of Hegelian Philosophy." In Paul Connerton (Ed.), *Critical Sociology,* pp. 51–72. New York: Penguin.

(1847) 1913   *The Poverty of Philosophy*. Chicago: Charles H. Kerr.

Marx, Karl, and Friedrich Engels
1968     *Selected Works*. London: Lawrence and Wishart.

Mumford, Lewis
(1922) 1962   *The Story of Utopias*. New York: Viking Press.

Proudhon, Pierre-Joseph
1845     *What Is Property?* Translated by Benjamin R. Tucker. New York: Howard Fertis.
(1848) 1927   *The Solution to the Social Problem*. New York: Vanguard Press.
(1863) 1979   *The Principle of Federation*. Translated and with an introduction by Richard Vernon. Toronto: University of Toronto Press.

Sennett, Richard
1981     *Authority*. New York: Random House.

## CHAPTER *15*

# ■ To Have and Have Not

With an understanding of conflict assumptions at hand, we can turn to the first group of theories that fits this paradigm. Each of the thinkers in this chapter offers explanations of what is arguably the central puzzle of the conflict tradition: that of *inequality*. We begin with Marx, only this time his work will be placed in historical context and followed by a synthesis and critique of his theory. This will be followed by a review of some of the twentieth-century works that address new dimensions of inequality only suggested in Marxist thought.

## ■ Karl Marx (1818–1883): Class Struggle

Marxism is a varied and intricate body of thought that escapes the categories imposed by academic specialization. Hence in most of today's universities, the ideas of Marx are probed by philosophers and historians, by economists and students of government, as well as by sociologists. Outside those universities, Marx has been cited (not always correctly) by revolutionaries and condemned by the leaders of threatened state governments since 1848, when with Friedrich Engels he published a pamphlet entitled *The Communist Manifesto*.

In the twentieth century, certain of these revolutions have been successful, and ideas variously attributed to Marx have been institutionalized. While this theory of change has never wanted for critics, institutional Marxism has on occasion even drawn fire from those who consider themselves Marxists.[1] Nevertheless, if ever there has been a body of intricately crafted social, political, and economic thought that shook the world, it is that of Karl Marx.

## History and Biography

Karl Marx was born on May 5, 1818, in Trier, located in the Prussian Rhineland.[2] Trier was a part of the Confederation of the Rhineland established by Napoleon. Marx's father was a free-thinking lawyer, and the family enjoyed a comfortable middle-class existence under a Napoleonic rule relatively free of anti-Semitism. With the fall of Bonaparte, the Rhineland passed to Prussia, which was not so kindly disposed toward the rights of its Jewish residents. In order to continue his practice of law, Heinrich Marx led his family to convert to the Lutheran faith.

The early years of Marx were played out in a distinctive frame of political history. While some of the European powers were seeking to suppress all remaining traces of the French Revolution and its Enlightenment ideals, a liberal movement toward unification in Germany surfaced. Inspired by the July revolution in France (1830) and with the watchwords, "Constitution, Parliament, Freedom for all," it gained momentum, especially in the Rhineland and Berlin. This movement was a part of the social ferment in which a group of academics at the University of Berlin fashioned a critical philosophy. Known as the *Young Hegelians,* they moved the now-deceased (1831) master's thought from the realm of ideas to a critique of religion, politics, and law. It was this group, whose number included Bruno Bauer, Ludwig Feuerbach, and Moses Hess, whose lives were to intersect that of the young genius, Karl Marx.

Marx was reared with an appreciation of Enlightenment ideals mediated through his father and an aristocratic neighbor, Ludwig von Westphalen. Marx later courted and married von Westphalen's daughter, Jenny, with whom he shared a life of singular devotion. It was later to be the remarkable strength of Jenny Marx that sustained her family through periods of poverty and grim persecution.

Marx graduated from high school at the age of 17 and enrolled as a student of law at the University of Bonn. He left after a year and entered the University of Berlin, where he became the protégé of Bruno Bauer. Even though Bauer was 10 years his senior, he saw (as did the other Young Hegelians) an enormous potential in Marx. In April of 1841, some three weeks before his twenty-third birthday, Marx received his Ph.D. from the University of Jena. In

---

[1] See, for example, Erich Fromm's criticism of the Soviet Union in *Marx's Concept of Man* (1966).

[2] Major references for this section include Toennies, 1974 (originally published 1921), and Berlin, 1963 (originally published 1939).

his dissertation, *The Difference Between the Democritean and Epicurean Philosophy of Nature,* he asserted (with Epicurus, and against Democritus and implicitly Hegel) that ideas are empty unless they contribute to an ethical foundation for life.

The young Marx continued to study and develop a highly progressive conception of democracy. He considered the revolutions in Europe and the United States. He turned the Hegelian dialectic (see Chapter 14) against the very traditions that the elder Hegel had come to revere. And he came to develop not only a dedication to study but a passion for the politics of change. Believing (most probably correctly) that he would be shunned in academia (a fate that had befallen his mentor, Bauer), Marx decided to become an itinerant scholar and journalist. Asked by Moses Hess to write for the paper *Rheinische Zeitung* in Cologne, he accepted and became its editor-in-chief. He wrote a number of pieces on the conditions of the peasants and the poor. When he branded the Russian government as reactionary, Emperor Nicholas I protested to the Prussian authorities. Marx soon was without a position.

In 1843 Marx married Jenny von Westphalen and moved to Paris, where he practiced his craft and associated with some of the leading social critics of the day (including Proudhon). Here, as editor of *The Paris Yearbooks,* he included two critical articles on capitalism written under the name of one Frederick Oswald. Oswald's true name was Friedrich Engels, the son of a wealthy textile manufacturer. Engels served as the manager of one of his father's concerns and was stricken by the brutality endured by the workers. It was through Engels that Marx was introduced to a problem so immense that it defied the critical philosophies of the Young Hegelians—for even they were often content with intellectual conflict only. Marx quickly saw the need for something more. Dialectically speaking, now a child of European socialism, he was to become its father.

In 1845 Marx was expelled from Paris by the government and traveled to Belgium. In Brussels, he worked with the German Workers' Educational Association, which was affiliated with the Communist League. Here he was chosen to write a position paper on the philosophy and program of communism. With the aid of Engels, he wrote *The Communist Manifesto* and the die of his life was now irrevocably cast. Expelled by King Leopold from Belgium, he returned to Paris and then to the Rhineland, where he edited a newspaper that quickly became an organ for revolutionary politics. His hopes dashed by the failure in France of the 1848 revolution, Marx was again exiled. In 1849 he moved with his family to London, which was to be his home for the remainder of his life.

By the time Marx reached London, he had already published in prolific fashion. A few of the more notable efforts include *Economic and Philosophic Manuscripts of 1844* (1844); *The Holy Family* (1845); "Thesis on Feuerbach" (1845); *The German Ideology,* with Engels (1845–1846); *The Poverty of Philosophy* (1847); and of course *The Communist Manifesto,* again with Engels (1848). But it was during the London years that his talent for theoretical explanation and the synthesis of divergent systems of social thought matured. Here he wrote *The Class Struggles in France: 1848–1850* (1850); *The Eighteenth Brumaire of Louis Bonaparte* (1852); *The Grundrisse* (1857–1858); *Theories of Surplus Value* (1861–1863); and the prodigious three volumes of *Capital: A Critique of Political Economy* (1867–1895).

If the London period represented the zenith of Marx's intellectual and political prowess, it was also an abyss of personal and familial hardship. Marx was compensated occasionally for his writing and served as a correspondent for the *New York Daily Tribune* for over 10 years. But those Marx championed were hardly able to pay him for his services. Inspired by the dreams of revolution and eventual justice, he spent long days at the British Museum, where samples of his handwriting are still displayed. Without the support of their benefactor, Engels, it is quite possible that even the miserable subsistence of the family would have been in jeopardy.

Yet to charge as some have that Marx reserved his passion for the revolution and in a real way abandoned his family does not appear accurate. Jobs for committed and convincing revolutionary intellectuals were in short supply. And Marx's impatience with those he thought to be uncommitted alienated more than a few supporters. It is ironic that the harshness of English working-class family life so well described by Engels in 1844 came to be mirrored in the poverty of his dearest friend. However, left with little else, Marx gave of himself and received in turn the devotion of a family of uncommon strength. (See selections drawn from family and friends in Fromm, 1966: 221–260.)

In 1864 Marx's lifelong conviction that intellectuals should serve real movements for change came to fruition. British, French, German, Italian, and other continental workers met to form an organization known as the International Working Men's Association, or the First International, based loosely on the ideology of collective ownership. Marx came as an invited delegate and wrote the inaugural address, which was adopted as a platform by the International. He soon became the principal figure of the organization's General Council, and as the International spread throughout Europe, Marx became more notorious than ever. And it was this notoriety that in part ensured that the first volume of *Das Kapital* would be taken far more seriously than his earlier efforts.

However, Marx's dreams for the International were not to be. In *The Civil War in France,* he wrote in strong support of the Paris Commune, a workers' movement not associated with the International that had taken political power. When the commune was destroyed by the French army, certain factions within the International (including some British labor leaders) grew worried. Faced with growing dissention, Marx fought to have the command of the organization moved to the United States. Although the members there were more loyal, they were also fewer and isolated. In 1876, in the city of Philadelphia, the International of Karl Marx ceased to exist.

In his twilight years, Marx knew somewhat the reverence of followers and freedom from the grinding poverty of the earlier London period. However, the years and illness had taken their toll. Jenny, the daughter of an aristocrat, who treated working people as nobility, suffered through the deaths of three of her children, and struggled to hold a family together, died in 1881. Within a year, Marx was also to lose his oldest daughter, the namesake of her mother. He was not to recover. Fifteen months after the death of his wife, Karl Marx shared her grave in Highgate Cemetery.

## Assumptions

Before we turn to that body of Marxist theory that has sociological implications, some comprehension of underlying assumptions is in order. On the issue of human nature, Marx held fast to the Enlightenment ideal of perfectability. As Zeitlin proposed (1968: 84–85), the potential of human powers appear in Marx as unlimited. He assumed that creativity and fulfillment, growth and enrichment, reason and cooperation were the very essence of the species. And against this higher standard he assessed the social systems of "prehistory" (before socialism), including capitalism.

Also crucial to understanding the Marxist vision of humanity is its *material* basis. To review a point made in Chapter 14, Marx was interested in how real, living human beings labored to master their environment and meet the real needs of survival and social existence. (The term *materialism* is often bandied about by critics of today's "conspicuous consumption." Marx's materialist conception of human nature is obviously no endorsement of the quest to possess the latest in consumer goods.)

In his "Thesis on Feuerbach" (1935, originally published 1845), Marx borrowed this Young Hegelian's materialism and transformed it. Ludwig Feuerbach had criticized Hegel's focus on consciousness by means of a critique of religion. He argued that what one knows as God is neither an idea nor a "spirit" (as Hegel would argue) but rather a *projection* of real human qualities. Thus, men and women create God in their own perfected image and in the process transform themselves into lowly and unworthy beings. This upside-down faith can only be overcome when the welfare of real people takes precedence over the search for purely spiritual meaning. Marx took the kernal of Feuerbach's materialism but went beyond a critique of religion to a materialist analysis of *political economy*. For him, economic systems and the political orders constructed thereon are always human products to be evaluated on their ability to provide real benefits to real people.

As have other conflict thinkers to come, Marx advanced a view of human nature marked by *sociability* and *activity*. Sociability does not merely mean that people need others to meet a basic need of companionship. More than this, the human social animal can develop as a person *only* within society (Marx, 1964b: 84). Also, for Marx, the nature of humankind is one of active being. As such, we are problem solvers who, through practical behavior, create both social history and self (Marx, 1935). This basic process, by which "mysteries" are solved rationally in practical human action, is known as *praxis*. Praxis becomes a standard for the evaluation of human thought and science as we shall see.

On the matter of the distinctiveness of the species, Marx believed that human beings must be set apart from other animals (Ollman, 1976). People can plan rationally, select from alternatives, and in a fully human society create a wider range of options. Unlike other animals, the human variety is flexible in solving problems, able to discover the often intricate connections between seemingly disparate events, and uses the mind to fantasize or even to set self apart from behavior. This particular view pits Marx against the contemporary work of George Homans and others (see Chapter 8) who have sought theoretical insight from works based on the study of other animal forms. However, it is not incompatible with certain of the pluralist assumptions examined in the previous section.

To this point, the Marxist portrait of the rational, self-conscious creator of social history may appear supportive of a "free will" argument. This is a misconception that follows only if we commit the cardinal error of isolating the individual from society, and human consciousness from real material conditions. Marx did not believe that individuals are free to choose the course of their lives, independent of external factors. To the contrary, when assessed in real economic and political terms, some societies can be considered freer than others, or some people in specific societies can be considered freer to make history. That is the Marxist dilemma: how to make a utopian society where all are free to realize their considerable human potential.

Marx conceived society in general as a practical solution to the problems of the human condition. It is self-evident, however, that the historical nature of specific societies represents a denial of human nature. For Marx, and his colleague Engels, this contradiction is clearly evident in the structure of modern capitalism. Where the nature of human being is assumed to be one of cooperation, the capitalist system institutionalizes competition. Where human nature flourishes only under conditions of collective enrichment, capitalism functions as a zero-sum game in which the misery of the many becomes a precondition for the opulence of the few. Where all people represent enormous potential for enlightenment, capitalism transforms an entire industrial working class into little more than beasts of burden.

To build a society consistent with human nature thus means to negate the capitalist essential: private ownership of the means of production. This is because in Marxist theory (as we shall see), the largely unrestricted acquisition of such private property logically leads to political and economic inequality. But also (in the process) the capitalist system promotes the divestiture of human talent and labor from the producer, the separation of worker from worker, and the self from personal control.

If capitalism is doomed to fail, then a utopian form of society might (depending on the praxis of real people) succeed. Although described by Marx and Engels in other ways, perhaps the most striking portrait is rooted in their critique of the division of labor under capitalism.

> For as soon as labor is distributed, each man has a particular, exclusive sphere of activity, which is forced upon him and from which he cannot escape. He is a hunter, a fisherman, a shepherd, or a critic, and must remain so if he does not want to lose his means of livelihood; while in communist society, where nobody has one exclusive sphere of activity, but each man can become accomplished in any branch he wishes, society regulates the general production and thus makes it possible for me to do one thing today and another tomorrow, to hunt in the morning, fish in the afternoon, rear cattle in the evening, criticize after dinner, just as I have a mind, without ever becoming hunter, fisherman, shepherd, or critic. (Marx and Engels, 1967: 22, originally published 1845–1846)

Because Karl Marx is our exemplar for the conflict assumptions underlying human science (see Chapter 14), it will suffice to briefly review his vision. You will recall that Marx rejected the unilinear form of causality associated with the positive theories of order. Instead, he embraced the *dialectic* both as a form of logic and as the inherent nature of social change. Hence social phenomena defy explanation by means of independent (causal) and dependent (effect) variables.

Marxist sociology is also historically specific, holistic, and macro-level. Societal structure is to be analyzed and understood in terms of its relationship to the particular events and ideas of the age in question. Societies as systems must be understood whole cloth; hence a study of the symbolic interactions of individuals runs the risk of separating minute social processes from the wider structural context. And while people do conceive, there is more to society than the conceptions of its members. Clearly, human beings are shaped by forces they do not consciously understand (Wilson, 1983: 166–175).

Marx holds in common with the functionalist, systems, and positive theories of order the assumption of a real, factual, material social world. However, as Zeitlin notes (1968: 90–91), Marx was more clearly aligned with Hegel (and the pluralists such as Schutz) in his style of thinking about those facts. Facts, for Marx, have a transient or changing nature; they are episodes in an ever-unfolding historical serial. As points in a process, facts cannot be taken as final, verifiable, and complete truth. New systems create new facts and redefine old ones. Nor are facts to be confused with notions of inevitability. Unemployment may be a historically specific fact of capitalism, but it is not universal for all systems. In addition, important social facts are not always discoverable by means of the empirical methods so crucial for order sociology. If direct, sensory experience is essential for knowledge, then historical research itself must be abandoned.

Finally, Marxist social science is marked by utopian standards. This does not mean that logic, evidence, and the quest for historical laws are not important to the evaluation of knowledge. However, "good" knowledge (including good social theory) should better the human condition. On the one hand,

Marx proposed the creation of a critical state of mind that will be used to build a consciousness of real social existence. On the other, mere "awareness" is not enough. Good theory should help people understand what must be changed, how the change can come about, and what the nature of a new order might be. At its best, theoretical science is indistinguishable from the praxis, the practical problem solving of social life. In the words of Marx, "Science should not be an egoistic pleasure. Those who are fortunate enough to be able to devote themselves to scientific work should be the first to apply their knowledge in the service of humanity" (Marx, in Israel, 1971: preface).

## Theoretical Content

In his eulogy for Marx, Friedrich Engels reduced the essence of Marxist thought to two crucial and original discoveries. We shall explicate these as a beginning point and proceed to demonstrate that other explanatory constructs within Marxist theory can be quite logically derived from these premises. The first discovery centers on the material basis for society, the second on the law of historical motion.

### THE MATERIAL BASIS FOR SOCIETY

Our earlier review of Marx has stressed the materialist nature of his assumptions. Accordingly, within the explicit content of his thought we can find the separation of societal systems into a *material base* or substructure and a *superstructure,* which ensues from and consistently reflects that base (Wilson, 1983: 187–191). Now the material base refers to a particular mode of production, a method of organizing the productive life of society. The mode of production assumes differing forms through history (the "antagonistic" ones being Asiatic, ancient, feudal, and modern bourgeois), but all societies are founded in the productive attempts of people to meet their basic needs.

The societal superstructure consists of political institutions (especially the state in modern industrial societies), normative frameworks ranging from formal law to moral and religious expectations, the arts, formal systems of knowledge (such as science), ideologies, and ideological institutions. Although the material base for society is primary, the relationship between the material base and the superstructure is dialectical. Through this consistent interaction, each level is shaped by the other.

The superstructure, although always consistent with the nature of the underlying mode of production, develops its own existence and interests. This introduces the possibility of periodic and episodic dissonance. For example, political action within the superstructure cannot be mechanically explained as a simple reaction to the wishes of those in positions of substructural dominance.

Over time, however, such dominant interests can be expected to prevail until there is a change in the society's mode of production.

For Marx, those collectively dominant at the substructural level will effectively control the means of ideological production within the superstructure. Under capitalism, for example, the organization of ideological institutions (such as the media, religion, and education) will reflect the interests of that class that privately owns and controls the major means of production. In the case of the broadcast media today, Gaye Tuchman has argued:

> The predominance of private ownership in the broadcast industry does not mean that radio and television are either socially or politically independent of the corporate capitalism that dominates the American economy.... [O]ne expects to find patterns of ownership within broadcasting that are similar to patterns in other industries. In fact, as in other industries, the ownership pattern of television stations is one of local monopolies, regional concentrations, multiple ownerships, multimedia ownerships, and conglomerates. Similarly, one might expect to find shared social and political values. (1974: 3)

The superstructure consists of more than the mass media. Marx considered religion under capitalism to be the "opiate of the masses." This does not mean that every religious teaching or leader unconsciously works to tranquilize believers concerning the real sources of their misery. But for Marx, religion routinely teaches people to focus on the afterlife and to accept material suffering as "natural." Paradoxically, as we shall see, attempts to separate material and spiritual well-being contribute to *alienation,* an impoverishment of the true spirit of human beings.

Also a part of the capitalist superstructure, laws profess equal justice but primarily benefit the dominant groups, and the more one owns, the more one benefits. Education becomes a tool for the training of a work force whose labor unfairly benefits others who use it to acquire great wealth. The schools reproduce inequalities by providing different tracks, channels, and expectations for the children of different social classes. Thus, through the institutional forms and processes of the superstructure, a form of consciousness permeates the whole of society. Such is the nature of *ideological hegemony,* a form of social control under which even the have-nots interpret events employing the definitions of the ruling class.

To understand the general relationship between base and superstructure, as well as the specific connection between the capitalist mode of production and ideology, is to set the stage for another advance. Now we can comprehend the relationship between being and consciousness, existence and thought. True to his materialist assumptions, Marx wrote: "It is not the consciousness of men that determines their existence, but their social existence that determines their consciousness" (1970: 21–22). This is not an attempt to explain the individual ideas of isolated men and women on the basis of their social status. Instead, it is an effort to account for entire worldviews, or whole ideologies, as systematically related to an underlying sociological reality.[3] A major part of that reality in capitalist society has to do with class position and class-based consciousness. We will turn to this more specific issue in due course.

## THE HISTORICAL LAW OF MOTION

Marxist social theory approaches human history as a process marked by stages of development. Consistent with the foregoing discussion, such stages can be conceived as modes of production divided in turn into the *forces of production* and the *social relations of production*. The productive forces consist of the "means" (factories, land, raw materials, and so forth) and "tools" (including technology and machinery), as well as the skilled labor, necessary to produce wealth. The social relations are the social conditions and relationships that exist between people because of their position vis-à-vis the productive forces.

Social relations within the capitalist system hinge primarily on the question of whether a class owns the means and tools of production or works for those who do. However, there are other relations to be explored, especially those involving forms of authority. For example, authority relations might include not only owners and workers but managers (especially today those in various positions in the corporation), divisions within occupational hierarchies, the movement of members of an economically dominant class into the institutions of state power, and so forth.

To understand the nature of the mode of production is to begin to understand the Marxist law of historical motion, for each mode is not some self-contained "system" but rather a dialectic set of relationships. On the side of the forces of production when such elements as technological science, equipment, factories, and the forms of division of labor mature, the social relations between classes of people will be transformed. This sets in motion the process of revolutionary change, that is, the movement from one mode of production to another. Whatever the mode, however, Marx did not believe it will disappear before its productive forces are fully developed (Marx, 1964b: 50–52).

Looking specifically at early capitalism, workers fleeing from declining feudal estates (which could no longer support a population surplus) sought refuge and employment in the cities, which were growing centers of commerce. Many laborers came to work within cottage-based industries, not infrequently mastering a craft. With industrialization, the factory system became the center of production. Working people were subjected not only to its fragmented division of labor (which transformed craft into piecework or pay for time) but to the new forms of *private ownership* under industrial capitalism.

The exploitation of cheap labor and its division under industrial capitalism contributed to more wealth, more growth, and more industry. Now this

---

[3] Karl Mannheim was later to develop this insight. (See Chapter 18.)

progress, from the Marxist vantage point, is one-sided and unjust. But there is more to it than a humanistic regard for those who are exploited. For Marx, the *very relations between owners and workers become historically limiting to the further development of the productive forces*. In other words, there comes a point in the time of a mode of production when further development on the productive side is inhibited by the now archaic nature of its social relations.

For example, under modern capitalism the social relations between owners and workers are no longer determined by what happens within the boundaries of a particular society or nation-state. They increasingly involve an "absentee" bourgeoisie or proletariat. This follows as the manufacturing sector of the economy is dismantled in the face of international competition or exported in search of cheap labor. Such changes in the (now) world-based division of labor (a component of the productive forces) have serious implications for social relations. Thus, on the domestic front, workers lose jobs in the higher paying manufacturing sector. On the global level, where the exploitation has also been "exported," revolutionary movements that threaten that world order have increasing significance for the capitalist "hub." (See Wallerstein's work later in this chapter.)

At another level, the technological "savior" may be used to displace and/ or degrade workers rather than create new opportunities and benefits. (See Braverman's work also later in this chapter.) And at still another level, crises that require cooperation, rational societal-wide planning, and new solutions may not be met.

Thus, numerous contradictions flow from the conflicting (now backward) social relations between an owning and a working class. Under the capitalist mode of production, people do not control their labor or its products. Hence, the "actualizing" potential of work is lost, and the creative nature of *Homo faber* is denied. At another point, mindless and wasteful consumption replaces both production for pride and work that endures. At yet another point, a competitive struggle for existence subjugates the harmony of mutual support.

It is apparent through it all that the "law of motion," for Marx, is not founded in industrialization or technological advance per se. It is always manifested in a distinctively sociological *context:* the historically specific conditions of a particular mode of production and the dialectic relations between the forces and relations therein. Yet the law itself is not confined to a particular mode of production (otherwise it would not be a "law").

Although Marx centered the lion's share of his life's work in a critical analysis of the capitalist order, we should not forget that each mode of production (founded in fundamental economic inequality) responds to the same law. The law of motion is thus the law of *historical* motion. Whether Asiatic, ancient, feudal, or modern bourgeois, each contains its own specific contradictions—a set of dialectical relationships that ultimately dig its own grave. Hence, each mode is but a passing era in historical time, a dynamic sequel in a larger production. And yet each in its passing contributes something to its successor.

For Marx, such conflict is not endless. Humankind may learn its historical lesson: Modes of production founded in inequality are both self-limiting and self-destructive. As we shall see, he held that the conditions of modern bourgeois society can ultimately give rise to a new consciousness and a new order. This time the emerging historical synthesis will be founded on the social ownership of the major means of production. Inequality, the terrible engine of prehistory, will be replaced by the infinite power of human cooperation.

## THE STRUCTURE OF CAPITALIST SOCIETY

Although Marx was concerned with a theory of history, he founded his life's work in the critical analysis of capitalist society. In this section, we shall focus on the specific structure of that mode of production, introducing the theoretical constructs Marx and some of his heirs used to understand its organization and processes. *Class* is the first of these ideas, and it will provide us with something of a framework for the concepts to come.

Georg Lukács (in Bottomore, 1973: 92) notes that Marx offered no formal definition of class. You might recall that Marx and Engels noted in *The Communist Manifesto* that "the history of all hitherto existing society is the history of class struggles." Used in this manner, the term is not specific to capitalism but refers to the basic divisions between antagonistic groups engaged in a struggle over resources. However, the "modern classes" under capitalism, those of owners and workers, do have distinctive properties.

Rather than representing simple differences in wealth and/or income, the Marxist conception of class suggests a number of criteria. These include (1) a shared position in the economic order determined by relationship to the means of production (for Marx, the mass of people have been transformed under capitalism to workers who are dominated by an owning class that exploits their labor) (2) a distinctive culture and world view, (3) common interests that conflict with those of other classes, and (4) membership in a "community of fate" with global as opposed to simply local or national standing.

In this theoretical system, class is real. It is an objective reality that exists independent of people's perceptions. However, this does not mean that people (specifically, workers) are *conscious* of their class position. If they are not, then they are members of a "class in itself." However, if they develop a consciousness of their common interests, a sense of community and solidarity, and organize politically to oppose the *bourgeois,* then they become a "class for itself" (Bottomore, 1973: 20–27). It should be clear that competition among members of the same objective class over scarce resources retards the development of class consciousness. The power of dominant ideologies also serves the same purpose.

If class conflict is the lever for the transformation of history, then *the private ownership of property* is the fulcrum. Here Marx is not concerned with personal items, housing, and other consumer goods but with who owns the means and tools of production. Under capitalism, the quest for private acquisition is the imperative that drives the system. Thus there can be no ultimate controls on the building of private wealth without a change from capitalism itself, for this system by definition is committed to ever-greater growth and ever-deepening concentration of wealth. Marx referred to this process as the *general law of capitalist accumulation* (1967: 595–601, originally published 1867–1879).

Yet Marx held that the ultimate source of wealth can be none other than the labor invested in production. Given this, the only way members of a non-producing owning class can continue to accumulate more wealth is to expropriate a portion of the labor value of workers. How then is this particular "transfer" done? Marx explained this quite simply by means of the *theory of surplus value*.

When the capitalist purchases labor in the marketplace, he or she does not pay the full value of the wealth (product) the worker creates. Now, this is not a problem in business ethics. Those who play the capitalist role are compelled by the structure of the capitalist system to hold down the cost of labor because there is a contradiction between profits and wages. Profits, in turn, make investors of capital happy while fueling growth and expansion. Marx argued that the difference between the cost of labor and the selling price of what is produced is surplus value.

Under the capitalist system, this differential may be called profit. But for Marx (and Proudhon), it is a form of theft. The first victims are not consumers (most of whom are also workers) but those whose labor is so exploited (Marx, 1952, originally published 1861–1863). Thus the ingenuity of the capitalist system is first to expropriate a part of the value of the labor of a working class and then to sell the products of their own creation back to them at inflated prices.

Marx noted other implications of this pressure to hold back the cost of labor. As mentioned earlier, technology is used to increase productivity (output per hour of human labor) by eliminating jobs. The growing number of unemployed then constitute an "industrial reserve army" driven through desperation to take what work they can find. To update Marx, in the modern era of multinational corporations, the surplus value created by workers is of course even greater in the developing and underdeveloped world. This exporting of jobs is again not a problem of business ethics. It is, as always, a structural issue. International and domestic competition, coupled with the demands to grow and increase the return on investment for shareholders, compels the owners (shareholders) and/or corporate managers (who are often one and the same) to seek cheap labor.

Finally, the quest for surplus value (together with a corresponding need to control the work force) is manifested in a uniquely destructive division of labor. The fragmentation of occupations into mindless, repetitive routines transforms people into pieces of machinery, paper shufflers, and cheerful robots. And there is more. The mind is separated from manual labor, work and "life" are ripped asunder, and the producer is divested of control over the product.

In the modern era, the labor market itself comes to be divided along the lines of skills, organization, sex, and race. The poorer jobs are predominantly held by women, a black underclass, migrants, and new immigrants. Within this divided market, higher paid workers (predominantly white, male, and native born) are threatened by cheaper labor.[4] Hence at the broader societal level, the division of labor contributes to conflict within the working class and the setting of particular interests against the public good. However, the division of labor has other implications, and this brings us to an examination of the dynamics of *alienation* in capitalist society.

## COMMODIFICATION AND REIFICATION

Given his repudiation of philosophical idealism, Marx has been accused of ignoring the spiritual side of the human condition. It is true that Marx remained true to his materialist assumptions and that he rejected mystical and metaphysical conceptions of being. However, his theoretical system deals at length with the thinking, feeling, motivating life of the inner person. It is to that sense of the human spirit that we now turn.

Remember that Marx shared with Hegel the assumption that our basic nature is manifested in the transformation of the material environment into what is needed to survive. However, the nature of *Homo faber* is not simply that of an animal seeking sustenance. Instead, through the process of production, nature itself comes to affirm the reality of our very existence. Through human efforts, it is transformed. And because such efforts are ordinarily organized in concert with others, our very *species being* is nurtured. Thus, through labor, we reproduce our very humanity in a real and objective world. For Marx, this *objectification* of species life means that we create not only an image of self in the conscious mind but that we see our reflection in the world we have made (Israel, 1971: 37–38).

However, not all objectification is created equal as far as the confirmation of human nature is concerned. Remember that for Marx, work must be under the control of the worker. This means that *authentic* objectification presupposes that work life is willful and consciously directed, that it represents creative expression (not merely survival), and that it is an avenue for sociability (Israel, 1971: 39).

Given an understanding of capitalist structure, what then are the implications for authentic objectification, for the realization of essential humanity? We have already discovered the nature of private property, the imperative of accumulation, and how the quest for surplus value is manifested in a division of labor that sets the person against self and others. This state of affairs has ob-

---

[4] For an analysis of the split labor market and the place of race and ethnicity in working-class antagonism, see Bonacich, 1972, 1975.

vious implications for the Marxist conception of spiritual impoverishment, but before we consider this issue a final preliminary argument is in order.

For Marxist theory, one of the most distinctive features of the capitalist mode of production is *commodification*. A commodity is something (usually a product) that is bought or sold, that is *exchanged* against the value of other products in the market. Not every product is made to be exchanged. Marx argued that before capitalism, goods were produced for their *utility*. Hence, the worth of goods and products was based on their *use value*. A system of barter allowed necessary products to be traded for other essential goods strictly on the basis of their immediate utility. Here there was little separation between the act of producing and the act of consuming (Israel, 1971: 41–45).

However, through the market structure of capitalism, products are converted into commodities. In their commodity form, products' *exchange value* is separated from their use value. Now production is primarily *for sale and resale*, distribution networks proliferate (on a global basis today), and the consumption is estranged from the act of producing. Marx was not opposed to world trade. (In fact, he foresaw the coming of a planned world economy.) And although there is more than a trace of the romantic in his writing, he was not proposing a return to the barter system. His critique of the capitalist market and its commodity form revolves on several crucial observations.

First of all, within the capitalist system, the major criterion of use value (whether it meets a basic human need) is subordinate to the different standard of exchange value (how much return can be expected when products are sold). It is clear that money is the most general form of exchange value, and the reason for being for capitalist production. The implications of this transformation are considerable. No matter what the use value of a product (how important or frivolous), its production is dependent on its exchange value. This reality is the basis for a $100-billion-a-year advertising industry in the United States. The purpose of that industry is to artificially create a market, adding to the exchange value of products.

All of this does not imply that capitalist products are without use value, but it does mean that the exchange side is the major determinant. For example, high-tech medicine has utility, but its potential for profit is what places it *above public, preventive care* in the medical industry. At another level, pet rocks, wall walkers (creepy-crawly toys that walk on walls), hula hoops, Trivial Pursuit, high fashion, sugar-loaded cereals, and romance novels may at one time or another be produced in abundance.

A second aspect of the Marxist critique of the commodity form involves the transformation of labor. Within the capitalist system, those who work sell their labor for a wage. Hence, *labor* itself assumes a commodity form complete with exchange value. One's labor is no longer authentic objectification but rather a mere element in the cost of production. And as with all other commodities, labor power is owned by the capitalist class because they own the jobs.

A third dimension of commodification has to do with the transformation of social relationships within the broader society. Not confined to workplace, commodified relationships come to permeate all social relationships. C. B. MacPherson observed:

> Whatever the degree of state action, the possessive market model permits individuals who want more delights than they have, to seek to convert the natural powers of other men to their use. They do so through the market, in which everyone is necessarily involved. Since the market is continually competitive, those who would be content with the level of satisfactions they have are compelled to fresh exertions by every attempt of the others to increase theirs. Those who would be content with the level they have cannot keep it without seeking to transfer more powers of others to themselves, to compensate for the increasing amount that the competitive efforts of others are transferring from them. (1962: 59)

Finally, Marx identified the *fetishism of commodities* (1967: 71–83). The great paradox of labor under capitalism is that the worker comes to be dominated by the products of his or her own hands. Reduced to a cog in the machinery of production, confining personal contributions to a tiny fragment of a process ever growing in complexity, the worker is both subordinate and expendable. Kept apart from the centers of command, those who sell their labor for a wage "are not paid to think." Or if they are, their thoughts become the property of someone else. The productive life assumes a mysterious nature, its organization appears beyond comprehension, and the finished product is vested with a power not its own.

In the early 1920s, Georg Lukács was to take Marx's fetishism to other levels. A student of Max Weber (see Chapter 10), Lukács focused on two crucial aspects of capitalism: rationality and bureaucracy. For Lukács, the dominance experienced by workers originates in the mode of production but (quite consistent with Marx) does not remain there. As the capitalist economy matures, its organization reflects more and more a bureaucratized form. This is correspondingly true for the superstructure (government, laws, and so forth) that ensues from the material base or substructure.

Within the bureaucracy, a set of rational processes is institutionalized so that tasks are divided and routines for problem solving are standardized. However, in the process of working within this structure, bureaucrats develop a reverence for its rules and a sense of obligation. Over time, it is treated as a living thing. The bureaucracy becomes the equivalent of a specter. It is in truth the product of purposeful, human organization, but people surrender unto this ghost of their imagination a nature and reality of its own (Israel, 1971: 269–282). Lukács termed this process, whereby bureaucracies (and other social formations) are empowered and brought to life, *reification*. By it, human creations are given suprahuman standing, a wholly abstract reality is made concrete, and social arrangements designed to meet real and immediate needs appear transcendent.

For example, "society" is given life when one considers its forces to operate independent of real human beings. The "office" is reified when it is given

an existence altogether independent of its occupant. (Thus one is asked to respect the "office" even if, for example, the president in it is facing impeach-
ment.) The "market" is reified to the extent that it supposedly determines
(when left alone) such things as the cost of goods, services, and labor. By
reification, human beings make symbols real (reverence for the flag), turn
ideologies into forces of absolute good and evil (democracy, free enterprise,
socialism, communism), and turn complex world political issues into simplistic ones (freedom fighters versus terrorists). Throughout this process, the
(falsely transcendent) status quo becomes insulated from the criticism of mere
mortals.

## ALIENATION

With a structural understanding of commodification and the related process of
reification now in hand, we can turn at last to the consequences for the spirit of
the worker. To do this we must grasp the Marxist construct of *alienation*. Now
this condition has a number of dimensions, but each is suggestive of an artificial and destructive form of separation. Alienation is rooted first of all in the
estrangement of people from the means of productive life. Without property,
the masses of men and women have no choice but to sell their labor to those
who own. Yet, the social relationship between owner and worker can only be
an alienated one. They are estranged by virtue of the irreconcilable differences
in their class interests.

 Under such a relationship, labor is invested in the production of increasingly fetishized commodities. Describing the condition on this level, Marx argued that alienation is an *emptying* process for the worker who toils under the
conditions of industrial capitalism. Coexisting with the material side of exploited labor (including the objective conditions of poverty and deprivation) is
the impoverished inner life of those who work. Simply put, as their structural
position requires the surrender of what they make, and as what they make is
the manifestation of their being, workers are selling bits and pieces of self. Or,
in the words of Marx:

> It is the same in religion. The more man puts into God, the less he retains in
> himself. The worker puts his life into the object, but now his life no longer be-
> longs to him but to the object.... Whatever the product of his labor, he is
> not.... The alienation of the worker in his product means not only that his
> labor becomes an object, an external existence, but that it exists outside him,
> and that it becomes a power on its own confronting him. (1961: 69, originally
> published 1844)

Simply put, what is produced, as well as the entire productive process
(what happens on the job), is *strange, foreign, and totally outside* one's control and
external to one's authentic needs. Confronted with a fragmented division of
labor dedicated essentially to increasing exchange value, and understanding
that individual workers are always expendable, those who work become the

gravediggers for their own soul. The malaise of this *alienation from the self* means that the worker

> does not affirm himself but denies himself, does not feel content but unhappy, does not develop freely his physical and mental energy but mortifies his body and ruins his mind. The worker therefore only feels himself outside his work, and in his work feels outside himself. He is home when he is not working, and when he is working he is not at home.... Its alien character emerges clearly in the fact that as soon as no physical or other compulsion exists, it is avoided like the plague. (Marx, in Zeitlin, 1968: 87)

Caught up in a competitive struggle for scarce jobs or better pay and transformed into an empty shell, the worker then experiences the final estrangement: alienation from others. This is the ultimate denial of species being. Now men and women become objectified "others" sharing social space but not social identity. The private interest contends with the public good, the "me" is wholly set apart from the "we," and the person turns from society. In the final analysis, alienation under capitalism is a form of social and psychic death.

## IDEOLOGY AND FALSE CONSCIOUSNESS

Given Marxist theory, the problem of alienation is only to be solved through successful class struggle. And, if you remember, successful class struggle in turn is dependent on the development of class consciousness. Now it should be obvious that Marx was aware of the considerable repressive power of the capitalist system. But he was more certain of the rational abilities of workers, brought together in the factory system, to define their class interests and organize to defend them. However, that consciousness of position and interests (which would transform a class in itself to a class for itself) is inhibited by the power of *ideology* and the corresponding production of a *false consciousness*. These final arguments will bring our synthesis of Marxist social thought to a close.

Earlier in this chapter we distinguished between the material base or substructure and the superstructure within a mode of production. The point was made that the latter includes (but is not restricted to) the systems of ideas and knowledge dialectically related to the material base. Such idea systems can be termed *ideology,* and although the material base is the primary partner in the relationship, ideology and the material base are mutually influential.

Quite early in his writing career, Marx collaborated with Engels in a study entitled *The German Ideology* (1967, originally published 1845–1846). Early in the manuscript he noted that idealist philosophers (even those who broke with Hegel) seldom looked at the *connection* between the "material reality" of German history and the content of their philosophy. *The German Ideology* is a watershed work in what we earlier identified as the sociology of knowledge. However, Marx and Engels were interested in more than the interrelationships between the emergence of knowledge (for example, philosophy and science) and the events and ideas of an era. Instead, they were interested in the ways in which ideas become external forces of coercion, serving the interests of dominant groups. Hence this well-known passage:

> The ideas of the ruling class are in every epoch the ruling ideas, i.e., the class which is the ruling material force of a society is at the same time, its ruling intellectual force. The class which has the means of material production at its disposal has control at the same time over the means of mental production, so that thereby, generally speaking, the ideas of those who lack the means of mental production are subject to it. (Marx and Engels, 1967: 39)

Ruling ideologies become, therefore, forces of social control. They (and their institutional forms, such as education, the media, and religion) are part of the superstructure of the capitalist mode of production and thus serve the interest of the capitalist class. However, in dialectic fashion, these ideologies both reflect and shape the material base or substructure. Perhaps we can demystify these processes if we employ examples of ideological content.

In Western societies today (and particularly in the United States), we often encounter the idea of *individualism.* Marx would argue that this is little more than an alienated conception that separates self-interest from the public good. However, as an instrument of ideological control, individualism has two clear consequences. It provides a ready-made justification for inequality, while inhibiting the recognition of common interests on the part of the subject population.

Other dominant ideas might include *progress,* which is often measured in commodity or technological growth. Given our earlier discussion, it should be clear that under the capitalist system, these forms of growth routinely retard *social* growth. But ideas based in commodity "happiness" and the powers of technology to solve problems serve to camouflage (for the moment) structural contradictions within the existing order. Finally, you might wish to consider the political/intellectual consequences of such notions as *equal opportunity* (routinely offered in lieu of equality), *trickle down* (which argues that to benefit the rich is to benefit the poor), and *careerism* (which means getting job skills and not learning how to think critically).

Now at the level of the mind, ideology is productive of a *false consciousness.* Very simply, when people uncritically accept the prevailing wisdom on its own terms, they take on false definitions of reality. False consciousness, however, is not a matter of *subjective processes* rooted in the individual mind (or minds). For Marx, it is founded in distinctively macrosociological conceptions. Hence a specific form of false consciousness is represented when people accept the illusions of an *age;* another form occurs when intellectuals uncritically incorporate the dominant ideology within systems of knowledge; and still another form emerges when an entire class fails to understand its societal and/or historical role (Szacki, in Israel, 1971: 95–96).

One important implication of this macrostructural conception of false consciousness is that "illusions" are not somehow purposely and consciously manufactured by the bourgeoisie for the express purpose of controlling the proletariat. Instead, as members of a class that controls, they *believe* those ideas that legitimate their dominance.[5] The bourgeois outlook can only be *uncritical, ahistoric, and self-centered* (Lukács, 1971, originally published 1922). Its members cannot be expected to develop class consciousness. This is not to say that members of this class cannot form alliances to more efficiently dominate the state and labor but that they can never be expected to acknowledge the structurally exploitative and inherently *superfluous* nature of their position. And of course, their solidarity is ultimately inhibited by the predatory nature of their roles. As Marx was fond of saying: "One capitalist finishes off many capitalists" (quoted in Acton, 1967: 104).

What then of "false consciousness" and the working class? It should be clear that members of this class also buy into the dominant ideology. When combined with the earlier forms of dehumanization we examined (fetishism of commodities, reification, the dimensions of alienation), the resulting mystification obscures what Marx believed to be true class interests. However, unlike the owning class and their allies, the *material position* of workers ensures both their exploitation and their potential as a force for change. As we have already seen, Marx argued that under advanced capitalism, the social relations between owners and workers become increasingly strained. Correspondingly, those relations become archaic and unable to support the further development of the productive forces. Such periods of crisis grow, and the brunt of course is borne by the working class.

Marx believed that such historically specific preconditions unleash repressed rational forces within labor. Then follows the development of class consciousness and its political organization into a revolutionary movement. In breaking their own chains, this class will realize the ideal they embody: the advent of social ownership and the beginning of true human history.

## Critique

If we consider the magnitude of the response to Marxist theory, it is fair to say that this is a most heuristic system of thought. Sometimes bent on explicating or extending the tradition, sometimes on revealing its logical and ideological difficulties, a century of scholarship has grappled with its explanations. Certain of the issues of Marxist thought remain controversial today, and some of the more important ones follow.

One long-standing criticism of Marxist thought centers on the issue of *economic determinism.* Noting the importance of the "mode of production,"

---

[5] There are many individual exceptions, as with Engels himself, but the Marxist focus is on what is typical of the class outlook as a whole.

some critics charge that this theory makes the whole of society and history a consequence of how a society organizes its productive life. Stated another way, critics have charged that, for Marx, the economy becomes the "independent variable" and culture and the entire superstructure "dependent variables." In truth, Marx constantly returned to the material base to *begin* his explanation of society. And this clear predisposition has drawn fire repeatedly. It is also true that there is much within the superstructure that Marx appeared to ignore, preferring instead to examine those particular dimensions with clear implications for social change (such as ideology and class consciousness).

However, it also must be acknowledged that Marx did not end his theoretical quest with an examination of the substructure. Remember that the logic of Marx is *dialectical*. That is, there is a dynamic and interactive relationship between the material base and the superstructure. Given dialectic assumptions, they (or their components) do not constitute variables that enter into a unilateral or unilinear relationship. In fact, the concepts of determinism and variable essentially belong to the language of *positive science*. Only with great caution should they be superimposed on the historical, holistic, and qualitative work of Marx.

The Marxist social historian George Rudé (1980) has argued that ideas and ideology, although grounded in material conditions, can at historically propitious moments take on a primary role. In a similar vein, Marx argued that "theory becomes a material force when it grips the masses" (in Rudé, 1980: p. 19).

Another common criticism of Marx centers on a vulgar interpretation of materialism. It should be clear by now that Marx did not reduce human nature and human history to simple greed. Nor did he ignore the spiritual/intellectual side of the species. To the contrary, it is a historically specific system that is productive of exploitation in the modern era. Stated simply, Marxist thought is not founded on a study of human motivations, greed or otherwise.

Another issue for Marxist thought centers on the *labor theory of value*. It gives rise to questions about the role of nonlabor factors in the production of wealth (capital and machines, for example) and to the question of skill and educational differentials among workers (human capital distinctions). In the capitalist system, wealth is routinely viewed as a consequence of investment decisions made by private owners or investors. Further, the making of wealth is linked in large measure to state-of-the-art technology. Finally, workers are assumed to be paid on the basis of "market factors": the relationship between supply (of the workers' skills) and the demand for them.

The Marxist conception of labor value turns these views on end. First of all, the capitalist system is distinctive by reason of the exalted role it gives to the private holder of wealth. Second, unlike private capital, labor is the common (and essential) property of all economic systems. Third, machines and technology are not self-creating or self-operating. They, too, represent the works of labor. Finally, Marx held to an egalitarian conception of labor, focusing again on the whole of productive life. In his words, the

... total labor-power of society, which is embodied in the sum total of the values of all commodities produced by that society, counts here as one homogeneous mass of human labor power.... Each of these units [individual workers] is the same as any other. Hence the value of any article [or service] is the "labor time socially necessary ... to produce an article under the normal conditions of production, and with the average degree of skill and intensity prevalent at the time. (1967: 39, originally published 1867–1879)

Now in clarifying the issue of surplus value, we cannot begin to resolve its controversy. On the one hand, there is more than a trace of single-mindedness and romanticism here. On the other hand, there are obviously ways to organize an economy that do not make the services of private investors superfluous. Perhaps most importantly, a reading of Marx reminds us that those who labor are routinely undervalued within the capitalist system.

As to skill differentials, Marx the humanist would remind us that the productive life of society is necessarily interdependent. All who produce what a society needs are essential—in their own right and because all "skilled tasks" are dependent on the "less skilled." Remember, too, that for Marx, some "skills" are invented or socially useless except in the capitalist system. From this argument, one cannot exact a technical formula for establishing income scales. But that is not the point. There is an egalitarian premise here: Those of different abilities are members first of a common and interdependent humanity. And the general material needs of all must be met *before* the issue of different compensation for the supposedly more skilled occupations is raised.

There are other issues to be addressed. Marx focused on the contradictions of the capitalist system. For this reason and for that of historical specificity, he did not consider problems common to all industrial systems. On a similar level, Marx gave only passing concern to the problem of the state and alienation. The *state* too may be fetishized (or, perhaps more accurately, reified), as a number of modern examples make clear.

As for the predictive power of this theory, in the more than a century since Marx's death many movements and nation-states (often having more in difference than in common) have been founded in his name. Nevertheless, to this point a Marxist transformation has not come to an advanced capitalist state (though some in the West have developed a "soft" socialism that blends private ownership, public planning and regulation, and a welfare state.) Still, as Marx would remind us, history has not stopped.

As for the ideological implications of Marxist theory, we need not speculate. Unlike Durkheim's call to order and Weber's insistence that human science be value free, its prime reason for being was to change the world. Ironically, this conception of revolutionary knowledge has brought about a paradox. Within the circles of power in the Western world, Marxism is often reduced to a label of delegitimation and a rallying cry for international adventures. Yet, when institutionalized within the state, the canons of Marx may be invoked to solidify power and close off critical debate (Kolakowski, in Bottomore, 1973: 119–122). Both such conditions represent a perversion of Marxist thought.

# ▪ Modern Voices on Inequality: Neo-Marxian Theory

Other shortcomings of Marxist thought have been recognized by twentieth-century scholars sympathetic to the tradition. Using Marx as a base, they have refined lines of thought, and explored what their mentor at a distance omitted or chose not to emphasize. Others appear to have found in Marxist theory the beginning point for more specialized works on modern monopoly capitalism and its internationalization as a world system.

In the pages to come, we shall briefly consider the works of the *structuralists* Louis Althusser and Maurice Godelier. Then we shall turn to the works of Paul Baran and Paul Sweezy on *monopoly capitalism* and to Harry Braverman's assessment of the *degradation of modern labor*. Finally, we shall explore Immanuel Wallerstein's conception of *global capitalism*. In the process, we will depart somewhat from our earlier format. Instead, we will look occasionally at groups of theorists rather than individuals, omit biographical information, and address more narrowly drawn questions in the Marxist tradition.

## The Structuralists

Some historians have argued that civil wars are the bloodiest of human conflicts. Whether true or false, within academic circles a corollary is often true: Those who share a theoretical perspective struggle among themselves with greater ferocity than those who do not. So it is with some modern-day Marxists in general and with the work of the French intellectual Louis Althusser in particular. However, it is not our purpose to explore squabbles that are peripheral to a body of thought. The work of Althusser, as well as that of Maurice Godelier, is representative of those who see in Marx's lifelong work a line of demarcation. And this remains a major issue.

### LOUIS ALTHUSSER ON IDEOLOGICAL AND SCIENTIFIC MARXISM

For Althusser, an *epistemological break* can be found in Marx's work. This means that the very *nature* of Marxist knowledge is transformed into "*two distinct theoretical disciplines.*" Althusser locates this break in *The German Ideology,* written by Marx and Engels in 1845–1846, and to a lesser extent in the earlier (1845) "Thesis on Feuerbach." He considers these works to be a critique by Marx not only of German philosophy (including the Hegelian and Young Hegelian varieties) but of Marx's own earlier ideology. Or, in the words of Althusser:

> By founding the theory of history [historical materialism], Marx simultaneously broke with his erstwhile ideological philosophy and established a new

philosophy [dialectical materialism].... This "epistemological break" divides
Marx's thought into two long essential periods: the ideological period before,
and the scientific period after. (1969: 343–344)

Hence, the pre-1845 period is portrayed as *ideological,* that is, *nonscientific.*
Simply put, Althusser has pitted Marxist thought against itself. He argues that
the works of the immature period are humanistic, at least somewhat infused
with German idealist philosophy, and hence *still influenced by external ideology.*
The increasingly mature work of Marx (on the other side of the break) constitutes both a philosophical and scientific revolution. And this new science is a
science of history.

Althusser has argued that the immature Marx (somewhat a prisoner of
ideology) held a romanticized conception of human *freedom* that he implicitly
discarded later. This earlier view led generations of later scholars to *mistakenly
give to the human actor far greater power than the scientific Marx would admit.* Stated
formally,

If we take seriously what Marx tells us about the real dialectic of history, it is
not "men" who make history, although its dialectic is realized in them and in
their practice, but the masses in the relations of the class struggle. (1972: 168)

What this means is that Althusser gives to Marx (and himself) what he
believes is essential for a true (nonideological) science. The essence of that science is an insistence on *laws* rooted in social structure that operate independent
of human will, consciousness, and purpose. When Althusser argued that people
do not make history, he was saying that the dialectic forces of history work
whether we are aware of them or not. Instead, the *masses,* caught in the structurally determined relations of the class struggle, are more the instruments than
the makers of history.

Now if we consider Althusser's position, we find certain criticisms are in
order. The first of these has to do with his conception of science. Althusser
cites Marx for the discovery of a new science of history, complete with a dialectic form of logic. Yet he is unwilling to abandon the determinism that he
implicitly believes marks *all* science. Consequently, he eliminates men and
women from their own history and yields to history an inevitability. Lukács (if
you recall) would no doubt call this portrayal, by which history becomes a pup-
peteer, a form of reification.

However, from the Marxist vantage point, there is a saving quality to
Althusser's work. Though he denies that the relationship between individuals
and society is reciprocal, he affirms that there is a dialectical relationship involving structural components. Specifically, this means (as Marx argued) that
the forces and relations of production, along with the elements within the
superstructure (such as the state and ideology), are mutually causal. However,
Althusser holds (also as Marx) the primacy of the economic base. This focus
does direct attention to the macrostructure of society in history and away from

a wholly phenomenological obsession with human consciousness (see the work of Alfred Schutz in Chapter 13).[6]

## MAURICE GODELIER ON THE "HIDDEN LOGIC" OF ECONOMIC SYSTEMS

A second figure among the French structuralists is Maurice Godelier. His works parallel those of Althusser in several important ways. He too believes that the young Marx was nonscientific, given too much to what some might call an Enlightenment image of human potential. And with Althusser, he has argued that the mature Marx passed on a science of history, founded in an understanding of social structures and free of philosophical speculation on human nature.

In his work, Godelier has employed a conception of structure common to both Marx and the anthropologist Levi-Strauss.[7] So conceived, a structure "is not a reality that is directly visible . . . but a *level of reality* that exists beyond the visible relations between men, and the functioning of which constitutes the underlying logic of the system ... by which the apparent order is to be explained" (1972: xix; italics added). This quest to uncover the *hidden structural logic,* specifically, that which determines the form and relationships of economic systems, distinguishes the work of Maurice Godelier.

Godelier's problem of structural logic takes the form of an inquiry into the *rationality and irrationality in economic systems.* This problem assumes two forms. On the one side, is the rationality of "economic behavior of individuals within particular economic systems." On the other, is "objective capacities for evolution possessed by these systems themselves." These are obviously connected, "for in order to understand the rationality of the economic behavior of individuals, we need to know the structure of the economic and social system in which they act" (1972: 25–26).

Godelier first considered the rationality of actors within the capitalist system (calculating entrepreneurs, participating workers, consumers with preferences) (1972: 30–47). He quickly showed that these *intentional and purposeful* rationalities are both *visible and individual based,* hence *nonstructured.*[8] His argument also leads to the conclusion that what is defined as rational economic behavior is quite obviously context bound. (For example, the Islamic banker

---

[6] Althusser also spoke to another criticism of Marxist theory, holding that a socialist revolution need not occur in the most developed of capitalist countries but at the "weakest link in the chain of imperial states" (1969: 97). By this argument, the Russian Revolution becomes consistent with the major thrust of Marxian prediction. Wallerstein's analysis of world systems speaks to this issue as we shall see at chapter's end.

[7] Godelier studied under Levi-Strauss and was inspired to develop a Marxist analysis of anthropological issues (1977).

[8] This is clearly a critique of the philosophy of idealism and the Weberian-pluralist vision of social order.

who charges no interest would appear quite irrational from the perspective of the Bank of America.)

Although Godelier has analyzed the rationalities of individuals, he does not believe that they are simply transformed into the rationalities of social systems. Instead, he cites Marx in turning from an individually based interpretation of structure to a structurally based interpretation of individuals:

> But here individuals are dealt with only insofar as they are the personifications of economic categories, embodiments of particular class-relations and class-interests. My standpoint ... can less than any other make the individual responsible for relations whose creature he socially remains, however much he may subjectively raise himself above them. (Marx, in Godelier, 1972: 46)

Thus, in Godelier's reading of Marx, the individual as an individual disappears. He or she is important only as the manifestation of larger historical forces, not as a conscious, willful actor. Hence, the problem of rationality is raised from the human level to the higher order of *systemic rationality*. What then is the nature of that rationality? Or put in another form, what specifically is the hidden structural logic that accounts for the rise and fall of the capitalist mode of production? For Godelier, the essence of the hidden logic of capitalism is found in his distinctive conception of *contradiction*.

> It is not a contradiction within a structure but *between two structures*. It is thus not directly a contradiction between individuals or between groups, but a contradiction between the structure of the productive forces (their more and more advanced socialization) and the structure of the productions-relations (the private ownership of the productive forces). (1972: 79)

In other words, Godelier holds (with Marx) that in early capitalism there was a structural correspondence or "functional compatibility" between these two Marxist "forces." However, as the capitalist mode of production matures, it changes and what was once compatible becomes incompatible or contradictory. For Godelier and Marx, the principal contradiction between structural forces appears at a certain stage of the maturity of the capitalist system, and that stage is the stage of *large-scale industry*. With the development of large-scale industry, the urban (now international) working class grows, and its members interact even as they are exploited by a more fragmented division of labor and increasing machine and other technical power. The fiction of unity between capital and labor is then dissolved and the revolutionary movement begins. Dialectically, the historic mission of capital is to "develop the productive forces of social labor" (Marx, in Godelier, 1972: 85). Stated simply, capitalism is the womb of socialism.

However, and this is the crucial point, Godelier sees in Marx a *science* that demonstrates both the *necessity and superiority* of a new mode of production compared to its predecessor (1972: 82). Now, Godelier does not mean this as a value judgment. Instead, economic systems evolve and are superseded (capitalism by socialism, for example) because each manifests an inherent structural logic. This logic, for Godelier, has nothing to do with assumptions about human nature, morality, or ethical principles. Just as Adam Smith was unscientific in making the claim that capitalism is a societal extension of rational human nature, so was the early Marx (and many of his heirs) wrong to claim that socialism must triumph because it is simply compatible with our *species being*.

As does Louis Althusser, Godelier seeks to eliminate the Marxist image of human nature from this theoretical system. And while he does a service in pointing up the structural nature of Marxist science, he is open to several criticisms. First, we are left with the question of what Marx really said. The answer is he said a lot. We often know only what specific interpreters think is important within his vast system. Still, it is clear that Marx did not see the sharp division between humanism and science that Godelier and Althusser emphasize. The volumes of *Capital* (in his supposed scientific period) ring with egalitarian premises and assumptions. Marx's scientific theory certainly matured, but it does not follow that this maturity came at the expense of his image of human nature.

Yet the problem of Godelier is deeper. In stressing the evolution of systems and the necessity and superiority of later modes of production, he appears to have assigned an *inevitability* to history and an *irrelevancy* to its makers. More specifically, Godelier may have replaced an economic with a broader *structural determinism*. Now Marx is partly to blame for this. In his preface to the first volume of *Capital* (1967, originally published 1867–1895), he spoke of the "natural laws of capitalist production … working with iron necessity towards inevitable results."

However, shortly thereafter, Marx saluted the English factory inspectors, medical reporters on public health, and various commissions of inquiry for their work. He also believed in English factory legislation and that one nation's success in legal reform can help others—the purpose being to eliminate "all legally removable hindrances to the free development of the working class." Although Marx did not believe such acts could be sufficient to remove "the obstacles offered by the successive phases of its [capitalism's] normal development," such intentional and purposive acts could "shorten and lessen the birth pangs."

What then is the solution to our puzzle? Marx is perhaps more a humanist than the structuralists wish to believe and more a structuralist than the humanists wish to believe. However, it is doubtful that Marx would have committed his life to the study of change if he believed that such knowledge made no difference in the forward march of history. In sum, human beings are not imprisoned in a vast historical machine. Nor are they free to build societies in their own image. They create both their own conceptions and their own history, but in the process they are ever "conditioned by a determinate development of their productive forces" (Marx, in Israel, 1971: 69).

# Monopoly Capitalism:
# Paul Baran, Paul Sweezy,
# and Harry Braverman

Important to the second group of neo-Marxian theories that follow is the transformation from competitive to monopoly capitalism. When Marx argued that "one capitalist destroys many capitalists," he was peering into the future from a nineteenth-century vantage point. And while he foresaw a continuing concentration of wealth and power in the hands of a few, Marx also clearly emphasized the role of competition in driving down prices and profits (which would lead in turn to the future exploitation of labor.) Although competition has not disappeared, modern economic reality is far removed from the early industrial form.

For some of its critics, capitalism is now centered in the world of the corporation or, perhaps more accurately, the *megacorporation*. Such giants are often linked by interlocking boards of directors[9] and commonly conduct business in national and international markets. The position of dominance held by a few giants in specific sectors of the economy has led some to argue that the *price competition* assumed by Marx is outdated. For Paul Baran and Paul Sweezy, *monopoly capital* means that when large corporations control an economic sector, price competition gives way to *price making*. The objective is to avoid the mutually destructive price warfare endemic to competitive capitalism.

> This objective is achieved by the simple expedient of banning price cutting as a legitimate weapon of economic warfare. Naturally, this has not happened all at once or as a conscious decision. Like other taboos, that against price cutting has grown up gradually out of long and often bitter experience, and it derives its strength from the fact that it serves the interests of powerful forces in society. As long as it is accepted and observed, the dangerous uncertainties are removed from the rationalized pursuit of maximum profits. (Baran and Sweezy, 1966: 58–59)

How precisely are prices made? The most obvious answer, that they are fixed through collusion, is also frequently the wrong answer. Pricing conspiracies involving collusion among supposed competitors are not all that rare (Simon and Eitzen, 1982). However, as Baran and Sweezy have argued, the *ideology* of competitive capitalism remains strong despite evidence of increasing concentration. Therefore, certain institutional practices have emerged to eliminate the need for collusion while checking price wars. One of these involves *price leadership*. Here, one leading member within an industry announces a price, and the others adopt it. For example, when a leading bank announces it

---

[9] Corporations are directly interlocked when a member of the board of directors of one also sits on the board of another (or others). Corporations are indirectly interlocked when different members of each board sit on the board of a third.

is raising or dropping its prime interest rate (the rate offered to its most favored corporate customers), other major banks follow suit.

Baran and Sweezy were quick to point out that the "abandonment of price competition does not mean the end of all competition" (1966: 67). (Hence, the announcement of the death of competitive capitalism is premature.) It simply assumes different forms. For example, industrial members compete in the spheres of *cost reduction* (such as acquiring new technologies of production), *new commodities* (whether introducing truly new products or simply "improved" versions designed to avoid market saturation), and *the sales process* (which includes market research, promotion, and an advertising industry).

When combined, high monopolistic pricing, cost control, product innovation, and sophisticated marketing provide the basis for an expanding *economic surplus*. This is defined as "the difference between total social output and the socially necessary costs of producing it" (1966: 112). How then is this surplus utilized? Baran and Sweezy argue that under competitive capitalism it was primarily accumulated or consumed by the capitalist class, with some of the surplus going to the church and the state. However, under monopoly capitalism, the disposal of surplus becomes a more complex issue. Truly, some of it goes to richly compensate corporate managers and large shareholders, who may then convert it into luxury goods to be consumed. A portion of the surplus may be constantly reinvested in new technology and the expansion of operations. Still more may be spent to further stimulate sales.

Yet, all of these forms of surplus–absorption are insufficient. Indeed, Baran and Sweezy argue that strategies such as investment in new technology and expansion, as well as marketing, may create an even greater surplus. The contemporary "solution," for these authors, is found in the role of the modern capitalist state. Government operates as a new sponge, absorbing much of the economic surplus and converting it into uses that are "narrowly circumscribed by the nature of monopoly capitalist society" (1966: 142). These uses consist of state support for a growing civilian government and a burgeoning military apparatus.

Now the state under monopoly capitalism becomes a major employer, purchases goods and services, and makes "transfer payments" (such as subsidies for corporations and farmers, unemployment compensation, and so forth). All of these reduce the economic surplus and quiet some social discontent while maintaining inequality. Yet despite the growth of civilian government, it competes for resources with a growing warfare state.

Baran and Sweezy hold that with the internationalization of capital (especially since World War II) and the rise of the Soviet bloc, playing the military card became increasingly crucial in maintaining and expanding a world economic system. Against this reality, vast expenditures on peacetime weapons (marked by bloated costs and quick obsolescence) offered the hope of both absorbing the economic surplus and ensuring the global order. Thus there emerges the irrationalism of the monopoly system. Overall, it is an economy based on the production and absorption of waste. Within this general structure there emerges a specific modern *warfare state*. In turn, the warfare state is capital-intensive (creates fewer jobs per dollar invested compared to other industries), is committed to planned obsolescence (especially in high-tech weapons systems), and drives an arms race that has little to do with legitimate national defense (Baran and Sweezy, 1966: 178–217).

The work of Baran and Sweezy raises a number of issues that must await a brief review of a second dimension of the monopoly capital debate. In his *Labor and Monopoly Capital* (1974), Harry Braverman addressed the problem most aptly described in his subtitle: *The Degradation of Work in the Twentieth Century*. Here the focus is on the modern world of work, not its subjective dimensions but rather the vast occupational changes that mark the labor process. And yet his is more than a study of the shifting of jobs in industrial society. Braverman's problem is that of a contradiction: the vision of the "scientific/technocratic" society with its demands for a highly skilled and intelligent work force and a corresponding view of growing dissatisfaction with the conditions of industrial, service, and white-collar work (Braverman, 1974: 3–4).

Braverman's view does not originate within the halls of ivy. He worked seven years as a coppersmith, and when that craft fell to change, he worked in related jobs such as pipefitting and sheet-metal work. Hence he experienced more than the "real world of work" with its craft skills, sweat and dirt, but the demise of the manual arts with their potential for satisfaction and mastery. Yet this is not a work that seeks to glorify the vision of the craft at the expense of science, technology, and automation. Braverman has attempted a *system-specific* analysis of what has happened to work under the conditions of monopoly capital in this century. His method is historical, his focus is structural, and his message is one of change.

Braverman shares the assumptions of Marx in other important ways. He holds to the vision of the *maker* who, in concert with others, fashions the material environment through unified mental and manual labor and *becomes* fully human. But under the conditions of degraded work, the mind is split off from "common" labor, and human beings are enslaved by machines or machinelike routines. Under monopoly capitalism, employers (increasingly the large corporation) can buy in the "labor market" a piece of the worker's labor life. This buying and selling of mindless labor, Braverman argues, is found not merely in the routine of factories but in other jobs held in abundance by a "new working class."

The Marxist conception of working class commonly elicits the image of those who toil in the factories, mines, and mills of capitalist society. Braverman argued that such a view is overly static and that the Marxist conception of class was instead "an expression for an ongoing social process" (1974: 24). In other words, if we consider the relationship to the means of production (and implicitly, the *source* of income), then the working class consists of those who sell their labor (or services) for a wage (or salary). However, the *composition* of this class, as well as the *nature* of the work performed, reflects the "transformation of sectors of the population" (1974: 24).

Hence, the conception of a working class must be a *dynamic* one. Only then can it encompass the realities of *growth* (at present fewer than 10 percent of the U.S. work force is self-employed). A dynamic conception of a working class can also deal with the *shifting* of occupations (for example, the rise of service and white-collar jobs) and the real changes within the *same* occupation (for example, today's cabinetmaker is more a semiskilled factory operative than a skilled craftworker).

The central problem for Braverman (as for Marx) is *who controls* the labor process.

> It thus becomes essential for the capitalist that control over the labor process pass from the hands of the worker into his own. This transition presents itself in history as the *progressive alienation of the process of production* from the worker; to the capitalist, it presents itself as the problem of *management*. (1974: 58)

It is the managerial control of labor, especially through the artificial divisions and occupational specializations within the work force, that Braverman relentlessly probes.

All societies develop some division of labor that translates into different role expectations for the various tasks (not just economic) that must get done. However, under capitalism the productive process itself is fragmented into routines, and workers are assigned to one routine or another irrespective of their human needs and abilities. Therefore, only a small piece of the worker's whole is used, and the rest is ignored and discarded. This transformation of the worker into a cog in the machine has the obvious consequence of increasing productivity. However, it has the more subtle function of strengthening the hand of management. Management now controls *more dispensable and vulnerable* workers and is able to pay them less for their *simplified* labor (1974: 78–83).

Braverman has also reviewed other dimensions of managerial control. These include *scientific management,* a set of organizational principles and techniques developed by Frederick Winslow Taylor beginning in the 1880s. "Taylorism" was based on the premise that work should be reduced to its simplest elements and that the work performance involving each element should be systematically improved. Taylor's conception of the dumb brute seeking to shirk a "fair day's work" would embarrass modern managers steeped in more enlightened imagery. But Braverman argued that the *organization of today's workplace* is historically grounded in scientific management, and he cited Peter Drucker, the eminent contemporary management consultant, who agreed (Braverman, 1974: 88).

Management also controls, argued Braverman, through science, technology, and mechanization. Rather than being employed to humanize the work process, science and technology are employed to "engineer the human factor in work design. This means that the motions, time, and labor cost ... have been precalculated for each job" (1974: 178). As for mechanization, once the work process has been organized for machines, workers may become automatons who must adjust to rather than use their tools. Furthermore, the fact that automation may cost jobs also enhances managerial control.

Perhaps Braverman's most intriguing argument flows from his analysis of the "universal market" (1974: 271–283). Under capitalism, the extent of commodification is such that the whole of society is transformed into a gigantic marketplace. Within this market, "services" previously provided by self, family, or community become the basis for a new and thriving industry. On the one hand this industry involves the reorganization of such things as food preparation, travel, and hospitality to accommodate those who actively serve the market. On the other hand,

> ... the massive growth of institutions stretching all the way from schools and hospitals on the one side to prisons and madhouses on the other represents not just the progress of medicine, education, or crime prevention, but the clearing of the marketplace of all but the "economically active" and "functioning" members of society, generally at public expense and at a handsome profit to the manufacturing and service corporations who sometimes own and invariably supply these institutions. (1974: 280)

What Braverman called the degradation of work is not restricted to the traditional manufacturing workers or to the poorly paid service workers who replace them in a modern shifting of occupations. In the rising clerical field, the routines of scientific management, as well as a burgeoning computer technology, represent again for Braverman the heavy hand of managerial control. Computers do not simply do office work but have the capacity to monitor it. As for other evidence of degradation within the clerical occupation, the modern poorly paid (frequently female) clerk is compared with the nineteenth-century clerks (frequently male) who had higher status and greater relative pay. However, there is more to degradation: Braverman's point is that the greatest growth in jobs is to be found in the new working–class occupations of clerical, retail, and service workers. These are somewhat removed (in dignity, skill, and pay) from the prevailing image of unlimited growth in new, exciting, and well-paying careers.

Certain of the criticisms raised earlier concerning the work of Marx are applicable to these inquiries into monopoly capitalism. However, there are other issues to be raised. Baran and Sweezy perhaps paint an overly *monolithic* view of the power of giant corporations. Certain sectors of the modern capitalist economy are clearly dominated by a few concerns (perhaps the term *oligopoly* or *shared monopoly* is more useful for that reason). However, for better or worse, competitive capitalism is certainly alive in the retail sector, the deregulated airlines, and many areas of the service economy. Nor do Baran and Sweezy consider the clear reality of international competition (as in electronics, automobiles, steel, and so forth) that clearly has an impact on prices. These criticisms may be more in the nature of qualifications than repudiations, but they demonstrate the difficulty this theory has in dealing with the nuances of modern corporation capitalism.

On the labor side of the monopoly issue, Braverman's work has proven to be somewhat prophetic in the period since its publication. There is clearly a growing (if silent) revolution in the workplace toward service-sector jobs. Taken as a whole, these jobs pay less than those in both the retail and manufacturing areas. On the down side, Braverman may have attributed to monopoly capital exclusive responsibility for the stifling atomization of labor commonly found in *industrial* societies. He has made a convincing case, however, that the specific conditions of modern capitalism oppose the rise of holistic workers who are practitioners of *self-management*.

## The Capitalist World–System: Immanuel Wallerstein

The issue of a "world market" is touched upon by Marx in Chapter 24 of the first volume of *Capital:*

> All the peoples are enmeshed in the network of the world market so that the capitalist regime assumes an international character. With the constantly diminishing number of the capitalist magnates who ... monopolize all the advantages of this transformative process, there is an increase in the mass of distress.... But there is also a rising of the working class, who will have been constantly growing in numbers and are schooled, united, and organized through the working of the capitalist process of production. (Marx, in Acton, 1967: 104)

From the vantage point of the present, the Marxist phrase "diminishing number of capitalist magnates" appears an awkward way of describing the internationalization of corporation-centered capitalism. However, it does contain the genesis of an idea pursued by others. Among the more sophisticated contemporary efforts to explore the capitalist world-system and its relationship to international inequality is the work of Immanuel Wallerstein.

Just as the Marxist concept "mode of production" recognizes no changeless societal, national, or cultural boundaries, so does Wallerstein's *world-system* transcend social and political structures, customs, and lines drawn on maps (1979: 1–7). Wallerstein's historical point of departure resides in a distinction between what he termed the *world empire* based on conquest and political subjugation (types of which were China, Egypt, and Rome) and the modern world system based on the economic subjugation of capitalism. As an illustration of this system, he argued that nineteenth-century "empires" (such as those of Great Britain and France) were not world empires. Rather, they were "nation-states with colonial appendages operating within the framework of a world-economy" (1979: 6).

However, Wallerstein did not locate the emergence of the modern world economy in the nineteenth century and the explosion of the industrial revolution (which began in Europe in the latter half of the eighteenth century). Instead, he centered on the sixteenth century and the development of *world market trade*.[10] "This was the [world] system called capitalism. Capitalism and a world-economy (that is a single division of labor but multiple polities and cultures) are obverse sides of the same coin" (1979: 6). For Wallerstein, world capitalism is a powerful system including various nation-states. These political structures work to facilitate modern trade, to defend the system, and to ensure against losses. Profits, of course, remain in private hands.

The best way to understand Wallerstein's world-system is to conceive of it in terms of a *one-sided international division of labor*. Within that *hierarchical* division, we find the core, the periphery, and the semiperiphery. The *core* of the world-system is the center of economic dominance. Those nations at the core (which clearly vary over time) prosper through the exploitation of the periphery. The *periphery* consists historically of regions and peoples that provide the core with plentiful and cheap natural resources and labor power. The *semiperiphery* refers to those areas or states that are intermediary in the world hierarchy and usually decline and ascend. They are neither dominant nor dominated. Remember that a constant feature of the world-system is the "shifting location of economic activity and consequently of particular geographic zones" (1980: 179).

Wallerstein (1974) has found the genesis of the modern world-system in the period 1450–1640, during which economic subjugation slowly replaced military conquest and political domination. This was a period first of *geographical expansion,* marked by European expeditions into Asia, Africa, and the Americas. With this colonial foundation established, there emerged a global division of labor featuring *unequal development*. As that division took shape, different regions contributed specialized organizations, raw materials, products, and labor to the system as a whole. For example, the western European core developed first as centers of trade and later along industrial lines. It was home to the early members of a world *ruling class,* as well as to a growing legion of workers. Peasant farmers in the semiperiphery (such as southern Europe) worked the land, while in the periphery, forced labor (based on serfdom and the African slave trade) flourished. It should be noted here that Wallerstein's international division of labor is more specifically the internationalization of *labor exploitation*.

A final developmental event in the early history of the world-system centers on the rise of centralized state structures in Europe. They dominated the economic stage for much of the sixteenth, seventeenth, and eighteenth centuries, establishing military monopolies, organizing bureaucracies, and facilitating commerce.

The consolidation of the capitalist world-system awaited the European era commonly termed mercantilism (between 1600 and 1750). Mercantilism

---

[10] Market trade must be distinguished from the administered and redistributive world trade of empires.

was conventionally defined by Wallerstein (1980: 37) to involve "state policies of economic nationalism" (simply put, the economic interests of the nation as a whole transcended those of individuals or parts of the whole), and "a concern with the circulation of commodities" (a balance of exports over imports and an accumulation of bullion). By the beginning of the seventeenth century, the core was located in northwest Europe. During the first half of the century, Dutch hegemony prevailed, but the period 1651–1689 was marked by a struggle within the core (Wallerstein, 1980: 75–125). Here, Britain and France challenged Holland in rounds of warfare intended to gain trade advantages.

This mercantile era was, for Wallerstein, a period of recession in the world-system (1980: 128–175). This forced retrenchment because "the decline in relative surplus allowed room for only one core state to survive" (1979: 26). In this struggle, the British ousted the Dutch and held off the French. At this point Great Britain emerged from the mercantile period as the dominant core power, poised by 1760 to rule over the coming industrial stage of the capitalist world-system. Until this time, the basis for the system had been agricultural production and trade. However, with expanding industrial production came a "required access to raw materials of a nature and in a quantity that could not be supplied within the former boundaries" (1979: 27).

Britain ruled over the now industrial-centered world-system until 1873, when the "hegemonic role was assumed by the United States" (1979: 31). Germany, which also aspired to core status, was defeated during World War I and lost much of its peripheral control (colonies). It was unsuccessful in the 1920s in finding new industrial markets in the Middle East and South America, setting the stage for the rise of nazism. As for a contemporary note, Wallerstein argued that the Soviet Union and Eastern Europe are also parts of the modern world-system because it has been historically the only global game going. The Soviet Union was reinstated as a strong semiperipheral power after World War II and may be poised to seek a core position. In the post–World War II era, the system has featured increasing freedom on the part of multinational corporations "which are able to maneuver against state bureaucracies whenever the national politicians become too responsive to internal worker pressures" (1979: 33).

Wallerstein's contention that there is only *one world system* today is arguable. But let us hear his case:

> There are today no socialist systems in the world-economy any more than there are feudal systems because there is only one world-system. It is a world-economy and it is by definition capitalist in form. Socialism requires the creation of a new kind of world-system, neither a redistributive world-empire nor a capitalist world-economy but a socialist world-government. I don't see this projection as being in the least utopian but I also don't feel its institution is imminent. It will be the outcome of a long struggle ... in all the areas of the world-economy. (1979: 35)

Certainly, an examination today of the international banking structure, as well as world patterns of trade, would support Wallerstein's conception of international dominance by an essentially capitalist system. Also compelling is his portrayal of socialist state managers who operate on the same economic premises as do their counterparts in the capitalist core. It is ironic, however, that a critic of the capitalist world-system has nonetheless fashioned (albeit unintentionally) a rather *conservative view of its dominance*. However, Wallerstein's world-system may be a bit more fragile than is portrayed here. For example, in the present era, international banks and banking organizations (such as the International Monetary Fund and the World Bank) have lent enormous sums to "semiperipheral and peripheral" states. The inability or refusal to repay those debts may constitute more than a passing threat to the financial institutions of the capitalist core. Further, Wallerstein considers but perhaps *underestimates* the potential for international alliances on the part of the labor- and resource-rich periphery and semiperiphery.

One has to be careful with concepts like world-system. They are on the one hand masterful analytic and explanatory devices. On the other, they may create hard and fast images of dominance and continuity. These are, of course, suggestive of the process of reification, a problem that Marxist theory identifies but does not always avoid.[11]

## ■ Bibliography

Acton, H. B.
1967            *What Marx Really Said*. New York: Schocken.

Althusser, Louis
1969            *For Marx*. London: Penguin Books.
1972            *Politics and History*. London: New Left Books.

Baran, Paul, and Paul Sweezy
1966            *Monopoly Capital: An Essay on the American Economic and Social Order*. New York: Monthly Review Press.

Berlin, Isaiah
(1939) 1963     *Karl Marx: His Life and Environment*. 3rd ed. New York: Oxford University Press.

Bonacich, Edna
1972            "A Theory of Ethnic Antagonism: The Split Labor Market." *American Sociological Review* 37:547–559.

---

[11] Wallerstein recognized this with the disclaimer, "Nor am I in any way suggesting the immutability of the capitalist system." But he went on to argue "that this system currently (but not eternally) is capitalist in mode" (1979: 74). However, arguing that capitalism is not "eternal" does little to shake its pillars, disclaimers notwithstanding.

1975                             "Abolition, the Extension of Slavery, and the Position
                                 of Free Blacks: A Study of Split Labor Markets in the
                                 United States." *American Journal of Sociology* 37:601–28.

Bottomore, Tom (Ed.)
1973                             *Karl Marx*. Englewood Cliffs, N.J.: Prentice-Hall.

Braverman, Harry
1974                             *Labor and Monopoly Capital: The Degradation of Work in the
                                 Twentieth Century*. New York: Monthly Review Press.

Fromm, Erich
1966                             *Marx's Concept of Man*. New York: Frederick Ungar.

Godelier, Maurice
1972                             *Rationality and Irrationality in Economics*. New York:
                                 Monthly Review Press.
1977                             *Perspectives in Marxist Anthropology*. Cambridge, England:
                                 Cambridge University Press.

Israel, Joachim
1971                             *Alienation: From Marx to Modern Sociology*. Boston: Allyn
                                 and Bacon.

Lukács, Georg
(1922) 1971                      *History and Class Consciousness: Studies in Marxist Dia-
                                 lectics*. Translated by Rodney Livingstone. Cambridge,
                                 Mass.: MIT Press.

MacPherson, C. B.
1962                             *The Political Theory of Possessive Individualism*. London:
                                 Oxford University Press.

Marx, Karl
(1844) 1961                      *Economic and Philosophic Manuscripts of 1844*. Moscow:
                                 Foreign Languages Publishing House.
(1845) 1935                      "Thesis on Feuerbach." In Friedrich Engels, *Ludwig
                                 Feuerbach and the Outcome of Classical German Philosophy*,
                                 pp. 73–75. New York: International Publishers.
(1847) 1913                      *The Poverty of Philosophy*. Chicago: Charles H. Kerr.
(1857–1858) 1971                 *The Grundrisse*. Edited and translated by David McLellan.
(1857–1858)                      *Pre-Capitalist Economic Formations*. Edited by Eric J.
1964a                            Hobsbawn. New York: International Publishers.
1964b                            *Selected Writings in Sociology and Social Philosophy*. Trans-
                                 lated by T. B. Bottomore. London: McGraw-Hill.
(1859) 1970                      *A Contribution to the Critique of Political Economy*. New
                                 York: International Publishers.
(1861–1863) 1952                 *Theories of Surplus Value: Selections*. Edited by Karl
                                 Kautsky. New York: International Publishers.
(1867–1895) 1967                 *Capital: A Critique of Political Economy*. 3 vols. New York:
                                 International Publishers.

Marx, Karl, and Friedrich Engels
(1845–1846) 1967   *The German Ideology.* New York: International Publishers.
(1848) 1971      *Birth of the Communist Manifesto.* New York: International Publishers.

Ollman, Bertell
1976            *Alienation.* 2nd ed. Cambridge, England: Cambridge University Press.

Rudé, George
1980            *Ideology and Popular Protest.* New York: Pantheon.

Simon, David, and D. Stanley Eitzen
1982            *Elite Deviance.* Boston: Allyn and Bacon.

Toennies, Ferdinand
(1921) 1974     *Karl Marx: His Life and Teachings.* Translated by Charles P. Loomis and Ingeborg Paulus. East Lansing, Mich.: Michigan State University Press.

Tuchman, Gaye
1974            *The TV Establishment: Programming for Power and Profit.* Englewood Cliffs, N.J.: Prentice-Hall.

Wallerstein, Immanuel
1974            *The Modern World-System: Capitalist Agriculture and the Origins of the European World Economy in the 16th Century.* New York: Academic Press.
1979            *The Capitalist World Economy.* London: Cambridge University Press.
1980            *The Modern World-System II: Mercantilism and the Consolidation of the European World-Economy, 1600–1750.* New York: Academic Press.

Wilson, John
1983            *Social Theory.* Englewood Cliffs, N.J.: Prentice-Hall.

Zeitlin, Irving
1968            *Ideology and the Development of Sociological Theory.* Englewood Cliffs, N.J.: Prentice-Hall.

# CHAPTER *16*

---

# ■ Coercive Politics

The issue of political coercion has fascinated many sociologists who labor in the conflict tradition. Although some are indebted to the theoretical insights of Karl Marx, many do not choose to focus on a dialectical relationship between state power and the material base of capitalist society. Each of the contributors to this chapter, however, disagrees with order and pluralist assumptions on the polity. To be explicit, order sociologists routinely assume a *consensual* basis for political life, where the will of the majority comes to prevail. Pluralists see a wide variety of *interest groups* forming shifting coalitions to influence governmental action. While a specific group or coalition may be extraordinarily influential at a given historical moment, no single class or elite is dominant over time.

From the conflict vantage point, the political organization of society assumes a different nature. Here the structure of power (routinely state power), is founded in *force,* including that force rooted in legal authority. Given this view, the nature of the polity cannot be reduced to a simple mandate from the people. Nor is the "conflict" involved merely a result of the divergent and opposing interests of such pluralist categories as parties, lobbies, political action committees, or business and labor groups. Thus conceived, politics is not the art of compromise. Rather, it concerns the *forms of domination* by which a typically *self-replenishing* circle of command press their will.

Theoretical conceptions of the forms of domination may share the assumptions of the conflict paradigm, but they will vary in conceptual content. In the pages to come, we will first examine C. Wright Mills's modern classic on the rise of a tripartite *power elite* in the United States. This will be followed in turn by Theda Skocpol's cogent treatise on the *international states system,* and Nicos Poulantzas' work on the *modern capitalist state.*

# ■ C. Wright Mills (1916–1962): The Power Elite

C. Wright Mills remains to this day a largely unrecognized contributor to sociological theory. Yet in a short lifetime he published a number of well-crafted works on divergent topics. Mills was no stranger to controversy. He was always a critic, not merely of the institutional structure of society but of those human scientists who too easily accept the status quo. Mills believed that the failure of intellectuals is part of the larger failure of "rationality" in the modern era. Such a condition emerges when the rationality of the existing order is assumed, and it becomes only reasonable to think and act to further that order. Hence, reason (for example, that manifested in science) may serve an irrational purpose in an irrational order (such as the development of high-tech weapons systems for profit and the "defense" of world markets).

In the broadest sense, Mills lived before his intellectual time. He struggled virtually alone to keep alive the conflict imagery of critical thought during one of the more conservative periods of American history. However, the fact that Mills became one of the intellectual fathers of the New Left in the 1960s remains both a blessing and a curse. On the one hand, his preliminary efforts were to inspire new critical scholarship. On the other, much of what is theoretically sophisticated in his work has been overlooked and the legacy of Mills relegated by critics to polemic. Yet during his life, this futurist inquired widely into the world of labor leaders, the rising legions of white-collar workers, personality and social structure (with Hans Gerth), the specter of world war, the Cuban revolution, and of course, the range of intellectual responsibility. However, among them all, one effort is distinctive: the rise to power of an elite triad in the modern era.

## History and Biography

Charles Wright Mills[1] was born on August 28, 1916, in Waco, Texas. His family was middle-class and Roman Catholic. During his youth, they moved frequently, requiring the young Mills to attend a number of public and parochial schools. He began his university career as an engineering student at Texas A&M but soon transferred to the University of Texas to major in philosophy.

Mills took his M.A. in philosophy in 1939, but his choice of disciplines is a bit deceptive. At the University of Texas he developed an interest in the social philosophy of George Herbert Mead (see Chapter 12) and the early critical so-

---

[1] Major references on the life and times of C. Wright Mills include Scimecca, 1976; Horowitz, 1963; Aptheker, 1960; and Wallerstein, 1968.

ciology of Thorsten Veblen. Although he found *The Theory of the Leisure Class* less than substantial, Mills was to become the heir to Veblen's critique of class-divided society.

Mills moved to the University of Wisconsin, this time to the Department of Sociology, where he studied with Hans Gerth. Gerth had studied under Mannheim (see Chapter 18) but remained somewhat Weberian (see Chapter 10) in his conception of the historical social actor seeking to make meaning of his environment. (Mills later collaborated with Gerth in *Character and Social Structure* [1953], a theoretical account of the relationships between psychic and social structure.) He took his Ph.D. in 1941, defending a dissertation entitled *Sociology and Pragmatism,* which was later published in book form (1964).

After a short stay at the University of Maryland, Mills became an assistant professor at Columbia University. There he directed the Labor Research Division of the Bureau of Applied Research, working under Paul Lazarsfeld. Mills later came to criticize the methodology exemplified by Lazarsfeld, strongly geared as it was to the surveys and quantitative analysis of positivistic sociology (1967, originally published 1959). However, during this period Mills conducted research on labor, urban power structures, and the rise of white-collar workers. He quickly grew weary of attempting to explain stratification by studying only the ordinary people who consented to be questioned. He came to insist on a macrostructural conception of political stratification based in historical interpretation. And he grew increasingly convinced that a largely inaccessible elite dominates societal affairs.

Mills had grown up in a populist region in a family of limited resources living in the shadow of the Great Depression. His training, first at the University of Texas and then at Wisconsin, initially bore the stamp of critical philosophy and then a European sense of history and social structure. Then came the horror of the Second World War. When it was over, Mills was not content to consign European fascism to the dustbowl of history. Instead, he saw a linkage between the rise of fascism and the nature of a wider system: that of international monopoly capital. However, he began with a more domestic focus. During the postwar era, when most people (including the intellectuals) were content to celebrate the victory of democracy, C. Wright Mills began to question the authenticity of the democratic vision. Perhaps people are free to make history, but then perhaps some are freer than others.

The decade following the Second World War was not a safe period for critical politics. It was a time when the Soviets tested their first atomic weapon, signaling the beginning of the end of U.S. nuclear and superpower monopoly. It was a time of media frenzy based on the dubious premise that the "secret" of the bomb had been stolen. It was a time that saw the execution (for conspiracy to commit espionage) of "atomic spies" Ethel and Julius Rosenberg. It was a time when the House Un-American Activities Committee was busily uncovering the threat of communist subversion. It was a time when a young congressman from California by the name of Richard Milhous Nixon gained notoriety as a staunch anticommunist. (This he did through spotlighting the allegations of Whittaker Chambers, a former editor of *Time* magazine and ex-member of the Communist party. Chambers charged that communists—including one Alger Hiss—were working for the U.S. State Department.) This was a time when the junior senator from Wisconsin, Joseph McCarthy, provided name and leadership to a political reign of terror. This was a time of blacklists, of loyalty oaths, of careers destroyed by innuendo. This was a time of madness.

Mills, perhaps shielded by his professorship at Columbia, escaped the fate of some. But as he considered the postwar scenario, he discerned more than the isolated influence of a twisted political movement headed by twisted minds. He saw the abdication by intellectuals of their required leadership of conscience. He saw the failure of liberalism and Marxism as modes of critical thought. He saw that rationality did not invariably serve the ends of freedom. At the wider level, he saw the rise of a "new cast of actors," for whom the *white collar* disguised only a new form of alienation and bondage.

> At the top of the white-collar world, the old captain of industry hands over his tasks to the manager of the corporation. Alongside the politician, with his string tie and ready tongue, the salaried bureaucrat, with briefcase and slide rule, rises into political view. These top managers now command hierarchies of anonymous middle managers, floorwalkers, salaried foremen, county agents, federal inspectors, and police investigators trained in law.... And in the lower reaches of the white-collar world, office operatives grind along, loading and emptying the filing system; there are private secretaries and typists, entry clerks, billing clerks, corresponding clerks—a thousand kinds of clerks. (Mills, 1951: ix–x)

Mills did not believe this white-collar world to be congruent with the democratic vision. Socially, it made for a widespread alienation, leaving its victims without roots, loyalties, or sense of history. Economically, it made for the death of craft and unpeaceful coexistence with a world shaped by alien forces. Politically, it made for a continuing sense of inaction on the part of voiceless masses. This, then, was the stage that Mills set in 1951 for his later treatise on the nature of power in American society.

C. Wright Mills was not to witness the impact of his ideas on a new generation of sociologists. He died in Nyack, New York, on March 20, 1962.

## Assumptions

Over and again, the dominant imagery of human nature to be discerned in the writing of C. Wright Mills is that of *rationality*. At the level of individual thought, the ability to reason, to analyze systematically, to form sound judgments and draw informed and logically consistent conclusions distinguishes the species. When applied at the political level, "the reasonable person" is a precondition for the participatory conception of democracy that Mills found so appealing. And it is the distortion of reason, by such as the "mass media of distraction," that he found so appalling (1959: 311–315, originally published 1956).

Indeed, Mills found that the value of the discipline of sociology is rooted in its ability to transmit a special form of rational analysis. At the intellectual level, sociological rationalism comes in the form of an "imagination" that allows its possessor to grasp the relationships: between history and biography, between institutional and psychic structure, between public issues and private troubles (1967: 3–24, originally published 1959). A part of that larger rationalism enables the individual to join with others in the creation of society, as well as the course of its future. Although the power of those social forces that constitute the status quo is formidable, they are never adequate to totally determine the range of reason.

Just as Mills insisted upon the rational actor, he further envisioned the rational society. At the level of societal structure, this form of rationality can be measured in both the economic and political spheres. For Mills, the productive life of a society is rational to the extent that it allows for independent control by independent producers. Accordingly, his historical exemplars include the owner-operators of small farms and business enterprises (1951: 3–59). Political life is envisioned as a form of "rational democracy," with participation expected at the local level and leaders drawn from the grass roots. The exemplar here is the "town hall" form of direct democracy (1959: 298–324).

We should recall that the conflict vision of society routinely assumes a coercive present and a utopian future. Mills is no exception. There is more than a trace of southwestern populism in Mills's conception of the independent property-owning middle class in the pre–Civil War United States. Yet for Mills, that era stretching from the final third of the nineteenth century to the mid-twentieth century was one of transformation. Gone are the small-interest economy and politics on a human scale. In their stead has risen a new social order: one that features giant managed corporations, an integrated nation-state, and a burgeoning organization of military power. And at the center can be found the modern *power elite,* exercising the authority that comes with their positions of command (1959: 7).

If the present coercive order is irrational, Mills hinted at the promise of change. If enlarged and centralized institutions are problematic, then smaller and decentralized ones are called for. If the present is plagued by a society of *masses* (where people are commanded, inactionary, and deceived), then the future holds the promise of a society of *publics* marked by free debate and informed choice. However, this future necessitates the reassertion of reason and the rebirth of independence in new historical circumstances. As leaders of this quest, Mills identified the young intelligentsia of the "New Left" (1960c). These he believed to understand the importance of change.

In the first section of this book, we examined certain of the Millsian conceptions of human science. Above all, Mills called for a rebirth of the *classical* tradition. By this he meant those interpretative ideas that orient their user to understanding social reality. Classic sociology is marked by an "attempt to state the general historical trend, the main drift of modern society" (1960b: 3). In service of that purpose, classicists developed general models of society and used these to construct theory. Even though the theories may prove inaccurate, the underlying models continue to be useful. Or stated in the language of this book, the great ideas are often to be found in the paradigm rather than the specific theoretical content.

Graham Kinloch (1981: 122–124) observes in Mills the methodology of *historical induction* (drawing general and interrelated conclusions from the particular events and ideas of history). This deduction is evident (as we have seen) in the linkage by Mills of social conditions and ideas, of historical trends and social structure, of biography and history, of hierarchical power and the elitist ideology, and of intellectual responsibility and rational democracy. Later in his career, Mills moved to a comparative sociology, examining noncapitalist ideas and their political consequences (as in the Cuban revolution).

Mills detected in the sociology of his time a reluctance to examine change and a corresponding abandonment of historical inquiry. His call for a classical renaissance in sociology occurred against the background of positivism (and its drive to uncover facts that were often left to speak for themselves). He critiqued such fact gathering not as unnecessary but as routinely atheoretical, narrow, expensive, and altogether dominant in fashioning the image of human science (1960b: 6–7). Directly stated, Mills was a rather lonely representative of a paradigm not (yet) in favor. Undaunted, he continued to conduct inquiry into the "trend of Western societies," to understand the present as history, and to insist that knowledge be used to usher in the good society.

## Theoretical Content

In a real sense, Mills founded his critique of the *power elite* in the "romantic pluralism of the Jeffersonian ideal" (1959: 260, originally published 1956). Such an ideal prevailed only in a society of independent proprietors. Yet the ideology remains. It is one of a "plurality of independent, relatively equal, and conflicting groups of the balancing society" (1959: 243). For Mills, it surfaced in the guise of David Riesman's *veto groups* (see Chapter 11), with its deceptive vision of a middle-class society of countervailing interests in which the "chiefs" have lost power.

Mills contended that the old independent property-owning middle class had become a new salaried and dependent middle class; that to the extent that veto groups existed, they were banished to the middle levels of power where the crucial issues were not resolved; and that instead of losing control, the chiefs had consolidated it. His argument is historical, and it is guided by a series of implicit questions, the answers to which are widely scattered and often camouflaged by a narrative style.[2]

Mills sought to explain the forms of elite domination. However, a guiding set of theoretical issues can be gleaned from *The Power Elite* and presented in the form of simplified questions. We shall begin with a summary point: Who are the "elite"? This aside, we can consider together the following: What are the origins of the elite, and how do they come to command? What is their style? At what levels do they exist? How are they to be identified? In what institutional structures are they dominant? What is the nature of the polity in a society ruled by an elite? What are the negative consequences of elite domination?

In attempting a definition, Mills noted what the elite are *not*. They are not an aristocracy or political nobility. They are not restricted to a small circle of great "old" families, though these can be identified and often rule. They come disproportionately from the upper classes of capitalist society (including those whose wealth is reasonably new). When not upper-class, the families of the future elite are routinely derived from the upper third of income and occupational groups. Their fathers are at the least from the professional or business stratum. They are routinely native born, as are their parents. They are typically eastern, Protestant (especially Episcopalian or Presbyterian), and urban (1959: 278–279).

Mills further argued that the elite form a cohesive social and psychological entity, that they are "self-conscious members of a social class" and possess a similar worldview (1959: 11). They are frequently perceived as they perceive themselves: as born to command, as higher types of individuals, as possessors of superior energy and morality. They are unified and, in many respects, interchangeable (1959: 12–15).

The issue of elite emergence is a matter of history, that of elite maintenance one of social structure and socialization. The Europeans who colonized the country were seldom of aristocratic lineage. They came to a land of vast resources, subjugated its native population, and claimed ownership. Thus perhaps 80 percent of the white male population of the eighteenth and early nineteenth centuries were property owners, an independent middle class. Faced with no aristocracy and done with British rule, this class did not confront the institutions of feudal privilege. Hence, the way was clear for an unfettered bourgeois revolution.

Mills noted the isolation of the continent and the difficulty of military invasion, the immense resources, and the later surges of immigrant labor. But these were not the only factors in the rise of a national bourgeoisie. The Revolutionary War finished the loyalists as a nobility (often finishing their estates as well), the Jacksonian status revolution challenged the dominance of old New England families, and the Civil War ended the claims of a southern aristocracy.

---

[2] The work of Mills represents good and provocative literature, but he was prone to sacrifice the tedium of logic and clear prose in the interest of dramatic effect.

Here, sometimes between the lines, Mills chronicled the "tempo" of capitalist development—for in the United States, laissez faire flourished early in the absence of crown-imposed mercantile restrictions, and industrialism ended the reign of southern planters. "No fixed ruling class, anchored in agrarian life and coming to flower in military glory, could contain in America the historic thrust of commerce and industry, or subordinate to itself the capitalist elite" (1959: 13).

However, the question of emergence does not address the question of maintenance. With the passing of the old middle class came the rise of giant corporations and the modern state, and the closing of positions at the top. The circles of command became largely self-replenishing. If their occupants were not born in the sense of shared heredity, they were destined by means of social position to experience both structural advantage and elite expectations. They are men and women of similar origin (more than ordinarily, upper-class) and education (often ivy-league), of career and life-style. They are trained to lead in the intimate context of family, exclusive clubs, and the right secondary schools.

Yet there is more to elite maintenance than common socialization and personality type. The elite remain in power by virtue of the coincidence of the various positions of power within the leading institutional structures of society. Simply put, these major institutions are interrelated and interdependent. They are hierarchical and bureaucratized. Their goals are often complementary and interconnected. As a consequence, those at the pinnacle in one sphere can, if called upon, routinely move to another. Hence, above all, the elite are *unified* by their socialization and institutional roles. That unification maintains their command (1959: 15–20).

Mills also argued the existence of what might be termed an elite "style." Those within the higher circles ordinarily deny that they are powerful (in the Weberian sense of forcing others to obey against their will). Those who seek office claim to be standing only as "public servants." And of course, they retain a body of image makers to sell that view to the "little people" (1959: 17). Those who command the military also commission public relations programs that sell the Pentagon (1959: 220).

As to the question of the scope or level of elite power, Mills held that elites are a common fact of community life. However, not all community elites are created equal (1959: 30–39). Rather, the *metropolitan* elite are predominant, and those from the eastern cities disproportionately comprise the national elite. Accordingly, Mills argued that the elite can be identified by means of their listing in metropolitan *social registers,* their memberships in restrictive clubs, and their background in exclusive schools.

Perhaps most important is the identification by Mills of those institutional structures subject to elite control. Not surprisingly, he argued that the elite dominate the national economy. The "number one stratum" here includes the *very rich* who routinely inherit sizable fortunes but add to them frequently by using other people's money as venture capital or loans. Also included are the chief executives of major corporations. Frequently from upper-class origins, these executives are served by elaborate networks of contacts and have access to and control over crucial information. As major corporations are typically interlocked (by means of directors who sit on a number of boards), the influence of leading executives is expanded. With the dominance of giant corporations, Mills argued, the very rich and the chief executives are now the "corporate rich" (1959: 94–170).

The second component of the elite triad is the *warlords* who command the military. In a bit of history, Mills noted that despite the assurances that the country is not a militarist nation, its credentials are not those of a staunch neutralist. (He cited the editors of *Fortune,* who observed in 1935 that the U.S. Army since 1776 "has filched more square miles of the earth by sheer military conquest than any army in the world, except only that of Great Britain" [1959: 177].) This would come as small surprise, of course, to the first Americans.

To be precise, since 1776, the United States has fought seven (now eight) wars against foreign powers, a civil war, and a century of intermittent conflicts with its indigenous peoples, and it has intervened repeatedly in Central America and the Caribbean (1959: 177). Given such history, it is logical that military service is routinely offered as a credential for political office (including that of the presidency).

Mills argued the ascendancy of the military elite, especially in the post–World War II era. Their increasing influence in societal affairs has emerged against the backdrop of the U.S.–U.S.S.R. balance of terror and the dramatic growth of *military capitalism.* Furthermore, just as industry has found in the military an enormous source of state capital, so too has higher education found funding for its research in the same source (1959: 171–224). (The so-called military-industrial complex can be enlarged to include technological, labor, managerial, and political dimensions.)

The last division within the elite consists of the *political directorate.* The contention here is that a small group is now effectively in command of those executive decisions "made in the name of the United States of America" (1959: 231). Mills defined them (as of 1953) as the 50 or so who head the executive branch, including the president, the vice president, the cabinet secretaries, the White House staff, and the heads of major administrative departments and agencies.

The political elite are not drawn from "party regulars." Nor do they come from bureaucracies, where the professional administrator spends a life in political service. They are, instead, routinely *outsiders* to such structures. Moreover, over the past two centuries, the political elite have tended to start at the top, that is, to begin on the national level. Increasingly, they bypass local, state, and congressional office. They are appointees who come and go but typically remain in the orbit of power.

What then is the nature of a polity dominated by an elite? A sameness of view and deed at the top will prevail, with the semblance of debate consigned only to the middle levels of power. At the base of the pyramid is the mass, subjected to the ideological control of the media, unable to give opinion or to answer back, with political action carefully channeled into the routines of referendum, petition, and election (1959: 298–324). (Remember that most elites are not subject to election and that the presidential race is ultimately a choice between elites or those controlled by them.)

Mills argued that the idea of the power elite should sensitize one to the expansion and centralization of institutional hierarchies (the giant corporation, the modern state, the high military). It should further raise the questions of the official secrecy that shrouds decision making, the absence of a politically neutral civil service, the curtailing of legitimate local interests, and the absence of professionals in government (1959: 296–297). But perhaps above all, this idea should clarify the nature of the *higher immorality,* which is not so much a matter of the "corruption" of leaders but an expected and systemic feature of elite-dominated society.

For Mills then, the higher immorality is manifested in a blunted sense of moral responsibility on the part of the elite. In characteristic fashion, Mills penned an eloquent indictment.

> It is not the barbarous irrationality of dour political primitives that is the American danger; it is the respected judgments of Secretaries of State, the earnest platitudes of Presidents, the fearful self-righteousness of sincere young American politicians from sunny California.... Such men as these are crackpot realists: in the name of realism they have constructed a paranoid reality all their own; in the name of practicality they have projected a utopian image of capitalism. (1959: 356)

## Critique

A number of points remain at issue after a close reading of Mills. In some ways, his vision of the future appears too greatly informed by the populist romanticism of the past. "Once upon a time," he argued, there was an independent middle class, politicians were statesmen, and entrepreneurs flourished. Other historians have been less sanguine. The land was, of course, taken by force of arms from its original inhabitants. And despite the beckoning of the frontier in the colonial period, not all landowners were created equal. Nor were the disenfranchised women and the large population of black slaves in the antebellum South. As for Jeffersonian pluralism and the political process, one key to the early reality of power in the postrevolutionary era can be gleaned from Charles Beard's historical interpretation of the constitution.

> The movement for the Constitution ... was originated and carried through by four groups ... money, public securities, manufacturers, and trade and shipping.

> The members of the Philadelphia Convention ... with a few exceptions ... derived economic advantages from the establishment.

> No popular vote was taken directly or indirectly on the proposition to call the Convention which drafted the Constitution.

> A large propertyless mass was, under the prevailing suffrage qualification, excluded at the outset from participation in the work of framing the Constitution.
>
> The Constitution was ratified by a vote of probably not more than one sixth of the adult males of the population.
>
> The Constitution was essentially an economic document based upon the concept that the fundamental private rights of property are anterior to government and morally beyond the reach of popular majorities.
>
> The Constitution was not created by "the whole people"; ... neither was it created by "the states." ... [I]t was the work of a consolidated group whose interests knew no state boundaries and were truly national in scope. (Beard, 1961: 324–325)

Mills also large ignored the factory system and the impact on the working class of the early nineteenth century. Particularly crucial was the depression of 1837. Employers responded by cutting wages by 30 to 50 percent and began the rapid introduction of machine technology, a process that was to hasten the demise of skilled labor (Foner, 1947: 121–172). And although Mills remains correct in asserting the more permeable nature of class boundary lines during the century before the Civil War, this fact alone should not obscure the realities of the southern plantation economy, the northern factory system, and the subjugation of powerless (typically propertyless) groups.

Another important criticism of Mills centers on his infatuation with the elite as the *personification* of power. Despite giving recognition to the institutional order, time and again he indulged a bent toward nonstructural analysis. He argued, for example, that although the elite may be influenced by institutional roles, they are not bound by them. Or in his words, "Far from being dependent upon the structure of institutions, modern elites may smash one structure and set up another in which they then enact quite different roles" (1959: 24).

Such personification often introduces a corollary problem: that of an *ahistorical use of history*. Ironically, Mills argued that it is not "historical necessity" but an identifiable elite who have made the notorious decisions of history (ranging from Napoleon's decision to transform his consulate into an emperorship to that of Truman and a few others to drop the atomic bomb) (1959: 24). There is a difference between noting the *relationship* between history and biography, and *reducing* history *to* biography. This is not to say that Mills was interested so much in the "life story" of the elite, but his theory may not be sufficiently far removed from a "great man" theory of events and ideas.

Finally, one should consider the nature of the role Mills prescribed for the intellectual. Quite aside from his eloquent insistence that criticism and activism should be expected is a seeming conviction that the makers and shapers of ideas hold the key to the utopian transformation of society. Now this point cannot be taken in isolation. Mills also rejected what he termed the "labor metaphysic": the Marxist proposition that the working class will play the decisive role in social change. He also faulted the modern elite for the limitation of their vision, the dearth of their reason. Taken together, this infatuation with the power of ideas and the omission of the working class and other ordinary people from history produces a metaphysic of its own. Perhaps this body of work turns on a rebirth of Plato's philosopher-king, the historical centrality of an *intellectual elite*.

# ■ Theda Skocpol (b. 1947): States and Social Revolutions

Theda Skocpol studied at Harvard, where she began her academic career in 1975. Her significant work *States and Social Revolutions* (1979) has the distinction of emerging from her doctoral thesis. She intended it as "a frame of reference for analyzing social-revolutionary transformations in modern world history" (1979: xi). In a general sense it is an exemplar for historical, comparative, and political sociology. And it presents us with a counterpoint to the inquiry of Mills. As we shall see, Skocpol is both transnational and consistently structural in her analysis of coercive politics.

In some ways, *States and Social Revolutions* stands as a rejoinder to Immanuel Wallerstein's inquiry into the "modern world-system" (see Chapter 15). Skocpol has taken issue with Wallerstein for his "attempt to explain in economically reductionist terms the structure and dynamics of this (originally European and ultimately global) international states system" (1979: 22). Rather than focus on the instrumental use of nation-states by dominant classes bent on controlling world markets, Skocpol focuses on an *international structure of military competition* not originally founded in the capitalist mode of development.

Thus, nation-states emerge in this system of thought as organizations driven by two imperatives. The first is the control of "home territories or populations," and the second is competition (of an essentially militaristic nature) with other nation-states in the international system. Simply stated, Skocpol attributes to the international states system an *analytically distinctive and autonomous* reality. Such a political focus does not prevent us from considering the interrelationships of world economics and world politics. It merely means that the latter does not emerge from and cannot be reduced to the former (1979: 14–40). This position thus embraces the conflict assumption of the ultimately coercive state. However, the focus on politics and (especially) war-making powers, represents a clear break with the Marxist contributions in the conflict tradition.

Skocpol expresses a debt to certain of Marx's arguments and does not hesitate to employ them throughout her work. However, she discerns a "lack of fit" between the real history of revolutions and Marxist theory. She notes, for example, that revolutions have not occurred in the most advanced of capitalist nations but rather in agrarian countries caught in a competitive disadvantage. Skocpol also argues that even should working classes in advanced societies become an effective revolutionary force, they would still be forced to contend with two problems. First, there is the possibility of new forms of state domination ensuing from the revolution itself. Second, a new order in an advanced industrial nation would face continuing political and military competition from other nation-states (1979: 292–293). Such views are reminiscent of Proudhon's conception of the natural incorrigibility of the state (see Chapter 14).

At the outset, Skocpol characterizes social revolutions as "rare and momentous occurrences" that have "transformed state organizations, class structures, and dominant ideologies" (1979: 3). Further, they are marked by "class-based revolts from below" (1979: 4). Skocpol argues that despite the historical importance of these transformations, theoretical attempts to explain them have fallen short. She demonstrates this in her review of four such attempts: Marxist (revolutions as class conflict), aggregate-psychological theories (which center on the motivations of revolutionaries), systems/value consensus theories (revolutions are considered to emerge from systemic disequilibrium), and political/conflict (which features the clash of government and organized interest groups) (1979: 9–14).

Skocpol observes that the common denominator among all theories of revolution is *voluntarism,* with its focus on the willful bringing of radical change by historical actors. "None of these perspectives ever questions the premise that ... a necessary causal condition is the emergence of a deliberate effort ... aimed at overthrowing the existing political or social order" (1979: 15). Such a "purposive image" is erroneous according to Skocpol. Furthermore, if the willful and deliberate efforts of people to "make a revolution" is irrelevant, it should come as no surprise to find that she rejects a place for ideology in her theory. For this theorist, ideas about structural crisis do not bring a revolution; the structural crisis produces the revolution.

Put explicitly, Skocpol rejects such voluntaristic images as leaders organizing mass movements for change, or people becoming aware or getting fed up with the existing order, or the rise of idea systems that challenge the status quo. She is not concerned with motives of social actors or the spread of revolutionary ideologies among the discontented. While such factors are concomitants of revolutions, they cannot be considered causal. Instead, hers is an *impersonal and nonsubjective effort to focus upon both the international and intranational institutional orders, and their impact on potentially revolutionary groups within society.* Thus revolutions are not made; they come. In trying to explain this historical coming, this theorist embarks upon a somewhat *nomothetic* course: the search for *regularities* of an institutional and historical sort among different social revolutions (1979: 18).

This interest in a *general* explanation of social transformations led Skocpol to select the French (1787–1800), Russian (1917–1921), and Chinese (1911–1949) revolutions. These she argues were sufficiently similar in terms of both their *old regimes* and their "processes and outcomes" to expect a "coherent causal explanation." To be precise, all three happened in somewhat wealthy agrarian states without a history of colonial subjugation. Also, they were to confront both external and internal crises of general similarity. On the transnational level, they faced more developed nations with strong military resources. Domestically, they faced specific political and economic contradictions that led to the weakening of the central state, peasant rebellions, and the emergence of "mass-mobilizing political leaderships" seeking to take state power. Once successful, the revolutionary new regimes were much more unified than the old orders they replaced. In fact each had great-power potential (1979: 40–41).[3]

Skocpol approaches her study systematically, specifying (A) the *conditions for political crisis,* (B) the *conditions for peasant insurrections,* and (C) the *societal revolutions* (resulting from A + B). As to political conditions (A), she centers on the situation of the dominant class, the state of the agrarian economy, and the nature of international pressures. The conditions for peasant revolt (B) include those of the agrarian class structures and local politics. With these explanatory categories in place, she approaches each of the historical cases.

In the case of each of the (prerevolutionary) old regimes, the dominant class was landed, and in the cases of France and China drew wealth from commerce. In addition to its commercial disadvantage, the Russian landed nobility had little political power in a rigidly bureaucratic and absolutist state. However, both French *proprietors* and the Chinese *gentry* exercised political leverage in their semibureaucratic and absolutist forms of government. As to their noncapitalist, agrarian economies, there was growth in France and Russia, while the Chinese population and land restrictions meant stagnation.

At the international level, eighteenth-century France had suffered repeated defeats in the War of the Austrian Succession (1740–1748) and the Seven Years War (1756–1763) and had suffered English commercial domination. Russia had been defeated in the Crimean War (1854–1855) and the Russo-Japanese War (1904–1905) and of course fell into the disaster of World War I. During the nineteenth century, late imperial China lost the Opium War (1839–1842) to Great Britain and then was forced to "open" the nation to free trade. By century's end, China had lost a war with Japan (1895–1896) and was dominated by the imperial powers (including France, Russia, and Japan).

Skocpol's second "cause" of this triad of revolutions is centered in the conditions that led to peasant insurrections. In France, the agrarian economy featured *proprietary wealth,* which meant that land and property were rented out to tenants. Peasant smallholders worked perhaps 80 percent of the land but owned only 30 to 40 percent. The conditions of the Russian peasants were stronger, because they owned 60 percent (and rented more) and had developed enduring communities based on collective holdings. In China, the peasants

---

[3] Skocpol's is a work in comparative sociology, and she proceeds by contrasting her selected cases with other nations (Prussia/Germany, Japan, and England) where revolutions did not occur.

owned half the land but worked all of it (renting the remainder from the gentry). As to local politics, French villages were somewhat autonomous (under royal supervision); Russian villages were sovereign (but controlled by the tsarist bureaucracy); and in China, the gentry and literati (educated people employed by the imperial state administration) were dominant.

Skocpol argues that these conditions explain the revolutions in question. Yet despite the importance of external and internal political conditions, she argues that in these primarily agrarian societies, the "crucial insurrectionary ingredient" has been the revolt of the peasantry. Hence, in 1787–1789, the breaking of the French monarchy was marked by peasant insurrection. In Russia, the unsuccessful 1905 "dress rehearsal" was followed in 1917–1921 by the fall of the tsarist regime in which the peasantry rose against private owners of land. And finally, the Chinese imperial state began to crumble in 1911. This period was marked by agrarian disorder rather than revolt. However, after 1927, the Chinese Communists (only one party among a number) left their urban base for the countryside, secured the support of the peasantry, and finally consolidated the revolution, which ended in 1949 (Skocpol, 1979: 47–156).

Summarizing broadly then, Skocpol's structural theory of revolutions operates on two levels. The first identifies the place of the old regimes in an international states system and the exploitative class relations featuring landlords and tenants. These she combines with a second level of prerevolutionary conditions: those that favor peasant solidarity, freedom from the dominant land-holding class, and the decline of punitive state control. This is a provocative and well-grounded argument but one not free of controversy.

Perhaps most open to question is the centrality of the peasantry in Skocpol's explanation of social revolutions. There can be little doubt that the peasants were a crucial force in the success of the communists under Mao in China. Nor should one underestimate the importance of "the great fear" in the French countryside that marked that revolutionary period. However, even in China it was necessary for the communists to "win" the peasantry, while Mao was aided greatly by urban cadres. And in France the role of the alienated nobility and especially the rising and dissatisfied bourgeoisie must be noted.

As for the Russian Revolution, Skocpol's version of history clearly downplays the role of soldiers and urban workers. Certainly she is correct that military defeat was destabilizing, yet it was precisely the defeats during World War I that precipitated the mutiny of Russian troops (including those in Petrograd) in 1917. The point is that huge contingents of the military joined the revolution. Further, it should be recalled that this predominantly agricultural nation was heavily dependent on its (admittedly backward) industrial sector. Some two million workers belonged to trade unions, and perhaps half of these engaged in crippling strikes in 1917. Although revolts in the countryside were crucial, one might question the conclusion of a peasant vanguard. It is certainly true that the peasantry was not alone.

Aside from the question of the peasantry is the more serious nullification by Skocpol of consciousness, ideology, and mass mobilization as revolutionary determinants. Although the elimination of the "subjective factor" might please such different sorts as Louis Althusser (Chapter 15) and George Homans (Chapter 8), this leaves us in the dubious position of arguing that minds and ideas are not really important. It is vital to note that this has certainly *not been the view of those carrying out revolutions.* What would have been the nature or direction of the French Revolution without the ideas of Voltaire, Montesquieu, the Encyclopedists, and Rousseau? Or of the Russian without those of Marx and Lenin? Or of the Chinese without the vision of Mao?

Furthermore, given Skocpol's argument (that ideology is not of major importance in the emergence of revolutionary movements), would the same argument not be posed for the use of ideology as a form of social control on the part of *existing regimes?* Would it not also follow that ideological socialization is unimportant, that what is taught in the schools or presented in the media has little bearing on the *maintenance* of the existing order?

As for the question of organization, leadership, and mass mobilization, without these, revolutions appear to be loose cannons rolling across the deck of history. Certainly there is more to a revolution than its spontaneous emergence along totally predetermined lines. Revolutions not infrequently hang in the balance. And their ultimate direction and success (if not their historical breakout) must reside in large measure on the organizational ability of revolutionary groups to mobilize support. This observation, of course, is consistent with the arguments of two rather successful revolutionaries: Lenin and Mao. But more than that, it is consistent with the superior organizational structure of the Bolsheviks (originally, the major branch of the Socialist Democratic party in Russia who followed Lenin) and the Chinese Communists.

# ■ Nicos Poulantzas (b. 1936): The Capitalist State

We conclude our review of conflict theories of politics with a brief examination of the work of the contemporary structuralist Nicos Poulantzas. Poulantzas has certain things in common with Theda Skocpol, as well as the French structuralists Louis Althusser and Maurice Godelier (see Chapter 15). Specifically, he does not assign causal standing to individuals and their attributes (motivations, consciousness, rational intent, and so forth). Instead, he joins with Skocpol (and departs to a great extent from C. Wright Mills) in a rejection of voluntarism.

Although Poulantzas does not consider Skocpol's "international states system," he shares her conception of structure in one respect. He does not focus on the *material base* that looms so large in the work of Althusser, Godelier, and Wallerstein. Instead, his theoretical center is the *political superstructure,* "the branches and apparatuses of the state, and the question of their relation to social classes" (1978: 24, originally published 1974). Yet unlike Skocpol, Poulantzas has constructed a system-specific theory of *the* capitalist state (as opposed to Skocpol's general look at a states system).

Now Poulantzas has a wide view of the "branches and apparatuses of the state." These range from the repressive (army, police, prisons, and even the civil service and judiciary) to the ideological (education, religion); from the informational (media) to the cultural (the arts and literature); and they include political parties, trade unions, and even the family. (It appears that most of what might be included in the Marxist *superstructure* is here.) These state apparatuses have no collective standing as an independent entity; nor do they represent a power of their own. Rather, they exist to concentrate and give sanction to *class domination*.

Simply translated, this means that Poulantzas does not see the state as a neutral force somehow corrupted by ruling classes. Instead, state apparatuses are the *embodiment of class relations*. As such, these structures constantly reproduce the *patterns of dominance and submission* endemic to class-based societies. In concrete terms, this means that the courts protect property owners, the union leadership cooperates with owners/managers, and so forth. Hence, a working-class revolution cannot be concerned with simply *replacing* those at the helm. Rather, a new state with new relations must be created. When this occurs, one can logically expect that the content of the arts and literature will be different, the role of trade unions changed, political parties will perhaps be replaced by more direct forms of democracy, and so forth (1978: 24–28).

Poulantzas distinguishes between the general role of the state under conditions of (early) competitive capitalism and (late) monopoly capitalism. Although the capitalist state in both stages has important repressive (political violence) and ideological functions, the changes in its economic role are noteworthy. Summarizing briefly, the state has never played the laissez-faire role ascribed to it by early liberal (now conservative) analysts.[4]

> From taxation through to factory legislation, from customs duties to the construction of economic infrastructure such as railways, the liberal state always performed significant economic functions, though of course not to the same degree in all capitalist social formations—the role of the state was far more important in Germany and France than in Great Britain, for example. (1978: 100)

Yet if laissez faire is a myth, so too for this theorist is the portrayal of the monolithic state that mechanically serves the interests of monopoly capital. Now please do not misunderstand. Poulantzas recognizes the increasing mo-

---

[4]The terms *liberal* and *conservative* are, of course, relative. When Adam Smith wrote *The Wealth of Nations* in the late eighteenth century, laissez faire represented liberal economics. This is because the conservative mercantilism of the time blocked the rising bourgeoisie. Of course, laissez faire *now is a feature of conservative ideology* (*though not necessarily practice*).

nopolization of capital in a growing corporate/international system. However, he rejects the conception of the state as an automatic instrument of a unified ruling class. Furthermore, he argues that the interventionist role of the state has changed historically in both degree and kind with a movement from competitive to monopoly capital.

During the competitive stage of capitalism, the economic structure plays a dominant and determinant role vis-à-vis the state. However, during the monopoly stage, this relationship is reversed. The state now becomes an economic force. It is directly engaged in the "extended reproduction of capital as a social relation" (1978: 100). In other words, rather than simply intervening to provide the infrastructure of capital (roads, bridges, sewers, and so forth), or to regulate the conditions of labor (through such devices as the welfare state and labor law), the modern capitalist state has new historic functions. For example, it plays a determining role in the internationalization of capital and, perhaps most important, seeks to reconcile the "contradictions and fractions within the bourgeois camp" (1978: 107).

Taken thus far, this structuralist theory of the state has several attributes. First of all, Poulantzas replaces the view of the state as a simple instrument wielded by a "power bloc" of big monopoly capital. In addition to the interests of monopolists, the state embodies those of nonmonopoly capital (which can be expected to resist simply being swallowed up). This means that the hegemony of big monopolies, although real, is often too simply expressed. Indeed, the monopoly fraction within the overall dominant bourgeois class may itself be divided. For example, big banks may prefer to lend to nations within the Third World rather than make cheaper money available to the large corporate manufacturing sector.

Second, just as the state consists of various apparatuses, so do classes represent certain internal divisions. For Poulantzas, things like networks, cliques, and family ties must be considered. Finally, both the state and its apparatuses, as well as class and class fractions, have *relative autonomy*. This does not imply independence but instead suggests that each structural component of the entire mode of production acts in part on its own agenda rather than simply reacting to some system-wide imperative.

There is more to the work of Poulantzas than we have sketched here, but we have identified the form of his explanation. A careful observer will note that he has moved the locus of *social relations* from the Marxist material base or substructure to the *state superstructure*. Such relations are not merely those of owners and workers. Rather, they involve the various fractions within both monopoly and nonmonopoly capital. Given this portrayal, Poulantzas is able to explain that despite the relative dominance of the monopolist fraction, state accommodation and compromise with other bourgeois forces are also a structural imperative.

As with the structuralists in Chapter 15, Poulantzas departs from much of the Marxist sense of science. Missing is a dialectical relationship between actors and objective structures. Also missing is the quest for *empirical evidence* so clearly a part of the very works (by Marx) the structuralists claim to admire. (One cannot read *Capital* without being struck by the attempt to ground and verify arguments.) And as is the case for Skocpol's theory of revolution, human actors and actions, minds and ideas disappear from the scene.

# ■ *Bibliography*

Aptheker, Herbert
1960                *The Social World of C. Wright Mills.* New York: Marzani
                   and Munsell.

Beard, Charles
1961                *An Economic Interpretation of the Constitution of the United
                   States.* New York: Macmillan.

Foner, Phillip
1947                *History of the Labor Movement in the United States.* New
                   York: International Publishers.

Gerth, Hans, and C. Wright Mills
1953                *Character and Social Structure.* New York: Harcourt, Brace
                   & World.

Horowitz, Irving Louis (Ed.)
1963                *Power, Politics and People: The Collected Essays of C. Wright
                   Mills.* New York: Oxford University Press.

Kinloch, Graham
1981                *Ideology and Contemporary Sociological Theory.* Englewood
                   Cliffs, N.J.: Prentice-Hall.

Mills, C. Wright
1948                *The New Men of Power: America's Labor Leaders.* New York:
                   Harcourt, Brace & World.
1951                *White Collar.* New York: Oxford University Press.
(1956) 1959         *The Power Elite.* New York: Oxford University Press.
1958                *The Causes of World War III.* New York: Simon &
                   Schuster.
(1959) 1967         *The Sociological Imagination.* New York: Oxford University
                   Press.
1960a               *Listen, Yankee: The Revolution in Cuba.* New York:
                   McGraw-Hill.
1960b               "Introduction: The Classic Tradition." In C. Wright Mills
                   (Ed.), *Images of Man,* pp. 1–17. New York: George
                   Braziller.
1960c               "Letter to the New Left." In Chaim I. Waxman (Ed.), *The*

|       | *End of Ideology Debate,* pp. 126–140. New York: Funk & Wagnalls. |
|-------|----|
| 1962  | *The Marxists.* New York: Dell. |
| 1964  | *Sociology and Pragmatism: The Higher Learning in America.* Edited and with an introduction by Irving L. Horowitz. New York: Oxford University Press. |

**Poulantzas, Nicos**

| (1974) 1978 | *Crisis in Contemporary Capitalism.* London: Verso. |
|-------------|----|
| 1976        | *The Crisis of the Dictatorships.* London: Verso. |

**Scimecca, Joseph**

| 1976 | *The Sociological Theory of C. Wright Mills.* Port Washington, N.Y.: Kennikat Press. |
|------|----|

**Skocpol, Theda**

| 1979 | *States and Social Revolutions.* Cambridge, England: Cambridge University Press. |
|------|----|

**Wallerstein, Immanuel**

| 1968 | "C. Wright Mills." In *The International Encyclopedia of the Social Sciences,* vol. 10, pp. 362–364. New York: Crowell Collier Macmillan. |
|------|----|

# CHAPTER *17*

---

# ■ Culture and Irrationality

An invaluable part of the Enlightenment heritage is the idea of the critique. Quite literally it implies *oppositional thinking* based in turn on the ability to distance or separate oneself in order to form a judgment. From a sociological perspective, a critique of society presupposes an ability to stand apart from the conventional social wisdom. It means a transcendence of societal time and space, a movement outside the confines of one's own history and biography. It means the suspension of a lifetime of ongoing socialization designed to fit one into a designated niche within a particular society—its institutions and its culture. Perhaps above all, it means to entertain alternative visions of the future, even as others are clinging hard to the present or seeking desperately to reclaim the past.

In a general sense, sociological theories in the conflict tradition are critical by definition. Yet in this chapter we will examine those for whom *informed judgment* is a reason for being, not the by-product of theoretical systems. These efforts in *critical sociology* are distinctive first of all in what they are not. Their predominant focus is neither structural nor institutional. Nor are they primarily grounded in the historical materialism that signifies Marxist science. Instead, these exponents of critical sociology address the cultural and ideological realms and the subjective impact of these forces on human consciousness and the human personality. This is not to say that critical sociology is not informed by the work of Marx, for it most assuredly is. However, unlike the structuralists examined in the preceding chapters, these critics fashioned an image of mind and ideas dialectically engaged with the objective social world. And for this passage, they turned to Hegel.

# ■ Georg Lukács (1885–1971): Reification and Class Consciousness

Foremost among Hegelian Marxists was Georg Lukács, whose major work emphasized the distinctively subjective dimension of Marxist thought. Not formally a member of the Frankfurt School, his work nevertheless established a firm foundation for the critique of knowledge, culture, and consciousness that marked the program of the Institute of Social Research. But more than the affiliates of the Frankfurt School (examined later in this chapter), Lukács developed an intricate theory of dialectics. Through it he fashioned an explanation of the interrelationships among the structures and ideologies of capitalism, class consciousness, and class action.

## History and Biography

Gyorgy Lukács[1] was born in Budapest in the then Austro-Hungarian monarchy. His family was Jewish, and his father was a wealthy and prominent director of the chief bank in Hungary. The young Lukács demonstrated an early talent for literary criticism, publishing his first work at age 18. In 1911, when he was still in his middle 20s, he published a two-volume work on modern drama. In preparation for that work, he studied *Capital*. (He noted that it was Marx the sociologist who appealed most to him, though he "saw him through spectacles tinged by Simmel and Max Weber" [see Chapter 10].) From approximately that point, he began to do most of his writing in German and became widely known as *Georg* Lukács.

Before the coming of World War I, Lukács was prone to dissociate politics and art. He believed, however, that bourgeois society was opposed to art and especially to artistic intuition as a form of truth. Lukács studied first in Budapest and then in Berlin and Heidelberg, where he was influenced by Max Weber and Georg Simmel. His studies in philosophy included both Husserl's phenomenology (see Chapter 13) and revisions of the thought of Immanuel Kant (see Chapter 9). Yet, two overwhelming events propelled him away from a pure philosophy of the mind and toward an Hegelian form of Marxism. The first was the desolation of World War I (1914–1918), which produced for most European intellectuals an attitude of pessimism. The second was, for Lukács, an answer to his despair: the Russian Revolution and the vision of Vladimir Ilyich Lenin.

---

[1] Important historical and biographical information on Lukács can be found in his preface to *History and Class Consciousness* (1971, originally published 1923) and in Lichtheim, 1968.

Lukács participated with enthusiasm in the Hungarian revolution of 1918 and held a position as minister of education in its communist government in 1919. However, he did not abandon the philosophical tradition of German idealism in favor of the materialism of Marx and Lenin. Instead, he came to see in Hegel a means of reconciling the idealist emphasis on the world of consciousness and interpretation with the Marxist conception of realism and objectivism. Hence, on the Hegelian side, Lukács argued that values and morality are parts of reality (not purely subjective experience). On the Marxist side, he held that "only a knowledge of society and the men who live in it is of relevance to philosophy" (1971: xvi).[2] This wedding of Hegelian-Marxism and the critique of society was to strongly inform the Frankfurt School.

The young Lukács's revision of materialism (see Chapter 15), together with his deviation from Lenin's conception of revolution, precipitated a fall from grace within the party. Whereas Lenin argued the necessity of a revolutionary *vanguard,* Lukács focused (as we shall see) on the importance of class consciousness. Thus Lenin's emphasis was party organization and leadership, while Lukács (driven by a Hegelian revision of idealism) sought to explain how the proletariat would ultimately negate the distortions of bourgeois thought. Lukács later recanted the strong Hegelian influence in his early treatise *History and Class Consciousness* (1971, originally published 1923), but this collection of essays remains his most important contribution to sociology and will be the object of our attention.

With the fall of the Hungarian regime (1919), Lukács was granted asylum in Vienna, where he remained in exile for the next decade. In 1930 he began his Moscow period, first as a member of the Marx-Engels Institute and then as an affiliate with the Philosophical Institute of the Academy of Sciences in the Soviet Union. He returned to Hungary after the war, taking a position as a professor of philosophy at the University of Budapest (1945–1956). Here Lukács joined the coalition government and became a member of the National Assembly. However, the Communist party again came to power in 1949, and he came to be identified with the insurrectionist forces that briefly toppled the pro-Soviet government in 1956. When the Soviets ended the Hungarian revolt, Lukács was deported to Romania. He returned to Hungary in 1957 and spent the remainder of his life as a professor. Georg Lukács died in Budapest in 1971.

## Assumptions

Inspired by the Russian Revolution, the young Lukács moved from his early existential despair to a more hopeful explanation of the "struggle for con-

---

[2] This position is a departure from Lukács's early existentialist work, in which he saw literature as an expression of the inner person and considered the social world to be without value.

sciousness" (1971: 68, originally published 1923) by the working class. Hence his first vision of human nature underwent a change, not simply in content but in spirit. He no longer saw human beings as destined by their nature toward alienation and isolation but instead as creatures of reason. Although reason could be distorted, the *structural position* of the working class made possible the emergence of a consciousness of the totality of history. Or as he stated in *History and Class Consciousness:*

> As the bourgeoisie has the intellectual, organizational, and every other advantage, the superiority of the proletariat must lie exclusively in its ability to see society from the center, as a coherent whole. This means that it is able to act in such a way as to change reality; in the class consciousness of the proletariat theory and practice coincide and so it can consciously throw the weight of its actions onto the scales of history—and this is the *deciding factor.* (1971: 69)

As for society, Lukács assumed the conflict stance of coercion in the present order, to be superseded by the historical processes of change. But it is the *ideological* nature of coercion that is central for this theory. First of all, Lukács assumed the Marxist vision of class-divided, capitalist society. The historical rise of capitalism represented a "unified economic structure" that brought with it a "unified structure of consciousness that embraced the whole society" (1971: 100). More specifically, the riddle of the *universal commodity structure* of capitalism, and its dialectical relationship with human consciousness, guides this theory, as we shall shortly see.

The vision of human science employed by Lukács assumes objective insight into subjective reality. His work combined Hegel's form of idealism and totality with the Marxist conception of history and insistence on praxis (practice). His "great realism" was rooted in two convictions: (1) that the truth of criticism would be borne out in historical events and (2) that the limitations of capitalism could never be clear to the bourgeois and petit bourgeois classes. Instead, only from the position of the working class could the totality of history be ultimately grasped. Put succinctly, truth and beauty (and their imposters) have a class nature. The critic, whether of social systems or their artistic and literary products, must grasp that nature and use it to better the life of humankind (1971: 64–66).

## Theoretical Content

The theoretical point of departure in *History and Class Consciousness* is the *universal commodity structure* of capitalist society. Rooted in the Marxist conception of exchange value (see Chapter 15), the commodity structure is at base a distortion of the natural, subjective relations between people. For example, under capitalism industry is organized so that those providing the labor do not control the why, what, or how of production. Instead, they are caught up in a division of labor in which even their own labor is bought and sold. Their purpose for being is to create increasing amounts of a product or service that somehow is more important than they are. If they are fired, or laid off, or cannot find a job, or work for low pay, the official explanations are those of mysterious market forces that are alleged to dominate mere mortals.

Simply stated, when relations between people are commodified, they acquire a "phantom objectivity" (1971: 83). This means that the products of human labor (whether automobiles, steel, or hamburgers) and the invention of the human mind (the form of economic organization that produces or tolerates "market forces") remain somehow *out there*. However, *people themselves appear to disappear*. In their own minds, they are caught up in what appears to be a rational, all-embracing, and autonomous structure (1971: 83–92).

Remember that for Lukács, the commodity structure is universal. This means that the conditions of structural powerlessness are not confined to the workplace or the economy. (If this were the case, the Marxist conception of *fetishism of commodities* would suffice because it explains the domination of the worker by the products of his or her own hands.) Instead, the commodity form invades every dimension of life, including the state, law, and bureaucratic organization.

It follows that just as workers do not fully comprehend that the economy is a human product, so do people under capitalism fail to understand that other social institutions are *made*. Instead, they attribute lawful rationality, power, and inevitability to the total range of social inventions. Thus the growing power of these inventions mirrors the increasing powerlessness of people; and institutional life diminishes in like measure the real life of human makers. In such instances, objective reality appears to function "*without the intervention of the subject*" (1971: 128). This general process of structurally imposed human surrender is termed, by Lukács, *reification*.

Left untouched, reification ensures the continued domination of people by social structures whose artificial nature is obscured. Revolutionary change is therefore dependent on the development of a freedom of the mind that places people in control. Ironically, Lukács saw capitalism as unique in its ability to polarize groups, increasing the probability of consciousness. Yet as noted earlier, all groups in capitalist society are not created equal in terms of their potential for "dereifying" the existing order. Lukács held with Marx that such a rebirth of reason (in lieu of a purely instrumental rationalism) is conditional. It is only from the *standpoint of the proletariat* (1971: 149) that a true consciousness, that is, a class-based consciousness, will emerge.

Unlike the "unhistorical and antihistorical character of bourgeois thought" (1971: 157), that of the proletariat will come to grasp the *present* as history. It will center on modern events, not as disconnected from the past but as the embodiment of more general processes. Lukács (like many touched by philosophical idealism) routinely avoided concrete historical examples. However, he would by his logic argue that the Russian Revolution of his era was not to be explained through immediate prerevolutionary conditions. Nor was it the ultimate product of a supposedly unique Russian history, featuring such factors as its tsarist past or the political rivalries of great states. Also "antihistorical" is the "great individual" theme of bourgeois historians (who might credit the blunders of Tsar Nicholas or the leadership of Lenin).

Instead, when it emerges, the proletariat conception of history is founded in a global understanding. Its totality readily comprehends the contradictions of an overarching capitalism, a system that transcends particular nations, national class interests, and individual leaders. It features understanding, not simply of the isolated past but the historical processes that unite the eras, ideologies, and destinies of those who share common modes of production. This knowledge of the present comes with the development by the proletariat of a *self-knowledge* of its own situation. Self-knowledge brings a critical comprehension of reified forces and insight into and repudiation of the universal commodity structure. Along with this comes the "abolition of the isolated individual," a recovery of the social nature of labor.

Finally, for Lukács, proletariat thought evidences an understanding of the necessity of the working class as a force for historical change. With its historical necessity clarified, the proletariat experiences its true beginning, its own emergence. No longer unconscious as a class, it rises to alter the course of future history (1971: 150–209).

## Critique

The sociology of Georg Lukács is open to certain of the questions raised later concerning the formal members of the Frankfurt School. The influence of German idealism often removes from center stage the real material events, ideas, and people of history so important to Marx. Caught in this dialectic, Lukács called for realism while resorting to abstractions not clearly connected to history. In this sense, his work has fallen prey to the reification of thought itself.

However, Lukács did not conceive of class consciousness as an emotional or psychological state. Hence, it is not a subjective condition of individuals. Instead of being the sum or average of what individuals in a class think or feel, class consciousness is a collective and rational sense of the historical mission of the class. In practical terms, this means the ability at critical historical moments to take state power and organize society as a whole. Critics might charge that Lukács has left us with a disembodied consciousness, somehow separated from the lives of real men and women. However, the enduring contribution of this theorist is the advancement of class consciousness from psychology to sociology.

# ■ The Frankfurt School

What came to be commonly known as the Frankfurt School was founded in 1923 in Weimar Germany as the Institute of Social Research.[3] Max Horkheimer (who became its director in 1930) provided the Frankfurt School with an unbroken continuity, first in pre-Nazi Germany, then in Geneva, then New York City, then California, and finally in the Federal Republic shortly after the Second World War. Under Horkheimer, the school was known for blending Marx's political economy with the German idealist tradition exemplified by Hegel.

Grounded in Hegelian Marxism, committed to a theoretical science bent on critique, and with many Jewish members, the Institute of Social Research was clearly vulnerable given the onslaught of national socialism in Germany. In early 1933, the Nazis expropriated many of its books, forcing the school to move to Geneva. In May 1934, the president of Columbia University, Nicholas Butler, invited Horkheimer to move the institute to New York City, where it was housed in one of the university's buildings. After a period in California, Horkheimer reestablished the institute in postwar Frankfurt. He was accompanied by T. W. Adorno, while others of its luminaries (including Herbert Marcuse and Erich Fromm) remained in the United States.

As we shall see, the members of the Frankfurt School were an interdisciplinary lot. Under the umbrella of Hegelian Marxism, other unlikely syntheses of thought took root. Thus, the Frankfurt critique drew from such disparate traditions as the empirically grounded social psychology, Freudian psychoanalysis, philosophical rationalism, phenomenology, law, and literary criticism. Yet the full measure of critical sociology in the Frankfurt tradition was essentially ignored by sociologists in the United States until the 1960s.

To be sure, the Frankfurt works on fascism, or better yet, the fascist or neofascist personality type, became standard features of the *psychological literature*. And an appreciation of the school could be discerned among philosophers, political economists, and students of literature. However, from the Frankfurt perspective, sociology in the United States during the exile years bore the priestly imprint of the order and pluralist paradigms. It was not a season for prophets.

Paul Connerton has argued (1976) that the work of the institute during the 1930s remained cohesive by steering a course between the extremes of empiricism/pragmatism on the one side and pure phenomenology on the other (see Chapter 13). Its members ignored the conventional wisdom that empirical research and philosophical speculation do not mix, seeing in the latter the basis for *critical theory*. The program of the institute further called for a critique of the

---

[3] This discussion of the Frankfurt School is informed by Brosio, 1980; Connerton, 1976; Jay, 1973; and Van Den Berg, 1980.

"totality" of culture and society in the sense of Georg Lukács (previous section) and found direction in Marx's *Critique of Political Economy*. Hence, social phenomena are not to be studied in isolation but related to an essentially *global* social structure understood as a historical whole.

However, it is the dual nature of the Frankfurt critique that should guide our coming inquiry. This form of oppositional thinking was not a simple embodiment of the skepticism of the Enlightenment. It was refined by German idealism in two important ways. First of all, the Frankfurt critique questioned the general *conditions of knowledge* common to all human perception. Borrowing from Kant, they raised questions about the *rules of order* imposed by the human mind on a world of formless and confusing sensations. Hence, we do not create reality, but instead we employ the innate, a priori rules or perceptual categories by which reality acquires its meaning (see Chapter 9). Second, the Frankfurt critique addressed the more particular *constraints of knowledge*. Influenced by Hegel (see Chapter 14), this view holds that knowledge may be distorted by coercive influences. Hence the slave may first be only an instrument of the master, but through labor, he or she transforms the environment and forms a new "self" grounded in a new understanding of humanity and new forms of practice. Thus, even the "negative" of destructive social conditions (slavery) gives rise to forces that negate and surpass those conditions (Connerton, 1976: 17–22).

Above all, the Frankfurt critique evaluates the social reality by recourse to a *tribunal of reason* (Jay, 1973: 63). The paramount measure of reason is those social forces that impel society to change along the lines of democracy, freedom, and cooperation. The alternative can only be that of the *irrational order,* a society based on forms of autocracy and coercion that pits class against class, men against women, race against race, and the human subject against his or her own nature. In formulating its analysis, the exponents of critical theory have sought no fixed and final set of intellectual answers. Indeed, this is an ever-open and expanding form of thought. Nor does critical theory represent an immutable political blueprint. However, it does offer a means of understanding why we are often unsuccessful in posing the issues or in framing more productive questions. This is why the Frankfurt School is not a place but a quality of mind.

Those whose thought constitutes the Frankfurt tradition represent a distinguished group. In addition to Max Horkheimer, it includes the social psychologist T. W. Adorno, the psychoanalyst Erich Fromm, the philosopher Herbert Marcuse, and the philosopher of science/social science methodologist Juergen Habermas. We shall only provide a brief overview of the works of the first three, before offering more extensive consideration of the others.[4]

---

[4]This is certainly not an exhaustive list of Frankfurt people. Others include the legal scholars Otto Kircheimer and Franz Neumann, political economist Friedrich Pollock, the sinologist Karl Wittfogel, and students of literature Leo Lowenthal and Walter Benjamin.

## Max Horkheimer on the Reification of Theory

In the work of Max Horkheimer one finds the Frankfurt critique of *traditional* theory in the human sciences. By traditional theory, Horkheimer meant the conception of positive explanation that has worked so well in the natural sciences and, for pragmatic and ideological reasons, has been adopted by the sciences of society (1976: 208, originally published 1937). Perhaps first established by Descartes (who sought to impose due order on a natural sequence of events ranging from the simple to the complex), traditional theory addresses only those "practical questions" that appear to emerge full-blown from life in the present-day society. The historical and social origins of such questions, as well as the ultimate uses of scientific knowledge, are defined as external to science (1976: 222). Instead, traditional theory (as adopted in the sciences of humanity) seeks to explain (if indeed it does not grow out of) the collection of facts by empirical inquiries (such as surveys).

In his critique, Horkheimer argued that the traditional conception of theory presents the scholar as somehow a value-free, disconnected bystander. As such, the traditional theorist does not address the meaning of theory for human existence, for to do so would require a holistic understanding of a society and its history. Instead, positive explanation functions "as if" the questions it resolves are those only of the isolated present. Critical theory, for its part, is seen by Horkheimer to be guided by a "concern for the rational organization of human activity. For this theory is not concerned only with goals already imposed by existent ways of life but with men and all their potentialities" (1976: 223). This necessitates a conception of human nature in which real beings in real situations are more than data to be verified and behavior to be predicted according to the laws of probability.

Stated succinctly, the traditional positive conception serves to *reify* theory. Theory is viewed as something other than a human product, the rules for its construction are seen as somehow absolute, and it appears as somehow inherent in knowledge. Given such conditions, theory is isolated from its historical and societal context. It supports and reflects "life in a society dominated by industrial production techniques" (1976: 208). Hence, theory becomes a form of *scientism* in which the trappings, vision, and language of science are used to create closed systems of thought.

## Erich Fromm on Escape from Freedom

If there is an integrating thesis in the varied works of Erich Fromm, it centers on the Marxist construct of alienation. By nature a social being, the human condition has historically been marred by a separation from nature, from others, and ultimately from self. The breaking of ties to others is ordinarily done in the name of freedom, but for Fromm such primary ties give "security and a feeling of belonging and of being rooted somewhere" (1969: 25, originally published 1941).

> They are the ties that connect the child with its mother, the member of a primitive community with his clan and nature, or the medieval man with the church and his social caste. Once the stage of complete individuation is reached and the individual is free from these primary ties, he is confronted with a new task: to orient and root himself in the world and to find security in other ways than those which were characteristic of his preindividualistic existence. (1969: 25)

Freedom then is ambiguous. Considered as a process of necessary independence, it assumes one meaning. Reconsidered as a form of estrangement, it assumes another. It is the "aloneness" of freedom from which modern humanity seeks to escape. And this produces the contemporary dilemma. Either human beings will use freedom to build a sane society founded in rational cooperation with others or seek security and belonging through submission to authority.

In characteristic Frankfurt fashion, Fromm placed the idea of freedom in specific historical context. Viewing the human being as both the product and producer of history, he argued that character and personality are also specific to their epoch. To be explicit, Fromm held that the rise of the Protestant Reformation is one root of the contemporary dilemma of freedom and separation. On the one hand, it taught autonomy and responsibility. On the other, it emphasized the evil, insignificance, and powerlessness of the individual.

Fromm argued that this period found vast segments of the population threatened by "revolutionary changes in the economic and social organization" (1969: 39). Those changes had their nexus in the increasing role played by capital in the late medieval economy. By the fifteenth century, large commercial companies had come to threaten the small merchants, and the guild ownership of industry (such as mining) was transformed. No longer were members of a guild paid a share for the work they did. Increasingly, those shares were owned by those who did not work, who paid wages to those who did. By the end of the sixteenth century, the guilds had changed from cooperative bodies of craftworkers and apprentices to more monopolistic and exclusive organizations.

Within this context, Protestantism became more than a revolt against the authority of the Catholic church. For Fromm, it enshrined individualism, taught self-degradation and distrust of others, and rationalized powerlessness as a natural part of the human experience. Thus the character traits that emerged were not primarily (as Weber had argued) those of a Protestant ethic that enabled believers to build modern capitalism. The asceticism, thrift, work compulsion, control of emotion, and overwhelming sense of duty were traits that "became productive forces in capitalistic society" (1969: 102).

Fromm argued that the collapse of the medieval social system and the rise of capitalism on the larger scale produced new anxieties and new answers to those anxieties. Protestantism, at least in part, was a response to these forces. As a private, individualistic, person-centered ideology, it prepared the believer psychologically for a changing economic role. And in the process, it questioned not only the authority of the Catholic church but the medieval ideal of community life on a human scale.

This then is the nature of the freedom that produces the human impulse to escape. The isolation and powerlessness of the individual (even more pronounced according to Fromm under modern monopoly capital), may be manifested in escapist forms such as *destructiveness* and *automaton conformity*. However, the most essential form of escape from freedom is that of *authoritarianism*. This means that the alienated are prone to seek other "secondary bonds" for the primary ones they have lost. But their attachments to others are twisted. Denied the authentic authority of cooperation, they admire the perverted authority found in the domination of others. Fromm's "authoritarian character" represents "the personality structure which is the human basis of fascism" (1969: 164).

## Theodor W. Adorno on the Authoritarian Personality

It was another member of the Frankfurt School who became noted in the United States for inquiries into authoritarianism. T. W. Adorno shared with Fromm the belief that fascism, with its emphasis on authority, its nationalism, its militarism, and its frequent racism, is the product of a decaying capitalism. Or in Adorno's words, "the fascist regimes of the first half of the twentieth century have stabilized an obsolete economic form, multiplying the terror needed to maintain it now that its senselessness is blatant" (1974: 34, originally published 1951). However, Adorno is not remembered for his critique but for his research that culminated in *The Authoritarian Personality* (1969, originally published 1950).

Adorno headed a team of social psychologists at the University of California at Berkeley whose research uncovered the authoritarian personality type. For these researchers, the authoritarian possesses a multidimensional constellation of stable and correlated personality attributes, including (among others) blind conformity, the belief in a clearly delineated hierarchy of authority, anti-Semitism, fascist political beliefs, rigidity, intolerance of ambiguity, and various forms of ethnocentrism and racism. Ironically, the Adorno study employed the positivist/empirical method of questionnaires/scales, in addition to interviews and projective techniques. Although somewhat historical and specific, at least in the examination of culture, this research centered on desperate needs for strength often channeled into forms of racial and ethnic prejudice.

## Critique

Trent Schroyer's book on the Frankfurt School is appropriately entitled *The Critique of Domination* (1973). Those who wrote in this tradition did not confine their analysis to the domination of economic exploitation. Instead, they believed that capitalism is marked by an irrationality that in its many forms inhibits the human animal. For Horkheimer, it is evident in an ahistoric and reified form of theoretical science. For Fromm, the confusion of individualism and privatism with authentic human freedom is irrational. For Adorno, the authoritarian personality is above all an irrational being, professing patriotic allegiance to democratic ideals while holding fast to various forms of inequality. However, for these and others in the critical tradition, the highest form of irrationality is the death of reason and the raising of its imposter: blind technocratic thought content to serve the ends of power (Tar, 1977). Yet despite the appeal of such work, certain points of controversy remain.

Horkheimer's work, for example, embodies one of the dilemmas of critical theory. On the one hand, Horkheimer demonstrated the context-bound nature of positive science and has led us to question its sacred standing. On the other, there is more to the explanation of society than a critique of other explanations. And the issue is still not fully drawn. Oppositional thinking is by nature reactive. It is dependent on the preexistence of other (by definition) limited visions.

As for the work of Fromm and Adorno on authoritarianism, despite intentions to the contrary, they appear to have installed a type of personality as the maker of fascism. Theirs is not a sharply constructed focus on history, structure, and ideology. Furthermore, Adorno's work on authoritarianism dominated academic circles in social psychology in the United States. And Fromm's many books of criticism found mass-market appeal in a society known for its interest in the private and the personal. Perhaps there is a relationship among these observations. It would appear that even a critical inquiry into character and personality remains just that: more a critique of individuals than a critique of society.

## ■ Herbert Marcuse (1898–1979): One-Dimensionality

As we have noted, Lenin believed that a sense of revolutionary purpose must be brought to the working masses by a revolutionary party. This view also emphasized the importance of intellectual leadership and science in the analysis of social systems. Leading members of the Frankfurt School, as well as the young Georg Lukács and Rosa Luxemburg, argued the contrary. They adhered to a *spontaneous* development of class consciousness (and its sense of world-historic mission) on the part of the working class. As did other members of the Frankfurt School, the social philosopher Herbert Marcuse remained a critic of both capitalist culture and Soviet Marxism.

Herbert Marcuse was born on July 19, 1898, in Berlin. Fleeing the Nazis, he came with Max Horkheimer and other members of the Frankfurt School to Columbia University in 1934. He joined the faculty at Brandeis in 1954 and moved to the University of California at San Diego in 1965. In the turbulence of the 1960s, Marcuse became something of a spiritual leader of the New Left movement on university campuses.

Marcuse's *One-Dimensional Man* (1964) was a continuation of the major theme of his life's work: the role of Hegelian "forces of negation" in modern technological society. For this critic (as for Marx), industrialization had introduced the historical opportunity for true reason and freedom. Properly used, sophisticated machine production could end material want and free humankind to pursue the intellectual side of its nature. However, Marcuse argued, the emergence of a more fully developed humanity is contingent on the replacement of capitalism by a socialist form of society (Israel, 1971: 164). Still, this meant more than the state ownership of the means of production. For Marcuse, and other members of the Frankfurt School, the Soviet Union had ended the traditional forms of capitalism, but it remained repressive.

Herbert Marcuse died in Starnberg, West Germany, on July 29, 1979.

## Assumptions

Consistent with the Frankfurt tradition, Marcuse assumed reason to be the measure of humanity. In *Reason and Revolution,* he expressed it as follows: "The life of reason appears in man's continuous struggle to comprehend what exists and to transform it in accordance with the truth comprehended" (1954: 10, originally published 1941). For Marcuse, reason is best understood as a force of history. That is, it matures and is perfected only in the real historical context of space and time. Thus, the historical world is not "a chain of acts and events" but *a struggle of the mind* to adapt the world to the ever-changing human potential.

What, then, is the nature of society? For Marcuse, "reason presupposes freedom" (1954: 9). Knowledge of the truth is meaningless unless human beings possess the ability to *act* on its precepts. In the free society, members are in control of their own development; reality may be shaped in accordance with the potentialities revealed by reason. In dialectic fashion, freedom also presupposes reason. Thus, the capacity for systematic, comprehensive analysis drives the subject toward enlarging the sphere of liberty. But for Marcuse, freedom is the first measure of society.

What, then, is the nature of the society in which liberation is denied? It is not the clearly totalitarian or authoritarian forms that intrigued Marcuse.

Instead, it is the advanced industrial society with its more subtle and self-legitimating forms of control. "The more rational, productive, technical, and total the repressive administration of society becomes, the more unimaginable the means and ways by which the administered individuals might break their servitude and seize their own liberation" (1964: 7). The alternative is a new state of consciousness among the members of industrial society founded in certain realizations: "Organization for peace is different from organization for war; the institutions which served the struggle for existence cannot serve the pacification of existence. Life as an end is qualitatively different from life as a means" (1964: 17).

As for the nature of human science, Marcuse advanced the critical theory characteristic of the Frankfurt School. His thought employed the "power of the negative," by which "contradiction becomes the distinguishing quality of reason" (1964: 171). With this Hegelian conception in mind, he held forth against the irrational culture as well as the one-dimensional forms of thought that mystify the human condition.

Marcuse argued that the irrational culture of the advanced technological society closes "the universe of discourse." In the place of critical debate it raises the "happy consciousness—the belief that the real is rational and that the system delivers the goods" (1964: 84). As for the style of positive sociology that prevailed prior to the tumult of the 1960s, Marcuse critiqued its *therapeutic empiricism:* the propensity to expose and correct abnormal behavior whether in the industrial plant, the criminal justice system, or wherever people needed to be adjusted to the existing order. This tendency to take an existing order as given and legitimate is to ignore that its systems and institutions might be "insane" or "criminal," or irrational.

## Theoretical Content

In typical Frankfurt fashion, Marcuse focused more on the cultural superstructure than the material base or substructure of society. It was from this foundation that he addressed the central issues in *One-Dimensional Man.*

One-dimensionality is a property of both a specific form of society and the individuals living within. Marcuse held that human beings possess both inner and outer dimensions. The first is "an individual consciousness and an individual unconsciousness," which can be distinguished from the second dimension. This "private space" is ordinarily *apart from* public opinion and behavior (1964: 10). In the modern era, this inner freedom or first dimension has been invaded and conquered by the second dimension of existence.

Marcuse held that an external world of mass production, mass distribution, and mass technology has come to claim the whole person, blending the two spheres of existence into a distorted whole. No longer can one stand outside the flow and tumult, critically considering the whole of society and weighing its promises. The new being has absorbed the prevailing ideology of the second, external dimension into reality, defining its existence as rational, its efficiency as good, its illusions as lawful necessities. In the last analysis, one-dimensionality signifies the death of reason.

One-dimensional thought thus pervades, distorts, and shapes the irrational culture. It is systematically promoted by the mass media, by politicians, by the makers and shapers of language and its symbols. The one-dimensional being, shorn of the ability to critically evaluate the conventional wisdom, internalizes a set of simple phrases and slogans by which the world is defined.

For example, the term *free* or *free world* is routinely applied to the Western world and its allies in the Third World of development who are receptive to and dominated by corporation capitalism. (Hence, apartheid in South Africa has been defined by some as part of the free world.) Vaguely understood, but impassionately offered, buzzwords such as *free enterprise, democracy, socialism,* and *communism* replace reasoned debate. They become the raison d'être for the full range of international and domestic state policies, whether economic, social, or military. Hence, by such processes, the movement of thought is replaced by the stagnancy of official dogma (1964: 1–18).

What, then, are the prospects of change in the one-dimensional society? For Marx, the working class in advanced capitalist societies represents the Hegelian "forces of negation." Stated simply, the proletariat will retain the technology of capitalism while discarding its irrational political structure. Marcuse, however, altered the Marxist view of change by arguing that the working class has been transformed in the modern era.

First of all, today's working class in advanced capitalist societies does not experience the physical pain and misery of nineteenth-century work life. Second, because of automation, today's working class consists more and more of white-collar and service workers, less and less of blue-collar production workers. The sophistication and complexity of the machine system means that the tool is no longer a simple instrument of the individual worker (which ties him or her to other workers doing the same work). Instead, the distinctive occupational identity of the nineteenth-century production worker is lost.

Third, technological change has a mixed impact on workers. On the one hand, it threatens jobs and power. On the other, it means greater interdependence and integration of the laboring class with both factories and capitalist society. (Marcuse cited "worker's participation" in decisions.) And finally, the old forms of class domination in which the owners and bosses were clearly defined have disappeared. In their stead have come new forms of domination, and a "technological veil" now disguises inequality and the new forms of slavery (1964: 22–34).

Marcuse thus saw an improved standard of living for the working class, together with their reification of the new forms of technological subjugation. In other words, the working class, having been bought off and mystified by the new forms of technology, is no longer equipped to play the role attributed to it by Marx in an earlier historical period.

Consistent with the Frankfurt tradition, most of *One-Dimensional Man* is a critique of culture. Marcuse identified one-dimensionality in art and literature, where artist and writer "entertain" rather than question. Those who do break the mold are met with the tolerance of indifference (1964: 60–71). One-dimensionality is also manifest in a closing of the "universe of discourse." Here the hypnotic language of progress and self-celebration is joined with "human relations research" to soothe anxieties and promote the "happy consciousness." (See Chapter 8 on human relations.) One-dimensional philosophy teaches that what exists is rational, and one-dimensional science finds its reason for being (and its funding) in the "ever-more-effective domination of nature" (1964: 158).

Standing against this one-dimensional onslaught is the hope of an advanced humanity, imbued with the power of negative thinking.

## Critique

Herbert Marcuse wrote eloquently in the tradition of critical theory. His impact was felt not merely by the counterculture student legions of the 1960s and early 1970s, but by a range of intellectuals who sought to recover the spirit of reason in an age of positivism. However, there are points of controversy that require a brief review.

First of all, despite an acknowledged debt to Marxist theory, Marcuse was not clearly system specific in his analysis of technological society. In other words, technology may have been reified not simply by the working class but by Marcuse himself. Hence, he appeared to quarrel more with technology per se than the specific societal forces that determine its uses. This, together with his ultimate faith in reason, reduces his argument to a variety of culture lag, in which the technological breakout appears to simply outdistance the values required to control it.

Marcuse also tended to empower technology with a sort of *vitalism*. It appears as efficient, purposive, and self-determining: a form of life. There was also a strong tendency to employ a Durkheimian argument (see Chapter 5), emphasizing the potential for technology to produce the integration of the working class with capitalist society. The divisiveness and fracturing are correspondingly played down. For example, Marcuse mentioned, but did not stress, the role of technology in what Braverman terms the *degradation of work* (see Chapter 15).

Also, Marcuse examined only briefly in later writings an important point missing in *One-Dimensional Man*: the emergence of a *new global proletariat*. As Immanual Wallerstein argued (see Chapter 15), in an international system, the new centers of industrial wage exploitation are increasingly found in the Third World of development. Finally, Marcuse's arguments on the increasing affluence of workers must be seriously qualified. In the United States at present, the massive shift toward a service economy means that the greatest job growth is occurring in occupations that pay lower wages than the shrinking manufacturing sector.

# ■ Juergen Habermas (b. 1929): Legitimations

The work of Herbert Marcuse shifted attention from the economic con-tradictions of capitalist society to the irrationality of its culture. This philo-sophical movement from realism to idealism deemphasized the importance of a revolutionary working class. Instead, social change would come from advances in reason. It should come as no surprise to find that university students of the 1960s found in Marcuse and others a sense of their own historical mission. (In-deed, Marcuse's critique of cultural conformity in the midst of prosperity may have more adequately described the concerns of university students than the conditions of the working class.) Caught up in the movements to oppose the Vietnam War and to press for the rights of women and racial/ethnic minorities, university campuses became the centers of new political agendas.

## Assumptions

The growth of the New Left was of course not confined to the campuses of the United States. In Europe, the work of another modern exponent of the Frank-furt tradition strongly influenced the student movement. Juergen Habermas has blended work in the methodology of the human sciences with a critique of sci-ence and technology. For this theorist, science and technology feature an *instru-mental rationality* too easily applied to the systematic control of people.

Influenced by his critical reformation of the work of Max Weber (see Chapter 10), Habermas argued that instrumental rationality (called *Zweck-rationality* by Weber) is a problem unto itself. It is expressed in a *technocratic con-sciousness* (1970: 111, originally published 1968), a form of ideology that makes a "fetish of science." Simply stated, technocratic consciousness includes the systematic development and application of techniques of problem solving within a routinely bureaucratic context. The technocrat conceives of science and its methods as purely instrumental.

Technocratic consciousness is opposed to reason (Weber's *Wertrationality*) because reason necessitates reflection and negation. Reason forces one to ask which problems are being solved and for whose benefit. For Habermas, the technocratic consciousness, marked by an instrumental rationality, does not consider the welfare of the whole. Nor is it confined to the scientific/tech-nological community. When, as an ideological form, it pervades society, the masses of people are depoliticized (noncritical of existing structures of power) and compliant. Ethics as a "category of life" is thus repressed (1970: 112–115).

# Theoretical Content

The technocratic consciousness is one dimension of a larger problem more fully explored in the later work of Habermas. Taking the Weberian conception of *legitimation*[5] as a point of departure, he sought to explore the various idea systems that maintain and preserve the status quo. In perhaps his most important analysis of modern capitalism, Habermas argued the existence of a *legitimation crisis* in a book so entitled (1975). This means that the commonly shared justifications for "why things are the way they are" become less convincing in the wake of rupturing contradictions found in contemporary institutions. In other words, legitimations are decreasingly effective in the preservation of a sufficient level of mass loyalty.

The crisis of legitimation is especially pronounced for state authority under late capitalism (1976, originally published 1973). Here, Habermas supported the thesis of Claus Offe. The state, as a system of legitimated force, requires an *input* of loyalty and confidence from the people to support its *output* of autocratic administrative decisions. Yet the legitimations that ensure such loyalty run up against powerful contradictions rooted in the conflicting functions attributed to the modern state.

For example, the state is required to play the role of the "individual capitalist" when it responds to the needs of specific firms or economic sectors. It must also function as the "total capitalist," defending the whole system, when conflicts among its powerful factions arise. Finally, it must appear to be responsive to the more *general interests* of the mass population.[6]

Habermas argued that the demands on the modern capitalist state are intensifying.

> It bears the cost of international competition and the cost of the demand for unproductive commodities (armaments and space research); it bears the cost of infra-structural activities directly related to production (transport systems, scientific and technical progress, occupational training); it bears the cost of social consumption which is only indirectly related to production (housing construction, health, leisure, education, social insurance); it bears the cost of social security for the unemployed; and finally it bears the cost of burdens on the environment created by private production. (1976: 376)

The state, responding to individual, total, and general interests, seeks to balance these demands and raise the tax revenues to pay for them. This intensifies the dilemma as the state establishes spending and taxation priorities in an attempt to relieve the pressure. We might cite the following contemporary examples not considered by Habermas that nevertheless are consistent with his theory.

---

[5] Weber conceived of legitimation in the context of authority. The issue is how people come to be convinced that they ought to be subjugated to the will of others.

[6] Habermas's conception of the state is quite similar to that of Nicos Poulantzas (see Chapter 16).

1. The "solution" of less spending does not resolve the question of where cuts are to be made (especially when arms of every description often have strong appeal for those who are "fiscal conservatives" on the social spending side).

2. The "solution" of raising taxes to pay as you go runs counter to the interests of wealthy (and powerful) corporations and individuals who provide (admittedly, at their discretion) investment capital for the system.

3. The "solution" of deficit spending means that the money not raised from taxes must be borrowed; thus government competes with business for funds in the financial marketplace. This has two important consequences. First, the national debt mounts and the yearly interest paid by government to lenders reaches staggering proportions. Second, the need for money by government and invested capital on the part of business creates a dependence on *external sources of capital* (foreign investment).

According to Habermas, the state is thus required to balance the imperatives of economic growth and stability against the demands of military capitalism and the welfare state. This occurs in the context of an increasingly global economy in which individual states (including superpowers) are less and less able to control events. As it fails to contain the breakout of these contradictions, evidence of legitimation crisis appears. Conflict will emerge over distribution and social reform will suffer (as the haves worry less about the have-nots). The unplanned economy, hooked on growth and nonproductive expenditures such as weapons systems, will appear unstable and unfair. Finally, the very *motivations* that maintain the capitalist system will disintegrate.

The argument advanced is that the sociocultural system of late capitalism motivates its members by means of *privatism*. The appeal to private interests is manifested in such things as family consumption and leisure, increased career status, and "civic concern" with little regard for the public good. However, the ideologies that support the "me generation" are losing their power of legitimation because of social change. Habermas is unclear in his argument, but change in his system appears to be both structural and cultural. In the former sense, the system cannot deliver what it promises. In the latter, the justifications for the failure to deliver do not wash, and/or people change their expectations (for example, expecting more state services) and are less responsive to various appeals to private interests.

For example, the class hierarchy is legitimated by the *ideology of achievement*. This idea system teaches that compensations are distributed according to the worth of one's contributions. If one works hard and is talented one will be rewarded. Yet at the same time, all must have the "equal opportunity to become unequal." This corresponds with such things as a demand for equal access to education and nondiscriminatory standards to evaluate performance in school and on the job. Yet, Habermas argues that the connection between education and occupational success is weakening. Hence a degree no longer carries with it a strong probability of a good job. Also, more and more jobs are fragmented and monotonous, while an *instrumental attitude* (the job is only a means to other ends) spreads. Hence the ideology of achievement is delegitimated.

Habermas also argues a delegitimation of *possessive individualism*. Simply put, the members of bourgeois society have been taught that private wealth is the key to the general welfare. Yet the conditions of urban life in complex societies are more and more reflective of reliance on public services (transportation, recreation, education, health, and so forth). No longer do financial incentives alone motivate people.

Finally, Habermas notes changes in science, art, and morality that will undermine the private motivations that drive capitalist society. *Scientism* may, clearly enough, serve to depoliticize the mass by legitimating both instrumental rationality (as above) and the authority of experts. Yet it may also set standards (reason, logic, evidence) by which the experts may be judged. Likewise, *modern art* has emerged as a symbolic critique of *bourgeois* society. Habermas also holds to a variation of the "global village" argument. People who come to develop a more cosmopolitan conception of the "human being" (citizens of the world) will develop a *universal morality*. This morality introduces loyalties that transcend those of private or even state interests.

## Critique

Once again, problematic issues common to other systems in critical theory can be raised. Habermas is somewhat painfully suspended between the theoretical worlds of Marx and Weber. This is a critique of *bourgeois* society, but it is fixed at the superstructural level (culture, ideologies, the role of the state). Largely absent are the structural forces that drive real people in the real events of history. Here the prime movers are those of the mind, and change awaits a rebirth of reason.

Habermas, like Mills and Marcuse before him, found in the student movement the impetus for change. Still, this view must be qualified. Students are a transient population whose relative privilege separates them from other disaffected segments within society. Moreover, as is evident in the contemporary period, the motivations attributable to privatism have taken new root, on campuses as well as off. This is an era of *old legitimations in new form,* of the New Social Darwinism.

The New Social Darwinism casts nations, groups, and individuals as winners and losers, successes and failures, good and evil. It addresses the problems of chemical-induced distortions (a personal affair), not the distortions of ideology. It projects its artificial systemic self to the whole range of human nature. It promises success to those who hone their supremely individual strengths (fitness, fashion, self-help, and self-hype). It offers private solutions for public issues.

Yet above it all, the vision of Habermas is a hopeful one. Perhaps, he has argued,

> the "pursuit of happiness" might one day mean something different ... not accumulating material objects of which one disposes privately, but bringing about social relations in which mutuality predominates and satisfaction does not mean the triumph of one over the repressed needs of the other. (1979: xxiv, originally published 1976)

# ■ Bibliography

Adorno, Theodor W.
(1951) 1974      *Minima Moralia: Reflections from Damaged Life.* London: NLB.

Adorno, Theodor W., et al.
(1950) 1969      *The Authoritarian Personality.* New York: Norton.

Brosio, Richard A.
1980      *The Frankfurt School: An Analysis of the Contradictions and Crises of Liberal Capitalist Societies.* Muncie, Ind.: Ball State University Press.

Connerton, Paul (Ed.)
1976      *Critical Sociology.* New York: Penguin Books.

Fromm, Erich
(1941) 1969      *Escape from Freedom.* New York: Holt, Rinehart and Winston.

Habermas, Juergen
(1968) 1970      *Toward a Rational Society.* Boston: Beacon Press.
(1968) 1971      *Knowledge and Human Interests.* Boston: Beacon Press.
(1971) 1973      *Theory and Practice.* Boston: Beacon Press.
(1973) 1976      "Problems of Legitimation in Late Capitalism." In Paul Connerton (Ed.), *Critical Sociology,* pp. 363–387. New York: Penguin Books.
1975      *Legitimation Crisis.* Boston: Beacon Press.
(1976) 1979      *Communication and the Evolution of Society.* Boston: Beacon Press.

Horkheimer, Max
(1937) 1976      "Traditional and Critical Theory." In Paul Connerton (Ed.), *Critical Sociology,* pp. 206–224. New York: Penguin Books.

Israel, Joachim
1971            *Alienation: From Marx to Modern Sociology.* Boston: Allyn
               and Bacon.

Jay, Martin
1973            *The Dialectical Imagination: A History of the Frankfurt School
               and the Institute of Social Research, 1923–1950.* Boston:
               Little, Brown.

Lichtheim, George
1968            Gyorgy Lukács. In *The International Encyclopedia of the So-
               cial Sciences,* vol. 9, pp. 488–492. New York: Crowell
               Collier Macmillan.

Lukács, Georg
(1923) 1971     *History and Class Consciousness.* Cambridge, Mass.: MIT
               Press.
(1924) 1970     *Lenin.* London: NLB.
(1954) 1976     *The Young Hegel.* Cambridge, Mass.: MIT Press.

Marcuse, Herbert
(1941) 1954     *Reason and Revolution.* New York: Humanities Press.
1964            *One-Dimensional Man.* Boston: Beacon Press.
1965            "Repressive Tolerance." In Robert Paul Wolff, Barrington
               Moore, Jr., and Herbert Marcuse, *A Critique of Pure Toler-
               ance,* pp. 81–117. Boston: Beacon Press.

Schroyer, Trent
1973            *The Critique of Domination.* Boston: Beacon Press.

Tar, Zoltan
1977            *The Frankfurt School: The Critical Theories of Max
               Horkheimer and Theodor W. Adorno.* London: Routledge
               and Kegan Paul.

Van den Berg, Axel
1980            "Critical Theory: Is There Still Hope?" *American Journal of
               Sociology* 86:449–478.

# CHAPTER *18*

---

# ■ Ideology

The thought of Juergen Habermas, considered at the conclusion of Chapter 17, is an appropriate bridge linking the Frankfurt School to other forms of critique. Thus, the theoretical analysis of *legitimations* would serve well as an introductory section for the pages that follow. However, the work to come is not best understood as an extension of the Frankfurt mind. It does not address the larger questions of culture. Nor does it consider the general artificiality of the "culture industry" (including the mass media). What is at issue now is the more narrowly drawn puzzle of *ideology*. And what distinguishes the authors we consider next (from the Frankfurt tradition) is a clear sense of the *connectedness* between idea systems and the class structure.

## ■ Karl Mannheim (1893–1947): Ideology and Utopia

Like Georg Lukács (see Chapter 17), Karl Mannheim was born in Budapest.[1] He was the only child of a Hungarian father and a German mother. After graduation from the humanistic gymnasium in Budapest, he studied at Berlin, Budapest, Paris, and Freiburg. His professors included Lukács and Edmund Husserl (see Chapter 13). Despite an early interest in philosophy, Mannheim turned to the human sciences, coming to be influenced by the thought of Weber and Marx. In 1925 he came to the major intellectual center of Germany, the University of Heidelberg, where he habilitated as an unsalaried lecturer.

---

[1] Biographical references include Wolfe, 1971, and Shils, 1968.

Karl Mannheim left Heidelberg for the University of Frankfurt in 1929, where he was a professor of sociology and economics. With the rise to power of the Nazis, he was dismissed in 1933 and fled to Great Britain, where he became a lecturer in sociology at the London School of Economics. Twelve years later, he became a professor in that university's Institute of Education. During his tenure at Heidelberg, Frankfurt, and the London School of Economics, Mannheim pioneered with systematic efforts in the sociology of knowledge. While in Great Britain, he was also editor of the International Library of Sociology and Social Reconstruction. This contributed to the growth and respectability of sociology in England.

Early in his career, Mannheim centered his analysis first in problems of interpretation, then in epistemology (the study of the origin, nature, methods, and limits of knowledge), and finally in particular kinds of knowledge. As his sociological interpretation matured, he made systematic inquiry into the social forces contributing to the emergence and shaping of certain forms of knowledge. These included (but were not limited to) the impact of generations, intellectual traditions, and class interests on differing conceptions of truth.

The modern classic *Ideology and Utopia: An Introduction to the Sociology of Knowledge* was published before Mannheim fled the Nazis. After the development of this masterpiece (1929–1931), he moved from a study of ideas to the study of social structure. Here the focus was on such issues as the bureaucratization of society, the structural formation of personality, the position and role of the intelligentsia, and the relationship between sociology and social policy. His work on the nature of democracy foresaw a coming elite disintegration and irrationality. Thus, before Mannheim's premature death in 1947, he had conceptualized sociology as a means for *planning* societies to avoid both the dangers of totalitarianism and the class system.

## Assumptions

The conception of human nature that prevails in *Ideology and Utopia* is one of reason, mediation, and self-reflection. Indeed, "scientific critical self-awareness" on the part of those who work in the social sciences presupposes a certain attribute of mind, an awareness of the relationship between social structure and systems of thought. This is not to argue that all those participating in social processes are doomed to falsify reality. Nor must they somehow suspend their value judgments and will to action. Instead, Mannheim held that to *participate knowingly* in social life presupposes that one can understand the often hidden nature of thought about society. Human beings have the potential for self-examination and contextual awareness. And only when these are understood can one have a comprehension of the formal object under study (Mannheim, 1968: 46–47, originally published 1936).

Simply put, there is a point in time, a moment of truth, when "the inner connection between our role, our motivations, and our type and manner of experiencing the world suddenly dawns upon us" (1968: 47). To be sure, some level of social determinism is real, for sociologists and all those who seek to unravel the puzzles of social life (including the puzzle of knowledge itself). None of us is free to exercise some metaphysical power of will. However, to the extent that one uses the power of reason to gain insight into the sources of such determinism, to that extent a *relative freedom from determinism* is possible. It follows that this potential for simultaneously comprehending self, the socio-historical context, and the object to be analyzed must be realized (especially by sociologists).

Certain assumptions concerning the nature of society remain constant throughout Mannheim's work. He returned again and again to the themes of conflict: of classes (and their systems of thought), of political movements, and of the necessary dissenting role of the intelligentsia. He addressed, as we shall see, the wider ground of the sociology of knowledge, but within that generality he considered the specific questions of ideological structure. However, for Mannheim the "ideological structure does not change independently of the class structure and the class structure does not change independently of the economic structure" (1968: 130).

This sense of the "structural totality of society" Mannheim attributed to Marx. He built his theoretical system on the threefold structural tendencies of Marx's earlier body of thought: first of all, that the mode of material production shapes the political sphere (and the rest of the "superstructure"); second, that change in the material base is closely connected with "transformations in class relations" and corresponding shifts in power; and third, that idea structures may dominate people at any historical period, but that these ideologies may be understood and their change predicted theoretically.

Nevertheless, unlike Marx, who emphasized that the ideas of the ruling class prevail, Mannheim held that class-divided societies contain a special stratum for "those individuals whose only capital consisted in their education" (1968: 156). As this stratum comes to draw from different classes, it will contain contradictory points of view. Hence, the social position of intellectuals is not merely a question of their class origin. Its "multiformity" provides the "potential energy" for members of the intellectual stratum to develop a social sensibility and to grasp the dynamic and conflicting forces of society (1968: 156–157).

Mannheim's conception of human science reflects a synthesis of idealism and materialism, spirit, and society (Wolff, 1971: xiv). Kurt Wolff has identified Mannheim's fundamental question: How can social conditioning be reconciled with the "inexhaustibility and unforeseeability" of ideas and spirit? And as a corollary, how can spirit and society be saved? Mannheim believed that a sociology of knowledge would resolve this question and advance the discipline as a science. Above all, a sociology of knowledge would enable its user to *realize a more accurate determination of the facts* (1968: 296).

Now, the task of a sociology of knowledge is not simply one of getting rid of bias, propaganda, or unrecognized values. Rather, even when knowledge is freed of all forms of "distortion," it will contain inherent "traces" that are an inevitable part of the structure of truth. For example, knowledge is never a matter of pure ideas that rise disembodied from their maker. It has implications for social action. Furthermore, it reflects the position in society of the knower as well as the corresponding events and dominant ideas of specific historical periods. Knowledge, even the scientific sort, does not exist in some separate sphere of truth. It is an intricate part of an altogether human process, bound up in the interrelationships of history, society, and psychology. Knowledge is truly of *this* world (1968: 292–309).

## Theoretical Content

In his attempt to explain ideology, Mannheim identified two distinct meanings: the particular and the total. The first of these refers to the common conception of ideology as distortion. The particular conception of ideology ranges in meaning from a more or less conscious attempt at manipulating others to un-witting self-deception. Those who employ it analytically seek to uncover *only a part* of an opponent's assertions. The particular conception also focuses on a purely *psychological* level, perhaps accusing the opponent of deception, but always assuming that *both parties share common criteria of validity.* Finally, the particular conception seeks to uncover the *hidden interests* or motivations of the opponent.

The total conception of ideology is far more inclusive. It refers to thought systems associated with an age or a specific sociohistorical group (such as a class). It focuses on the "total structure of the mind" as it occurs for an epoch or a group. (Hence, it is not the mind of an individual or association of individuals but the constellation of ideas and their processing that reflects a period or group.) The total conception of ideology will call into question the opponent's "total *Weltanschauung,*" including the mode of thought. (Thus, the opponent is not seen as an individual or concrete group as much as a perspective that reflects a collective life.) From this total conception, it follows that there may exist essentially different intellectual universes, each with a distinctive set of criteria by which truth is judged. Finally, the total conception is not concerned with "motivations" or "interests" at a psychological level but rather seeks the relationship between social forces and worldview.

While the meaning of particular ideology is self-evident, the total conception is more troublesome. However, it becomes clearer when used analytically to understand a class-based conception of reality. For Mannheim, the owning and working classes represent different worldviews, different modes of thinking, and different criteria for "truth." Hence their ideologies are not to be understood in terms of individuals or motivations.

For example, the individual proletariat does not necessarily possess all of the elements of the working class *Weltanschauung.* Each may participate only fragmentally in the whole outlook of the group. What then of the "motivations" that are "behind" a particular view? For Mannheim, idea systems (or any specific piece of one) are rather the function of different social categories, situations, or settings. The *interests* reflected in ideas are those of the larger spheres of age, class, and other sociological forces (1968: 55–75).

It should be clear from the foregoing discussion that Mannheim's sociology of knowledge will employ a total conception of ideology (1968: 265–266). But it does something more. It advances a distinctively sociological conception of epistemology, a way of understanding the relationships between historical and social structure and the *very grounds by which knowledge is judged.* Mannheim did this by making the critical distinction between *relativism* and *relationism.*

To argue that knowledge is relative today is to say that "all historical thinking is bound up with the concrete position in life of the thinker" (1968: 78–79). In an older sense, relative thought was the knowledge that came from the purely subjective standpoint of the knower. But whether considered alone or in combination, these forms of relativism mean either (1) that subjective knowledge is untrue, or (2) that certain historical and biographical events "taint" the knowledge of an era. Both conceptions of relativism assume that there is an absolute "truth" that is being compromised.

In order to free thought from relativism, Mannheim introduced the concept of relationism. By "relationism" he meant that the grounds for knowledge are not invariant, continuing from age to age. Hence to argue that knowledge is relational is to say that "there are spheres of thought in which it is impossible to conceive of absolute truth existing independently of the values and position of the subject and unrelated to the social context" (1968: 79). However, this does not mean that "anything" goes, for once one understands that historical knowledge is relational, one must discriminate between what is true and false. In other words, "which social standpoint" (with its corresponding perspective) comes closer to the *truth?* (In this case, Mannheim's conception of the "perspectivization" factor is clearly informed by the work of Lukács; see Chapter 17.)

Truth seeking, for Mannheim, is obviously not an asocial process. But there is more. The questions of knowledge and truth are often bound up in political forms of struggle (1968: 36) and their corresponding views of the world. (Hence, the title of the book, *Ideology and Utopia.*) By "ideology" Mannheim meant those total systems of thought held by society's ruling groups that obscure the real conditions and thereby preserve the status quo. "Utopian" thinking signifies just the opposite. Here, total systems of thought are forged by oppressed groups interested in the transformation of society. From the utopian side, the purpose of social thought is not to diagnose the present reality but to provide a rationally justifiable system of ideas to legitimate and direct change.

Thus, for Mannheim, "ideology" means that ruling groups become blind to knowledge that would threaten their continued domination, whereas "utopia" means that oppressed groups selectively perceive "only those elements in the situation which tend to negate it" (1968: 40). Remember that Mannheim was *not* arguing that both sides are simply biased. And there is *more* to his position than the argument that there are *different* truths. (Admittedly, it is not unusual for those interested in the preservation of the existing order to have a different agenda of questions, thus different answers, than do those interested in change.) To be clear, because of its structural position, one "side" may be closer to a specific truth than another. However, when both sides address the same question, then judgments still must be made concerning the truth of their answers.

## Critique

Throughout his career, Mannheim sought to establish relationships between structural categories and modes of thought. Thus, he looked at classes, sects, generations, and parties to conceptualize differences in their worldviews. In *Ideology and Utopia,* for example, he identified different forms or ideal types (see Max Weber in Chapter 10) of the "utopian mentality." For example, early religious sects (such as the Anabaptists) joined with other oppressed groups in the "spiritualization of politics." Their revolutionary conception of society was fixed on the establishment of a millennial kingdom on earth.

The bourgeois thinkers of the Enlightenment also struck at the waning power of the aristocracy. They represented a socially ascendant class whose utopian mentality took the form of a "liberal-humanitarian" ideal. This ideal featured a reasoned form of progress, and it was advanced by the middle stratum of society. This stratum, in turn, was disciplined by a "conscious self-cultivation" and sought justification in a new ethics and intellectual culture that undermined the world of the nobility.

Other forms of utopian mentality include the "conservative mode," bent on controlling the anarchism of "inner freedom" that threatens the utopian dream. The last is the "socialist-communist mode," which locates human freedom in the breakdown of capitalist culture (1968: 247). Given this range, it is clear that thought which is utopian in one context may be ideological in another.

Despite this promising delineation of ideal types of utopian thought, Mannheim proved historically imprecise in associating ideas and social position. This problem can be generalized to his work as a whole. Put clearly, Mannheim was routinely content to interpret knowledge from the vantage point of idealist philosophy. He struggled with the content of ideas and their interrelations within the structure of an overall system of thought. When he introduced the larger questions of structure, he did little more than claim that knowledge is bound up in social position. When he dealt with specific classes or movements, he was content to use them more as illustrations of how thought systems differ. He seldom specified the real, material conditions that give rise to ideological and utopian visions.

# ■ Antonio Gramsci (1891 – 1937): Ideological Hegemony

Unlike most of those whose ideas have contributed to our passage, Antonio Gramsci was neither an academic nor a university graduate. Instead, his life was that of a journalist, worker organizer, member of the central committee of the Italian Communist party, and political prisoner for over a decade in an Italy ruled by Benito Mussolini. Yet the eloquence of his writing and especially the depth and power of his *Prison Notebooks* were to attract much posthumous attention among students of ideology.

## History and Biography

Gramsci[2] was born in 1891 in Sardinia, an island wracked by the general poverty of the south of Italy. Here he was to know firsthand the disunity and inequality that marked his native land. After completing his elementary education in 1903, he interrupted his schooling to work in support of his family. After two years, he returned to secondary school and in 1911 was awarded a scholarship at the University of Turin. Now on the mainland, Gramsci found in Turin an urban center of the factory system, the natural crucible for the formation of an industrial working class.

While a student of literature and linguistics, Gramsci was influenced by Benedetto Croce's liberal philosophy. Croce had developed a critique of both positivism (see Chapter 8) and the vulgar forms of historical materialism (see Chapter 14) common in early twentieth-century Italy. He also conceived of history as an intellectual imperative. For Croce, the understanding of ethics, art, literature, politics, and culture presupposes an understanding of history. So influenced, Gramsci developed his own increasingly sophisticated critique of bourgeois culture. Yet he found in Croce more a philosophy of spirit than one of praxis. (Indeed, Croce believed that history is a movement toward rationality, and as such irrational evil cannot prevail.) In time, as Marx had done with Hegel, Gramsci took from his master a conception of historical movement and superimposed the Marxist measure of thought: its relevance for social action.

Gramsci became active in the Italian Socialist party and by 1916 was writing for the socialist newspaper *Avanti*. In the coming years, he continued his political journalism and became a dominant figure in the *factory council movement* in Turin.[3] Gramsci believed that authoritarian industries only prepare

---

[2] A succinct reference on Gramsci's life and times is Joll, 1977.

[3] For an excellent account of Gramsci's emergence in this movement, see Clark, 1977.

workers for subjugation, and he argued that the workers, managers, and professionals in industry are the real producers and should combine against the owners of capital. In 1920 he supported the national *occupation of the factories,* which had a strong impact on Turin. However, despite initial success, the movement failed. The Socialist party failed to seize power, and when it split in 1921, Gramsci became a leading figure in the new offshoot, the Italian Communist party. Yet in the turbulence of the post–World War I period, new forces of change were to seize command. In October of 1922, the fascists marched on Rome and Benito Mussolini formed a new government.

After treatment for his chronically poor health in a Moscow clinic and a short stay in Vienna, Gramsci returned to Italy in 1924. He had been elected in absentia to Parliament, and here he led the political resistance to the fascisti. However, as Mussolini's control became absolute, the opposition crumbled. In November of 1926, Gramsci was arrested in Rome and sent to a camp for political prisoners at Ustica. In the next year, he was transferred to a Milan prison, and in 1928 he was tried in Rome and sentenced to 20 years. At the Special Penal Establishment at Turin, he began to write some 32 prison notebooks and a number of poignant personal letters.

Gramsci's frail condition continued to deteriorate in prison, and an international campaign on his behalf resulted in his transfer to clinics, first in Formia in 1933 and then in Rome in 1935. Even as he lay dying, Gramsci was considered a political threat worthy of guards. Two years later, the man E. J. Hobsbawn called the Great Gramsci died of a cerebral hemorrhage at the age of 46.

## Intellectuals, Hegemony, and the Modern Prince

Basic to the whole body of Gramsci's work is the Marxist conception of historical specificity (see Chapter 14). Given a comprehension of the real historical conditions, human beings through enlightened practice can proceed to change the world. Basic to this process are both the intellectuals as a stratum in society and the intellectual potential in every human being. Each person

> ... carries on some form of intellectual activity; that is, he is a "philosopher," an artist, a man of taste, he participates in a particular conception of the world, has a conscious line of moral conduct and therefore contributes to sustain a conception of the world to modify it, that is to bring into being new modes of thought. (From the *Prison Notebooks,* quoted in Joll, 1977: 120)

As to the formal intellectual stratum, Gramsci argued that its members would execute one of two ideological roles. On the one hand, some would join the new intellectuals who emerged from revolutionary struggle to form the leadership for the movement. On the other hand, some would continue to create and disseminate the ideas that sustained the ruling class. The first position on the role of intellectual leadership is, of course, informed by Lenin. The second argument (that intellectuals may be interest bound to the class structure of society) bears the stamp of Marx.

Gramsci's conception of the role of intellectuals is basic to comprehending what he meant by *hegemony,* and especially the *ideological forms of political dominance.* First of all, from the Leninist standpoint, hegemony is a revolutionary strategy. Considered in the thought of Gramsci, hegemony in practical terms means a class alliance between a leading proletariat and the peasantry.

More generally on the question of strategic hegemony, Gramsci argued that successful revolution presupposes the formation by the intellectual vanguard (now within the proletariat) of a bloc of forces. Intellectuals would also be students of history, comprehending the differences in the historical conditions of Russia and those that prevailed in the West (in the post–World War I era). In sum, as the first duty of revolution is the taking of state power, a class intent on this mission must be tightly organized and ideologically sound. And this is the responsibility of the party intellectuals (Salvadori, 1979).

However, Gramsci in the *Prison Notebooks* (1971, originally published 1923–1929) moved the question of hegemony beyond the issue of strategy. Instead he broadened the problem, conceiving of hegemony as *a moment of new ideological integration* when the allied revolutionary classes (such as workers, soldiers, peasants) seek awareness on a universal level. Through ideological struggle (led by the vanguard), the specific and autonomous interests of the specific classes within the alliance vanish. They are replaced by a new hegemony based on a shared vision. The alliance is thus transformed: from *peaceful coexistence* to a *new* existence, from a plurality of interests to unification (Mouffe, 1979).

This form of ideological transformation, this new collective will, is forged in the context of the political party. Drawing on the imagery of Machiavelli (see Chapter 6), he described the party as a modern prince (1967, written 1929–1935). Of course, the new "prince myth" had little in common with the sixteenth-century aristocratic elite instructed by Machiavelli. Nor did Gramsci subscribe to the politics of cunning and duplicity often attributed to the Florentine. He did believe (as did Machiavelli) that a false sense of morality (often based in the doctrines of the church) served to conserve the status quo. And he did reserve for the modern prince a leading role in social change, as did Machiavelli for the Medicis.

Finally, there is in the work of Gramsci the theoretical basis for a critique of ideological social control on behalf of ruling forces. Controlling systems of thought are mediated through society by different structures of hegemony, including the media, education, and religion. For Gramsci, ideological hegemony means that the principal themes of domination (essential to the continuing control of a ruling class) are redundant in the culture.

On the modern scene in the United States, such labels as the "me generation," "looking out for number one," "competitors," and "survivors" exemplify a vocabulary of privatism. Movies, television, and popular novels feature themes of human interest, escapism, the magical transformation of lives, and the triumph of will. Athletic events offer the opportunity to identify with (or degrade) competitors and to legitimate competition. But above all, Gramsci would be sensitive to the promises of fairness and opportunity that become a part of the economic, political, and social structure, for these ensure the continued support of the existing order by its common people.

## Critique

Norberto Bobbio (1979) has perceived in Gramsci's thought a "double inversion" of Marxist theory. First, the ideological superstructure appears to have primacy over the material substructure. That is, Gramsci more clearly refutes the *economism* that some critics find in Marx (see Chapter 15). Second, the *consensual basis of civil society* has primacy over the *coercive basis of political society*.

For Gramsci, civil society and political society represent the two major divisions or levels of the superstructure. The first is the center of the "private" institutions of ideological hegemony (for example, the modern corporate media or the church in the Middle Ages). Here Gramsci centers on the role of ideology in building a consensus among the population that advances the hegemony of a dominant class. Conceived broadly, civil society refers to the whole of ideological-cultural relations. The second level, that of political society, refers to direct domination on the part of the state and its apparatuses.

Perhaps now it is clear that, for the *structural* Marxists (see Chapter 15), Gramsci's conception of society is too greatly informed by the Hegelian emphasis on the world of ideas. For the same critics, Gramsci's continuing emphasis on *coalition building* and a new synthesis of interests is questionable. That is, Gramsci's attempts to enlist the "new middle classes" (engineers, technicians, foremen) meant that he perceived them as potential revolutionaries. His argument that different interests would succumb to a new collective synthesis within the party bears this out. But for some "orthodox" Marxists, some of the more privileged groups are not structurally disposed toward class struggle. This does not mean in practical terms that more privileged individuals (for example, intellectuals) cannot break with the existing order. But as a group, it is not expected.

Gramsci also conceived of power in terms of *democratic centralism*. This refers to a political structure in which power is exercised centrally but one that is continuously open to new ideas and new leaders from the "depths of the masses" (Gramsci, in Joll, 1977: 133). This focus on participatory institutions, when combined with the primacy of ideological control, has produced new interest in Gramsci in an era of increasing corporate, state, bureaucratic, and media power.

Gramsci's impressive, if unsystematized theory, offers enough of a pluralist vision to appeal to those in the West who perceive in capitalism a decaying economic system but wish to retain the institutions of political democracy. Hence, the thought of Antonio Gramsci is theoretically relevant for modern

*Eurocommunism* (especially in Italy), a movement that seeks to steer a course independent of the Soviet Union.

# ■ Alvin Gouldner (1920–1980): The Ideology of Sociology

We will conclude with a brief review of a work conceived by its author as a critique of sociology. In one sense, Alvin Gouldner's best-known book is a specialized effort in the sociology of knowledge. In the continuing turbulence of the 1960s, marked by struggles against the Vietnam War, against racism and sexism and the degradation of the planet, Gouldner found a sociology tied to an earlier time and place. Its old assumptions, those of order, consensus, integration, and control, appeared sadly out of place. These and the equilibrium theories of society in which they found expression were being driven inexorably toward a more critical stance—hence, *The Coming Crisis of Western Sociology* (1970).

Alvin Gouldner wrote in a period when theories of order were heavily entrenched in academic sociology. For example, in 1964 a survey of American sociologists revealed that 80 percent were favorably disposed toward functionalist/systems theories (see chapters 5 and 6). This followed an observation by Kingsley Davis (in his presidential address to the American Sociological Association in 1959) that functionalism and academic sociology had become one (Gouldner, 1970: 373).

For Gouldner, all social theories have embedded in their formal arguments certain *background assumptions*. These are "unpostulated and unlabeled" preconceptions that operate as "silent partners in the theoretical enterprise" (1970: 29). Background assumptions include both world hypotheses (primitive presuppositions about the nature of the world and everything in it) and *domain assumptions* (which are more limited in terms of conceptual sphere). For example, Gouldner would call our tripartite configuration of assumptions about human nature, society, and human science domain assumptions.

By this point, we should need nothing further from Gouldner to understand the role of assumptions in the construction of theory. However, what he said about the "subtheoretical level" is provocative. For Gouldner, these domain assumptions, or set of subtheoretical beliefs, determine whether or not a theory is *intuitively convincing*.

Hence, even for trained sociologists, theories do not necessarily appeal on the grounds of "formal logic and supporting evidence." Rather, the intuitively convincing theory is

> ... commonly experienced as déjà vu, as something previously known or already suspected. It is congenial because it conforms or complements an assump-

tion already held by the respondent, but an assumption that was seen only dimly by him precisely because it was a "background" assumption. (1970: 30)

Simply put, the background assumptions of social theory comprise an *ideological infrastructure* (1970: 46–49).

Gouldner's concern with ideology did not end with the infrastructure of social theory. He extended his critique to the *professional socialization* of new sociologists. Clearly stated, the professional ideology transmitted to the apprentices of human science is an extension of nineteenth-century positivism and its reaction to the Enlightenment. In the place of the reasoned criticism of negation is raised up the positive affirmation of *continuity, convergence, and cumulation*. Thus for Gouldner, the socialization of new sociologists conveys an abiding conviction. It is that *over time, the ideas of the truly great thinkers form a discernable pattern of agreement and that later discoveries simply build upon the past*. So conceived, sociology has no rightful place for critique because its knowledge emerges not from conflict but from a historically validated consensus (1970: 16–18).

Yet for Gouldner, the events of his day and the corresponding changes in social theory foretold the end of a functionalist academic stance. From his vantage point, he saw an "emerging alienation of young sociologists from Functionalism" (1970: 410). This discontent was no longer confined to individual expression but found collective demonstration. Within the universities, new visions of society were supposedly taking root among "middle-class youth," and these ideological shifts were to be a new component of the milieux in which social theory is made. On the outside, the development of the *welfare state* made resources available to sociology. However, the premise of social research for social change contradicts order assumptions (which are ill fitted for the explanation of change). It features instead the values of freedom and equality.

# ■ Critique and Endnote

Gouldner's work on the ideology of sociology convincingly documents the decline of functionalism and the emerging respectability of critical forms of thought. However, Western sociology (at least in the United States) may have resolved its crisis more by raising up other varieties of order and pluralist theory than by warmly embracing the conflict paradigm. Gouldner himself acknowledged the growth of alternatives (such as Homans's, Goffman's, and Garfinkel's) that in no sense attempt a critical, macrostructural appraisal.

But it is the broader conception of a sociology of knowledge that is most intriguing here. Gouldner believed that the larger events and ideologies of an age, mediated through the student consciousness of the university, form the crucible for social theory. Today there appears to be a changed societal and university milieu. The new welfare state is the warfare state, and along with this shift has come a new set of priorities for government-sponsored research. The War on Poverty is over. Poverty won—and sociologists now speak of a permanent underclass. The exploration of space now portends the militarization of the heavens. And the new idealism is defined in terms of nationalism, patriotism, and the celebration of self. Given these conditions, perhaps the next coming crisis of Western sociology will feature a resurgence of social Darwinism.

But there is clear folly in a narrow vision of history that sees tomorrow as a simple extension of today. The conditions of present crisis, whether in academic disciplines, social theories, or societies, also present the opportunity for historical breakouts. The direction of future history may be untoward and unclear but one thing appears sure. Crisis will not be resolved by ideologues blindly committed to distorted conceptions of eras long past, safe in the assumption that history has stopped. Instead, it will be engaged by those who hold humane and reasoned visions of alternative tomorrows. If a new generation of sociologists is to play a role in the new global society to come, if its members are to realize their place in the historical moment, they must learn to seize the future. And that is why the sociological passage is a journey without end.

# ■ *Bibliography*

Bobbio, Norberto
1979       "Gramsci and the Conception of Civil Society." In Chantal Mouffe (Ed.), *Gramsci and Marxist Theory,* pp. 21–47. London: Routledge and Kegan Paul.

Clark, Martin
1977       *Antonio Gramsci and the Revolution That Failed.* New Haven, Conn.: Yale University Press.

Gouldner, Alvin
1965       *Enter Plato: Classical Greece and the Origins of Social Theory.* New York: Basic Books.
1970       *The Coming Crisis of Western Sociology.* New York: Basic Books.
1976       *The Dialectic of Ideology and Technology: The Origins, Grammar, and Future of Ideology.* New York: Seabury Press.
1979       *The Future of Intellectuals and the Rise of a New Class: A Frame of Reference, Theses, Conjectures, Arguments and an Historical Perspective on the Role of Intellectuals and Intelligentsia in the International Class Contest of the Modern Era.* New York: Seabury Press.

Gramsci, Antonio
(1929–1935) 1967    *The Modern Prince and Other Writings*. Translated by Louis Marks. New York: International Publishers.
(1929–1935) 1971    *Selections from the Prison Notebooks of Antonio Gramsci*. Edited and translated by Quintin Hoare and Geoffrey Nowell Smith. New York: International Publishers.

Joll, James
1977                *Antonio Gramsci*. New York: Penguin Books.

Mannheim, Karl
(1923–1929) 1952    *Essays on the Sociology of Knowledge*. New York: Oxford University Press.
(1935) 1967         *Man and Society in an Age of Reconstruction*. New York: Harcourt, Brace & World.
(1936) 1968         *Ideology and Utopia: An Introduction to the Sociology of Knowledge*. Translated by Louis Wirth and Edward Shils. New York: Harcourt, Brace & World.
1950                *Freedom, Power, and Democratic Planning*. New York: Oxford University Press.

Mouffe, Chantal
1979                "Hegemony and Ideology in Gramsci." In Chantal Mouffe (Ed.), *Gramsci and Marxist Theory*, pp. 168–204. London: Routledge and Kegan Paul.

Salvadori, Massimo
1979                "Gramsci and the PCI: Two Conceptions of Hegemony." In Chantal Mouffe (Ed.), *Gramsci and Marxist Theory*, pp. 237–258. London: Routledge and Kegan Paul.

Shils, Edward
1968                "Karl Mannheim." In *The International Encyclopedia of the Social Sciences*, vol. 9, pp. 557–561. New York: Crowell Collier Macmillan.

Wolff, Kurt H.
1971                "Introduction." In Kurt H. Wolff (Ed.), *From Karl Mannheim*, pp. x–cxxxiii. New York: Oxford University Press.

# ■ Name Index

# ■ Subject Index